A HISTORY OF CANADIAN LEGAL THOUGHT

Collected Essays

A HISTORY OF CANADIAN LEGAL THOUGHT

Collected Essays

R.C.B. RISK

Edited and introduced
by G. Blaine Baker and Jim Phillips

Published for The Osgoode Society for Canadian Legal History by
University of Toronto Press
Toronto Buffalo London

Printed in Canada

ISBN-13: 978-0-8020-9424-7
ISBN-10: 0-8020-9424-4

Printed on acid-free paper

Library and Archives Canada Cataloguing in Publication

Risk, R.C.B., 1936–
A history of Canadian legal thought : collected essays / R.C.B.
Risk ; edited and introduced by G. Blaine Baker and Jim Phillips.

ISBN-13: 978-0-8020-9424-7
ISBN-10: 0-8020-9424-4

1. Law – Canada – Philosophy – History. 2. Law – Canada – History.
3. Law – Study and teaching – Canada – History.   I. Baker, G. Blaine
II. Phillips, Jim   III. Osgoode Society for Canadian Legal History
IV. Title.

KE394.Z85R48 2006   340'.10971   C2006-903499-0
KF345.R48 2006

University of Toronto Press acknowledges the financial assistance to its
publishing program of the Canada Council for the Arts and the
Ontario Arts Council.

University of Toronto Press acknowledges the financial support for its
publishing activities of the Government of Canada through the
Book Publishing Industry Development Program (BPIDP).

Contents

PART TWO
The Challenge of Modernity: Canadian Legal Thought in the 1930s

PART THREE
Postwar Developments

Foreword

THE OSGOODE SOCIETY
FOR CANADIAN LEGAL HISTORY

Richard Risk, a true pioneer in the writing of Canadian legal history, has contributed more than anyone else to the discovery of often neglected Canadian thinkers about law, and to explanation and analysis of their thought as well as that of better-known legal thinkers such as Frank Scott, Bora Laskin, W.P.M. Kennedy, John Willis, and Edward Blake. Some years ago the Osgoode Society and Risk's colleagues recognized his contributions to legal history with the publication of a festschrift – *Essays in the History of Canadian Law: In Honour of R.C.B. Risk*, edited by G.B. Baker and J. Phillips. Collected in this volume are Risk's major published essays describing the distinctive ways that Canadians have thought about the nature and function of law. Covering the immediate post-Confederation period to the 1960s, these essays range in subject matter from legal education to the British North America Act, and include discussions of such diverse topics as estoppel, the administrative process, and statutory interpretation. An introduction by Blaine Baker and Jim Phillips situates Risk's work in Anglo-American legal history and within Canadian history, and explores common themes in the essays reproduced here.

The purpose of The Osgoode Society for Canadian Legal History is to encourage research and writing in the history of Canadian law. The Society, which was incorporated in 1979 and is registered as a charity, was founded at the initiative of the Honourable R. Roy McMurtry, a former attorney general for Ontario, now chief justice of Ontario, and officials of the Law Society of Upper Canada. Its efforts to stimulate the study of legal history in Canada include a research-support program, a graduate student research-assistance program, and work in the fields of oral history and legal archives. The Society publishes volumes of interest to its members that contribute to legal-historical scholarship in Canada, including studies of the courts, the judiciary, and the legal profession; biographies; collections of documents; studies in criminology and penology; accounts of significant trials; and work in the social and economic history of the law.

Until earlier this year the editor-in-chief of the Osgoode Society for Canadian Legal History was Professor Peter Oliver, who served in that role since 1979. Professor Oliver passed away in May 2006, but not before he worked extensively with the authors of our 2006 books. He is primarily responsible for seeing them through from inception to publication, as he was for all of the other sixty-three books published during his tenure of more than a quarter of a century. The Society is much indebted to him for all his contributions.

Current directors of The Osgoode Society for Canadian Legal History are Robert Armstrong, Kenneth Binks, Patrick Brode, Michael Bryant, Brian Bucknall, Archie Campbell, David Chernos, Kirby Chown, J. Douglas Ewart, Martin Friedland, Elizabeth Goldberg, John Honsberger, Horace Krever, Gavin MacKenzie, Virginia MacLean, Roy McMurtry, Brendan O'Brien, Jim Phillips, Paul Reinhardt, Joel Richler, William Ross, James Spence, Richard Tinsley.

The annual report and information about membership may be obtained by writing: The Osgoode Society for Canadian Legal History, Osgoode Hall, 130 Queen Street West, Toronto, Ontario. M5H 2N6. Telephone: 416-947-3321. E-mail: mmacfarl@lsuc.on.ca. Website: Osgoodesociety.ca.

R. Roy McMurtry
President

Jim Phillips
Interim Editor-in-Chief

A HISTORY OF CANADIAN LEGAL THOUGHT

Collected Essays

Introduction

G. BLAINE BAKER AND JIM PHILLIPS

This anthology of 12 historical studies of Canadian legal thought, all the work of University of Toronto Professor of Law Emeritus R.C.B. Risk, collects work published over a span of some 20 years.[1] Selected by the author and the editors of this volume, at the request of the Osgoode Society, these articles represent a major corpus of writing on the history of Canadian legal culture, and are therefore best understood as contributions to Canadian intellectual history. The purpose of republishing them is to make a valuable, and in many ways unique, body of scholarship on the late-nineteenth- and mid-twentieth-century Canadian legal mind both more visible and more accessible, to Canadian and international audiences.

The essays have been grouped in this volume in three categories, and the order in which they appear within those categories is thematic rather than reflecting the date of publication. The categories are 'The Classical Age: Canadian Legal Thought in the Late Nineteenth Century' (six papers);[2] 'The Challenge of Modernity: Canadian Legal Thought in the 1930s' (five papers);[3] and 'Postwar Developments' (one paper).[4] They therefore survey, collectively, a period of almost one hundred years. Risk was ultimately most interested in the decades straddling the turn of the twentieth century and in the 1930s, a preoccupation reflected in the temporal focus of the scholarship reproduced here. He did, however, establish something of a bridgehead into the postwar period late in his career, and others have begun to explore more fully his themes for the second half of the twentieth century.[5] Geographically, Risk's emphasis when dealing with the common law tended to be central Canada, especially Ontario, but that focus was frequently transcended in his work on Canadian public law thought. Hopefully other scholars will eventually be inspired to identify and assess in detail regional similarities or differences in national private and public law thought.

A note about the format of the essays reproduced here is necessary. The articles are essentially in their original form. Inevitably in a series of pieces that deal with related topics but were written over a long span of time, there is some overlap among them and occasionally some repetition. We considered editing out this repetition and referring the reader to other articles in the collection. That would have made the book shorter and have been helpful to the reader who wants to take it all in one go. But it would also have required the reader who looks only at selected articles at any one time to go back and forth, and we decided that keeping each article coherent was the better course. The text is therefore mostly unaltered in any substantive way. There are, however, some small changes to the original articles. The notes have been edited for consistency of style, and a few minor mistakes corrected, and we have added cross-references to other papers in this collection where appropriate. But in all substantial respects the essays are in their original form.

This introduction was written with three goals in mind. A first purpose is to locate Risk's work methodologically in the contemporary writing of Anglo-American intellectual history. A second goal is to provide a more concrete description of ways that Risk's studies relied on or complemented, and continue to interact with, scholarship in British, American, and Canadian intellectual history. The final aim, with which the largest part of this introduction is concerned, is to survey the principal themes within Risk's work.

Theory and Method in Intellectual History

A useful starting point for this reflection is the straightforward insight of American historian David Flaherty that, depending on how it is done, legal history can find itself closely aligned with cultural, social, political, or economic history, or with a combination of those forms of scholarship.[6] Indeed, Risk's earliest historical research, which led to a series of four seminal articles on law and the market in mid-nineteenth-century

Ontario, were more like contributions to Canadian economic or political history than additions to intellectual history.[7] That writing was influenced by the work of leading American legal historians such as Lawrence Friedman, Morton Horwitz, and Willard Hurst, whose interest in ideas was secondary to their curiosity about the instrumental deployment of legal doctrine or institutions to affect social change in the nineteenth century.[8] That tendency has continued to dominate mainstream scholarship in modern American legal history during the intervening 30 years.[9] Its impact in Britain is more difficult to assess, owing primarily to the slower pace at which interest in most species of modern legal history has developed there.[10]

The reasons for the relative preoccupation with the role of law in political, social, and economic history in Canada's sibling jurisdictions are also complex.[11] But part of the explanation for that historiographical tilt is probably that 'there was a tendency among historians to deride rather than try to understand the thought processes of the law, and the ideas and culture of the legal profession, that are essential to any understanding of the history of law and society.'[12] In contrast, even in Risk's early work there was latent concern about legal consciousness and ideology. His studies of law and the economy in mid-nineteenth-century Ontario were, for example, peppered with references to lawyers' engagement with the Canadian Loyalist myth, the Victorian idea of progress, and North Atlantic liberalism.[13] Alongside a new history of culture and political ideas pioneered by Canadian scholars such as Leslie Armour, Elizabeth Trott, Carl Berger, and Brian McKillop, Risk set out anew in the early 1980s to describe several distinctively Canadian forms of legal consciousness through a study of judicial mindsets, short biographies of noteworthy legal scholars, and a history of constitutional thought.[14] In the course of doing so, he said a great deal about the emergent administrative state and the rule of law, the contingency of conceptions of judging on competing assumptions about legal knowledge, discursive models for debates about constitutional divisions of power, and the ideologies of private and public rights.[15]

Risk's work on the history of Canadian legal thought most closely resembles the strand of contemporary intellectual history that is generally known as contextualism. In that methodology a historian's task is to reconstruct the cultural context in which his or her historical subjects worked and to explain or interpret texts and ideas with reference to it. The products of that kind of intellectual labour typically take the form of histories of the belief systems of particular communities or of discussions organized by the linguistic assumptions shared by the relevant conversationalists. Well-known international practitioners of that methodology include Joyce Appleby, Quentin Skinner, and John Pocock.[16] Although Risk was typically parsimonious in his provision of references, his reliance on the work of several of those contemporaries can be traced through the notes to his articles.[17]

Alternative approaches to intellectual history that have found expression in recent American and Continental writing on legal history include the structuralism often associated with Michel Foucault, Jacques Derrida's textualism, and the techniques of new criticism and deconstruction.[18] Risk has not been given to lengthy forays into theories of historical knowledge or historiography, but there are a couple of features of his work that suggest he was not oblivious to modern debates about method. One such quality is playful references to protagonists in his arguments, such as his description of Foucault as a 'straw scarecrow,' and occasional mention of the 'structure' of legal thought.[19] Another is the consistency and precision with which he provided context for his 'portrait gallery' of Canadian legal thinkers.

Canadian and Anglo-American Cultural Historiography

Risk made selective use of leading overviews of Canadian historiography, such as Carl Berger's *Writing of Canadian History*.[20] But those references most often involved factual detail rather than epistemological debate.[21] Nor was Risk much interested in periodic published hand-wringing by practising Canadian intellectual historians over issues like the relationship between state-building nationalism and regional identity.[22] Risk was keen to promote interdisciplinary dialogue among diverse species of historians, and he was mildly sensitive to the handicap he bore by virtue of the perennial status of Canadian cultural history as a poor relation to other sub-themes in Canadian history. He attempted to close those gaps by engaging promptly with new monographs in Canadian intellectual history as they appeared with increasing frequency during the 1980s and the 1990s. But that engagement on Risk's part was rarely reciprocated by fellow-travellers doing other forms of Canadian cultural history.[23]

A first and modest use that Risk made of companion scholarship in local intellectual history was biographical. An essay on the judicial outlook of Chief Justice of Ontario William Ralph Meredith, for example, was based on some 750 reported late-nineteenth- and early-twentieth-century judgments that Meredith authored.[24] But personal context was provided by an unpublished doctoral thesis on Meredith's pre-judicial career.[25] In a companion overview essay on Canadian constitutional thought, also set in the late nineteenth century, Risk had much to say about teacher, pamphleteer, and parliamentarian David Mills.[26] Reliance on an unpublished biography of Mills provided context for Risk's dissection of Mills' Canadian public law theories.[27] Similarly, when Risk brought forward his studies of local constitutional scholars into the 1930s,[28] he was able to flesh out his commentary on Francis Reginald Scott's academic writing by reference to work by literary and political historians on Scott's poetry and social activism.[29] What is most striking about Risk's turn to cultural history for assistance with biographical context for his legal scholars is, however, the infrequency with which he was able to do it. Leading Canadian legal writers, many of whom also had high-profile careers in business and politics, have not yet attracted the sustained attention of mainstream social or economic historians.

A second use that Risk made of scholarship in Canadian intellectual history was pin-point and thematic. That reliance often involved older monographs whose treatment of topics like the compact theory of federalism or the provincial rights movement played directly into new work that Risk was doing on public law scholarship.[30] Again, however, the engagement that Risk was able to achieve with those kinds of sources was modest, a state of affairs consistent with the overwhelmingly positivistic character that historiographers of Canadian constitutionalism have consistently attributed to that literature.[31]

A third use that Risk made of related writing in Canadian intellectual history involved reference to a handful of articles in legal history that offered professional context for what his scholars were doing.[32] That context was sometimes remote, and Risk can occasionally be seen to be reaching to integrate the work of fellow law school travellers into his accounts of turn-of-the-twentieth-century Canadian legal thought.[33] The community of legal historians in which Risk worked who were interested in ideas was not large.[34]

Finally, and most ambitiously, Risk integrated into his expanding historical essays on local legal thought path-breaking studies in the history of Canadian religion,[35] public administration,[36] philosophy,[37] political theory,[38] and imperialism.[39] Sometimes those monographs were deployed to suggest that Risk's judges and legal scholars shared beliefs with larger and more professionally diverse groups of Canadian intellectuals. On other occasions they were used to reveal contrasts in the ways that different disciplines embraced history or interpreted texts. As often as not, however, those complementary studies in Canadian cultural history became footnotes without much elaboration.[40] Risk routinely made these kinds of gestures of scholarly extroversion, presumably in the belief that they would encourage others to work harder to more fully integrate histories of legal thought into accounts of Canadian political, social, and religious theory.

Contrary to emerging tendencies in other species of Anglo-American intellectual history, Risk's engagement with companion British scholarship was minimal. He occasionally used ranking sources in English analytical jurisprudence for definitional assistance.[41] But integration of publications in modern English legal history was limited to a couple of works by David Sugarman and Harry Arthurs, because there is not much other British material that is relevant to Risk's work on the history of Anglo-Canadian legal thought.[42] He made more extensive and productive use of contemporary publications in the history of modern British political thought, but that is not a literature to which Risk was seeking to contribute significantly.[43]

American source material for the history of modern legal thought, both primary and secondary, was by far Risk's preferred comparative sounding board. That choice makes sense for two reasons. Canadian legal scholars were, by many indications, reading American legal literature during the periods in which Risk was interested. Indeed, several of Risk's historical subjects attended graduate school in the United States and came under the direct influence of leading American thinkers of the day.[44] There is also more and better secondary literature on the history of United States legal thought than there is intellectual history for any aspect of the contemporary Canadian or British experience. That American literature offers the potential of rewarding comparative insight, and it therefore made doubly good sense to work through it carefully.

Risk made selective but potent use of the mission statements of sociological jurisprudence and American legal realism by leading spokespeople for those movements such as Roscoe Pound, Felix Cohen, Benjamin Cardozo, and Jerome Frank.[45] That recurrence to 'primary' sources is helpful to readers, since the tone and content of publications by Risk's twentieth-century Canadian subjects can routinely be shown to be similar to the American manifestos. Risk made another more precise use of American sources when he turned to the examination of particular topics. Three examples should make the point. Risk's Canadian writers were often administrative process enthusiasts, keen to enhance the state's role in redistributive initiatives through refinement of non-constitutional public law. Issues of institutional design, instrument choice, and statute construction were therefore standard fare in their writing. To assist interpretation of the Canadian scholarship, Risk often brought leading American academic sources into his analysis.[46] A similar technique was deployed by Risk in his assessment of emerging Canadian private law theory, such as that underlying private international law.[47] Conflict of laws was an appropriate aspect of private law to examine comparatively, not only because Risk had an original Canadian scholar in that subject in the person of Moffat Hancock, but also because legal realism had a greater impact on choice of law than on most other aspects of American private law. Risk could probably have done more in that regard, but he appears to have chosen instead to emphasize close reading of his Canadian texts and to integrate further comparative material by working from a rich and diverse selection of recently published secondary sources on the history of modern United States legal thought.

Americans have written a lot about their history of legal education – scholarship that was relevant to Risk because a couple of the essays in this collection are obliquely about Canadian law schools and because most of his historical subjects spent substantial parts of their careers in this country's struggling faculties of law of the early and mid-twentieth centuries.[48] Indeed, it would have been difficult for Risk to have assessed the 'Harvardization' of Canadian legal thinkers such as Caesar Wright or Bora Laskin without reliance on those American sources. Risk made similarly selective but effective use of recent publications in twentieth-century American constitutional history.[49] United States jurisprudential models described in that literature enabled him to see quickly that a similar model of balance, shorn of legal realism's political edge, featured Canadian scholars skilled in the workings of legal processes and the institutional implementation of social preferences.

Secondary literature on twentieth-century American legal thought at large was, however, the most important source of comparison and inspiration for Risk. The first cluster of essays in this anthology, grouped under the heading of 'The Classical Age: Canadian Legal Thought in the Late Nineteenth Century,' features writing motivated by what Risk characterized as 'rule of law' thought – thought that was said to have involved the deduction of rights from abstract first principles. Legal analysis was thought to be neutral, apolitical, and autonomous, and judicial decisions, in turn, were held to be shaped entirely by the play of formal logic on common law doctrine. Risk found trans-systemic support for those conclusions in published histories of late-nineteenth-century American legal formalism.[50] But he also used related American writing to assist description and explanation of a transition from formalism to realism that characterized Canadian legal scholarship of the early twentieth century.[51] Since that process was characterized by the importation of American ideas about progressivism in law, sociological jurisprudence, and legal realism – which focused on the identification, evaluation, adjustment, and balancing of interests by academics participating in a reconstruction of functional law – it also made sense for Risk to have made substantial use of histories of twentieth-century American legal thought in his production of the second cluster of articles in this anthology, 'The Challenge of Modernity: Canadian Legal Thought in the 1930s.'[52]

Canadian Legal Scholarship's Philosophical Themes

Risk's goal in scrutinizing neoclassical Canadian case law and extrajudicial writing of the late nineteenth century was to determine how judges and scholars understood the methods and limits of legal reasoning. Adjectives that provide common ground among the six articles in the first section are ones such as *positivistic, apolitical, autonomous,* and *objective*. The doctrine of strict precedent had been settled in Britain before the last quarter of the nineteenth century, and it was applied in a rigorously derivative fashion in English Canada. Law was thought by Risk's historical subjects to exist independently of commentators who organized it or the judiciary who applied it. But law work was repeatedly said to be scientific, in two ways. The coordination, arrangement, and systematization of case law and general principles was said merely to reveal state law's inherently orderly and thus scientific character. Augustus Henry Fraser Lefroy's public law triumph, *Legislative Power*, was a comprehensive constitutional treatise organized around 68 propositions for interpretation of the *British North America Act*.[53] John Skirving Ewart's private law milestone, *Estoppel*, was likewise constructed in a near-codal manner around 11 principles that were said to give clarity to what Anglo-American courts had done in thousands of disputes involving estoppels by misrepresentation.[54] *Scientific* meant, in part, 'coherent and orderly.'

But Risk concluded that his late-nineteenth-century Canadian law-yers also saw a form of Baconian natural science in the processes of induction from previously decided cases to first principles and the subsequent deduction from those abstract rules to settle new disputes that characterize *stare decisis*.[55] Inductive generalization was, said Risk, thought to be a purely logical exercise in synthesis. Deduction from general principles to new cases was apparently thought to involve a little more judicial flexibility, because the implications of the existing stock of rules were not always fully understood. Courts and commen-tators were therefore obliged to elaborate on broad principles, but once an application had been settled, it could not be modified. Social needs, interests, and the comparative merits of alternative potential results formed no part of the calculation. Indeed, in respect of Chief Justice of Ontario William Ralph Meredith, Risk was able to report that that judge gave no hint of any belief that his work had public importance, and that he conceived of his vocation as a search for the authoritative single case whose similarity to the conflict at hand imbued it with the weight of adjudicative authority.[56] Because it examines the thought of a judge, Risk's work on Meredith is perhaps the place where he also considers most systematically the relationship between legal ideas and the effect those ideas had on the law as applied by courts. But this was a theme explored, in varying degrees, throughout his work.[57]

Risk's late-nineteenth-century legal thinkers were uniformly taci-turn, a characteristic that made the task of explaining their commitment to 'rule-of-law' thought a challenging one. But almost none of what they said or did was original, making it possible for Risk to look for explanations for local legal formalism largely in Britain, from whose bar, courts, and schools Canadian habits were derivative. Most elite, late-nineteenth-century Canadian lawyers were imperialists, with loy-alty to Britain and British models, and conceived of law as a major link of empire. Insofar as they engaged in theoretical self-reflection, their legal consciousness seems to have been structured upon the earlier work of English laissez-faire positivists such as John Austin, John Stuart Mill, and Jeremy Bentham.[58] Risk was otherwise able to report that they spoke regularly of legal science, both in terms of the systematic organi-zation of normative information and in terms of inductive method. But the Canadian scholars do not seem to have been as crassly ambi-tious for their profession as leading lawyers elsewhere in the North Atlantic world who used scientific ornamentation for public relations advantage.[59]

In addition to a superior court judge, two private law textbook writers, and ten constitutional scholars, Risk factored the political commentary of David Mills and Edward Blake into his studies of neoclassical Canadian legal thought.[60] Parliamentary proponents of provincial rights had, by 1900, constructed a model of autonomous Canadian federalism based on coordinate governments, independent of one another, each exercising exclusive and supreme authority in its sphere of power. That provincial rights rhetoric was, said Risk, derivative of the dominant form of Anglo-American legal reasoning of the day, which was built around autonomous and equal juridical people, sharp notional boundaries between public and private spheres of action, overwhelming respect for courts and state law, and an appreciation of legal relations as transactions among seats of power divided by sharp lines. Federal intrusions into fields of provincial jurisdiction were therefore characterized as assaults on the integrity of legal liberalism rather than mere *ultra vires* actions under the *British North America Act*. Risk concluded that late-nineteenth-century Canadian public law involved a constitutionalization of the common law in which was implicit an extension of the legal and political power of provincial parliaments. But he also concluded that effective discursive innovation or theoretical manoeuvring by erudite Liberal orators such as Mills and Blake was about nothing more or less than decontextualized federalism. Consistent with general patterns of private law scholarship about which Risk was simultaneously writing, the range of literature and sources on which provincial rights advocates relied was limited, and there is no indication that material preferences like friendly regulation of manufacturing concerns in expansive provincial jurisdictions or favouritism for resource extraction, transportation, or financial enterprises had much to do with the technical legal culture of provincial rights.[61]

A close link between that political rhetoric and legal doctrine was ultimately forged by constitutional text writers such as Lefroy. His *Legislative Power* was said by Risk to have been doctrinally pedestrian, but Lefroy did untangle an undigested jumble of division of powers case law by imposing on it provincially sympathetic interpretive frameworks that structured twentieth-century debates about Canadian statebuilding around legal terms of art like ancillarity, pith and substance, double-aspects, and concurrency.[62]

A second distinctive public law theme that Risk was able to unearth, mostly from political debate, had to do with the sovereignty of parliament, responsible government, and the role of legislatures in the facilitation and protection of private autonomy.[63] He observed early in his research that Canadian private law reasoning was typically deferential rather than hostile towards parliamentary action, and that legislatures were regarded as protectors of personal liberty.[64] Contrary to what constitutionally empowered 'Lochner-era' American courts were doing with judicial review of legislative action to protect individual rights, mainstream Canadian legal thinkers tended to rely on parliaments as guardians of personal freedom and arbiters of the limits of rights.[65] Private autonomy was routinely limited by the needs of the broader community expressed in statutory form, and, perhaps even more uniquely Canadian, debates that began as arguments about individual rights often ended as claims for the autonomy of provincial legislatures. Even more enigmatically, late-nineteenth-century Canadian civil and political liberties were also said by Risk to have been mutually reinforcing in that active participation in government was regarded as constitutive of personal identity. Freedoms such as those of life, person, property, speech, conscience, and religion were thought by Risk's historical subjects to have been transplanted eighteenth-century British constitutional claims against the state, but they were not understood to be absolute liberties. The real issues for the legal thinkers were by whom and according to what process could limits be imposed by the will of the community assembled in a democratically authorized setting. Civil liberty was therefore a kind of unnatural and bridled freedom to live within the restraints of laws made and applied by a government responsible to the population at large. The only restraints on legislative power were said to be 'the good sense and right feeling of the people,' expressed in public discourse about shared values. An important corollary of that point of view is that the executive branch of government cannot have statutory or quasi-legislative powers, since that would make for despotic and arbitrary government.

The circle of provincial rights, civil liberties, and political freedoms was thus closed insofar as the federal cabinet's exercise of its *British North America Act* power to disallow provincial laws on grounds of division of powers (and the related capacity of provincial lieutenant-governors to reserve provincial acts) offended basic principles such as responsible government and the sovereignty of parliament. The movement by provincial rights advocates of division of powers disputes from executive to judicial settings was thus shown by Risk to have been not merely a matter of pragmatic forum-shopping, but a principled application of emergent civil and political rights thought.

Risk's initial work on the 1930s (completed in 1984 and 1987) preceded his studies of late-nineteenth-century Canadian legal thought.[66] He was therefore not, at least in the first instance, obliged to address directly issues of transition or comparison that later became major themes in his writing on the 'challenge of modernity.' Risk commenced study of Canadian legal thought in the 1930s biographically, with a tribute to his former teaching colleague John Willis and a prosopogrophy of nine contributors to the inaugural (1935) volume of the *University of Toronto Law Journal*. Sub-themes about the administrative or welfare state and law teaching or legal education quickly emerged in that writing alongside Risk's predominant interest in Canadian legal thought.[67] His most sweeping conclusion in the five articles collected in this volume under the heading 'The Challenge of Modernity: Canadian Legal Thought in the 1930s' is that traditional faith in the shaping of judicial decisions by the application of formal logic to common law doctrine was replaced by concern about values, context, and human choices. Law, both judicially made and statutory, came to be understood as a means to achieve social ends, which, by definition, lay outside state law. The focus of legal reasoning thus became human interests in need of identification, evaluation, adjustment, and balancing, rather than formal rights. That reorientation meant, in turn, that the character and worth of official law should be assessed by its social effects and its coherence with contemporary values. Risk's Canadian legal scholars of the 1930s therefore quite naturally developed a confident enthusiasm for their roles in debates about policy and social context. A new appreciation of the material world's fluidity and law's facilitative and regulatory capacities provoked a penchant for functional and realistic law, in whose making and management law school academics were increasingly determined to participate. Legal scholarship thus came to be epitomized by political passion.[68]

Alongside that increasingly progressive or sociological mandate for judicially administered private law, modern Canadian legal thought featured broad acceptance of the public sector and a willingness to invest extensive powers in the state. The daily routine of legislative and administrative business effectively displaced judicial *cause célèbres* as the focus of academic inquiry.[69] Expressed bluntly, scholars' shared hope seems to have been that increased legislative and administrative activity would circumscribe market-related, common law values, and thus change the relationship of individuals to their communities. The expertise and accountability of administrative delegates became new, corollary issues for Risk's legal thinkers of the 1930s, challenges with which they may have dealt incompletely but nonetheless treated in a thoroughly functional rather than judicial or conceptual manner.

Risk found that constitutional scholarship had changed purpose and tone dramatically in the 1930s. Insofar as there was an established approach to writing about the Canadian constitution, it involved legal practitioners producing treatises by extracting doctrine from judicial decisions. Constitutional texts and legal rules were thought to exist independently of temporal contingency, context, or values, making jurisprudential analysis an objective and apolitical task.[70] Reoriented public law scholarship of the interwar period became the prerogative of a small group of full-time Canadian legal academics who were concerned about the federal government's constitutional incapacity to undertake crucial social functions in a time of economic depression. That paralysis was blamed almost uniformly on the preference for provincial rights manifested by the Judicial Committee of the Privy Council in division-of-powers litigation over the previous half-century. The scholars insisted that the Privy Council had failed to consider history, context, or interests.[71] This failure, together with its positivistic approach to textual interpretation, drew nationalistic, legally realistic, and socially progressive fire from Risk's scholars of the 1930s. Those critics were attempting at the same time to rehabilitate the Dominion government through the promotion of fiscal federalism, enhanced legislative union through uniformity of laws projects, agitation to abolish appeals to the Privy Council, and left-leaning political action.[72]

Although Risk rarely wrote comprehensively or even explicitly about Canadian legal education or law schools, his twentieth-century subjects were almost all career law teachers. They typically worked in geographic and intellectual isolation from each other, in a handful of small faculties. By highlighting the cultural and professional assumptions that underlay the scholarship of writers like William Paul McClure Kennedy, John Willis, Alex Corry, Percy Corbett, and Frank Scott, Risk was able to suggest that there was more interdisciplinarity, academic inspiration, and pedagogical variety beyond the mainstream of the Law Society of Upper Canada's Osgoode Hall Law School than received wisdom about the history of Canadian legal education had allowed.[73] He also began to expose a political wedge in attitudes toward the administrative state between the nascent community of professional legal academics and the rank and file of the practising bar. The dominant response of Canadian lawyers to the rise of the regulatory state, said Risk, was to insulate their thinking from its implications, while academic lawyers more often assumed responsibility through teaching, writing, and political activism for construction of the institutional apparatus of public welfare. The recent appearance of a number of Canadian law firm histories should facilitate further reflection on that theme, which made a large impression upon the legal periodicals and popular press of the interwar years.[74]

Perhaps naturally in view of the pioneering character of Risk's writing on Canadian legal thought, he was cautious in his attribution of causes of the significant shifts in ethnic loyalty, moral responsibility, and epistemological assumptions that occurred among his scholars between 1890 and 1940. He noted parallels between the activities of his group and those of other Canadian social scientists during the relevant period, but also observed no apparent contacts among members of those groups. Instead, Risk concluded that, insofar as his revitalized Canadian legal writers of the 1930s had models, they tended to be university-based American legal scholars. Harvard's Roscoe Pound, a changeable theoretical mentor, was identified as an early influence on Canadians such as W.P.M. Kennedy and Caesar Wright, as were Felix Frankfurter and Thurman Arnold upon John Willis.[75] A recent study by Robert Gordon of Willis' American counterparts is one of the few other attempts to work out those patterns of intellectual cross-pollination, and Risk himself has been cautious in the attribution of direct influence.[76] Local experience with the economic depression of the 1930s and the related mobilization of private, charitable, and public sectors to cope with welfare issues no doubt also placed a new premium on institutional design. Deeper excavation of the bases for the transformation in theoretical orientation of Canadian legal scholars as between 'neoclassical' and 'modern' writers initially identified and documented by Risk will likely show them to have been multiple rather than unicausal.

Risk's treatment of post–Second World War developments was not quite as sustained, topically diverse, or extensively grounded in source material as was his work on the earlier periods. But 'On the Road to Oz: Common Law Scholarship about Federalism after World War II' was a similarly path-breaking study of Canadian legal culture, and it brings forward in a manner recognizable to contemporary students of Canadian constitutionalism several themes that characterized previous eras of scholarship.[77] Risk's mid-twentieth-century subjects – Frank Scott, Bora Laskin, and William Lederman – had different approaches to

public law scholarship, but shared the belief that the central constitutional questions of the day had to do with the prevailing allocation of
federal–provincial power and with techniques for the achievement of a
preferred division of that power that was responsive to social welfare
issues rather than to the imperatives of legal doctrine. Scott tended to
write about social values and contemporary politics, without dissecting
legal doctrine or processes. Lederman also tended to eschew intensive
analysis of rules and case law in favour of the identification of sweeping trends and general appeals to broad-based public sentiment. Laskin
was said by Risk to have been more conventional and even encyclope-
dic in treatments of hard law than either of his contemporaries, with a
target audience of law students, lawyers, and judges. But he was frequently critical of courts for their techniques of constitutional interpretation, their styles of reasoning, and the political implications of their
decisions

All three of Risk's mid-twentieth-century commentators believed
that the meanings of words were ambiguous, incomplete, and even
indefinite, that judges made political choices that should not be masked
by barren logic or abstract reasoning, and that the judiciary was obliged
to take account of current social conditions and needs as its members
balanced overlapping or competing federal and provincial claims to
power. Risk characterized that preference for non-textual balancing of
extra-legal considerations as the scholarly version of cooperative federalism in the political sphere, and as a tamed version of the academic
ferment associated with the interwar years. It trimmed legal realism's
iconoclastic or cynical edges, and featured scholars skilled in the workings of legal processes and the institutional implementation of social
preferences.[78] That 'model of balance' came to dominate Canadian
constitutional adjudication and scholarship during the 1960s and 1970s.
A substantial amount of intellectual history has been undertaken by
chroniclers other than Risk on very modern local public law, with the
result that a comprehensive historiographical account would not need
to end with 'Road to Oz.'[79]

Conclusion

Neither lawyers nor legal scholars in the Anglo-American tradition have
been much interested in socio-legal history writ large, and there has traditionally been even less enthusiasm for cultural histories of law. Internal 'lawyers' histories' of keystone concepts such as freedom of contract

or the inviolability of property have not only sufficed, but have dominated that department of the history of ideas. Typically devoid of context and built on undemonstrated assumptions about the social or cultural relevance of ideas, those kinds of accounts tended to postpone or foreclose more rigorous inquiries into the thought processes of the law or the ideas and beliefs of the legal professions. Even instrumental accounts of the history of law and society are prone to be skewed in the absence of appropriate attention to related habits and structures of legal thought. Risk intuited that shortcoming over three decades ago and urged his contemporaries to do something about it in a widely read initial agenda for Canadian legal history.[80] When too few people responded to that solicitation for support, Risk effectively created the cultural history of Canadian law as a field of insightful and comparative scholarship by doing the work himself. The contents of this anthology are offered as a representative cross-section of that intellectual entrepreneurialism.

NOTES

1 The essays reproduced here represent about half of Risk's work in modern legal history. A complete list of Risk's publications to 1999, including writings on contemporary administrative, constitutional, and property law that do not form part of his historical dossier, can be found in 'R.C.B. Risk Bibliography,' in G.B. Baker and J. Phillips, eds., *Essays in the History of Canadian Law: In Honour of R.C.B. Risk* (Toronto: Osgoode Society for Canadian Legal History and University of Toronto Press, 1999) 583. Four citations must now be added to that bibliography to bring it up to date: R.C.B. Risk, 'Here Be Cold and Tygers: A Map of Statutory Interpretation in Canada in the 1920s and 1930s' (2000) 63 *Sask. L.R.* 195; 'On the Road to Oz: Common Law Scholarship about Federalism after World War II' (2001) 51 *U.T.L.J.* 143; 'Canadian Law Teachers in the 1930s: When the World Was Turned Upside Down' (2004) 27 *Dalhousie L.J.* 1; and 'My Continuing Legal Education' (2005) 55 *U.T.L.J.* 313.

2 In the order in which they appear in this volume, these essays are 'Constitutional Scholarship in the Late Nineteenth Century: Making Federalism Work' (1996) 46 *U.T.L.J.* 427; 'A.H.F. Lefroy: Common Law Thought in Late-Nineteenth-Century Canada – On Burying One's Grandfather' (1991) 41 *U.T.L.J.* 307; 'Rights Talk in Canada in the Late Nineteenth Century: "The Good Sense and Right Feeling of the People"' (1996) 14 *Law & Hist. R.* 1 (with R.C Vipond); 'Blake and Liberty,' in J. Ajzenstat, ed., *Canadian*

Constitutionalism, 1791–1991 (Ottawa: Canadian Study of Parliament Group, 1992) 195; 'John Skirving Ewart: The Legal Thought' (1987) 37 *U.T.L.J.* 335; 'Sir William R. Meredith C.J.O.: The Search for Authority' (1983) 7 *Dalhousie L.J.* 713.

3 In the order in which they appear in this volume, these essays are 'Volume One of the Journal: A Tribute and a Belated Review' (1987) 37 *U.T.L.J.* 193; 'The Scholars and the Constitution: POGG and the Privy Council' (1996) 23 *Manitoba L.J.* 496; 'John Willis: A Tribute' (1984) 9 *Dalhousie L.J.* 521; 'The Many Minds of W.P.M. Kennedy' (1998) 48 *U.T.L.J.* 353; 'Canadian Law Teachers in the 1930s: "When the World Was Turned Upside Down,"' supra note 1.

4 'On the Road to Oz,' supra note 1.

5 See 'On the Road to Oz.' For recent work see most notably J. Benedickson, 'From Empire Ontario to California North: Law and Legal Institutions in Twentieth-Century Ontario' (1995) 23 *Manitoba L.J.* 620; P.V. Girard, *Bora Laskin: Bringing Law to Life* (Toronto: Osgoode Society for Canadian Legal History and University of Toronto Press, 2005); M. MacLaren, 'A History of the University of Toronto Faculty of Law Review' (1997) 55 *U. of Toronto Faculty of L.R.* 375.

6 See D.H. Flaherty, 'Writing Canadian Legal History: An Introduction,' in D.H. Flaherty, ed., *Essays in the History of Canadian Law: Volume One* (Toronto: Osgoode Society for Canadian Legal History and University of Toronto Press, 1981) 3 at 4.

7 See R.C.B. Risk, 'The Nineteenth-Century Foundations of the Business Corporation in Ontario' (1973) 23 *U.T.L.J.* 270; 'The Golden Age: The Law about the Market in Nineteenth-Century Ontario' (1976) 26 *U.T.L.J.* 307; 'The Last Golden Age: Property and Allocation of Losses in Ontario in the Nineteenth Century' (1977) 27 *U.T.L.J.* 199; 'The Law and the Economy in Mid-Nineteenth-Century Ontario: A Perspective' (1977), 27 *U.T.L.J.* 403.

8 Compare L.M. Friedman, *A History of American Law* (New York: Simon and Shuster, 1973); M.J. Horwitz, *The Transformation of American Law, 1780–1860* (Cambridge: Harvard University Press, 1977); J.W. Hurst, *Law and the Conditions of Freedom in the Nineteenth-Century United States* (Madison: University of Wisconsin Press, 1956).

9 See, for example, T.A. Freyer, *The Federal Courts and Business in American History* (Greenwich, CT: JAI Press, 1979); M.J. Horwitz, *The Transformation of American Law, 1870–1960: The Crisis of Legal Orthodoxy* (Oxford: Oxford University Press, 1992); H. Hovenkamp, *Enterprise and American Law, 1836– 1937* (Cambridge: Harvard University Press, 1991).

10 See generally D. Sugarman and G.R. Rubin, 'Towards a New History of

Law and Material Society in England, 1750–1914,' in G.R. Rubin and D. Sugarman, eds., *Law, Economy and Society, 1750–1914: Essays in the History of English Law* (Abingdon, UK: Professional Books, 1984) 1.

11 For useful speculations see R.W. Gordon, 'Historicism in Legal Scholarship' (1981) 90 *Yale L.J.* 1017; M.J. Horwitz, 'The Conservative Tradition in the Writing of American Legal History' (1973) 17 *Am. J. Legal Hist.* 275; S.N. Katz, 'The Problem of a Colonial Legal History,' in J.P. Greene and J.R. Pole, eds., *Colonial British America: Essays in the New History of the Early Modern Era* (Baltimore: Johns Hopkins University Press, 1984) 457.

12 R.W. Gordon and D. Sugarman, 'Richard C.B. Risk: A Tribute,' in Baker and Phillips, supra note 1, 3 at 4.

13 See, for example, Risk, 'Golden Age,' supra note 7 at 337, 339; Risk, 'Last Golden Age,' supra note 7 at 236; Risk, 'Law and the Economy,' supra note 7 at 421, 427, 430. See also R.C.B. Risk, 'This Nuisance of Litigation: The Origin of Workers' Compensation in Ontario,' in D.H. Flaherty, ed., *Essays in the History of Canadian Law: Volume Two* (Toronto: Osgoode Society for Canadian Legal History and University of Toronto Press, 1983) 418 at 421– 2; R.C.B. Risk, 'Lawyers, Courts and the Rise of the Regulatory State' (1984) 9 *Dalhousie L.J.* 31 at 38; R.C.B. Risk, 'New Directions for Legal History,' in D. and R. Gagan, eds., *New Directions for the Study of Ontario's Past* (Hamilton: McMaster University Press, 1988) 117 at 122, 125.

14 See, for example, L. Armour and E. Trott, *The Faces of Reason: An Essay on Philosophy and Culture in English Canada 1850–1950* (Waterloo: Wilfrid Laurier University Press, 1981); C. Berger, *The Sense of Power: Studies in the Ideas of Canadian Imperialism, 1867–1914* (Toronto: University of Toronto Press, 1970); A.B. McKillop, *A Disciplined Intelligence: Critical Inquiry and Canadian Thought in the Victorian Era* (Montreal and Kingston: McGill-Queen's University Press, 1979).

15 For an overview of that writing, which takes account of Risk's entire oeuvre and situates in it the twelve essays that comprise this volume, see G.B. Baker, 'R.C.B. Risk's Canadian Legal History,' in Baker and Phillips, supra note 1 at 17.

16 See, for example, J.O. Appleby, *Capitalism and a New Social Order: The Republican Vision of the 1790s* (New York: New York University Press, 1984); J.G.A. Pocock, *The Machiavellian Moment: Florentine Political Thought and the Atlantic Republican Tradition* (Princeton: Princeton University Press, 1975); Q. Skinner, *The Foundations of Modern Political Thought* (Cambridge: Cambridge University Press, 1978).

17 See, for example, 'Blake and Liberty,' in this volume at 149, citing Appleby, supra note 16, and J.H. Hexter, 'Republic, Virtue, Liberty, and

the Political Universe of J.G.A. Pocock,' in J.H. Hexter, ed., *On Historians* (Cambridge: Harvard University Press, 1979) 255.

18 Good overviews of those developments and their reception by modern legal historians can be found in W.W. Fisher, 'Texts and Contexts: The Application to American Legal History of the Methodologies of Intellectual History' (1997) 49 *Stanford L.R.* 1065, and R.W. Gordon, 'Critical Legal Histories' (1984) 36 *Stanford L.R.* 57. See also R. Darnton, 'Intellectual and Cultural History,' in M. Kammen, ed., *The Past Before Us: Contemporary Historical Writing in the United States* (Ithaca: Cornell University Press, 1980) 327; M. Ermath, 'Mindful Matters: The Empire's New Codes and the Plight of Modern European Intellectual History' (1985) 57 *J. Modern Hist.* 1065; J.G.A. Pocock, 'Introduction: The State of the Art,' in J.G.A. Pocock, ed., *Virtue, Commerce and History: Essays on Political Thought and History, Chiefly in the Eighteenth Century* (Cambridge: Cambridge University Press, 1985) 1.

19 See, for example, 'Road to Oz,' in this volume at 427; Risk, 'New Directions,' supra note 13 at 121.

20 C. Berger, *The Writing of Canadian History: Aspects of English-Canadian Historical Writing since 1900* (Toronto: University of Toronto Press, 1986). See also M. Bliss, *A Living Profit: Studies in the Social History of Canadian Business, 1883–1911* (Toronto: McClelland and Stewart, 1974).

21 See, for example, 'Many Minds of W.P.M. Kennedy,' in this volume at 325; 'Scholars and the Constitution,' in this volume at 263; 'Volume One,' in this volume at 232.

22 See, for example, C. Karr, 'What Is Canadian Intellectual History?' (1975) 55 *Dalhousie R.* 55; C. Karr, 'What Happened to Canadian Intellectual History?' (1989) 17 *Acadiensis* 174; A.B. McKillop, 'Nationalism, Identity, and Canadian Intellectual History' [1974] *Queen's Q.* 81; A.B. McKillop, 'So Little on the Mind,' [1981] *Trans. Royal Society* (4th ser.) 19; D. Owram, 'Intellectual History in the Land of Limited Identities' (1989) 24 *J. Can. Stud.* 114.

23 Mostly because all of Risk's historical work was published in article form, few reviews that touch on his scholarship exist and it is not therefore possible to assess the impact of his work through those mediums. The observation in the text about limited reciprocity is impressionistic, but that sense is based on 20 or 25 years of general reading in Canadian history, and in the history of education, the professions, and public administration in particular.

24 'Sir William R. Meredith C.J.O.,' in this volume.

25 W. Demski, 'William Ralph Meredith: Leader of the Conservative Opposition in Ontario' (PhD thesis, University of Guelph, 1977).

26 'Constitutional Scholarship,' in this volume.
27 D.J. McMurchy, 'David Mills: Nineteenth-Century Canadian Liberal' (PhD thesis, University of Rochester, 1969). See also R.C. Vipond, *Liberty and Community: Canadian Federalism and the Failure of the Constitution* (Albany: State University of New York Press, 1991); R.C. Vipond, 'David Mills,' in *Dictionary of Canadian Biography*, vol. 13 (Toronto: University of Toronto Press, 1994) 707.
28 See, for example, Risk, 'Scholars and the Constitution,' in this volume.
29 Compare S. Djwa and R. St J. Macdonald, eds., *On F.R. Scott: Essays on His Contributions to Law, Literature, and Politics* (Montreal and Kingston: McGill-Queen's University Press, 1983); M. Horn, 'Frank Scott, the League for Social Reconstruction, and the Constitution,' in Ajzenstat, supra note 2 at 231.
30 See, for example, G.P. Browne, *The Judicial Committee and the British North America Act: An Analysis of the Interpretive Scheme for the Distribution of Legislative Powers* (Toronto: University of Toronto Press, 1967), in 'Scholars and the Constitution,' in this volume at 267–8; R. Cook, *Provincial Autonomy, Minority Rights, and the Compact Theory, 1867–1921* (Ottawa: Queen's Printer, 1969), in 'Constitutional Scholarship,' in this volume at 62; R. Simeon and I. Robinson, *State, Society and the Development of Canadian Federalism* (Toronto: University of Toronto Press, 1990), in 'Scholars and the Constitution,' in this volume at 267; A. Smith, *The Commerce Power in Canada and the United States* (Toronto: Butterworths, 1963), in ibid. at 251.
31 Compare M. Gold, 'Constitutional Scholarship in Canada' (1985) 23 *Osgoode Hall L.J.* 495; P.H. Russell, 'Overcoming Legal Formalism: The Treatment of the Constitution, the Courts and Judicial Behaviour in Canadian Political Science' (1986) 1 *Can. J. Law & Soc.* 5.
32 See, for example, G.B. Baker, 'The Reconstitution of Upper Canadian Legal Thought in the Late-Victorian Empire' (1985) 3 *Law & Hist. Rev.* 219; G.B. Baker, 'So Elegant a Web: Providential Order and the Rule of Secular Law in Early Nineteenth-Century Upper Canada' (1988) 38 *U.T.L.J.* 184; G. Bale, *Chief Justice William Johnstone Ritchie: Responsible Government and Judicial Review* (Ottawa: Carleton University Press, 1991); B. Hibbitts, 'Progress and Principle: The Legal Thought of Sir John Beverley Robinson' (1989) 34 *McGill L.J.* 454.
33 See, for example, 'Constitutional Scholarship,' in this volume at 63; 'A.H.F. Lefroy,' in this volume at 87, 88, 93; 'Scholars and the Constitution,' in this volume at 259.
34 Canadian cultural history that dealt with Risk's law-related themes but did not find its way into his texts would include J.E. Bickenback and

C.I. Kyer, 'The Harvardization of Caesar Wright' (1983) 33 *U.T.L.J.* 162;
P. Horwitz, 'Bora Laskin and the Legal Process School' (1995) 59 *Sask. L.R.*
77.

35 See, for example, M. Gauvreau, *The Evangelical Century: College and Creed in
    English Canada from the Great Revival to the Great Depression* (Montreal and
    Kingston: McGill-Queen's University Press, 1991), and M. Van Die, *An
    Evangelical Mind: Nathaniel Burwash and the Methodist Tradition in Canada,
    1839–1918* (Montreal and Kingston: McGill-Queen's University Press,
    1989), both in 'Constitutional Scholarship,' in this volume at 64.

36 See, for example. D. Owram, *The Government Generation: Canadian
    Intellectuals and the State, 1900–1945* (Toronto: University of Toronto Press,
    1986), in 'Law Teachers,' in this volume at 396; 'Scholars and the Constitu-
    tion,' in this volume at 264; 'Volume One,' in this volume at 232. See also
    Risk, 'Cold and Tygers,' supra note 1 at 209.

37 See, for example, Armour and Trott, supra note 14 in 'Volume One,' in this
    volume at 232; McKillop, supra note 14 in 'Blake and Liberty,' at 150; and
    'Volume One,' at 232.

38 See, for example, B. Ferguson, *Remaking Liberalism: The Intellectual Legacy of
    Adam Short, O.D. Skelton, W.C. Clark, and W.A. MacIntosh, 1890–1925*
    (Montreal and Kingston: McGill-Queen's University Press, 1979), in
    'Rights Talk,' and 'Volume One,' in this volume at 129, 232; J.A.W. Gunn,
    *Beyond Liberty and Property: The Process of Self-Recognition in Eighteenth-
    Century Political Thought* (Montreal and Kingston: McGill-Queen's Univer-
    sity Press, 1983), in 'Rights Talk,' in this volume at 122.

39 See, for example, Berger, supra note 14 in 'A.H.F. Lefroy,' in this volume at
    90.

40 See, for example, the following, all in this volume: 'Blake and Liberty,' at
    148, 150; 'Constitutional Scholarship,' at 60, 62, 63, 64; 'Law Teachers,' at
    396; 'A.H.F. Lefroy,' at 88, 90, 93; 'Rights Talk,' at 121, 122, 129; 'Scholars
    and the Constitution,' at 259, 260, 264, 267; and 'Volume One,' at 232.

41 See, for example, C.K. Allen, *Law in the Making* (Oxford: Clarendon Press,
    1958), in 'William Meredith,' in this volume at 201; R. Cross, *Precedent in
    English Law* (Oxford: Clarendon Press, 1961), in 'Scholars and the Constitu-
    tion,' in this volume at 262, and 'William Meredith,' in this volume at 201;
    L. Goldstein, *Precedent in Law* (Oxford: Clarendon Press, 1987), in 'A.H.F.
    Lefroy,' in this volume at 87. See also J.P. Dawson, *Oracles of the Law* (Ann
    Arbor: University of Michigan Law School, 1968), in 'William Meredith,' in
    this volume at 201.

42 See, for example, D. Sugarman, 'Legal Theory, the Common Law Mind,

and the Making of the Textbook Tradition,' in W. Twining, ed., *Legal Theory and Common Law* (Oxford: Basil Blackwell, 1986) 26, in the following, all in this volume: 'Constitutional Scholarship,' at 63; 'John Skirving Ewart,' at 173; 'A.H.F. Lefroy,' at 87, 90; 'Scholars and the Constitution,' at 259; 'Volume One,' at 232. See also H.W. Arthurs, *Without the Law: Administrative Justice and Legal Pluralism in Nineteenth-Century England* (Toronto: University of Toronto Press, 1985), in 'John Willis' in this volume at 296; D. Sugarman, 'The Legal Boundaries of Liberty: Dicey, Liberalism, and Legal Science' (1983) 46 *Modern L. Rev.* 102, in 'John Willis,' ibid. 293.

43 Compare J.W. Burrow, *A Liberal Descent: Victorian Historians and the English Past* (Cambridge: Cambridge University Press, 1981), in 'Many Minds of W.P.M. Kennedy,' in this volume at 327, and 'Blake and Liberty,' in this volume at 148; S. Collini, *Liberalism and Sociology: L.T. Hobhouse and Political Argument in England, 1880–1914* (Cambridge: Cambridge University Press, 1979), in 'John Skirving Ewart,' in this volume at 178; H.T. Dickinson, *Liberty and Property: Political Ideology in Eighteenth-Century Britain* (London: Methuen, 1977), in 'Blake and Liberty,' in this volume at 148; D. Forbes, *The Liberal Anglican Idea of History* (Cambridge: Cambridge University Press, 1952), in 'Constitutional Scholarship,' in this volume at 64; M. Francis, 'The Nineteenth-Century Theory of Sovereignty and Thomas Hobbes' (1980) 1 *Hist. Pol. Thought* 517, and A.D. Kriegel, 'Liberty and Whiggery in Early Nineteenth-Century England' (1980) 52 *J. Modern Hist.* 253, both in Risk, 'Blake and Liberty,' at 148, 150; D. Lieberman, *The Province of Jurisprudence Determined: Legal Theory in Eighteenth-Century Britain* (Cambridge: Cambridge University Press, 1989), in 'A.H.F. Lefroy,' in this volume at 87; M. Loughlin, *Public Law and Political Theory* (Oxford: Clarendon Press, 1992), in 'Many Minds of W.P.M. Kennedy,' in this volume at 331, 336, and 'Scholars and the Constitution,' in this volume at 265; G.J. Postema, *Bentham and the Common Law Tradition* (Oxford: Clarendon Press, 1986), in 'A.H.F. LeFroy,' in this volume at 87.

44 Risk made reference on several occasions to the influence of American scholars such as Oliver Wendell Holmes, Benjamin Cardozo, Felix Cohen, Karl Llewelyn, Jerome Frank, and Thurman Arnold on members of a first generation of full-time Canadian legal academics such as Bora Laskin, John Willis, William Lederman, and Frank Scott. See, all in this volume, 'Law Teachers,' at 359; 'Many Minds of W.P.M. Kennedy,' at 311–12; 'Road to Oz,' at 419–422; and 'Volume One,' at 228.

45 Compare B.N. Cardozo, *The Nature of the Judicial Process* (New Haven: Yale University Press, 1921), in 'Law Teachers,' in this volume at 388, and 'Road

to Oz,' in this volume at 420; F. Cohen, 'The Ethical Basis of Legal Criticism' (1931) 41 *Yale L.J.* 201, in 'Road to Oz,' in this volume at 432; J. Frank, *Law and the Modern Mind* (New York: Brentano's, 1931), in 'John Willis,' in this volume at 274; R. Pound, 'Mechanical Jurisprudence' (1908) 8 *Columbia L.R.* 101 in 'Law Teachers,' in this volume at 338, and 'Road to Oz,' in this volume at 420; R. Pound, 'The Scope and Purpose of Sociological Jurisprudence' (1911) 24 *Harvard L.R.* 591, and (1912) 25 *Harvard L.R.* 160, in 'Road to Oz,' in this volume at 420, and 'Law Teachers,' in this volume at 388.

46 See, for example, T.W. Arnold, *The Symbols of Government* (New Haven: Yale University Press, 1935) and *The Folklore of Capitalism* (New Haven: Yale University Press, 1937), both in 'John Willis,' in this volume at 281; J.M. Landis, *The Administrative Process* (New Haven: Yale University Press, 1939), in ibid. 297; J.M. Landis, 'A Note on Statutory Interpretation' (1930) 43 *Harvard L.R.* 886, in 'Law Teachers,' in this volume at 393, and 'Volume One,' in this volume at 230; M. Radin, 'Statutory Interpretation' (1930) 43 *Harvard L.R.* 863, in the following, all in this volume: 'Law Teachers,' at 393; 'Road to Oz,' at 432, and 'Volume One,' at 230.

47 See, for example, D.F. Cavers, 'A Critique of the Choice-of-Law Problem' (1933) 47 *Harv. L. Rev.* 173, W.W. Cook, 'The Logical and Legal Basis of the Conflict of Laws' (1924) 33 *Yale L.J.* 457; W.W. Cook, 'Substance and Procedure in the Conflict of Laws' (1933) 42 *Yale L.J.* 333; E. Lorenzen, 'Territoriality, Public Policy, and Conflict of Laws' (1924) 33 *Yale L.J.* 736; H. Yntema, 'The Hornbook Method and the Conflict of Laws' (1928) 37 *Yale L.J.* 468; in 'Law Teachers,' in this volume at 389.

48 See, for example, W.L. Chase, *The American Law School and the Rise of Administrative Government* (Madison: University of Wisconsin Press, 1982), in 'John Willis,' in this volume at 294; L. Kalman, *Legal Realism at Yale* (Chapel Hill: University of North Carolina Press, 1986), and R. Stevens, *Law School: Legal Education in America from the 1850s to the 1980s* (Chapel Hill: University of North Carolina Press, 1983), both in 'Many Minds of W.P.M. Kennedy,' in this volume at 331, 334.

49 See, for example, T. Aleinkoff, 'Constitutional Law in the Age of Balancing' (1987) 96 *Yale L.J.* 943, in 'Scholars and the Constitution,' in this volume at 268; H. Gillman, *The Constitution Besieged: The Rise and Demise of Lochner Era Police Powers Jurisprudence* (Durham: Duke University Press, 1993), in 'Rights Talk,' in this volume at 121; G. Peller, 'Neutral Principles in the 1950s' (1988) 21 *Mich. J.L. Reform* 561, in 'Scholars and the Constitution,' in this volume at 268.

50 Compare C.C. Goetsch, 'The Future of Legal Formalism' (1980) 24 *Am. J.*

Legal Hist. 221, in 'William Meredith,' in this volume at 208; R.W. Gordon, 'Legal Thought and Legal Practice in the Age of American Enterprise,' in G. Geison, ed., *Professions and Professional Ideologies in America* (Chapel Hill: University of North Carolina Press, 1983) 70, in 'Constitutional Scholarship,' 'John Willis,' 'Scholars and the Constitution,' and 'A.H.F. Lefroy,' all in this volume at 63, 293, 259, 87; D. Kennedy, 'Towards an Historical Understanding of Classical Legal Thought in America, 1850–1940' (1980) 3 *Research in L. & Soc.* 3, in 'Scholars and the Constitution,' 'John Willis,' and 'A.H.F. Lefroy,' all in this volume at 259, 293, 87; A.J. Sebok, *Legal Positivism in American Jurisprudence* (Cambridge: Cambridge University Press, 1998), in 'Law Teachers,' in this volume at 391.

51 See, for example, D. Kennedy, 'Form and Substance in Private Law Adjudication' (1967) 89 *Harvard L.R.* 1685, in 'William Meredith,' in this volume at 208; L.S. Paine, 'Instrumentalism v. Formalism: Dissolving the Dichotomy' [1978] *Wisconsin L.R.* 997, in 'William Meredith,' in this volume at 208; E.A. Purcell, *The Crisis of Democratic Theory: Scientific Naturalism and the Problem of Value* (Lexington: University of Kentucky Press, 1973), in 'Scholars and the Constitution' and 'John Willis,' in this volume at 265, 298.

52 See, for example, R.W. Gordon, 'New Developments in Legal Theory,' in D. Kairys, ed., *The Politics of Law* (New York: Pantheon Books, 1982) 281, 'Scholars and the Constitution,' in this volume, at 268; G. Peller, 'The Metaphysics of American Law' (1985) 73 *California L.R.* 1151, in ibid. in this volume at 264; J.H. Schlegel, 'American Legal Realism and Empirical Social Science: The Singular Case of Underhill Moore' (1980) 29 *Buffalo L.R.* 195, in ibid. at 265; J.H. Schlegel, *American Legal Realism and Empirical Social Science* (Chapel Hill: University of North Carolina Press, 1995), in 'Many Minds of W.P.M. Kennedy,' in this volume at 331, 334; J.H. Schlegel, 'American Legal Realism and Empirical Social Science: From the Yale Experience' (1979) 28 *Buffalo L.R.* 495 in 'Scholars and the Constitution,' in this volume at 265; J. Singer, 'Legal Realism Now' (1988) 76 *California L.R.* 465 in ibid. at 265; G.E. White, 'From Sociological Jurisprudence to Realism: Jurisprudence and Social Change in Early Twentieth Century America' (1972) 58 *Virginia L.R.* 999, in ibid. at 265.

53 A.H.F. Lefroy, *The Law of Legislative Power in Canada* (Toronto: Toronto Law Book and Publishing, 1897).

54 J.S. Ewart, *An Exposition of the Principles of Estoppel by Misrepresentation* (Chicago: John Skirving Ewart, 1900).

55 See generally H. Schweber, 'The Science of Legal Science: The Model of the

Natural Sciences in Nineteenth-Century American Legal Education' (1999) 17 *Law & Hist. R.* 421.

56 See 'William Meredith,' in this volume.

57 See, for example, the discussion of the impact of Edward Blake's ideas on division of powers jurisprudence in 'Blake and Liberty,' and the conclusion that the scholars' critiques of the Privy Council in the 1920s and 1930s had no effect on the work of the courts, in 'Scholars and the Constitution,' both in this volume. It should be conceded that the relationship between legal ideas and legal doctrine was of necessity an issue treated less fully in some articles than in others, although it appears throughout the period most studied by Risk, c. 1880–1940.

58 Compare J.L. Austin, *The Province of Jurisprudence Determined* (London: J. Murray, 1832); J.S. Mill, *On Liberty* (London: John W. Parker, 1859): J. Bentham, *Principles of Morals and Legislation* (London: W. Pickering, 1780).

59 Compare C.M. Cook, *The American Codification Movement: A Study of Antebellum Legal Reform* (Westport, CT: Greenwood Press, 1981); R. Berkowitz, *The Gift of Science: Leibniz and the Modern Legal Tradition* (Cambridge: Harvard University Press, 2005); R.W. Gordon, 'The Ideal and the Actual in the Law: Fantasies and Practices of New York City Lawyers, 1870–1910,' in G.W. Gawalt, ed., *The New High Priests: Lawyers in Post–Civil War America* (Westport, CT: Greenwood Press, 1984) 51.

60 See 'Blake and Liberty,' 'Constitutional Scholarship,' and 'Rights Talk,' all in this volume.

61 For a more expansive gloss on that assessment, see G.B. Baker 'The Province of Post-Confederation Rights' (1995) 45 *U.T.L.J.* 77.

62 See 'A.H.F. Lefroy,' in this volume. See also R.C.B. Risk, 'Canadian Courts under the Influence' (1990) 40 *U.T.L.J.* 687; Vipond, supra note 27; R.C. Vipond, 'Alternative Pasts: Legal Liberalism and the Demise of the Disallowance Power' (1990), 39 *U. of New Brunswick L.J.* 126.

63 See, for example, 'Blake and Liberty' and 'Rights Talk,' in this volume.

64 See, for example, 'John Skirving Ewart,' 'A.H.F. Lefroy,' and 'William Meredith' in this volume, and Risk, 'Nuisance of Litigation,' supra note 13.

65 Compare Gillman, supra note 49.

66 See, for example, 'John Willis' and 'Volume One,' both in this volume.

67 See 'Many Minds of W.P.M. Kennedy' and 'Volume One' in this volume. See also Risk, 'Continuing Legal Education,' supra note 1.

68 See 'Law Teachers,' 'Scholars and the Constitution,' and 'Volume One,' all in this volume.

69 See generally 'John Willis' and 'Law Teachers' in this volume. See also

R.C.B. Risk, 'Lawyers, Courts, and the Rise of the Regulatory State' (1984) 9 *Dalhousie L.J.* 31, and Risk, 'Continuing Legal Education,' supra note 1.

70 Compare 'Constitutional Scholarship,' 'A.H.F. Lefroy,' and 'Rights Talk,' all in this volume.

71 It bears noting that Risk took no position on whether the scholars of the 1930s were correct in their view that the original intention of the *BNA Act* was to create a strong central government. What mattered was that they took that view, and that their advocacy of it derived at least in part from changes in ideas about the nature and function of law. For the most recent contributions to the debate over the meaning of Confederation and the role of the Privy Council see P. Romney, *Getting It Wrong: How Canadians Forgot Their Past and Imperilled Confederation* (Toronto: University of Toronto Press, 1999); and J. Saywell, *The Lawmakers: Judicial Power and the Shaping of Canadian Federalism* (Toronto: Osgoode Society for Canadian Legal History and University of Toronto Press, 2002).

72 See generally 'Law Teachers' and 'Scholars and the Constitution' in this volume.

73 See, for example, 'Law Teachers,' 'Many Minds of W.P.M. Kennedy,' and 'Volume One' in this volume. See also C.I. Kyer and J.E. Bickenbach, *The Fiercest Debate: Cecil A. Wright, the Benchers, and Legal Education in Ontario, 1923–1957* (Toronto: Osgoode Society for Canadian Legal History and University of Toronto Press, 1987); W.W. Pue, 'Common Law Legal Education in Canada's Age of Light, Soap and Water' (1996) 23 *Manitoba L.J.* 654; J. Willis, *A History of Dalhousie Law School* (Toronto: University of Toronto Press, 1979).

74 See, for example, C. Cole, *Osler, Hoskin and Harcourt: Portrait of a Partnership* (Toronto: McGraw-Hill Ryerson, 1995); C. Moore, *McCarthy, Tetreault* (Toronto: Douglas & McIntyre, 2005); R.W. Pound, *Stikeman, Elliott: The First Fifty Years* (Montreal and Kingston: McGill-Queen's University Press, 2002).

75 See 'John Willis,' 'Many Minds of W.P.M. Kennedy,' and 'Volume One' in this volume. See also Risk, 'Continuing Legal Education,' supra note 1.

76 Compare R.W. Gordon, 'Willis's American Counterparts: The Legal Realists' Defense of Administration' (2005) 55 *U.T.L.J.* 405. See also G.B. Baker, 'Willis on Cultured Public Authorities' (2005) 55 *U.T.L.J.* 335.

77 'Road to Oz,' in this volume. That article also contains less contextual material than most of Risk's other writings, presumably because it was a beachhead in the post–World War Two era rather than a first instalment of comprehensive coverage.

78 See also 'Scholars and the Constitution,' in this volume.

79 See, for example, E. Anderson, *Judging Bertha Wilson: Law as Large as Life* (Toronto: Osgoode Society for Canadian Legal History and University of Toronto Press, 2002); Girard, *Bora Laskin*, supra note 5; R.J. Sharpe and K. Roach, *Brian Dickson: A Judge's Journey* (Toronto: Osgoode Society for Canadian Legal History and University of Toronto Press, 2003); F. Vaughan, *Aggressive in Pursuit: The Life of Justice Emmett Hall* (Toronto: Osgoode Society for Canadian Legal History and University of Toronto Press, 2004).

80 See R.C.B. Risk, 'A Prospectus for Canadian Legal History' (1973) 1 *Dalhousie L.J.* 227.

PART ONE

The Classical Age: Canadian Legal Thought
in the Late Nineteenth Century

1

Constitutional Scholarship in the Late Nineteenth Century: Making Federalism Work

Introduction

> During a period of twenty years the constitution of Canada has been put to many tests. It is less difficult to say now than it was ten years ago, that our federal constitution may turn out to be something different from what the framers of it intended.

This shrewd observation was made in 1887 by Dennis O'Sullivan, in the preface to the second edition of his book *A Manual of Government in Canada*.[1] In the text that followed, he described the institutions of Canadian government and advocated a model of federalism – the model he believed was the basis of the changes he was observing. This article is about O'Sullivan's book and all the other books and articles written by common law lawyers about the constitution from Confederation to 1900. I plan to study not only this writing, but through it, the ideas about federalism that were shared by all lawyers.

I want to stress two themes. First, much in this early writing about the Constitution is illuminated by reading it against the background of a struggle for power between Dominion and provinces. This struggle, often known to historians as the provincial rights movement, provoked many of the issues that seemed important to my writers, and as the century came to an end, they recorded the constitutional doctrine of its outcome: the triumph of the provinces.

If the first theme appeals to readers interested in history, the second may appeal to constitutional scholars. In short, it is about ways of thinking about federalism, and about legal reasoning. The triumph of the provinces at the end of the century was also the triumph of the model of federalism O'Sullivan saw emerging. This model remained dominant during the first half of the twentieth century, and it still has significant power. The basic elements of the model, which I shall call the model of autonomous federalism, were coordinate governments, independent of each other, each having exclusive and supreme authority in its own sphere of power. These elements alone, though, can be the basis for significantly different versions. The distinctive edges of the Canadian model were an emphasis on the autonomy and equality of the governments, and the exclusiveness and sharp boundaries of the spheres. Moreover, the model was closely related to the dominant beliefs about legal reasoning and the proper functions of courts. My colleagues who do not care much about history, but who do care about twentieth-century federalism and its fate, may be interested in reading about the beginnings of ideas that may seem to them to be abstract and timeless.

Much that these two themes might include is hardly startling. Historians and political scientists have already written extensively about the appearance of the model, usually using the term coordinate federalism, and debating whether it was a betrayal of Confederation. I can hardly make an article out of substituting a new label, even though I think it is more expressive. What I do hope to contribute is an account of the origins of the model and its distinctive elements; the ways in which the lawyers, especially my writers, contributed to its construction; the relation between the substance of the model and legal reasoning, and the relation between these two and political argument.

The Writers and Their Writing Introduced

For more than a decade after Confederation, neither lawyers nor anyone else wrote much about the constitution. Books and articles began to appear regularly around 1880, and by 1900, four major books had been published. First, in 1879, came O'Sullivan's *A Manual of Government in Canada*, the first edition of the book from which my epigraph is taken.[2] O'Sullivan practised law in Toronto, as well as being a prominent lay official in the Roman Catholic Church. His first edition began with an historical sketch stressing the rise of responsible government, and then turned to a survey of the major institutions: the Crown, federalism, the legislatures, the government departments, and the judiciary, concluding with an account of individual rights. Throughout, the survey was flat, undertaking little analysis and suggesting no tension or controversy. The second edition, which appeared in 1887 as *Government in Canada*, retained the same basic structure, but it was much more thoughtful and ambitious, especially in its treatment of federalism. As we shall see, the difference seems to have been caused by O'Sullivan's politics, and in particular, his strong support of the claims of the provinces.

Next, in 1884, came *A Law Treatise on the Constitutional Powers of Parliament and of the Local Legislatures under the British North America Act, 1867*, by Jeremiah Travis,[3] from St. John, who studied law at Harvard, did some earlier academic writing, and played an important role in bringing a 'scientific' legal education to New Brunswick.[4] His *Treatise* was a reply to *Letters Upon the Interpretation of the Federal Constitution*, a widely read statement of the constitutional claims of Quebec, by T.J.J. Loranger,[5] a Quebec politician and judge. Loranger's interpretation of the division of legislative powers seemed to Travis to have gone badly astray, and Travis devoted the entire book to presenting his own version – one much more favourable to the Dominion.

The next author, William Henry Pope Clement, wrote *The Law of the Canadian Constitution* in 1892,[6] while practising law in Toronto. Later, in 1897, he wrote a prize-winning introduction to Canadian history that was widely used in Canadian high schools, and he eventually became a judge in British Columbia. His declared purpose was to present Canada's constitution 'in reference as well to our position as a Colony of the Empire as to our self-government under the federal scheme of the *BNA Act*.'[7] Nonetheless, the book sprawled in ways that made this simple beginning an awkward frame at best. Beginning with a short introduction composed of variations on the theme of federalism and a claim that the governments of Canada and the United States were fundamentally different, he divided the bulk of the book into two large parts. The first described Canada's colonial status, including such topics as the application of British statutes to Canada and the prerogative and powers of the Governor-General; the second was a long account of the *British North America [BNA] Act* (under the rubric of self-government), section by section and case by case. The final part was a short account, based almost entirely on the statutes, of the addition of provinces and territories after Confederation. Like O'Sullivan, Clement favoured the provincial cause, although not as pervasively and forcibly.

The author of the last of the four major books, A.H.F. Lefroy, was educated in England and became a teacher, albeit late in his career. Born in Toronto, he took a BA at Oxford, and was called to the bar in England in 1877, and in Ontario the following year. During the 1880s and 1890s, he practised law in Toronto in a series of small partnerships and wrote extensively about constitutional law, especially federalism. His first and by far his most important book was *The Law of Legislative Power in Canada*,[8] which was written throughout the 1890s and appeared in 1898. Although an introduction described the glories of the British constitution, especially its union of liberty with legislative supremacy and its superiority to the American constitution, the body of the text, as its title promised, was an extensive and rigorous account of the doctrine about the division of legislative powers. In 1900 Lefroy was appointed professor of Roman law at the University of Toronto, where he expanded his writing to include common law theory and Roman law, as well as three more books about constitutional law.[9] In addition to these four writers, a few other lawyers wrote books, none of which needs to be discussed.[10]

Two major legal periodicals were published in this period, both in Toronto: the *Canadian Law Journal* and the *Canadian Law Times*. Discussion about constitutional law began in both of them around 1881, and by 1900 about a hundred notes and articles had appeared. E.D. Armour, a Toronto lawyer, was particularly prolific; in addition to editing the *Canadian Law Times*, he lectured at Osgoode Hall and wrote both texts and articles, the latter often about constitutional law.[11]

Last I come to law teachers, although only to begin by expressing my disappointment. Constitutional law was taught at all four of the common law schools – Dalhousie, Saint John, Osgoode Hall, and Toronto – but unfortunately notes have survived for only two of the teachers. One was Richard Weldon, who was appointed dean at Dalhousie when it was established in 1883 and was its 'professor of constitutional and international law,' as well as a Conservative member of Parliament. A set of student notes for his course on Canadian constitutional law have been preserved, but they are often confusing and fragmentary; whether the reason was the student's inattention or Weldon's own failure cannot now be known.[12] The other was David Mills, who taught a course in federalism at Toronto during the 1890s and kept his own typed notes. He was also a Liberal member of Parliament, a practising lawyer, a teacher, a newspaper editor, and, eventually, minister of justice and a judge of the Supreme Court. He has never escaped the reputation of being a pedantic bore, lacking imagination and insight; he was, nonetheless, one of the most learned and intelligent of the lawyers.[13]

Non-lawyers as well wrote about the constitution, and among them, the two dominant ones were Adolphous Todd and John George Bourinot. Todd, the Dominion parliamentary librarian, wrote a classic study of parliamentary government in England and a study of responsible government in the Dominions, both of which emphasized the Crown, the prerogative, and responsible government.[14] Bourinot's writing covered a wide range of history, government, political commentary, and fiction, but only two of his many books need to be mentioned here, *A Manual of the Constitutional History of Canada* and *Federal Government in Canada*. Both were surveys, and both were read by lawyers – or at least they were books that students were supposed to have read.[15] I can anticipate one of my major conclusions by saying that this writing did not express the concept of autonomous federalism in any significant way and did not make any significant contribution to its development, especially in contrast to the writing by lawyers.

The Writing Surveyed

These writers shared one basic belief, and all lawyers would have agreed with them: the essence of the Canadian constitution was the British constitution coupled with federalism, an essence captured by the Preamble to the *BNA Act*, which declared that the colonies wished to be 'federally united … with a Constitution similar in Principle to that of the United Kingdom.' The writers took great pride in this distinctive coupling: O'Sullivan saw 'a new departure in colonial government,' and Clement began by declaring that 'a new thing under the sun' had been created in 1867.[16]

Whatever their leanings in Canadian politics, they all professed loyalty to the glories of the British constitution. One small, but revealing manifestation of this faith was their reaction to a stray comment by A.V. Dicey, the leading English constitutional writer. In the first edition of his great text, *The Law of the Constitution*, published in 1885, he said that Canada's constitution was modelled on the constitution of the United States.[17] The Canadians were outraged and took great pains to demonstrate Dicey's error: their constitution was essentially British – and therefore not only different from the American, but far superior. Both Lefroy, in his introduction, and Clement, in his opening chapter, argued at length that the essential difference between the United States and Britain was parliamentary government, and measured in this way, Canada could hardly be similar to the United States. Clement even went so far as to argue that Britain and her Empire was 'as truly federal ... as the United States,' and therefore federalism or a written constitution could hardly mark a crucial difference. Relying on Bagehot and Woodrow Wilson, he lauded the flexibility, the harmony, and the focusing of responsibility in parliamentary government, which he contrasted to the rigidity, friction, and diffusion of leadership in congressional government. Lefroy said much the same, stressing as well the capacity of parliamentary government for 'organic growth.'[18]

It was federalism, though, that commanded the attention of the writers. Even though O'Sullivan and Clement wrote about a wider range of topics, it was federalism that stimulated them and provoked their most careful and most lively efforts. Travis and Lefroy, the other two major authors, wrote entirely about federalism, and so did almost all of the writers in the periodicals. In contrast, there was very little discussion of basic constitutional theory, the British constitution, or individual rights.[19]

This emphasis on federalism was a product of three factors. First, and more important, it was federalism that was both distinctive and challenging. The British constitution invoked by the preamble seemed well settled, and it was recorded in a myriad of familiar books. Federalism, the other element of the Canadian constitution, was unexplored. True, the example of the federalism of the United States was close at hand, but its appeal had been dimmed by the Civil War and by a pervasive turning away from things American, and much of Canada's federalism was not only different, but deliberately different. Moreover, the union of federalism and parliamentary government seemed to be not only distinctive, but, as we shall see, problematic: how could a monarchy be combined with federalism?

Second, the struggle between the Dominion and the provinces was ultimately, as we shall see, a struggle about the nature of Canadian federalism, and it created a pressing need to articulate claims and to synthesize doctrine. Third, most of the work of the courts was about federalism. That is, most of the cases that might be called 'constitutional' were about federalism in one way or another, and this generation of lawyers put the courts at the centre of the legal universe and made analysis of the cases the primary focus of scholarship.

The Nature of Canadian Federalism: The Model of Autonomous Federalism

The analysis of federalism can be divided into two major questions: first, what was the nature of Canadian federalism, which I shall consider in this part; and second, what was the division of legislative powers between the Dominion and the provinces, which I shall consider later.

The first question, about the nature of Canadian federalism, had at its basis queries that might be asked about any federation: what was the relation between the local and the central governments, and the relation of both to the citizens? Given this general frame, it took its particular form in Canada in three overlapping sets of questions. The first set were about the provincial legislatures: what sort of institutions were they? Were they the same as the Dominion Parliament? That is, were they Parliaments – with all the inherent powers and capacities of the British Parliament – or, instead, were they merely law-making bodies, created by the *BNA Act* and having only the powers it gave them?[20] Second, what were the executive powers of the provincial governments, and in particular, were their executives independent of the Dominion executive? Section 58 of the *BNA Act* specified that the lieutenant-governors were to be appointed by the Governor-General in Council. Having been appointed in this way and not by Her Majesty herself, did they have prerogative powers, or did they have only the powers granted to them by the Governor-General? And third, what were the appropriate uses and limits of the Dominion's power of disallowance? One grand question stood for all three questions, and its answer was the sum of the answers to all of them: were the provinces subordinate to the Dominion, or equal and autonomous? These questions have been settled so long that they have disappeared from the day-to-day thinking of constitutional lawyers and from constitutional law courses. Nonetheless, for the lawyers in the late nineteenth century they were urgent, much more urgent than the second question, about the division of legislative powers.

I can best introduce the writing about them by beginning with the conclusion I anticipated in my introduction. The eventual answer, or the principle that underlay all the answers, was the model of autonomous federalism. The provincial legislatures and their executives were independent of the Dominion, and had exclusive authority in their own spheres. This was certainly not the model of Confederation. The *BNA Act* gave the Dominion extensive powers of supervision: power to appoint the judges of the superior courts as well as the lieutenant-governors, and powers to disallow provincial legislation and to create a Supreme Court with comprehensive jurisdiction. Autonomous federalism was, though, the model proclaimed by the provinces, and by the mid-1880s, it was central in lawyers' thought and the dominant model for interpreting the *BNA Act*.

My account of the writing about this model needs to be preceded by an account of its early appearances in politics and the courts. David Mills was the first to present it, in speeches in Parliament in the late 1860s and early 1870s, and in a remarkable letter to Sir John A. Macdonald about Macdonald's proposal for a Supreme Court, where he argued that the model demanded separate courts for the provinces and for the Dominion. Until he left politics at the end of the century, Mills espoused his beliefs consistently and passionately, in politics and in his teaching.[21] In the early and mid-1870s, Oliver Mowat, the premier of Ontario and one of the major figures in the campaign for the provinces, presented fragmentary versions in debates with the Dominion and the Colonial Office, claiming that the provinces could appoint Queen's Counsel, and that they, not the Dominion, had the right to escheats. (The contrast between the trivial substance of these issues and the significance of the principles at stake is remarkable indeed.) The claim to appoint Queen's Counsel involved the claim that the lieutenant-governors had prerogative powers independent of the Governor-General, and the claim to escheats involved both interpretation of a couple of sections of the *BNA Act* and the argument that the provinces were the original colonies, retaining their original properties and powers, except so far as they had granted them to the Dominion in the *BNA Act*.[22]

As the campaign of the provinces mounted, the late 1870s and early 1880s saw much uncertainty and confusion. Mowat presented the model in a fuller way in 1877, arguing before the Supreme Court in *R. v. Severn*.[23] During the next few years, though, the Court demonstrated a contrary leaning. In 1879, it considered the question of Queen's Counsel in *Lenoir v. Ritchie*.[24] Although procedural issues confused the outcome, three members said that the lieutenant-governors had no prerogative powers, and Gwynne J., the strongest supporter of the Dominion, went out of his way to use the dreaded word 'subordinate.' In 1883, the right to escheats was presented in *A.G. Ontario v. Mercer*, where the claim succeeded in the Supreme Court, and the same three members denied the autonomy and primacy of the provinces. The Privy Council reversed, but limited itself to interpreting the specific sections of the *BNA Act*.[25]

In contrast, the Ontario Court of Appeal adopted the model enthusiastically from 1878 onwards.[26] In 1882, in *Hodge*, which gave the provinces authority to regulate taverns, it declared that their legislatures had the same kind of authority as the Dominion Parliament and were supreme within the limits of their powers. Two years later, the Privy Council affirmed, using much the same language.[27] This declaration settled the questions about the legislatures, leaving the questions about the provincial executives unanswered.

Turning from politics and the courts, the writing in the late 1870s and early 1880s did not contain much sustained consideration of these issues, but what was said supported the Dominion. In his first edition, O'Sullivan said calmly that the provinces were subordinate and not sovereigns, and their lieutenant-governors were deputies of the Governor-General.[28] A few years later, Armour attacked *Hodge* several times, unable to accept the pronouncement that the provincial legislatures were the same as the Parliament.[29]

The first sustained exposition of autonomous federalism after Mills' speeches was Loranger's *Letters*, which appeared in 1883. As I said earlier, he was impelled to write by a fear that the Supreme Court was threatening Quebec's autonomy and the French race, especially by its decision in *Mercer*. He claimed passionately that the basic principles of Confederation were the equality of the Dominion and the provinces, the autonomy of the provinces, and mutually exclusive spheres of power. The provincial legislatures were Parliaments, and the lieutenant-governors representatives of Her Majesty. These principles had been made in a compact among the original provinces, and were a condition of Quebec's acceptance.

In his second edition, in 1887, O'Sullivan abandoned the support he had given the Dominion in his first edition, and proclaimed the model of autonomous federalism and support for the provinces elegantly and aggressively:

> A federal union then means two perfectly independent co-ordinate powers in the same state. The powers of each are equally sovereign and neither are derived from the other. The state governments are not subordinate to the general government, nor the general government to the state governments. They are co-ordinate governments standing on the same level and deriving their powers from the same sovereign authority. In their respective spheres neither yields to the other. Each is independent in its own work; incomplete and dependent on the other for the complete work of government.[30]

O'Sullivan saw a struggle between two visions of Canada: one characterized by unity, a dominant Dominion government, and the subordination of the provinces, and the other by the autonomy of the provinces. Moreover, he saw each of these visions as an expression of one of the two elements of the preamble to the BNA Act: the British constitution, and federalism. 'It is difficult to conceive of forms of government more radically opposed to each other than a federal union and a constitutional monarchy.'[31]

The parliamentary sovereignty of the British constitution seemed to O'Sullivan to be contrary to the existence of the two equal legislatures and to judicial review, and the unity of the Crown seemed contrary to a division of executive functions. Because the BNA Act was 'invitingly open to a difference of opinion,' these visions could be used to justify different interpretations. O'Sullivan's preference was clear: the principles of federalism must prevail over the principles of the British constitution.[32]

He made two kinds of arguments to justify his choice. One, which he revisited several times, was directed primarily at the unsettled questions about the executives. Beginning with the basic principle of responsible government, supplemented by Bagehot's claim that the executive and the legislature were linked, he argued that executive functions must be divided in the same manner as legislative powers. In the other argument, a secondary one, he shared much with Loranger. Here, he saw Confederation as a compact. The original colonies continued, keeping their original Parliaments, properties, executive capacities, and prerogative powers, except to the extent that they had granted them to the Dominion at Confederation.

The explanation for O'Sullivan's strong support for the provinces cannot be simply his reading of the cases, because the question about the executives wasn't settled in 1887, and because his support went far beyond the requirements of simply reporting. His associations in practice and as lay official in the Roman Catholic Church put him in the midst of tangled webs of support for the Mowat administration, but there is no firm evidence of his beliefs apart from what he wrote.

Clement, writing in 1892, shared the same general model, and for him, even more than for O'Sullivan, the pressing question was the stature of the provincial executives. In the first part of the book (the account of the consequences of Canada's colonial status) he claimed that the executives were complete and independent in the same two ways as O'Sullivan had argued, although more explicitly and at greater length. While he was writing the second part (the account of the cases about the *BNA Act*), the Privy Council declared in *Liquidators of the Maritime Bank* that the lieutenant-governors were representatives of Her Majesty, and, expanding their declaration in *Hodge*, the provinces were not subordinate.[33] Reading this, Clement announced that the 'peaceful warfare' had come to an end. It was 'hopeless' to argue any longer that the provinces did not have 'full autonomy' in relation to the subjects assigned to them.[34]

For Lefroy, writing in the late 1890s, all these questions were replaced by settled doctrine, which he elaborated at length. The Dominion and the provinces were 'co-equal and coordinate'; each was supreme in its sphere; their legislative powers were mutually exclusive; and there were no overlapping powers (except for section 94). Executive powers were derived from legislative powers, and the lieutenant-governors were 'just as much representatives of Her Majesty as was the Governor-General …'[35] Both the provinces and the model of autonomous federalism had triumphed.

Among all the writing and speeches on federalism, the writing by these lawyers expressed the model most powerfully and comprehensively. Politicians supporting the provincial cause often invoked fragments, but speeches and pamphlets were not appropriate vehicles for analysis and exposition. The judges, even when they adopted the model, were not expansive, perhaps because the Canadian judges seemed to lose heart sometime in the 1880s, and because the Privy Council had little sustained interest or knowledge of Canada. Nor did the writers who were not lawyers perceive or record the model in any significant way; it did not, for example, appear in Bourinot's writing.

Not all the writers perceived the model clearly and consistently – nor would it be realistic to expect anything different. The periodical literature especially lagged; much of it seemed little more than an effort to understand the most recent Privy Council cases without any apparent general framework. From the perspective of the twentieth century, perhaps the beginnings of competing models can be perceived, particularly models involving extensive overlapping of legislative powers and judicial balancing. Nonetheless, this effort distorts these writers and their times more than it illuminates them. For example, Travis argued that the legislative powers overlapped extensively, but he did not have the understandings about legal reasoning that support the twentieth-century models.

The Sources of Autonomous Federalism, and the Distinctive Edges

Mills, O'Sullivan, Clement, and Lefroy were not original, creative thinkers, and they did not expound the model of autonomy in isolation. Its general structure had accumulated since the making of American federalism in late eighteenth century; for example, language about exclusive spheres first appeared in Madison's *Federalist*. For the Canadians, the most common sources of this structure were the great American constitutional texts by Cooley and Story, and a history of federalism by the English historian E.A. Freeman. A connection between Cooley and Mills is a more specific source. After spending his early adult years as a schoolteacher and superintendent in Southwestern Ontario, Mills went to law school at the University of Michigan in the early 1860s. There he studied constitutional law under Cooley and faithfully recorded much of the basic elements of the model in his notes.[36]

An emphasis on particular authors and particular connections, and a search for who read which book first, must not obscure the widespread acceptance of this model. By the time that it was articulated in its classic form for English and Canadian lawyers by Dicey in 1885,[37] it was already firmly established in the minds of most lawyers in England and Canada. When the provinces made their arguments in *Hodge, Maritime Bank*, and the *Local Prohibition Reference*,[38] they appealed to an understanding of federalism that was already established in the judges' minds.

These sources did not, however, contain the entire model. The emphasis on the autonomy and equality of the governments, and the exclusiveness and sharp boundaries of the spheres, gave the Canadian model a distinctive sharpness or fighting edge that made it different from the U.S. experience. Examples are the way O'Sullivan framed his definition, the way Clement argued about the provincial executives, and the way Lefroy used the model so rigorously throughout his extensive analysis. The notes that Mills took from Cooley contained the elements of spheres of power, but not these distinctive edges. Nor did they appear in any other of the major texts.

I can suggest three reasons for this difference. The first and major one is that the model was being used in the political debate. Even though the general structures and particular pieces of the model were already available, they had been shaped in different contexts and for different purposes. The Canadians' job was to articulate a theory of federalism in a context in which there was no serious thought of separation, at least after the first few years, and no doubt about the power of the national government to affect the citizens directly, or about the legitimacy of judicial review, as there had been in the United States. Instead, their context was the struggle between the model of Confederation and the ambitions of the provinces. The advocates for the provincial cause, in whatever forum they appeared, presented their cause as forcibly and comprehensively as they could.

The second reason is mid-nineteenth-century liberalism: the spheres of power and their sharp limits that defined the relation between the Dominion and the provinces were shaped by ideas about the relation among individuals in the liberal state. Except for one remarkable footnote by Clement and an equally remarkable set of articles by F.W. Wegenast written shortly after 1900, this relation was not described, but it may explain why the model was so appealing to lawyers.[39] The third reason, closely related to the second, was that the model was congruent with lawyers' ways of thinking about law generally in the late nineteenth century. I shall come to this topic later, but here, it is enough to say that spheres of power, autonomy, and sharp, binary distinctions were all part of lawyers' understandings about law and legal reasoning generally, and were manifested in the analyses of federalism. The second and third reasons explain much of the power of the provincial claims: the arguments appealed to deep and pervasive strands in lawyers' thought.[40]

Of Sovereignty and Compacts

I have set aside two topics about the nature of federalism, because they were too large to intrude until now: sovereignty and the compact theory. Sovereignty was a central concept in nineteenth-century legal and constitutional thought, especially the version formulated by John Austin: in every state there must be one sovereign, whose power is absolute and unlimited. In Britain, the sovereign was Parliament, and because Canada was a colony, Parliament was its sovereign, even though in day-to-day government practice, Canadians enjoyed a large measure of self-government.

If sovereignty was a central principle, though, how could federalism exist, particularly in the model of autonomy? How could one state contain equal and autonomous spheres of power? Americans had answered the question in several different ways, principally by constituting the people as the sovereign; but for Canadians, this answer was fundamentally inconsistent with the sovereignty of Parliament. O'Sullivan perceived these difficulties clearly enough and knew about the American solutions, but did not worry much. He claimed in one context that sovereignty could be divided among Britain, the Dominion, and the provinces, and in another that the governments in a federalism could be sovereign, although he acknowledged that this sovereignty 'falls short of the English theory of sovereignty in as much as it is limited.' In his argument about the executive power, he claimed that sovereignty was irrelevant, anticipating the eventual resolution by suggesting that 'a number of tenants may unite as well as a number of landlords.'[41] At the end of the period, Lefroy gave the authoritative answer. In his introduction, he contrasted the sovereignty of the people and the sovereignty of Parliament, proclaiming his faith in the British constitution that was also Canada's constitution. In the text, he recognized the ultimate sovereignty of the British Parliament, and described the powers of the legislatures by saying that they were supreme in their spheres. This phrase, 'supreme in their spheres,' established the basic element of the model of autonomy, giving each legislature absolute power over the subjects assigned to it, and at the same time denying them sovereignty.[42] The analysis was adequate to resolve the question, and modest and unimaginative. No one considered the late-nineteenth-century challenges to Austin's theory.

The compact theory was a more distinctive topic. Its foundation was a claim about the way the Dominion had been created: the colonies had made a compact, ratified by the British Parliament, creating the Dominion and conferring powers and property, and after Confederation, they continued to exist as the new provinces. A few years after Confederation, the provincial rights advocates began to use this compact as support for a wide range of claims.[43] One, which subsequent scholars have often taken to be the essence of the theory or its only claim, was that the *BNA Act* could not be amended without the consent of each of the parties: the provinces. Other claims, though, loomed larger in the 1880s, all of them directed at interpretation of the *BNA Act*: the provinces were entitled to government property not clearly allocated to the Dominion, and to the residue of the legislative powers – all powers not specifically granted to the Dominion. As well, their lieutenant-governors had the stature and powers they possessed before Confederation.

The theory played a substantial role in the early writing, and then faded in the late 1880s and the 1890s. Loranger spoke of Confederation as a compact, especially as a compact to preserve Quebec's distinctive culture. O'Sullivan and Clement also used the compact, especially in their arguments about the independence of the provincial executives, although not as often, and not in such a central way. For the common law lawyers the compact was typically a supplementary argument and not necessary to autonomous federalism. David Mills, for example, who expressed the model most elegantly, did not made the theory a central part of his argument.

Lefroy's book virtually removed the compact theory from constitutional argumentation among the common law lawyers. His first proposition declared that the *BNA Act* was the 'sole charter' for determining the rights of the Dominion and the provinces. Given the basic understandings of sovereignty, constitutions, and interpretation, this principle was both basic and inescapable, but it was an assertion about both the origins of the nation and the interpretation of its constitution that excluded any consideration of a compact. The second proposition was that the *BNA Act*, because it was founded on the Quebec resolutions, 'must be accepted as a treaty of union between the provinces,' but once enacted, it became a 'wholly new point of departure. The contrast between the two branches seemed to acknowledge a compact, but only as an historical event, irrelevant to interpretation. As I shall seek to demonstrate later, these propositions were expressions of fundamental beliefs about interpretation, and in this light, the compact foundered because it was at odds with the dominant common law thought.

The Division of Legislative Powers

The second of the two major federalism topics was the division of legislative powers between the Dominion and the provinces. It, too, was a battleground in the struggle between them, and here, too, the provinces triumphed, although the triumph was not nearly as great or as clear as their triumph about the nature of the federalism.

The first questions to be considered in a substantial way were about the structure of sections 91 and 92: what were the relations and priorities among their various parts? What did 'notwithstanding' and 'deemed' mean? These questions can seem wonderfully arcane now, especially because many lawyers today have little faith that the answers can determine outcomes for particular cases; but for the lawyers at the time, who had a larger faith in the power of doctrine, they were forums for fighting grand questions of principle and power. The text permitted different readings, and the differences often seemed to entail large consequences for the struggle between the Dominion and the provinces.

The most interesting question was whether sections 91 and 92 were a grant of two general powers, or, instead, did the Dominion have power to legislate over the enumerated subjects in section 91, together with the residue of the power remaining after the grant of specific powers to the provinces? In 1883, as part of his defence of the autonomy of Quebec and the French race, Loranger claimed that sections 91 and 92 each conferred one basic power: the power to legislate about 'matters of general interest' was given to Parliament, and power over 'matters of local interest' was given to the provinces. This division had been achieved by the compact at Confederation, in which the provinces had granted powers to legislate about subjects of common concern to the Dominion, and retained those that remained. This claim was closely related to the compact theory, and it supported the campaign of the provinces by suggesting that they were the same kinds of institutions as the Dominion, exercising the same kinds of powers – independent legislatures exercising independent powers.

Travis's book was, as I have already said, a response to Loranger. Throughout, he displayed immense self-esteem and little patience with fools, whom he saw all around him. Loranger's arguments were 'most extraordinary and utterly untenable,' 'very pretentious and utterly absurd,' and 'dreadfully weak.' Even the Privy Council was not spared: its reasoning in *Russell v. The Queen*,[44] a major case permitting the Dominion to impose prohibition, was 'manifestly incorrect,' demonstrating 'actual, stupid, stolid, ignorance,' and reading as though it had been prepared by an 'ignorant secretary.' Only William Ritchie, chief justice of the Supreme Court, emerged with much praise. But Travis's self-esteem by far outran his ability. The book was endlessly repetitive, poorly organized, and distorted by a tendency to make extreme, if not far-fetched, interpretations of the cases and his opponents' writing.[45]

Loranger had assumed, without saying so, that two classes of powers were entirely separate and did not overlap or affect each other. Travis disagreed, arguing that the subjects enumerated in section 92 overlapped 'extensively' with the subjects in section 91. To the extent that the subjects overlapped, both the Dominion and the provinces could legislate, but if both did, the Dominion was paramount. This argument made the Dominion's powers as extensive as the overlap and entailed a rejection of the idea that there were two basic powers. Travis continually denied that he had any objective except the demonstration of pure legal science, and if he had any political loyalties, they weren't widely known. Nonetheless, his analysis was a challenge to the provincial rights campaign and the model of autonomy. He rejected as 'absurd' all talk of the sovereignty of the provinces, for how could they be sovereign if much of the legislation that might be enacted under section 92 might be overridden by Dominion legislation? Nonetheless, his challenge was at odds with the dominant trend and persuaded no one.

A few years later, in 1887, O'Sullivan wrote his second edition, and here too, his stance was radically different than it had been in his first edition in 1879, where he suggested that the division of powers was a simple, uncontroversial issue.[46] Like Loranger, he saw two classes of powers, created at Confederation: the provinces agreed to grant general powers to the Dominion, retaining local powers for themselves, and Great Britain simply approved what had been done. He amplified Loranger's exposition by saying that these two classes each included a grant of residue and together comprised all possible subjects of legislation. It was misleading, therefore, to speak in the way Macdonald had at Confederation, of the provinces having only specified powers and the Dominion having the residue.[47]

In the 1890s, Clement said very little about this claim about two general powers. A few years later, Lefroy firmly rejected it by declaring that the Dominion had a residue of all the powers not specifically granted to the provinces and that section 92(16), which had been the source of the provinces' general power, was merely 'a minor residuary gift of power.'[48] Its fate was closely related to the waning of the compact theory, and due primarily to changes in legal reasoning. In short, the dominant approach to interpretation excluded the story about Confederation and the compact that gave the claim power. The very discussions in the books illustrate this shift: from the argument and history of O'Sullivan to the flat, abstract doctrine of Clement and Lefroy.

During the late 1880s and early 1890s, the grand questions of structure that were at stake for Loranger, Travis, and O'Sullivan were replaced by more confined questions about how to decide particular cases. A large pile of judgments had accumulated, but no widely accepted general principles for understanding them had emerged. An example of the uncertainty was a debate in the journals about the work of the Privy Council in the early 1890s: several eminent lawyers, including Armour, complained that they were unable find a pattern in its judgments. Most striking to a modern reader, they were unable to find any common ground between *Russell* and *Hodge*. *Russell* seemed to give power to regulate liquor to the Dominion and *Hodge* seemed to give the same power to the provinces. The aspect rule, which was announced in *Hodge* itself and which any first-year student would now use to reconcile them, was not part of the shared language of doctrine.

In 1891, Armour surveyed the cases and sought to order them by such terms as 'inferential or incidental jurisdiction,' 'concurrent jurisdiction,' and 'auxiliary jurisdiction.'[49] His scheme seems unfamiliar or impenetrable to a modern reader, at least it does to me, and it had no effect at all in its own time. A year later, Clement stated a few principles and discussed them intelligently in a couple of pages, but fell far short of a comprehensive analysis. In his turn, Lefroy undertook a synthesis, and set out principles that have endured for nearly a century, and continue to be standard fare in teaching materials: mutual modification, pith and substance, the difference between 'in relation to' and 'affecting,' necessarily incidental powers, aspects, and paramountcy. And *Hodge* and *Russell* were made consistent. Lefroy's work, as he understood it, was simply to synthesize the cases faithfully, but he gave the doctrine a coherence and internal consistency that it did not have before. Armour was an intelligent lawyer; the reason his principles now seem impenetrable to me may not be entirely because they were not a competent synthesis of the cases. Another reason is that my mind has been shaped by Lefroy's principles.[50]

These principles were closely related to the model of autonomous federalism: mutual modification was based on the assumption that the powers did not overlap, and Lefroy struggled at length to explain necessarily incidental powers in a way that separated the definition of the powers from their effects.[51] The aspect doctrine might seem from a twentieth-century perspective to be a concession to overlapping powers, but it was not: for Clement and Lefroy it was derived from their understanding that the legislative powers were about subjects or legal relations, not things, and throughout their discussions the powers did not overlap.[52]

What Was at Stake?

What sorts of ideas and interests were at stake for my writers? My answer is simple: the stakes were federalism. I do not mean, though, that abstract principles alone were at stake. The struggle was also for independence and power. Another possibility, however, is that the debate was a mask for economic interests, especially corporations that wished to be free from regulation.[53] The crucial battleground is the interpretation of sections 91 and 92. One hypothesis might be that regulatory legislation was declared *ultra vires* simply because of hostility to regulation, regardless of the reasoning; a second might be that regulatory powers were granted to the provinces, which were more vulnerable to political pressure. These two possibilities are at odds with what the courts had done before the mid-1890s. No significant decision had declared a regulatory measure *ultra vires*, and no lawyer in 1895 could have thought that the provinces had the extensive scope that Chief Justice Duff and Lord Haldane would give them in the twentieth century. In the long run, perhaps, provincial regulation was less of a threat to business than Dominion regulation, but there are no significant and particular linkages between this outcome and what the courts thought or did before 1900.

Another possibility is that autonomous federalism itself might have frustrated effective regulation, by sharply dividing powers between separate spheres. Whether the model has this effect is debatable, because much depends upon an assessment of the aspect rule, and especially upon whether a restricted use of aspects is an essential part of the model. The debate can be finessed by the realization that nothing in what the text writers said, nothing in what they perceived the stakes of their work to be, and nothing of substance in their immediate relations suggests that they had any sense that the stakes were anything but federalism. They should not be understood by what the twentieth century made of their work.

What, then, did these writers do to justify federalism as a distinctive form of government? Expressly, they said little. O'Sullivan concluded his second edition by justifying federalism in functional terms: a large and diverse country could not be governed by a single legislature ('the provinces are too scattered and their interests too diverse').[54] Instead, local matters should be dealt with by local legislatures and national or general matters dealt with by a common government – the Dominion. Weldon and Mills said much the same in their lectures, but Clement and Lefroy said nothing. Yet for all of them, the justifications were embedded throughout the topic. The claims for the provinces and the model of autonomy were essentially claims for self-government, albeit with a limited scope, for groups defined by history, culture, and geography. The division of powers and functions between local and general was self-evident to them, even though they realized that there could be differences of opinion about precisely where to draw the line. The meanings were derived from geography, from the experiences that led to Confederation, and from English history, especially the experiences with the police power and local government.

Legal Reasoning Introduced

So far, my account of the writers and their writing has been primarily about the substance of their thought. I turn now to their beliefs about law and legal reasoning. What did lawyers think that judges did, and should do, when they decided cases? What kinds of reasoning and arguments were appropriate for talking about law, and what kinds were simply unimaginable? What were the sources of their ideas? What was the relation, if any, between these beliefs and the beliefs about federalism?

The answer to the question about sources is clear: all these writers derived their ways of thinking primarily from England. They were familiar with the major constitutional writers in the United States, such as Cooley, Story, and Kent, but they typically referred to their writing in footnotes, and never preferred it to the English texts. Late in the period, they seem to have been entirely unaware of some of the American scholarship that challenged their ways of thinking. Lefroy, for example, in all his writing up to his death in 1917, never cited Holmes or Pound.

In England, a general mode of thinking emerged during the second half of the nineteenth century, which has been given different names, among them the rule of law, the black letter tradition, and classical legal thought. Whatever its name, its basic elements were the equality and autonomy of individuals (or, more abstractly, legal entities, including the state), a division between the public and private realms, and a pervasive perception of legal relations as spheres of powers separated by sharp, bright lines. In this thinking, the courts and the common law were paramount, and the work of courts in deciding individual cases was objective and apolitical – determining facts and applying the general principles of the common law or the words of a statute.

The typical form of scholarship was marked by the synthesis of cases into general principles of doctrine, divorced from time and context, and exemplified by a small group of scholars at Oxford, including Frederick Pollock and Dicey, who wrote classic texts about common law and constitutional law.[55] To begin at the end of the story in Canada, this mode of thinking was dominant by 1900, and Lefroy's book is the prime example – even Dicey gave praise.[56] Having said in the preface that his objective was to 'extract' general principles from the cases, he put these principles in 68 numbered propositions, each set in bold type, and followed by extensive commentary, almost all paraphrases or quotations from the judgments. He presented this doctrine with only a few small glimpses of the social and political context; the struggle between the Dominion and the provinces was barely mentioned, for example, and the Manitoba Schools Crisis, which was raging at the time he wrote, did not appear at all. He did not refer to any literature from other disciplines, nor to any of the constitutional writing in Quebec except for Loranger's *Letters*, and only because Loranger had said something about Lefroy's own issues. He did not seek illumination for his work from Quebec's distinctive experience, and did not wonder about a threat to the French race.

The differences among O'Sullivan, Clement, and Lefroy demonstrate how understandings of legal reasoning and the appropriate roles of scholarship had changed. Less than twenty years spanned their three books, but their education and experience put them in different eras. O'Sullivan and Clement were educated in Canada, O'Sullivan in the 1850s, and Clement a decade later. In contrast, even though Lefroy was educated only a few years later than Clement, he studied at Oxford, when it was the centre of the scholarship articulating the new ways of thinking.

The objectives, the contents, and the likely readers of the books were essentially different. O'Sullivan sought to describe the basic principles and the institutions of Canadian government, and only occasionally considered doctrine and cases. Clement's contents were much less disciplined, but the major topics and divisions were narrower and more in the domain of lawyers and their analysis: colonial status, federalism, and the *BNA Act*. Throughout the first part, he included description and analysis of doctrine, and the treatment of the *BNA Act* was a section-by-section exposition of all the cases. Lefroy's text, except for his introduction about the British constitution, was avowedly limited to the division of powers and to unremitting doctrinal analysis, a limitation that was emphasized by exiling history and overt expressions of faith and preference to the introduction. Instead of Clement's section-by-section compilation of cases, Lefroy sought synthesis, in the manner of his great English exemplars.

The range of subjects narrowed from the principles and institutions of government to doctrine about the division of legislative powers; courts and their doctrine came to be more and more central; and a sense of context and history virtually disappeared. None of these writers expressly specified his expected readers, but the differences clearly suggest a change from educated citizens and, perhaps, law students to practising lawyers and judges.

Interpretation

The emphasis on courts and federalism made their beliefs about interpretation crucial to a reconstruction of their beliefs about legal reasoning. The existence and legitimacy of judicial review itself was not a substantial issue, despite the scholarly attention it has received in the twentieth century. O'Sullivan and Clement gave it only a few paragraphs, treating it as settled and unproblematic, and it was not mentioned at all by Lefroy, by the writers in the periodicals, or by Weldon or Mill in their lectures.[57] The crux of the justification, expressed or assumed, was that the legislatures had limited powers; that is, the *BNA Act* granted powers to legislate about specified subjects – and only those subjects. The rule of law gave the courts the power and the duty to enforce the limits, and to declare that any purported statute was not law because it was not authorized by the *BNA Act*. Clement stated this thinking best:

> In a country under the rule of law, it necessarily devolves upon the courts which administer law, to enquire and determine ... whether an Act of a legislature having authority over a limited range of subject matters, is within or without its powers – is or is not law.[58]

In 1892, the Privy Council announced that the *BNA Act* must be interpreted 'by the same methods of construction and exposition which they apply to other statutes.'[59] These 'methods' were not discussed at any length by the Canadian writers, because they needed no discussion: they were widely shared and the English texts were conveniently at hand and unproblematic. One of the standard texts, Maxwell's *On the Interpretation of Statutes*, can serve as an example, even though no single source can embody all the complexity, detail, and variations of the period. Maxwell's first sentence was, 'Statute law is the will of the Legislature; and the object of all judicial interpretation is to determine what intention is either expressly or by implication conveyed by the language used.' This single sentence encapsulated his basic faiths: the legislature had a will, which could be expressed in words; the task of interpretation was discovering the meanings of these words, and these meanings were independent of the interpreter and the process of interpretation.

Maxwell continued by saying that if the meaning of words of a statute was 'free from ambiguity' it must prevail, even though it might be unreasonable or unjust. Contrary to some caricatures drawn by twentieth-century scholars, neither Maxwell nor any other writer of his period believed that meanings were always plain, awaiting discovery. A few lines later, he said, 'language is rarely so free from ambiguity as to be incapable of being used in more than one sense.' When language was 'open to doubt, and capable of receiving more than one construction, the true meaning' was to be sought by considering the words in their context within the statute, their history, and 'certain general principles.'[60] Most of the remaining 350 pages of the text elaborated these sources of meaning.

Throughout this elaboration, the courts and the common law were central. In particular, the 'certain general principles' were largely common law presumptions, made by courts. Much of the content of these presumptions was a consolidation of widely shared constitutional values, but as well much was an expression of economic and class preferences, which were often at odds with the manifest intention of the legislature.

The process of determining meaning was independent of context, values, and needs. In particular, ideas about the kind of federalism that might be appropriate for Canada were simply irrelevant. In the course of a debate about a controversial decision about the power of provinces to regulate sittings of courts, one British Columbia lawyer declared that Todd's opinion deserved no respect: he lacked 'long years of legal training,' and his work as a historian might have given him a 'broader range' but it might also have given him a 'tendency to look at expediency or policy.'[61]

Another example is Lefroy's encounter with Story's different faith. In his Proposition 38, Lefroy declared that, because a constitution could not expressly provide for every possibility, 'use was made ... of general language, containing in principle the conferred powers, and leaving to legislation and judicial interpretation the task of completing the details.' His understanding here was that the *BNA Act* contained the essential meanings, and he did not imagine that the courts were to have any original or creative power. Near the end of his discussion he quoted Story, especially about the need for interpretation, 'influenced by the demands of public policy and public welfare.' But for Lefroy such matters were irrelevant to interpretation, and he retreated quickly to his basic belief in the general principles.[62]

One tempting source of information about legislative intention was the debates preceding Confederation, which were within memory of most judges and writers. The settled doctrine, however, was firm: the only kinds of history that could be considered were the common law and earlier statutes. Social and economic history, and evidences of the plans and intentions of the legislators, were utterly inadmissible, a limitation that made interpretation seem apolitical and supported the power of the courts, by preferring the common law presumptions to evidence of legislative intention. In Canada, the firm exclusion of context and history was required by their faithful following of English models, but this obligation does nothing to explain the limitation itself. Ultimately, it was based on the nature of the threat history presented. To consider debates and context, in preference to the common law principles and presumptions, threatened to deny the lawyers' power, and to erode the property of their clients and friends. These were formidable costs, and formidable pressures to eschew history.[63]

The separation of interpretation from value and history did not entail a belief that law was entirely autonomous. A passage from Clement suggests that the thought was not so simplistic. Speaking about Confederation, he said, 'opinions may very reasonably vary at different periods as to where the line should be drawn that is to divide matters of common or "national," from matters of "local" concern.' The choice of the line was a matter of opinion – contingent and political – and there was no essential nature of local and general. Yet once the line was expressed in the *BNA Act*, it became law, 'a thing certain,' to be determined by the objective legal science, and arguments about where the line should be drawn in order, for example, to encourage economic development or to protect distinctive cultures became entirely irrelevant. The line between general and local expressed in the *BNA Act* was at the same time both an expression of values and an objective standard.[64]

The Unity of Federalism and Legal Reasoning

The model of autonomous federalism and the beliefs about the functions of the courts in review and interpretation were closely related – integrated might be more expressive. The powers given to the Dominion and the provinces were spheres with sharp limits, which were independent of each other and did not overlap. The term 'sphere' was common, but any other spatial figure would have expressed the same idea.[65]

The function of the courts was to determine the location of the boundaries of these spheres, and not to balance competing claims to power, or to make decisions of degree, or to consider whether an allocation of power might be 'better' by some other standard.

Balancing and degrees were fundamentally at odds with the idea of lines and the faith that judges did not make choices. Lefroy provides two examples. He perceived, astutely and with little help from the cases, that the doctrine that permitted Dominion statutes to 'affect' the domain of the provinces needed some limit, but confessed that he was unable to say any more than that the power permitted only reasonable and necessary intrusions; and he was unable to explain what sort of considerations might be relevant in making the determination. The reason for his inability is that questions of degree were inescapably at stake. The other example was his reaction to the famous comment by Lord Watson, in the *Local Prohibition Reference*, that some matters 'might attain such dimensions as to affect the body politic of the Dominion.'[66] Despite his immense respect for the Privy Council, Lefroy was deeply troubled, because this inquiry might 'bring before the Courts very difficult questions and questions of a very political character.'[67] He saw the decision as political because attaining dimensions suggested measurement and the question, how much? – a question that was fundamentally inappropriate for courts to be asked.

The Legacy for the Twentieth Century

The model of autonomous federalism and these beliefs about legal reasoning were dominant throughout much of the twentieth century. In the courts, they were manifested, for example, by the doctrine of mutual modification; by the contrast between definition of scope of the powers and the doctrine about necessarily incidental effects; by the avowed rejection of considerations of degree; and by the exclusion of history, context, and value from interpretation. Their most profound legacy, from the perspective of twentieth-century legal culture, was not so much any particular results, but the restrictions of lawyers' capacity to think in ways that related their doctrine to history, to political and economic change, and to beliefs about the kind of nation Canada should be. Throughout the century, their hold on lawyers' minds waned. First the scholars and then the courts came to see the powers overlapping, and to see courts as making choices about appropriate balances and allocations of power. The first scholarly challenges came in the late 1920s and 1930s, from Herbert Smith, Frank Scott, W.P.M. Kennedy, and Vincent MacDonald. The watershed came two decades later, in an article by William Lederman written in 1954.[68] In the courts, the dominance of the model was eroded during the 1960s, and it had faded into the background in major cases that came afterwards, such as *Crown Zellerbach* and *General Motors*.[69] It remains in lawyers' minds, but divorced from its origins, and often used as a surrogate for faiths that its makers might not recognize.

NOTES

1 D.A. O'Sullivan, *A Manual of Government in Canada* (1st ed., Toronto: J.C. Stuart, 1879; 2nd ed., Toronto: Carswell, 1887).

2 Supra, note 1. For a short biography of O'Sullivan, see *Dictionary of Canadian Biography* (Toronto: University of Toronto Press, 1990), vol. 12, 811.

3 J. Travis, *A Law Treatise on the Constitutional Powers of Parliament and of the Local Legislatures Under the British North America Act, 1867* (Saint John, NB: Sun Publishing, 1884).

4 See D.G. Bell, *Legal Education in New Brunswick* (Fredericton: Faculty of Law, University of New Brunswick, 1992) at 44–46.

5 T.J.J. Loranger, *Letters upon the Interpretation of the Federal Constitution* (Quebec, 1883). The *Letters* appeared first during 1882, as a collection of articles in newspapers. For an account of Loranger, see *Dictionary of Canadian Biography* (Toronto: University of Toronto Press, 1982) vol. 11, 529–31.

6 William Henry Pope Clement, *The Law of the Canadian Constitution*, 1st ed. (Toronto: Carswell, 1892). A second and third edition followed, in much the same form, from Carswell in 1904 and 1916. In the third edition, which was extensively rewritten, the section-by-section treatment of the *BNA Act* disappeared, but the Act itself remained dominant.

7 Ibid. at v.

8 A.H.F. Lefroy, *The Law of Legislative Power in Canada* (Toronto: Law Book and Publishing, 1897–8). The preface was written so late in 1897 that the book could not have appeared until 1898.

9 A.H.F. Lefroy, *Canada's Federal System* (Toronto: Carswell, 1913); *Leading Cases in Canadian Constitutional Law* (Toronto: Carswell, 1914); and *A Short Treatise on Canadian Constitutional Law* (Toronto: Carswell, 1918). *Leading Cases* was little more than excerpts from cases, and the other two were

essentially shortened versions of *Legislative Power*. Much of their text was taken from *Legislative Power*, and most of the shortening was done simply by omitting other text. For an account of Lefroy's thought and a complete bibliography, see Risk, 'A.H.F. Lefroy,' in this volume.

10 The major ones were A.R. Hassard, *Canadian Constitutional History and Law* (Toronto: Carswell, 1900); O.A. Howland, *The New Empire: Reflections upon Its Origin and Constitution and Its Relation to the Great Republic* (Toronto: Hart & Co., 1891); J.E.C. Munro, *The Constitution of Canada* (Cambridge: University Press, 1889); W.S. Scott, *The Canadian Constitution Historically Explained* (Toronto: Carswell, 1918); and G.J. Wheeler, *Confederation Law of Canada* (London: Eyre & Spottiswoode, 1896).

11 As well as the two central Canadian law reviews, two were published in the West, both of them in Winnipeg: the *Manitoba Law Journal*, edited by John Skirving Ewart, which lasted less than two years, from 1884 to 1885, and the *Western Law Journal*, which lasted from 1890 to 1895. Both of them contained only a few pieces about constitutional law.

12 For an account of Weldon's career, see J. Willis, *A History of Dalhousie Law School* (Toronto: University of Toronto Press, 1979) at 25–7, 34–5, and 62–4. He taught two courses: constitutional history and constitutional law. Notes for the constitutional law course taken by J.E. March are kept at the library of Dalhousie Law School. March seems occasionally to have 'tuned out' – to speak as a student now might speak. His notes for three successive lectures late in the course read, for example, 'the Act and discussed cases,' 'Read the Act,' 'Reading of the Act & discussion of cases.' The first 12 lectures were a romp through a vast and eclectic range of topics, and the remaining 28 were a section-by-section account of the *BNA Act*, including the cases. No notes from the history course survive, but the contents are suggested by Weldon's address at the opening of the law school in 1883: *The Inaugural Addresses Delivered at the Opening of the Law School ...* (1883), a copy of which is kept at the library of Dalhousie Law School. It was an account of the British constitution, stressing its progress towards justice and liberty from the misty Norman beginnings forwards.

13 Little writing has been done about Mills, and much less than he deserves. There is no biography, except for a short note in the *Dictionary of Canadian Biography* (Toronto: University of Toronto Press, 1993) vol. 13 at 707–11, and a PhD thesis, D.J. McMurchy, 'David Mills: Nineteenth-Century Canadian Liberal' (University of Rochester, 1969). The best account of his constitutional thought is in R.C. Vipond, *Liberty and Community: Canadian Federalism and the Failure of the Constitution* (Albany: State University of New York Press, 1991). Throughout the 1890s, he taught a course in

federal constitutional law, although the loss of a crucial calendar prevents knowing precisely when the course began. The course was composed of two parts, the first about Canada and the second about the United States. For the Canadian part, Mills began with a lengthy justification of federalism, and then turned, like Weldon, to a section-by-section discussion of the *BNA Act*. His own typed notes for the Canadian part of the course are in his papers, in the Regional Collection of the Weldon Library of the University of Western Ontario, although the papers are not organized in any way that enables particular references.

14 Adolphous Todd, *On Parliamentary Government in England: Its Origin, Development, and Practical Operation* (London: Longmans, Green, 1866); and *Parliamentary Government in the British Colonies* (Boston: Little Brown, 1880). For a brief account of Todd, see *Dictionary of Canadian Biography* (Toronto: University of Toronto, Press 1982) vol. 11 at 883–5.

15 John George Bourinot, *A Manual of the Constitutional History of Canada* (Montreal: Dawson Brothers, 1888); and *Federal Government in Canada* (Baltimore: Johns Hopkins University, 1889). For an account of Bourinot, see *Dictionary of Canadian Biography* (Toronto: University of Toronto Press, 1982) vol. 11 at 105–6. At Osgoode and Toronto, the texts most frequently specified were Bourinot's *Manual* and O'Sullivan, but at Dalhousie and Saint John, none was required.

16 Clement, supra note 6 at 1; and O'Sullivan, supra note 1, 2nd ed. at 29.

17 A.V. Dicey, *The Law of the Constitution* (London: Macmillan, 1885) at 153.

18 Clement, supra note 6 at 3–21; and Lefroy, supra note 8 at lxiv.

19 O'Sullivan wrote several chapters on rights, but they were no more than short assertions about the content of some of the major rights, without any analysis or consideration of the implications of parliamentary supremacy. Both Clement and Lefroy briefly expressed a faith that individual rights were protected in the British constitution, but did not explain how; Lefroy, for example, said simply that it 'guards the liberty of the subject without destroying the freedom of action of the legislature' (supra note 8 at lx). Even the ways in which federalism offered protection to individuals and cultures were barely mentioned.

20 This question was thoroughly vented in two books by non-lawyers. The first, F. Taylor, *Are Legislatures Parliaments?* (Montreal: John Lovell, 1879), suggested the answer by a dedication to John A. Macdonald, the prime minister of Canada throughout most of the period. The legislatures of the colonies were bodies assigned law-making powers, but no more. A reply came quickly in S.J. Watson, *The Powers of Canadian Parliaments* (Toronto: C.B. Robinson, 1880), dedicated to Edward Blake, one of the major leaders

of the provinces, making the argument that the key was functions, not labels.

21 The letter to Macdonald is discussed in R.C.B. Risk, 'The Puzzle of Jurisdiction' (1995) 46 *South Carolina L.R.* 703. Mills also introduced the model in speeches in Parliament about dual representation, the composition of the Senate, and disallowance of New Brunswick legislation about separate schools. In his lectures (Mills, supra note 13), he declared his views strongly and continuously. At every turn, he argued for the continuation of the original colonies, the autonomy of the provinces, the sovereignty of their legislatures, the independence of their executives, and the priority of section 92, all of which will be considered later in the text.

22 For an account of these quarrels and references, see P. Romney, *Mr Attorney: The Attorney-General of Ontario in Court, Cabinet and Legislature, 1791– 1899* (Toronto: University of Toronto Press, 1986) at 248–59.

23 (1879) 2 S.C.R. 70. Adam Crooks, Mowat's lieutenant, argued that the Dominion and the province were 'two sovereign bodies ... [T]here is no question of one being subordinate to the other ... [T]he jurisdiction of [the provinces] must be absolute and complete.' *Severn* was in effect an appeal from *Taylor*, (1875) 36 U.C.Q.B. 183 at 190, where Wilson J. said that the provincial powers must be 'exercised subject and subordinate to the power and authority of the Dominion Parliament.'

24 (1879) 3 S.C.R. 575.

25 (1883) 5 S.C.R. 538; 8 A.C. 767 (P.C.).

26 See *Leprohon v. City of Ottawa* (1878) 2 O.A.R. 522; and *Citizens Insurance v. Parsons* (1880), 7 O.A.R. 246; aff'd (1880) 4 S.C.R. 215; aff'd (1881) 7 A.C. 96 (P.C.).

27 (1883) 9 A.C. 117 (PC); aff'g (1882) 7 O.A.R. 246.

28 O'Sullivan, supra note 1, 1st ed. at 40–2, 57–8.

29 'Editorial Review: Regina v. Hodge – Regina v. Frawley' (1882) 2 *Can. L. Times* 376; 'Provincial Jurisdiction over Civil Procedure' (1882) 2 *Can. L. Times* 560; 'Editorial Review' (1884) 4 *Can. L. Times* 166; and 'The Constitution of Canada' (1891) 11 *Can. L. Times* 113. See also, Editor, 'Delegation of Legislative Power' (1882) 18 *Can. L.J.* 431; and T. H[odgins], 'Delegation of Legislative Functions and Disallowance' (1883) 3 *Can. L. Times* 279.

30 O'Sullivan, supra note 1, 2nd ed. at 7–8.

31 Ibid. at 10.

32 Ibid. at 22.

33 [1892] A.C. 437 (P.C.).

34 Clement, supra note 6, 2nd ed. at 46. See also 21–2, 45–7, 129, 141–4, 199, 201, and 301.

35 Lefroy, supra note 8 at propositions 7, 8, 17, 19, 27, 28, and 65.
36 See T.M. Cooley, *The General Principles of Constitutional Law in the United States of America* (Boston: Little Brown, 1880); *A Treatise on the Constitutional Limitations* ... (Boston: Little Brown, 1868); E.A. Freeman, *A History of Federal Government from the Federation of the Achain League to the Disruption of the United States* (London: MacMillan, 1863); and J. Story, *Commentaries on the Constitution of the United States* ... (Boston: C.C. Little, 1851). O'Sullivan read Pommeroy, Cooley, and Freeman; he was the only one to cite Freeman, although Mills referred to him in Parliament. Clement cited Cooley often, and Lefroy ranged more widely among the American texts. Mills' notes from the Cooley lectures are in his papers, supra note 13.
37 Dicey, supra note 17 at 128–43.
38 *Liquidators of the Maritime Bank v. New Brunswick* [1892] A.C. 437 (P.C.); *A.G. Ontario v. A.G. Canada (The Local Prohibition Reference)* [1896] A.C. 348 (P.C.).
39 In his preliminary discussion of the British constitution, Clement appended this footnote, which had little connection to its context: 'The federal idea is nothing more than the logical outcome of the "individualistic" idea, which lies at the bottom of self-government; and it would be an interesting task to trace the growth of this idea from its root in the belief that man has certain "natural rights," and that society controls his exercise of those rights only to the extent to give proper play to the rights of his fellow-men, up through the growth of municipal self-government to the establishment of a federal system of government, logical from root to topmost branch' (Clement, supra note 6 at 5). Wegenast's article is 'The Federal System' (1910) 30 *Can. L. Times* 11 at 120. His analysis was sustained and rich, supported by an impressive display of references, including classical and European philosophers, which took him far beyond the reach of any other Canadian writer.
40 The story of this appeal in the political arena has been told in Vipond, *Liberty and Community*, supra note 13.
41 O'Sullivan, supra note 1, 2nd ed. at vi and 97; see also 9 and 20.
42 Lefroy, supra note 8 at propositions 12, 17.
43 The only extensive and recent study of the compact theory is R. Cook, *Provincial Autonomy and the Compact Theory, 1867–1921* (Ottawa: Queen's Printer, 1969).
44 (1882) 7 A.C. 829 (P.C.).
45 Travis, supra note 3 at 3, 11 163, 168, 174. According to Travis, the New Brunswick court did not contain 'a single lawyer possessing anything like a thorough scientific legal knowledge'; some of its decisions were 'su-

premely ridiculous,' and its decisions in *Fredericton* were the 'most ridiculous of all ... delivered on this *ultra vires* question' (at 37, 51).

46 He said, '[A]t Confederation, the powers had been divided in "the best possible way for the country," and there was no "discontent or jealousy"': O'Sullivan, supra note 1, 1st ed. at 20.

47 O'Sullivan, supra note 1, 2nd ed. at 106–10.

48 Lefroy, supra note 8 at 343.

49 E. Armour, 'The Constitution of Canada' (1891) 11 *Can. L. Times* 113, 137, and 233; and (1892) 12 *Can. L. Times* 153.

50 All these writers paid far less attention than modern scholars do to the particular heads of power, for example, the regulation of trade and commerce; or to questions about the powers to legislate about particular topics or issues, for example, morality. For the earlier writers, Loranger, Travis, and O'Sullivan, preoccupied with the structure of sections 91 and 92, they were simply not a topic at all, and Clement considered the heads of power only in the course of commenting on the *BNA Act*. None of Lefroy's propositions was about a head of power, although in the commentaries he discussed several of the more important ones, especially regulation of trade and commerce and taxation.

51 Lefroy, supra note 8 at 347–64.

52 Clement, supra note 6 at 213–17, and Lefroy, supra note 8 at 394–415.

53 This possibility is considered by Blaine Baker in his review of Vipond's *Liberty and Community* (supra note 13), in (1995) 45 *U.T.L.J.* 77. This review is remarkably thoughtful and stimulating, and its 'hortatory' suggestions have been a formidable challenge throughout revising this article. My interpretation is much the same as Vipond's.

54 O'Sullivan, supra note 1, 2nd ed. at 295.

55 Of course this description is a model, and even as a model, it is greatly simplified. See G.B. Baker, 'The Reconstitution of Upper Canadian Legal Thought in the Late-Victorian Empire' (1985) 3 *Law & Hist. R.* 219; R.W. Gordon, 'Legal Thought and Legal Practice in the Age of American Enterprise,' in G. Geison, ed., *Professions and Professional Ideologies in America* (Chapel Hill: University of North Carolina Press, 1983) at 70; D. Kennedy, 'Towards an Historical Understanding of Legal Consciousness: The Case of Classical Legal Thought in America, 1850–1940' (1980) 3 *Research in L. & Soc.* 3; and D. Sugarman, 'Legal Theory, the Common Law Mind, and the Making of the Textbook Tradition,' in W. Twining, ed., *Legal Theory and Common Law* (Oxford: Basil Blackwell, 1986) at 26.

56 A.V. Dicey 'Book Review' (1898) 14 *Law Q.R.* 198.

57 Nor was review a substantial issue for the courts themselves, apart from

one early and sharp controversy in New Brunswick; see G. Bale, *Chief Justice William Johnstone Ritchie: Responsible Government and Judicial Review* (Ottawa: Carleton University Press, 1991) at 107–26 for an account of this episode.

58 Clement, supra note 6 at 202. O'Sullivan spoke in the same way; see O'Sullivan, supra note 1, 1st ed. at 21, and 2nd ed. at 25. See also Dicey, supra note 17 at 147. Most of the cases made or assumed the same sort of analysis. Some, however, invoked conflict as a justification for review – conflict between a Canadian statute (made by a subordinate legislature) and a British statute (made by the dominant or supreme legislature). Usually, although not always, this conflict was a way of expressing the limitation of power; see Clement, supra note 6 at 202.

59 *Bank of Toronto v. Lambe* (1887) 12 A.C. 575 at 579 (P.C.).

60 P.B. Maxwell, *On the Interpretation of Statutes* (London: Wm. Maxwell, 1875), 1.

61 An Exile, 'Administration of Justice in British Columbia' (1882) 18 *Can. L.J.* 244 at 245.

62 Lefroy, supra note 8 at 475. Lefroy did, though, favour a 'liberal' interpretation. In Proposition Three, he quoted the Privy Council about interpretation, and added, '[other statutes] of a similar character, that is to say, statutes conferring constitutional charters. The *BNA Act* cannot be construed in a rigidly technical manner.' This awkward formulation was probably more than a muddled attempt to synthesize inconsistent cases. Lefroy seemed to hope that constitutions were a distinctive kind of statute, which was just what the Privy Council sought to deny.

63 This limitation was a sharp contrast to understandings of interpretation in other disciplines, especially literature and religion. Throughout the nineteenth century, the Protestant churches in England, the United States, and Canada struggled with the question whether the history of doctrine could affect its meaning. Was the Bible just like any other book, to be read by the understandings that guided reading other books? Throughout the second half of the century, the churches accommodated these challenges and their doctrine. See D. Forbes, *The Liberal Anglican Idea of History* (Cambridge: Cambridge University Press, 1952); M. Gauvreau, *The Evangelical Century: College and Creed in Canada from the Great Revival to the Great Depression* (Montreal and Kingston: McGill-Queen's University Press, 1991); and M. Van Die, *An Evangelical Mind: Nathanael Burwash and the Methodist Tradition in Canada, 1839–1918* (Montreal and Kingston: McGill-Queen's University Press, 1989).

64 In his discussion of the aspect rule, Clement said, 'Of any number of laws

put forward as determining the "legal relation," only one is the law which governs. The views of advocates, and even judges, may conflict, but the law, though it may be, from time to time, varied at the will of the law-making body in the state, is at any given moment of time, a thing certain': Clement, supra note 6 at 214.

65 O'Sullivan said that the spheres must be 'separated and fenced off with all the accuracy of language that is possible' (supra note 1, 2nd ed. at 176), and Mills, speaking in the House of Commons, said that the line of division 'was as distinct as if it was a geographical boundary marked out by a surveyor': Canada, House of Commons, *Debates*, 8 March 1875, 576.

66 Lefroy, supra note 8 at 361.

67 A.H.F. Lefroy, 'Prohibition: The Late Privy Council Decision' (1896) 16 *Can. L. Times* 125 at 133.

68 William Lederman, 'Classification of Laws and the British North America Act,' in J.A. Corry, F.C. Cronkite, and E.F. Whitmore, eds., *Legal Essays in Honour of Arthur Moxon* (Toronto: University of Toronto Press, 1953) 183, as reprinted in W.R. Lederman, *Continuing Canadian Constitutional Dilemmas* (Toronto: Butterworths, 1981) 229. This story is told in a preliminary way in R.C.B. Risk, 'The Scholars and the Constitution,' in this volume. The models and their relation to the doctrine are discussed in B. Ryder, 'The Demise and Rise of the Classical Paradigm' (1991) 36 *McGill L.J.* 309.

69 *R. v. Crown Zellerbach Canada* [1988] 1 S.C.R. 261, and *General Motors of Canada v. City National Leasing* [1989] 1 S.C.R. 641.

2

A.H.F. Lefroy: Common Law Thought in Late-Nineteenth-Century Canada – On Burying One's Grandfather

Introduction

Augustus Henry Fraser Lefroy was one of the leading common law scholars in Canada in the late nineteenth and early twentieth centuries, but he is now virtually unknown. Among modern Canadian lawyers, probably only a few specialized constitutional scholars have ever heard of him, and doubtless only a few of them have looked at his books. Among modern Canadian historians, most know him as a minor figure among the late-nineteenth-century Imperialists, if at all.

Lefroy was born in Toronto in 1852, and educated in England, at Rugby and at New College, Oxford, where he took a BA degree in 1875. He was called to the bar in England in 1877, and in Ontario in the following year. During the 1880s and 1890s, he practised in Toronto in a series of small partnerships, and was also a court reporter for much of that time. In 1900 he became a professor of law at the University of Toronto, although he continued to practise as well. In 1912 he was a candidate for principal of the law school at Osgoode Hall, but the benchers chose John Delatre Falconbridge instead. Later, in 1915, he became editor of the *Canadian Law Times*. He died in 1919.[1]

Lefroy demonstrated his scholarly inclinations at the very outset of his career, publishing three articles in his first few years in Ontario, and several more in the 1880s and 1890s. His most productive period was from the late 1890s to 1911, in which he published his major book, *The*

Law of Legislative Power in Canada, and fifteen articles. Most of these articles were about constitutional law, and most of the rest were about Roman law, jurisprudence, and the theory of the common law.[2]

My purpose in this article is to reconstruct Lefroy's ways of thinking about law, especially his thought about the common law and the constitution, through an analysis of his writing. And I can begin to explain my title by revealing that John Beverley Robinson was his grandfather.[3] Robinson was a dominant figure in early-nineteenth-century Ontario, performing many roles in government, including that of chief justice. Their relation has an ironic twist: Lefroy respected his grandfather greatly, but his own writing helped make a gulf that today obscures Robinson from our understanding.

The Common Law

Lefroy's two major articles about the common law were 'Judge-Made Law' and 'The Basis of Case Law,' published in the *Law Quarterly Review* in 1904 and 1906. Those two were supplemented by 'Rome and Law,' published in the *Harvard Law Review* in 1907, and 'Jurisprudence,' which appeared in the *Law Quarterly Review* in 1911. 'Judge-Made Law' and 'The Basis of Case Law' dealt with the questions whether judges made law and how they made it, questions that engaged many of the English and Canadian common law scholars of his generation. Lefroy declared firmly that they did make law. His conclusion was based on the claim that the existing common law was not complete; that is, there were cases for which the existing stock of rules gave no answer. The judges had an obligation to decide those cases, and in deciding them they made law. Virtually all the common law had been made in this way, and even though such questions might be expected to grow fewer over time, they were not infrequent and would never disappear. The claim that judges made law was not startling in the early twentieth century. Lefroy's major effort and his distinctive contribution was an analysis of the methods and the sources for judicial lawmaking.[4]

In the first of the two articles, 'Judge-Made Law,' Lefroy described the methods for the lawmaking; he claimed that the law made by the judges 'consists in part of the gradual explanation and definition of the vague general terms in which broad principles of law are conceived of and expressed, and in part of the interpretation of the various transactions and relations of men *inter se*, by which latter process has been built up that great body of law, which may be called the law of implications and equities.'[5] These 'broad principles' were propositions that were so indefinite that they might be understood as governing cases in which 'in truth they do not apply' or 'which do not satisfy the requirements,'[6] and the courts made law by elaborating these principles to make them govern only the appropriate cases. For example, 'the whole law of nuisance may be regarded as based upon the maxim *sic utere tuo*.' The second mode, the interpretation of the 'transactions and relations of men,' was a richer and more complex concept. It was divided into two parts: relations arising from contract, and other kinds of relations, such as trusts. The function of the courts was to determine the obligations inherent in the relations. For example, if parties entered into a contract of sale – a 'generic contract' –without specifying any terms, 'all is left to the law,' and the terms that governed their relation was made by the courts; for example, the law about implied warranties.[7] The lawmaking power was, however, sharply limited in one way that Lefroy asserted but did not discuss: once they made the common law, the judges could not change it.[8]

In his second article, 'The Basis of Case Law,' he described the sources for making common law. They were 'the great basic principles':

   i) Justice, humanity, and other moral obligations,
   ii) Common sense, and the reason of the thing,
   iii) Public convenience and other practical considerations.[9]

Again, the bulk of the article was examples. Representative examples of justice, humanity, and other moral obligations as sources were cases about underground waters and spring guns. 'Common sense, and the reason of the thing' was a source in cases where 'scarcely ... any question of right or wrong arises; or else justice or other moral considerations are so evenly balanced between the parties as not to form a basis for decision,'[10] and one instance of this 'common sense' was the mutual rights of support of adjoining land owners. Examples of the use of public convenience (for which he tended to substitute 'public policy') as a source were contracts in restraint of trade, *Rylands v. Fletcher*, and cases in which 'the law ... sacrifices not only the convenience of individuals, but their just claims, to considerations of public convenience, and the general good,' such as privilege in the reporting of parliamentary debates, caveat emptor, and *Winterbottom v. Wright*.[11]

These two articles were entirely about lawmaking, and Lefroy did not write much about the general structure of the common law or its reasoning. His beliefs were, nevertheless, apparent enough. The settled common law (that is, the common law the judges had made) was, or could be, scientific; that is, it could be 'knowledge that was coordinated, arranged and systematized,' and it could be an internally coherent and consistent system of rules, from which subsidiary rules could be deduced.[12] As well, Lefroy believed that individual cases alone were binding, although he did not consider any tension between the authority of individual cases and a scientific common law composed of coherent general rules.

Lefroy's understanding of the common law was deeply rooted in English common law thought, and it can be illuminated by a short account of ways of thinking in the late eighteenth and nineteenth centuries. In the late eighteenth century, Blackstone and Mansfield were dominant. For them, the common law was composed of principles derived by the judges from reason and justice, and from the collective experience of the English people. In *Rust v. Cooper* Mansfield declared, 'The law does not consist in particular cases, but in general principles which run through the cases and govern the decision of them.'[13] Precedents should be respected, because they gave certainty and because they were a concrete record of reason and experience, but they did not have authority simply by virtue of having been decided, as they did for Lefroy. Blackstone said, 'The decisions of courts of justice are the evidence of what is common law,' but 'the law and the opinion of the judge are not always convertible terms, or one and the same thing.'[14] In cases for which no settled pattern of cases existed, judges drew directly on reason, justice, and experience.[15]

During the nineteenth century, understandings of the common law and the authority of precedent slowly changed. The positivism of Bentham and Austin became dominant, and the common law came to be understood as embodied in the cases. Precedent became binding authority, rather than persuasive, and by the end of the century, courts were obligated to follow the ratios of individual cases decided by courts at the same level or higher in the judicial hierarchy.[16]

As well, during the second half of the century, a widely shared way of thinking about such topics as the nature and proper functions of legislatures and courts, and the appropriate materials and ways of legal reasoning, became dominant among lawyers in England, the United States, and Canada. This way of thinking was expressed primarily by scholars, especially a small group at Oxford that included William Anson, Albert Venn Dicey, William Markby, and Frederick Pollock, and it paralleled and overlapped the positivism and strict precedent in the courts. Its basic elements were the equality and autonomy of individuals (and legal entities generally), a division between the public and private realms, and the paramountcy of the common law and the courts. Legal reasoning was distinctive, and sharply separated from politics and context. The common law was a set of internally consistent and coherent general rules, which expressed important moral and social standards, but which were autonomous or independent from their immediate context. The reasoning of the courts in elaborating and applying the common law was objective and apolitical. Of course, this description is a model, and even as a model it is greatly simplified. The minds of individual lawyers were much more complex and muddled, and included inconsistent elements. There were differences among individuals and between generations, and between practising lawyers and the profession. It has no widely accepted name, and for convenience I shall call it the 'rule of law thought,' in honour of Dicey, one of its primary makers.[17]

Lefroy's thought was primarily this late-nineteenth-century rule-of-law thought. He was a deeply committed positivist who taught from Frederick Harrison's lectures until he died.[18] Throughout his writing, the work of the courts in applying the settled common law appeared to be objective and apolitical. Judges found facts and applied the appropriate general rule, and the scientific process ensured that there would be only one appropriate rule, even though determining it might be difficult and debatable.[19] The common law was autonomous, although that concept does not mean that Lefroy believed the law did not express values about society, for he clearly did: the sources from which it was made were all statements of values, but they all seemed to be abstract and independent from their immediate context of place and time. There was no suggestion in any of the examples of lawmaking that there was a choice between social interests or classes at stake.

This autonomy was fortified by a sense that lawyers, especially judges, were the custodians of the legal science and the process of making law from these values and applying it. The autonomy was probably also related to the explanation for the rule that settled law could not be changed. Considering change, conceived as anything different from correcting an error in reasoning, would involve considering some particular social and political context, and might ultimately suggest that the common law and its basic principles were contingent upon the conditions of each society.

Lefroy's positivism, his faith in precedent, and his general understanding of the common law all might have been found in any common room or text in England. His major effort and his claim to distinctiveness was his discussion of lawmaking. How could judges make law, and at the same time be objective and apolitical? Many thinkers of his generation considered that problem, perhaps because the dominant positivism had made it pressing. Lefroy found the resolution in the process of reasoning from the basic principles and understandings. The courts did not declare their own personal wills or choices. Instead their work was 'discovering the implications and equities inherent in the transactions and relations of mankind,' and declaring 'the law's intention' that was embodied in the terms of the broad principles.[20]

Much of Lefroy's analysis of lawmaking was derived from earlier thought. Recall that the sources Lefroy specified for lawmaking were justice, humanity, and other moral obligations; common sense, and the reason of the thing; and public convenience and other practical considerations. These phrases were taken – and he acknowledged the source – from the late eighteenth century, especially Mansfield's famous judgment in *Millar v. Taylor*.[21] The methods of lawmaking Lefroy specified were 'the gradual explanation and definition of the vague general terms in which broad principles of law are conceived of and expressed, and in part of the interpretation of the various transactions and relations of men *inter se*.' The second branch of this proposition, the interpretation of transactions and relations, was taken from Sohm's *Institutes of Roman Law*, and again Lefroy acknowledged the source.[22] The first branch, the only major element that does not have a specific source, seems to be derived from the faith, dominant in the late eighteenth century, that the common law was a set of principles.

In this light, Lefroy's understanding of the common law was composed of layers from different times. The most recent and the thickest layer was from the late nineteenth century, and another was from the late eighteenth century. The layers were blended, however, and not separate geological deposits. Mansfield's vision of the entire common law as principle became a corner in a structure made by the positivism, the faith in precedent, and the objective and apolitical common law of late-nineteenth-century thought. He would have recognized his words in Lefroy's writing, but not the context. Nor would John Beverley Robinson.[23]

Lefroy's writing about Roman law illuminated the structure of his understanding of the common law in ways that were only implicit in these two articles. Interest in Roman law, especially in its use as an ideal, had become common in the second half of the century. Lefroy claimed that the Romans were 'the first people who ever arrived at a correct conception of ... the true nature of private law ... a conception of the utmost value to the welfare of mankind.' His definitions of private and public law were the established ones of contemporary jurisprudence: private law was the law that dealt with 'the mutual relations and transactions of private individuals *inter se.*' Lefroy claimed that its true nature was what it would be if its maker were 'perfectly wise,' and that its true nature had several illuminating characteristics. First, it would be 'simple and natural,' and for Lefroy what was natural was 'the natural ways of doing business ... [in] such ways as people spontaneously adopt when not obliged to conform to any express legal requirements.' Second, the proper method for the development of the common law is 'a process of juridical analysis of the transactions and relations of mankind, or in other words ... the discovery of the true nature of those transactions and relations from a juridical point of view ... in the light of reason, justice, common sense, and public policy.' Once rules were made in this way, 'other rules may be deduced by a process of reason and analogy' from the rules discovered through this process, and 'thus a completed system of law ultimately built up.' Such a system of law was to be distinguished from one composed mainly of usage or custom, which for Lefroy were either fortuitous or arbitrary, and pervaded by religious belief or superstition and distinguished from one composed of 'regulations imposed at will by the legislator.'[24]

Whatever merits this conception of private law may have had as a description of Roman law, it seemed to be as well a description of the ideal common law, illuminating Lefroy's understandings of its structure, reasonings, and politics. It also made the distinction between the public and the private worlds crucial. The relations among individuals were to be governed solely by the common law and the courts, and the content of the common law was what private individuals would will for themselves if they were unconstrained by legislation or custom. Lefroy distinguished this ideal common law from 'regulations imposed at will by the legislator,' 'rules imposed from above,' and 'rules arbitrarily imposed by authority.'[25] He said that the common law could be derived from the 'natural ways of doing business,' and traced to 'the ultimate laws of human nature.'[26]

This ideal common law was the legal structure of mid-nineteenth-century English liberal political economy, and especially the legal structure of the belief that individuals should be free to choose within spheres of power unconstrained by the state and that their obligations should be based on the expressions of their wills. It was another element in the justification of courts that made them objective and apolitical, central to the Constitution, and different from legislatures. Yet its detachment from the conflicts and swirling change of the late nineteenth and early twentieth centuries suggests that the structure was a defence – or a lament.[27]

The range of literature and ideas Lefroy used was sharply limited. He had an unbounded loyalty to Britain and British models, which pervaded his constitutional scholarship as well. All his examples were English cases, and virtually all the references to secondary literature were to English legal scholarship or to continental writing about Roman law. There were virtually no references to the rich legal literature in the United States, and none at all to Canada.

He was not an imaginative or original thinker, and the major outlines of his thought about the common law were derived from English scholarship; but his account of lawmaking was ambitious, and the most elaborate and sustained of his generation, in England or Canada. Ironically, however – or is it the fate of a Canadian? – it made little or no impact on his own generation, and remains virtually unknown. I know no reference to it in scholarly writing or in judgments of courts.

During the twentieth century, legal thought has changed substantially, and scholars, no matter where they fit in the current range of tastes and camps, think about the common law differently than Lefroy and his generation did. The crucial difference is the loss of faith in the web of understandings that for Lefroy made the common law a science. Yet much of the tension in Lefroy's articles remains: he and his generation sought a way to explain how judges could make law and yet be objective and apolitical. Because law expressed values, the problem was to explain how judges could talk about values and yet not be legislators or express their own wills. How could they find an objective standpoint? This has been one of the pervasive themes of scholarship since the 1930s, even though Lefroy's particular standpoint in the 'great basic principles' seems distant now.[28]

The Constitution[29]

The fate of Lefroy's common law scholarship has meant that whatever faint knowledge we have of him now comes from his constitutional writing. *The Law of Legislative Power in Canada* was the centrepiece of that writing; it was praised when it was published in 1897,[30] and quickly became a standard text. There were three other books. One, *Leading Cases in Canadian Constitutional Law*, published in 1914, was little more than excerpts from the leading cases, and the other two, *Canada's Federal System*, published in 1913, and *A Short Treatise on Canadian Constitutional Law*, published in 1918, were essentially shortened versions of *Legislative Power*.[31] There was a total of fifteen articles about constitutional law, seven published before *Legislative Power* and eight after, and all tended to be the same sort of analysis about the same sorts of topics. Therefore, I have concentrated on the one book, with occasional references to the other writing.

Lefroy began *Legislative Power* with a dedication, which must wait until the end of this paper to be revealed. Next came a preface, which was a statement of his purposes and a fulsome tribute to 'our beloved Queen, during whose glorious reign the constitutional foundations of the Empire have been laid broad and deep by the loyal wisdom of British statesmen and the wise loyalty of British people.' The next part, the introduction, continued the display of loyalty to British institutions. Its immediate purpose was to refute Dicey's assertion that the Canadian Constitution was a 'copy, though by no means a servile copy of the Constitution of the United States,' and it became an extended essay on the British Constitution, the *British North America (BNA) Act*, and the government of the United States.[32]

The cornerstone of the essay was Lefroy's fundamental belief that the British Constitution was the foundation of the *BNA Act*. 'The founders of Confederation faithfully followed by preference, and with much ingenuity, the principles of the British Constitution.'[33] He cherished the Constitution, and often seemed to look back especially to the 'matchless constitution,' demonstrating little understanding of ways his ideal had been transformed, especially by the powers of the cabinet and by political parties.[34] He stressed four elements: flexibility and organic growth, legislative supremacy, responsible government, and freedom, and all four were closely related and mutually supporting. Organic growth was a product of slow accumulation and adaptation, and this faith in growth, or progress, was pervasive even though he never specified clearly the direction in which the Constitution was progressing. Flexibility was a product of legislative supremacy and the lack of a written constitution,[35] and responsible government ensured that the people assembled in Parliament controlled the executive. Legislative supremacy and public power need not be feared: 'the principle of the British constitution seems to be that good servants ought to be trusted.'[36]

Freedom was an unbounded and unqualified blessing, of 'unspeakable value,'[37] and the *BNA Act* secured Canadians 'as a heritage for ever the precious forms of British liberty.'[38] Lefroy did not discuss freedom at any length in the introduction – or in any other writing, and his understanding must be gathered from short passages scattered throughout his writing. He saw two major forms of liberty: the first was the freedom of the people, or 'the power of the nation to make its deliberative will effective upon the government,' which was achieved through responsible government. The second was the freedom of the individual. He did not consider carefully how individual freedom was to be achieved, except to claim that it was 'in harmony' with legislative supremacy and did not depend upon constitutional guarantees of contract and property. The constitution 'guards the liberty of the subject without destroying the freedom of action of the legislature.'[39]

The *BNA Act* combined this British Constitution and federalism, and preserved allegiance to Empire. Dicey was simply wrong:

> The framers of that Act could not of course create a legislature precisely similar to the British parliament in respect to supreme control over all matters whatever in Canada, because they were bringing into existence not a legislative union but a federal union of the provinces. But they adhered as closely as possible to the British system in preference to that of the United States ... [T]hey restrained their hands and allowed as free scope as in the nature of the case was possible for that process of organic growth of the Constitution coincidently with the organic growth of the nation, which is one great virtue of the Constitution of the United Kingdom ... The preamble of the British North America Act embodies ... the simple truth, in intimating that in its federal character the Constitution of the Dominion is similar to that of the United Kingdom.[40]

Lefroy's pride had no bounds. The *BNA Act* was 'the most successful piece of constitutional legislation which has ever emanated from the Parliament at Westminster,' and 'a great triumph of British constructive statesmanship.' It was flexible enough so that 'so far as their internal affairs are concerned, Canadians could live and work under it within Empire until the crack of doom.' A few months before he died, he was pleased to think how the Constitution 'has worked so smoothly and happily, and has been developed in more than half a century of recorded decisions.'[41]

Allegiance to Empire accompanied the faith in the British Constitution. Lefroy rejoiced in 'the relations of complete confidence and respect, and true British heartiness, which prevail between the Imperial authorities and the government and people of this Dominion,' and he believed that Canada would be disrupted 'should any movement for Canada's independence and separation from the British Empire ever receive the support of a majority of her people.' His faith was for the future as well as the past. 'The greatest pessimist ... cannot any longer doubt the glorious future which lies before the British Empire ... nor the place which this Dominion is destined to hold within it.' He never described a structure for the Empire, although he seemed to prefer a closer relation and some form of Imperial federation. Within the Empire, Canada was to be free to mature, and the flexibility of the *BNA Act* enabled maturity to be achieved without constitutional disruption. The Judicial Committee of the Imperial Privy Council was an important part of the Imperial relation, and it had 'done splendid work upon the interpretation and development of our constitutional system [and established] great and fundamental doctrines of our Constitution.'[42]

Lefroy's faith in the British Constitution and the British Empire was paralleled by a thorough disapproval of the United States' government. In the making of the *BNA Act*, 'little was to be gained, except by way of warning, from the Constitution of the United States.'[43] Congressional government and the separation of legislative and executive powers, contrasted to responsible government, encouraged the president, the speaker, and the committees to become uncoordinated centres of power, and to diffuse responsibility and initiative. The written Constitution, the constitutional guarantees and limitations of power, and the limited powers of amendment produced rigidity, contrasted to flexibility and balance. More generally, the ultimate power of the people was contrasted to parliamentary supremacy, in which the people had no ultimate or residual power, and a lack of respect for public power and institutions was contrasted to the trust of 'good servants.' American cases were useless and even misleading as guides to the interpretation of sections 91 and 92, because of the great differences in the division of the powers: the powers of the Dominion and the provinces were exclusive, not overlapping; the residue of power was assigned to the Dominion, not the provinces; and the terms of important powers, for example the powers over criminal law and trade and commerce, were different.[44]

Faith in the British Constitution and its liberty, allegiance to Empire and a sense that Canada could mature within it, mistrust of the United

States, and a pervasive faith in progress, all made Lefroy a typical Canadian Imperialist of the late nineteenth century. It is hardly surprising that a lawyer should be among the Imperialists; and Anglo-Canadian legal culture, especially the respect for authority generally and the Privy Council in particular, did much to preserve and communicate the Imperialist faith. The very choice to quarrel with Dicey is suggestive: Dicey's *The Law of the Constitution* was one of the great English texts of the rule of law tradition and might well have served as a powerful model and ideal. Lefroy's choice to quarrel, despite his general loyalty to Britain and British lawyers and scholarship, was a small demonstration of the paradoxical independence of the Imperialists.[45]

The differences between the introduction to *Legislative Power* and *The Law of the Constitution*, and especially their treatments of liberty, may suggest even more about Lefroy's thought and about Canadian constitutional traditions. Dicey wrote about two great principles: legislative supremacy and rule of law. Despite a short and awkward effort to reconcile them, they seemed to conflict: the rule of law and the courts protected individual rights, especially liberty, but they were ultimately at the mercy of legislative supremacy. In his introduction, Lefroy did not write about the rule of law and he did not make courts central to the protection of the individual in the way Dicey did. Instead, he chose to write about responsible government, and about the way liberty was protected in Parliament, through responsible government. This choice reflected powerful strands of English constitutional thought, especially the struggle to control arbitrary governments. Perhaps, as well, it reflected a distinctive Canadian tradition. Throughout the nineteenth century, Canadian courts were not central in the understandings about protecting individual liberties, or establishing and defining our nation and its values. In contrast, Canadians tended to emphasize legislatures. A lot of work needs to be done to understand the reasons for this tendency, but it may be crucial to our understandings about rights.

But the introduction was, after all, only an introduction to a long book. The text of *Legislative Power* (and most of Lefroy's other constitutional writing) was about the division of legislative powers between the Dominion and the provinces. In the preface he announced that his objective was to 'extract' from the cases on the *BNA Act* whatever is of 'general application upon the law governing the distribution of power … [and] to formulate the results so arrived at in general Propositions.'[46] This undertaking was a part of the rule of law scholarship of the late nineteenth century. Scholars such as Dicey, Anson, and Pollock had written great texts that might have been his model, and Dicey himself reviewed *Legislative Powers* and praised it highly.[47] In this undertaking, the legal profession was a clearly defined hierarchy, headed by the judges, in which the scholars assumed the subservient role of scribes to the oracles and sought to consolidate the common law as a service to the legal profession.[48]

The text was just what Lefroy promised. It was composed of sixty-eight numbered propositions, which were a synthesis of the cases, each followed by extensive commentary. The commentary was virtually all doctrinal analysis, that is, descriptions of the cases and the principles that could be 'extracted,' and much of it was simply copious excerpts from cases. Contrary to the expectations that might be suggested by contemporary constitutional texts and casebooks, the propositions were not a series of discussions of the specific powers in sections 91 and 92. Even the general nature of the division was not introduced until the twenty-fifth proposition. Instead, they were essentially general principles about interpretation, and the nature and relations of the powers. The major powers were considered only occasionally, in an apparently random order as parts of the commentaries on the propositions.

The most useful illustrations are the propositions about the general terms of the division of the powers and their basic nature. Propositions 24, 25, and 26 described the general terms of the division. Section 91 gave the Dominion power to make laws about matters of 'general quasi-national importance,' and section 92 gave the provinces powers to legislate about 'particular subjects, all of a purely provincial, municipal, and domestic nature.' These powers were powers to legislate about subjects or matters, and they had an objective and almost tangible substance embedded in the *BNA Act*. Those two sections (together with sections 93 and 94) were an exhaustive grant of all legislative power, because section 91 was a 'general, undefined and unrestricted power,' and there was no ultimate residuum of power in the people.[49]

The provinces had 'authority as plenary and as ample ... as the Imperial Parliament ... possessed and could bestow,' and the Dominion had powers 'as large and of the same nature as those of the Imperial Parliament itself.'[50] The Dominion and the provinces were each supreme within the limits of their assigned powers. The supremacy was a product of the express terms of the *BNA Act* and the supremacy of the British Parliament. Its most dramatic manifestation was the absence of any constitutional guarantees for private rights, especially property, which was declared in proposition 21, and which a few judges had regretted or even doubted. In the introduction, Lefroy believed that legislative supremacy enabled flexibility and was 'in harmony' with individual freedoms, but in the text, it was a threat to private rights, which he occasionally openly regretted, but from which he could imagine no protection except disallowance. This difference was, I believe, a specific example of a difference between the introduction and the text that I shall return to later.

The power was different from the motive for its exercise, and if a legislature acted 'within the powers conferred ... we have no right to inquire what motive induced it to exercise its powers.'[51] This distinction seemed natural and clear, and it was ultimately based on the distinction between the subjective will of the legislature, and the objective subjects of the powers and the 'true nature' of the legislation. In this way the power was essentially the same as the power of an owner of property.[52]

The powers of the Dominion and the provinces were mutually exclusive, and 'there is no subject-matter over which there can [strictly speaking ...] exist concurrent powers of legislation.'[53] This exclusivity was declared by the express terms of the *BNA Act*, and supported by the general structure of thought about powers and the function of courts. Lefroy conceived these powers as spheres, which were bounded by sharp bright lines, and within which the powers were absolute. But his reservation – '[strictly speaking ...]' – revealed some crucial uncertainty and difficulty. The thirty years of experience since Confederation had suggested that the powers to legislate might overlap, and he struggled at length both to preserve the ideal and to make sense of the cases.

His struggles are illustrated by his discussion of two doctrines. The first was the doctrine of ancillary powers. The powers of the Dominion to legislate included 'by necessary implication' power to encroach upon subjects assigned to the provinces, and the provinces had the same power to encroach on Dominion subjects. Here the vision of spheres as property was unusually clear, and Lefroy spoke throughout of encroachments and invasions, and 'the right actually to invade ... territory.' These invasions were to be limited to whatever was 'reasonable and necessary' to enable legislation under section 91 to be effective, and the Dominion must not encroach 'unduly.' Lefroy was openly uncomfortable with this limitation, because it seemed to him to be a question of degree and judgment, and therefore to require the courts to make a decision that was deeply different from a determination about the location of a sharp line. He openly regretted that he was unable to think of a way of making the decision that pleased him more.[54]

The other example of the struggles about exclusivity was the aspect doctrine. Proposition 35 declared: 'Subjects which in one aspect and for one purpose fall within the jurisdiction of the Provincial Legislatures may, in another aspect and for another purpose, fall within the jurisdiction of the Dominion Parliament.'[55] The rule was first declared in *Hodge v. The Queen*,[56] and its immediate purpose was to determine the allocation of the powers over liquor, and especially to distinguish *Russell v. The Queen*.[57] It enabled lawyers to make sense of the Act and the cases in a way that preserved the exclusivity of the spheres of power. The powers did not conflict or overlap, even though statutes might happen to affect the same piece of the material world.[58]

All of Lefroy's analysis of legislative powers was essentially about the work of courts – judicial review and statutory interpretation. The text did not contain any sustained discussion of these topics, but many of his understandings and assumptions are apparent. Review was essentially a determination by the courts of the limits of powers: whether a challenged statute was within a power was an objective determination whether a boundary established by the *BNA Act* had been crossed. Proposition 36 declared that the court should first determine 'true nature and character ... to ascertain the class of subject to which it really belongs.' This nature was inherent in its terms, and could be discovered by reading it. Its validity was then determined by applying the general structure of sections 91 and 92.[59]

Proposition 3 declared that courts must interpret the *BNA Act* 'by the same methods of construction and exposition which they apply to other statutes, [of a similar character that is to say, statutes conferring constitutional charters].' Apart from the brackets, this proposition drew on widely shared understandings. A statute was the expression of the intention or will of the legislature, expressed in its words, and interpretation was discovering that will. Words in statutes had natural or usual meanings, which must prevail. Again, the courts' function was objective; the meaning was embedded in the statute, to be discovered by the courts.

This approach excluded consideration of the context of a statute unless the meaning of the words was doubtful. Yet context was often a tempting illumination, and some of the Canadian judgments, especially early ones, had openly considered the debates about Confederation and legislation in the colonies.[60] Lefroy's discussion of this experience was confused and inconclusive. He eventually said simply that such material 'may sometimes have to be considered,' and seemed to suggest that it was appropriate only when the terms were 'doubtful.'[61]

A more pervasive issue about interpretation was the general approach to interpreting the *BNA Act*. The prevailing understandings were that interpretation could be narrow and rigid, or broad and liberal.[62] A few Canadian judges had quoted and approved this passage from Emerich de Vattel: '[W]hile we may resort to the meaning of single words to assist our inquiries, we must never forget it is an instrument of government we are to construe; and … that must be the truest exposition which best harmonizes with its design, its objects, and its general structure.'[63]

Lefroy did not expressly approve this grand vision but, out of a mass of conflicting comments in the cases, he purported to derive the conclusion that the interpretation of the *BNA Act* should be liberal, which he integrated into his proposition by adding the bracketed qualification for 'statutes conferring constitutional charters.' In effect, he smuggled a glimmer of Vattel into his approach to interpretation.

In proposition 38, however, Lefroy reached the limits of liberal interpretation. It provided that because a constitution could not expressly provide for every possibility, 'use was made … of general language, containing in principle the conferred powers, and leaving to future legislation [and judicial interpretation] the task of completing the details.'[64] Lefroy's understanding here was that essential meanings were embedded in the terms of the Act, to be discovered or expounded by interpretation. Most of his discussion of this proposition was quotations from judgments about the need to elaborate the general terms, and resembled (though he made no express connection) his understanding of the elaboration of common law principles. But near the end of the discussion he quoted Joseph Story about the need for interpretation 'influenced by the demands of public policy and public welfare, according to the changes of time and circumstances.' This passage took him to the edge of a cliff, because here Story called for a creative or original role for the courts, which was deeply different from Lefroy's understanding of their proper role. Having looked over the edge of the cliff, he returned to his faith and said, '[W]ith reference to our constitution what is stated in Proposition 3 … must be remembered.' And it was in proposition 3 that he had invoked the traditional understandings about the discovery of meaning.[65]

Throughout the text, Lefroy demonstrated the same respect for judges and courts that pervaded his common law writing. This respect was implicit in the very nature of his undertaking: he sought no more than to synthesize their decisions. The *BNA Act* was the ultimate authority, but it tended to be pushed into the background, and the courts became dominant. He was reluctant to contemplate any proposition about the division of powers that could not be supported by a case, regardless of his own reading of the Act. Moreover, he tended to be reluctant to find any inconsistencies or departures from precedent, and he often made the cases appear to be more coherent than they were. The Privy Council, naturally enough for an Imperialist, was given the utmost respect. Each judgment was an oracle to be studied and accommodated. In 1913, when he did dare to criticize one of its decisions, he said that he had never before 'seen the smallest loophole for criticism or for doubt as to the correctness of any one of them before this last judgment.'[66] In 1915 he praised its objectivity by saying that it 'is about as much affected as any prejudice for or against corporations as the adding machine in a bank.'[67]

The text tended to make the doctrine seem changeless, even though by the late 1890s some substantial changes had begun, especially in the interpretations of the power to make laws for peace, order, and good government, and of the trade and commerce power. This tendency paralleled Lefroy's writing about the common law, and was a product of several causes, including the undertaking to synthesize, the general respect for courts, the faith in the rules about precedent, and, perhaps, a reluctance to approach anything that might seem to be an expression of personal values. In his understanding of the common law, the 'great basic principles' were expressions of values, but they were universal values derived ultimately from human nature. Values about the division of powers between the Dominion and the provinces might have seemed too particular and too contestable – too political – to be a part of legal reasoning.[68]

Closely related to this appearance of lack of change was a separation of the text from its historical, political, and social context, which continued the parallel to the common law. The propositions were stated in abstract form, and the commentary was limited to justifying them by listing and describing the cases used as sources. There was nothing about Confederation, except as part of a discussion of the appropriate sources for interpretation, and even there it was not discussed; it was simply a subject that cases had or had not considered. There was nothing about the political history of the preceding thirty years, and only a few small and oblique references to the provincial rights movement. This autonomous nature of doctrine was emphasized by the very form of the propositions, which were printed in larger and darker type than the commentary, and set off from it by generous spacing. A specific example of the separation from contexts was the treatment of the decision of the Privy Council in the *Local Prohibition Reference*, decided in 1896.[69] It had been anxiously awaited, and Lefroy held up printing half the book for months until it was decided.[70] It differed from the decision of the Supreme Court; it had important consequences for the prohibition movement; and it suggested changes in the interpretation of several terms of sections 91 and 92. Yet little of this was suggested in the text. It was simply one case, albeit an important one, among the others that made the system of doctrine.

The nature of the undertaking, the form of the text, the extensive use of excerpts, the presence of some overlapping and repetition – all may have combined to make *Legislative Power* seem pedestrian to subsequent generations. In retrospect, that appearance is misleading. By the mid-1890s the cases were a jumble, and the existing attempts at synthesis, comprehensive or not, were little less jumbled. The texts and articles written in the preceding decade tended to string cases and excerpts together in chronological order, or in the order of the sections of the *BNA Act*, or in no apparent order at all. Lefroy ordered the doctrine in the framework of rule of law thought, and much of what seemed simple after he wrote had not been nearly so simple before.

Two examples of his accomplishment are his treatments of the general nature of the spheres of power and the aspect doctrine. The structure of spheres of power seemed to be permitted or even encouraged by the *BNA Act*, for it specified that the powers of the Dominion and the provinces were exclusive, but much experience and thinking was needed to develop working doctrine. The components of that doctrine were scattered throughout the cases, and Lefroy gathered and ordered them much more clearly than they had been before he wrote. The aspect doctrine was one part of the doctrine. Throughout the twentieth century it has been a simple sentence taken from *Hodge*, but the retrospective simplicity is misleading. During the 1880s, lawyers' understandings of *Hodge* were full of confusion and disagreement.[71] Lefroy's text presented the aspect doctrine as part of a relatively coherent system, and separated it, for example, from the 'necessarily incidental' doctrine.[72]

The entire text of *Legislative Power* was an expression of the late-nineteenth-century rule of law thought. The undertaking to synthesize, the faith in meanings embedded in a text, the objectivity of the judicial function, the mutually exclusive and absolute spheres of power, and the distinctions between law and context and values were all familiar elements of English scholarship in the late nineteenth century. Earlier Canadian texts about the Constitution had a wider scope and had included; for example, history and the structure of government. Lefroy's text marked the coming of ways of thinking that were dominant throughout most of the twentieth century. As well, it began the lawyers' preoccupation with the division of powers that was dominant until the 1980s and the advent of the Charter.

The text of *Legislative Power* was different from its introduction, which contained no mention of analysis of doctrine, and much about context, history, and constitutional faiths. Like Lefroy's writing about the common law, the book was composed of different layers of ways of thinking. The text was an expression of the late-nineteenth-century thought, and the introduction invoked constitutional faiths that began centuries before. And here, again, a suggestion of a distinctive Canadian understanding of rights appears: perhaps our understandings have not been simply Dicey's, despite his great influence on the legal profession.

Lefroy's beliefs about interpretation, precedent, and the structure of spheres were challenged by scholarship in the 1920s and 1930s, by the same moods and movements that challenged his understandings of the common law. Much doctrine remains, though, in a form that he would find familiar. But the significance of him and his generation is not limited to our understandings and his. His work has significance for his own past as well as his future, and it is suggested by the dedication of *Legislative Power*: 'To the memory of Sir John Beverley Robinson, Bart, formerly chief justice of Upper Canada this work is dedicated albeit an unworthy tribute by his grandson the author.' Dedications to judges were part of the apparatus of the texts written by late-nineteenth-century legal scholars,[73] and if Lefroy had not been Robinson's grandson, he might have found another judge to whom to offer his tribute. But his dedication is ironic. We have only begun to understand legal thought in Ontario in the early and mid-nineteenth century, but we do know that it was distinctive and that it was embodied in Sir John Beverely Robinson.[74] Yet he is now obscured from us, and much of what obscures him is the ways of thinking that were established in the late nineteenth century. Lefroy paid tribute to his grandfather, and then buried him – in a coffin of paper.

NOTES

1 I have not found much information about Lefroy's life beyond the most formal dates and activities. This account is assembled primarily from a short note, (1900) 1 *U. Tor. Monthly* 54, and letters in the Falconer papers and newspaper clippings in the archives of the University of Toronto. I am grateful to John Honsberger for information about Lefroy's practice and about his candidacy for principal at Osgoode Hall.

2 A bibliography of Lefroy's writings includes the following texts, articles, and book reviews, and subsequent formal citations to them will be by title only. (Not listed here are Lefroy's editorial notes, his column 'By the Way,' or the short case comments that he wrote in the *Canadian Law Times* throughout his tenure as editor.)

    Texts: *The Law of Legislative Power in Canada* (Toronto: Toronto Law Book and Publishing, 1897‑8) (hereafter *Legislative Power*); *Canada's Federal System* (Toronto: Carswell, 1913) (hereafter *Canada's Federal System*); *Leading Cases in Canadian Constitutional Law* (Toronto: Carswell, 1914); *A Short Treatise on Canadian Constitutional Law* (Toronto: Carswell, 1918) (hereafter *Canadian Constitutional Law*).

    Articles: 'The Charitable Spirit of the Law' (1878) 14 *Can. L.J.* 285, 15 *Can. L.J.* 6 and 121; 'Dominion Control over Provincial Legislation' (1881) 17 *Can. L.J.* 217; 'Mortgage or No Mortgage: Admission of Parole Evidence' (1881) 1 *Can. L. Times* 403 and 459; 'The British versus the American System of National Government' (paper read before the Toronto branch of the Imperial Federation League, 18 December 1890); 'Constitution of Canada: Aspect of Legislation as Determining Jurisdiction' (1892) 12 *Can. L. Times* 12; 'Law of the Canadian Constitution: General Legislative Power of the Dominion Parliament' (1892) 28 *Can. L.J.* 353; 'The Correlation of Executive and Legislative Power in Canada' (1894) 30 *Can. L.J.* 537; 'The Privy Council on Bankruptcy' (1894) 30 *Can. L.J.* 182; 'Legislation and Liquor Dealers' (1896) 32 *Can. L.J.* 430; 'Prohibition: The Late Privy Council Decision' (1896) 16 *Can. L. Times* 125; 'Canadian Fisheries Appeal' (1898) 14 *L.Q.R.* 386, and 34 *Can. L.J.* 763; 'Canadian Forms of Freedom,' *Transactions of the United Empire Loyalist Association of Ontario* (1899); 'Commonwealth of Australia Bill' (1899) 15 *L.Q.R.* 155, 281; 'Remedies of Creditors of an Individual Partner of a Firm' 17 *Wash. L.R.* 719; 'Manitoba Liquor Act Case' (1901) 37 *Can. L.J.* 217; 'A University Training as a Preparation for the Legal Profession' (1901) 1 *U. Tor. Monthly* 263; 'Personal Liability of Contracting Agents' (1903) 2 *Can. L.J.* 250; 'The Rhodes Scholarships – Symposium' (1903) 3 *U. Tor. Monthly* 5; 'Judge-Made Law' (1904) 20 *L.Q.R.*

399, and 3 *Can. L.J.* 602, 673; 'The Basis of Case Law' (1906) 22 *L.Q.R.* 293, 416; 'A Century of Constitutional Development upon the North American Continent' (1906) 42 *Can. L.J.* 449; 'The Jottings of an Old Solicitor' (1906) 6 *Can. L.J.* 342; 'Rome and Law' (1907) 20 *Harvard L.R.* 606; 'Roman Law' (1908) 7 *University [of Toronto] Mag.* 598; 'Jurisprudence' (1911) 31 *Can. L. Times* 483 and 27 *L.Q.R.* 180; 'The Alberta and Great Waterways Railway Case' (1913) 29 *L.Q.R.* 285, and 49 *Can. L.J.* 561; 'Points of Special Interest in Canada's Federal Constitution' (1913) 33 *Can. L. Times* 898; 'Should Canadian Women Have the Parliamentary Vote?' (1913) *Queen's Q.R.*; 'Damages Recoverable in Contract' (1915) 35 *Can. L. Times* 739; 'Ex-President Taft at the University of Toronto' (1915) 35 *Can. L. Times* 216; 'James Manning Aikins – Sketch' (1915) 15 *J. of Comp. Leg.* (NS) 65; 'The John Deere Plow Company Case' (1915) 35 *Can. L. Times* 148; 'The Marriage Laws of Canada' (1915) 35 *Can. L. Times* 503; 'Mr A.V. Dicey on the Latest Phases of the British Constitution Ante Bellum' (1915) 35 *Can. L. Times* 812; 'The Anglo-Saxon Period of English Law' (1918) 26 *Yale L.J.* 291, 388, and 38 *Can. L. Times* 753; 'Flaws in the Common Law' (1918) 38 *Can. L. Times* 169.

   Book Reviews: (1917) 37 *Can. L. Times* 739; (1918) 38 *Can. L. Times* 64, 190, 282, 434.

3 His mother was Robinson's daughter, his father an Englishman who was the first Dominion astronomer. One of his partnerships during the 1890s was with Christopher Robinson, John Beverley's son, a leading counsel, with whom Lefroy argued a few important constitutional cases.

4 The term 'modes' is not Lefroy's, but it seems appropriate; see infra note 11.

5 'Judge-Made Law,' at 399.

6 Ibid. at 408. These propositions took two forms: propositions that were conceived in general terms, and propositions that contained a general term, such as 'unjust,' 'unreasonable,' or 'negligent.'

7 Ibid. at 408, 494.

8 Ibid. at 414.

9 'The Basis of Case Law,' at 296.

10 Ibid. at 303.

11 Lefroy did not carefully relate the two articles, and the designation of the first one as dealing with methods is mine, not his. However, his writing about Roman law supplies a useful illumination. In describing the ideal private law, he said, '[The proper method] of its development ... is a process of judicial analysis of the transactions and relations of mankind, or ... the discovery of the true nature of those transactions and relations, with

the object, that is, of bringing to light … rights and obligations … in the light of reason, justice, common sense and public policy': Lefroy, 'Rome and Law,' supra note 2 at 607. Here the intended relation is more clearly a relation of methods and sources. There was, however, some overlap.

12 Lefroy, 'Jurisprudence,' supra note 2 at 484. Such a science would 'enable us to codify the law on a complete and rational plan,' and enable 'making a logically consistent and complete ground-plan of the whole field of law': Ibid. at 488. The clearest statement about deduction of subsidiary rules is in Lefroy, 'Rome and Law,' supra note 2 at 607.

13 (1774) Lofft 383 at 385.

14 W. Blackstone *Commentaries on the Laws of England* (Oxford: Clarendon Press, 1765–9) vol. 1 at 71.

15 This description seeks to make common ground for Mansfield and Blackstone. See D. Lieberman, *The Province of Jurisprudence Determined: Legal Theory in Eighteenth-Century Britain* (Cambridge: Cambridge University Press, 1989); G.J. Postema, *Bentham and the Common Law Tradition* (Oxford: Clarendon Press, 1986); and G.J. Postema, 'Some Roots of Our Notion of Precedent,' in L. Goldstein, ed., *Precedent in Law* (Oxford: Clarendon Press, 1987) 1. There were other currents of thought in the late eighteenth century, but for understanding Lefroy, Blackstone and Mansfield are crucial.

16 See J. Evans, 'Change in the Doctrine of Precedent During the Nineteenth Century,' in *Precedent in Law,* supra note 15 at 35.

17 For descriptions of this thought, see G. B. Baker, 'The Reconstitution of Upper Canadian Legal Thought in the Late-Victorian Empire' (1985) 3 *Law & Hist. R.* 219; R.W. Gordon, 'Legal Thought and Legal Practice in the Age of American Enterprise,' in G. Geison, ed., *Professions and Professional Ideologies in America* (Chapel Hill: University of North Carolina Press, 1983) 70; D. Kennedy, 'Towards an Historical Understanding of Legal Consciousness: The Case of Classical Legal Thought in America, 1850–1940' (1980) 3 *Research in L. & Soc.* 3; and D. Sugarman, 'Legal Theory, the Common Law Mind, and the Making of the Textbook Tradition,' in W. Twining, ed., *Legal Theory and Common Law* (Oxford: Basil Blackwell, 1986) 26. The term 'rule of law' has at least one great disadvantage: it is also an important concept (or a multitude of concepts) that runs throughout constitutional theory and history. Confusion is clearly possible, but the term is certainly not used to suggest that this generation discovered the rule of law. Yet all the other terms in use seem even more inappropriate; for example, in the legal community, 'formalism' is too often used with pejorative connotations, and 'classical liberalism' may stress the associa-

tion with political economy without specifying a version and may also encourage asking what is meant by the adjective 'classical.'

18 Lefroy made his own edition of Harrison: F. Harrison, *On Jurisprudence and the Conflict of Laws, with Annotations by A.H.F. Lefroy* (Oxford: Clarendon Press, 1919). His analysis of lawmaking wavered, however. His claim that judges made law seemed based on a positivist understanding, but his claims about the sources seemed often to include a different faith; for example, his claim that the sources were 'the ultimate principles of case-law.'

19 Lefroy, 'Judge-Made Law,' supra note 2 at 414.

20 Ibid. at 400, 410. The writing about Roman law had similar passages.

21 (1769) 4 Burr. 2303.

22 Lefroy's citation was 'Ledlie's Trans 2ed 105–107.'

23 For a recent study of Robinson and references to earlier literature, see B. Hibbitts, 'Progress and Principle: The Legal Thought of Sir John Beverley Robinson' (1989) 34 *McGill L.J.* 454.

24 Lefroy, 'Rome and Law,' supra note 2 at 606, 607, 608.

25 Ibid. at 608, 610, 615.

26 Lefroy, 'Jurisprudence,' supra note 2 at 484, and 'Rome and Law,' supra note 2 at 607.

27 In his editorial column 'By the Way' in the *Canadian Law Times* Lefroy occasionally lamented invasions of private property by the legislatures.

28 There is another way to interpret the scholars of the late nineteenth century, which seems to be predominant in recent American writing. This interpretation claims (expressly or by implication) that those scholars believed the common law was ultimately a comprehensive set of ordained general principles, from which rules could be derived and outcomes could be determined in some mechanical way for all possible cases. (Who or what seems to have ordained these principles does not matter here.) In this interpretation the tension I see in Lefroy does not appear until the twentieth century. That may be sensible for the American scholarship, although it does seem to make a lot out of a few paragraphs in the introduction to Langdell's casebook; but it does not seem to be an accurate reading of the English scholars. They talked about judges making law, and had a closely related concern to make the courts and the common law objective and apolitical.

29 *Editors' Note*: For a general review of constitutional scholarship in this period, see R.C. Risk, 'Constitutional Scholarship in the Late Nineteenth Century,' in this volume.

30 The major reviews were Dicey, 'Book Review' (1898) 14 *L.Q.R.* 198 ('Mr

Lefroy has written an admirable book, which will at once become the leading authority on its subject'); Editor, 'Book Review' (1898) 18 *Can. L. Times* 108 ('Mr Lefroy's work is altogether an exceptional one'); and O'Brien, 'Book Review' (1898) 34 *Can. L.J.* 256 ('the author has done his work excellently well').

31 Much of the text of these two books is taken from *Legislative Power*, and most of the shortening was done simply by omitting text. The one useful contribution of the first, *Canada's Federal System*, was a rearrangement of the principles. Some catalogues also have a vague reference to a book on federal systems. I have been unable to find it, and it may be *Canada's Federal System*.

32 *Legislative Power*, preface and xliii. Lefroy's reference to Dicey was to Albert Venn Dicey, *The Law of the Constitution*, 5th ed. (London: Macmillan, 1897) at 157.

33 *Legislative Power* at xlv.

34 The only suggestion of an understanding of the passing of these ideals came late in his life, in 1918, when he lamented not only the passing of a limited franchise and a strong social and political aristocracy and ruling class but also the increasing control of both the legislature and the government by 'popular labour and political organizations.' 'By the Way' (1918) 38 *Can. L. Times* 447 at 447–8.

35 In his later writing Lefroy also suggested that the vague and overlapping powers of the *BNA Act* were a source of flexibility, and that the power to make laws for peace, order, and good government could be power to make constitutional amendments.

36 *Legislative Power* at xlv.

37 Lefroy, 'Canadian Forms of Freedom,' supra note 2 at 2.

38 *Canada's Federal System* at 749; similar comments appeared in 'By the Way,' (1915) 35 *Can. L. Times* 953, and (1916) 36 *Can. L. Times* 177.

39 'Book Review' (1917) 37 *Can. L. Times* 739; *Legislative Power* at lx.

40 *Legislative Power* at lx–lxiv.

41 *Canadian Constitutional Law* at vi, 154; 'By the Way' (1917) 37 *Can. L. Times* 333, and (1919) 39 *Can. L. Times* 68.

42 'By the Way' (1917) 37 *Can. L. Times* 261 (here Lefroy was agreeing with sentiments expressed by Zebulon Lash) and (1918) 38 *Can. L. Times* 133; *Canadian Constitutional Law* at v–vi; and *Canada's Federal System* at 758–9. About Imperial union he said, '[T]he choice for Canada is continental union and subordination to the United States or Imperial Federation.' (Lefroy, 'The British versus the American System of National Government,' supra note 2); see also 'By the Way' (1916) 36 *Can. L. Times* 744

(hope for closer union) and (1918) 38 *Can. L. Times* 616 (Imperial federation is coming). For his respect for the Privy Council, see also Lefroy, 'Commonwealth of Australia Bill,' supra note 2 at 164; 'By the Way' (1917) 37 *Can. L. Times* 621, and (1918) 38 *Can. L. Times* 434. Lefroy singled out Lord Watson especially for praise and thanks.

43 *Canada's Federal System* at 742.
44 The most extensive expressions of this attitude towards American cases were *Legislative Power* at lxv–lxvi; Lefroy, 'The British versus the American System of National Government,' and 'Canadian Forms of Freedom,' both supra note 2.
45 See C. Berger, *The Sense of Power: Studies in the Idea of Canadian Imperialism, 1867–1914* (Toronto: University of Toronto Press, 1970) for a description of the Imperialists.
46 *Legislative Power*, preface, 1.
47 See supra note 30.
48 This tradition is described wonderfully well in Sugarman, supra note 17.
49 *Legislative Power* at 306, 310.
50 Ibid. at 224 at proposition 17. Lefroy never speculated in any rigorous and abstract way about questions of sovereignty, although the general structure of his thought and his jurisprudence courses suggest that he accepted without question that there always must be a sovereign power. He was, however, clear about Canada. Proposition 12 stated clearly that the British Parliament was sovereign, even though the sovereignty would never be exercised. After all, the *BNA Act* was merely a statute of the Parliament, and could be amended or repealed.
51 *Legislative Power*, 273 (proposition 20). The sharp distinction between motive and the exercise of the power was declared in *Fredericton v. The Queen* (1880) 3 S.C.R. 505, one of the early decisions of the Supreme Court. The later cases consider the purpose of legislation in determining pith and substance in a way that undermined *Fredericton*, or at least any reading that considered only effect, but Lefroy did not describe that development. Perhaps the reason was his unwillingness to contemplate change or inconsistency.
52 This understanding of power, and much of the rule of law thinking generally, was expressed in one short passage from another late nineteenth-century Canadian text: 'The federal idea is really nothing more than the logical outcome of the "individualistic" idea, which lies at the bottom of self-government; and it would be an interesting task to trace the growth of the idea from its root belief that man has certain "natural rights" and that society controls the exercise of those rights, only to the

extent necessary to give proper play to the like rights of his fellow-men, up through the growth of municipal self-government to the establishment of a federal system of government, logical from root to topmost branch.' W.H.P. Clement, *The Law of the Canadian Constitution* (Toronto: Carswell, 1892) at 5.

53 *Legislative Power*, 347 (proposition 28). The brackets here are Lefroy's.

54 *Legislative Power*, 425 (proposition 37), 462, 448, 447. Another illustration of his reluctance to contemplate distinctions of degree was his comment on the famous passage about peace, order, and good government in the *Local Prohibition Reference* case (*Attorney-General of Ontario v. Attorney-General of Canada* [1896] A.C. 348 (P.C.)). The prospect that 'some matters in their origin local and provincial may attain such dimensions as to affect the body politic of the Dominion' was problematic because it might 'bring before the Courts very difficult questions, and questions of a very political character.' The term 'questions of a very political character' seems to mean distinctions that were not sharp lines between powers of different kinds: Lefroy, 'Prohibition: The Late Privy Council Decision,' supra note 2 at 130–1, 133.

55 *Legislative Power* at 393.

56 (1883) 9 A.C. 117 (P.C.).

57 (1882) 7 A.C. 829 (P.C.). Lefroy's analysis revealed his understanding of legislative powers: 'By "aspect"' must be understood the aspect of point of view of the legislator in legislating, – the object, purpose, and scope of the legislation. The word may be said to be used subjectively of the legislator rather than objectively of the matter legislated upon': *Legislative Power* at 394. This faith in objective 'subjects' of legislation, and the distinction between these subjects and the subjective will of the legislator, paralleled Lefroy's distinction between power and motive.

58 These two doctrines – ancillary powers and aspects – meant that valid statutes of the Dominion and a province might conflict. The *BNA Act* did not make express provision for this kind of conflict, perhaps because it was based on an assumption that the separation of the spheres of power would be unproblematic, but during the 1890s the Privy Council declared what lawyers had assumed: that the Dominion legislation would prevail. Lefroy duly recorded the pronouncement: *Legislative Power* at 347, 526, propositions 28 and 46. The cases in the 1980s returned to the meaning that Lefroy suggested: 'But this rule would seem to apply and be only meant to apply, to the case of absolutely conflicting legislation *in pari materia*, when it would be an impossibility to give effect to both the Dominion and the provincial enactments': *Legislative Power* at 533.

59 *Legislative Power* at 416.
60 These judgments are discussed in R.C.B. Risk, 'Canadian Courts under the Influence' (1990) 40 *U.T.L.J.* 687.
61 *Legislative Power* at 2, 41.
62 This belief was never clearly integrated with the dominant task of determining the will of the legislature, except by asserting that the legislature must have wanted or intended a strict or liberal interpretation.
63 The use of this quotation in the early cases is discussed in Risk, supra note 60.
64 *Legislative Power* at 469.
65 Ibid. at 475, 476.
66 Lefroy, 'The Alberta and Great Waterways Railway Case,' supra note 2 at 288.
67 'Case Comment' (1915) 35 *Can. L. Times* 235, 236.
68 In making his claim that judges make law, Lefroy had been careful to say that interpretation also was lawmaking ('Judge-Made Law,' at 401), but this understanding would not have made it any easier to discover values about federalism.
69 Supra note 53.
70 *Legislative Power*, preface.
71 For examples of this confusion, see E.D. Armour, 'Editorial Review: The Privy Council Decisions' (1894) 14 *Can. L. Times* 323; Editor, 'Delegation of Legislative Functions and Disallowance' (1883) 13 *Can. L. Times* 279; Editor, 'Editorial Review: The Liquor License Question' (1886) 6 *Can. L. Times* 18; Editor, 'The Constitution of Canada' (1891) 11 *Can. L. Times* 113, 136, 233, and (1892) 12 *Can. L. Times* 323; Editor, 'The Judicial Committee of the Privy Council' (1894) 30 *Can. L.J.* 294; Editor, 'The Supposed Inconsistencies of the Privy Council' (1894) 30 *Can. L.J.* 619; Editor, 'Note' (1886) 22 *Can. L.J.* 32; Paterson, 'Ultra Vires, Part III' (1886) *Can. L.J.* 88; T.H., 'Delegation of Legislative Power' (1882) 18 *Can. L.J.* 431.
72 Another example of his contribution, closely related to the aspect doctrine, was his careful distinction between situations in which the Dominion had power to legislate on a matter 'that would otherwise fall within the classes of provincial subjects' because the power 'necessarily included in any complete definition' of a power in section 91, and situations in which 'a provincial area of legislative power … may nevertheless be legitimately invaded … so far as required to complete by ancillary provisions the effectual exercise of the powers given to it by the enumerated subjects in section 91': *Legislative Power* at 431. This kind of distinction now seems simple (even though much modern scholarship does not believe that it is

coherent), but it had not been made before so clearly and as part of an attempt to make a consistent system of doctrine.

73 See, for example, Pollock's exuberant dedications described in Sugarman, supra note 17.

74 See, especially, G.B. Baker, 'So Elegant a Web: Providential Order and the Rule of Law in Early Nineteenth-Century Upper Canada' (1988) 38 *U.T.L.J.* 184.

3

Rights Talk in Canada in the Late Nineteenth Century: 'The Good Sense and Right Feeling of the People'

with R.C. Vipond

I am a friend to the preservation of the rights of property ... but I believe in the subordination of those rights to the public good ... I deny that the people of my Province are insensible to or careless about the true principles of legislation. I believe they are thoroughly alive to them, and I am content that my rights of property, humble though they are, and those of my children, shall belong to the Legislature of my country to be disposed of subject to the good sense and right feeling of the people of that Province.[1]

Edward Blake made this declaration about property in 1882. Presumably his beliefs were widely shared by Canadian lawyers, for he was the leader of the Liberal party, the treasurer of the Law Society of Upper Canada (Ontario), and one of the leading counsel. We seek to explore his beliefs and to reconstruct the understandings of rights in late-nineteenth-century Canada, and especially the understandings of common law lawyers.

In addition, we seek to pursue this undertaking in ways that will illuminate, and be illuminated by, American experience. The last decade has witnessed an impressive renaissance of interest in late-nineteenth-century American constitutional thought and reaffirmed the central position of *Lochner v. New York*.[2] Howard Gillman's award-winning treatise on the rise and demise of the Lochner-era police powers jurisprudence, to cite but one example, demonstrates clearly that the interpretive debate surrounding Lochner and its legacy remains very much alive.[3]

From a comparative perspective, what strikes us most forcefully about this debate is its court-centredness. However intense the debate surrounding *Lochner* and its legacy may be, virtually all of the participants accept that a constitutional era, indeed a way of thought, was defined or epitomized by a United States Supreme Court decision. The beauty of *Lochner* as a focus for comparison is not simply that it encapsulates a doctrinal moment and so provides a particularly useful vantage point to understand the development of American constitutional law. The larger value of *Lochner* is that it opens a window on themes that are 'deeply ingrained in the constitutional order, indeed in the very concept of constitutionalism.'[4] In that sense, *Lochner* is not just about the doctrinal issues raised in the context of substantive due process; it is also about the place of liberty, equality, and the redistribution of wealth in the larger American constitutional order. Courts may not have been the only arena in which these constitutional questions were discussed, but they were at the centre of the debate. And most *Lochner*-era legal scholars appear content to keep their attention fixed right there.

Consider, by contrast, the Canadian experience. Many of the issues that excited controversy in the United States – property rights, railroad rates, religious liberty, and protective social legislation among them – rose to public prominence in Canada as well. And lawyers, some of them trained in the United States, played a dominant role in the public debates. Yet in Canada there was no *Lochner*, much less a *Lochner* era, and most Canadian lawyers implicitly or explicitly rejected judicial review as a way of protecting individual rights.

There were, to be sure, differences in where Americans and Canadians drew the line between individual liberty and state power, but they were not large. More important for us is a stark and central difference about who should draw this line. For most prominent Canadian lawyers, an American-style judicial review was ultimately unthinkable. To them, liberty meant both individual autonomy apart from government and active participation in self-government. They believed strongly that individual and political liberties were at once mutually reinforcing and mutually limiting. It followed that legislatures, not courts, were the appropriate bodies to determine the limits on rights, and at the same time to protect individual liberty, for they were the bodies through which political liberty was expressed. In a phrase, late-nineteenth-century Canadian lawyers were devoted to the protection of 'constitu-tional liberty.' It is this faith, now essentially lost even in Canada, that we seek to retrieve and re-examine. And it is this faith that would have made Blake's declaration seem bizarre or outrageous to elite lawyers in the United States, and that would make it seem at odds with the Canadian Charter of Rights and Freedoms, established almost exactly one hundred years after he spoke.[5]

In addition to this central thesis about the role of legislatures, we make several more claims about rights, all closely related, and all suggesting contrasts to the American experience. First, individual rights did not play as large a role in defining public issues or the nation; second, the courts played a correspondingly lesser role. So much is relatively simple. The remainder of these claims involves a complex tangle of rights and federalism. In short, ideas about federalism speci-fied which legislatures should determine the limits about rights and, more generally, contributed to beliefs about how rights were protected. But struggles between the Dominion and provinces also obscured or pre-empted thinking about individual rights.

We pursue our undertaking by analysing seven episodes in the late nineteenth century. Our materials are primarily debates in legislatures, especially Parliament, an emphasis which reflects our conclusion that the important discussions took place in the political process. We also consider the decisions of the courts about these episodes, and discus-sions in legal and popular journals. We make no claim to be exhaustive. The constitution, rights, and law were not a confined realm. They permeated society and were discussed in countless places.

Lawyers contributed mightily to the debate – in Parliament, in jour-nals and newspapers, on the hustings, and, of course, in court. We emphasize lawyers because they were articulate, because they had power, and because we believe they best illustrate the distinctiveness of Canadian constitutional thought. We limit ourselves to common law lawyers, not only because of the limitations of our knowledge, but because the task of understanding civil law traditions and making comparisons to the common law would expand this article into a book.

The first of these seven episodes is the debate about Ontario's Rivers and Streams Bill, which we use as an introduction to our analysis. We continue with shorter discussions of the next four episodes: debates about prohibition, Sunday, regulation of conditions of work in facto-ries, and regulation of railway rates and contracts. We then come to some conclusions about rights and legislatures. In our discussion of the last two episodes, language in the Northwest, and the Manitoba schools crisis, we continue the analysis that informs these conclusions, turning as well to some conclusions about rights and about the nation and the courts. Last, we consider the writing of the late-nineteenth-century scholars.

The Constitutional and Political Context

In 1867 a handful of British colonies north of the United States were made into a federal state, the Dominion of Canada, by the *British North America Act* (the *BNA Act*), a statute of the British Parliament. The major reasons for Confederation were the apparent need for a defensive alignment against the United States, a hope for expansion to the west, and a deadlock between the English and the French, who had been combined in the province of Canada since 1841, and who were now divided between provinces of Ontario and Quebec. The general nature of the federalism that was created has been much debated among historians, but a relatively safe interpretation is that the objective was to create a powerful Dominion and at the same time to permit the provinces to determine their local affairs.

The constitution of the Dominion and each province was to be, as the preamble to the *BNA Act* declared, 'similar in Principle to that of the United Kingdom.' All lawyers would have understood this phrase to mean a combination of responsible government, common law rights, and parliamentary supremacy. At the heart of this constitution and its history was liberty. The British peoples had struggled since Anglo-Saxon times to defend their liberty against arbitrary and despotic rulers, and in the most common telling of this story, the Glorious Revolution of 1688 was the central symbol of this struggle.

Legislative powers were divided by sections 91 and 92. 'General' matters (especially powers to establish a national economy) were assigned to the Dominion, and 'local' matters (especially powers to regulate cultural and religious affairs) were assigned to the provinces. Schools established by minority religions were protected by section 93, and duality of language was given modest recognition in section 133. The Dominion was given substantial controls over the provinces, including, in section 90, a virtually unlimited power to disallow their legislation.

Shortly after Confederation, a struggle for power began between the Dominion and the provinces, especially Ontario. For most of this struggle the Dominion was governed by the Conservative party, led by Sir John

A. Macdonald, and Ontario was governed throughout by the Liberals, led by Oliver Mowat. Some historians argue that the struggle was a product of political opportunism by the provinces and inconsistent with the agreement at Confederation. Others, understanding Confederation differently, see it as a continuation of a long tradition of local autonomy. Whatever the reasons, a wide range of issues was involved, including the financial terms of Confederation, the location of the boundary between Ontario and Manitoba, the nature of the provincial legislatures, the powers of the provincial executives, the use of the disallowance power, and the division of legislative powers. These issues were contested on a wide range of battlegrounds, including newspapers, election platforms, legislatures, and courts. By 1900 the provinces had triumphed, and both the struggle and the outcome are an important part of the background of our story.

The Rivers and Streams Act

The first episode began in the late 1870s as a quarrel between two loggers about the use of the Mississippi River, a small stream in eastern Ontario. One of these loggers, Peter McLaren, owned extensive timber lands on both sides of the stream. After making it usable by blasting rocks and constructing dams and slides, he used it to float his own timber downstream. The other, Hugh Caldwell, owned timber lands upstream and attempted to drive his logs down the river through the improvements. After some squabbling, McLaren sought an injunction against Caldwell. Their quarrel had serious implications, for timber was a crucial staple in Ontario's economy, and the streams were crucial highways for transporting the logs to mills and markets.[6]

In December 1880 Vice-Chancellor Proudfoot granted the injunction. At the same time, prompted by the quarrel, the government of Ontario enacted the *Rivers and Streams Act*, giving anyone a right to use any stream, whether it was usable in its natural state or because improvements had been made. The owner of improvements was granted a right to 'reasonable tolls.' The Dominion then disallowed this Act. A parliamentary debate about the disallowance followed in April 1882, exposing fundamental beliefs about federalism (especially disallowance and provincial autonomy) and rights (especially common law rights).

For our purposes, the major speech for the Conservatives was made by Dalton McCarthy, a fiery orator, a leading counsel, a fervent believer in a British Canada, and an erratic political colleague. Every lawyer in the House would have unhesitatingly agreed with his opening argument: McLaren had a common law property right (a 'vested right') but the Ontario legislature, 'sovereign so far as its jurisdiction extends,' had absolute power to modify or terminate it. Having established this much, he then made a distinction between this power and constitutional obligation. The legislature was obliged to exercise its power according to principles found in the 'spirit of the constitution,' and one of these principles was that rights should be respected: property should be expropriated only with compensation and for public purpose. 'The primary object of all government is the protection, not merely of life and liberty, but of property.' The *Rivers and Streams Act* violated this principle in three ways: it expropriated property without reasonable compensation, for a private purpose, and retroactively (it extinguished rights declared by a court).

McCarthy justified disallowance as a way of enforcing the spirit of the constitution and as a remedy for the violation of the right. It was a protection against attacks on a minority, especially its property, which corresponded to the constitutional guarantees in the United States. 'It is perfectly certain that, across the border, this Statute would be deemed unconstitutional and void ... [in the United States] the Courts ... have power to determine whether the parties are properly compensated or not ... Either we are unfit to exercise the right of disallowance ... without violating the rights of private property, or we will have, by a law, to prevent the possibility of a hostile majority in any Local legislature despoiling a man of his property.'[7]

For the Liberals, the major speech was made by Edward Blake. He began by attacking disallowance, making the same distinction between power and constitutional obligation that McCarthy made; the *BNA Act* gave a power to limit or extinguish rights, but it was subject to a limitation, which he too found embedded in 'the spirit of the Constitution.' Here, though, he parted ways with McCarthy. The limitation he invoked was the respect for Ontario's liberty to make the determination about limiting McLaren's rights. He derived this liberty from British constitutional history, invoking the slow and peaceful progress toward 'the principles of freedom' and 'popular rights,' toward liberty and responsible government. As he spoke, the liberty of the British people to determine their affairs free from despotic monarchs was transformed into the liberty of the people of Ontario to determine their affairs free from a despotic Dominion. Next, the powerful language of liberalism was used to support history, and Ontario's liberty became the 'right as a state which each of us has as a man – the right to go wrong.' He agreed that McLaren had a common law property right, but the choice whether to limit the right, whether to enact the *Rivers and Streams Act*, was a choice for Ontario to make, free from arbitrary interference from the Dominion. Coming to the end of his argument, Blake spoke the words from which we have taken our opening quotation.[8]

Even though Blake and McCarthy were enemies in this debate, they shared a large measure of constitutional beliefs. At bottom, they shared a faith in the British constitution invoked in the preamble to the *BNA Act*.[9] More particularly, they shared a belief in common law rights, which they divided into two groups. The constitutional rights were claims to participate in government, especially responsible government, and included rights of representation, voting, and freedom of speech. The individual rights, our major concern, were the claims of individuals to liberty from restraint by government, especially freedoms of the person, speech, religion, and property, including McLaren's riparian rights.[10] For Blake and McCarthy, these rights – and all constitutional law – had been made not in a revolution, not in the streets, and not by a philosopher in a code, but by judges in an accumulation of decisions about individual cases. They were common law rights.[11]

These individual rights were not understood to be absolute and unrestricted. For centuries the common law had limited them by the needs of the community. Blackstone had contemplated restraints that were 'necessary and expedient for the general advantage of the publick.'[12] Generations of law students had read Paley's argument, in his *Moral and Political Philosophy*, that only restrictions for the public good were permitted and they had memorized the example he gave justifying quarantine.[13] Their understandings of permissible restrictions were narrow by our current beliefs or by the beliefs of the late nineteenth century, but the principles and the language were firmly settled.

McCarthy and Blake also shared beliefs about legislative supremacy and constitutional obligation. Dicey said in 1885 that Parliament has 'the right to make or unmake any law whatever, and further ... no person or body is recognized by the law of England as having a right to override or set aside the legislation of Parliament.'[14] Therefore, Parliament had, beyond any doubt, the power to extinguish McLaren's right to exclusive use of the stream and his improvements. At the same time, it had an obligation that both McCarthy and Blake recognized, a constitutional duty to respect rights and the principles of the constitution, even though this duty could not be enforced by courts.

If Blake and McCarthy shared all this, how did they differ? Of course, the politics of the moment made sharp and obvious differences, but their deeper differences can best be described by considering two questions about limits on rights, which we suggested in our introduction: Where should the limits be drawn? Who should have the power to make this determination?

The first question can be phrased as follows: Was the limitation of McLaren's rights legitimate? Blake did not respond at any length to McCarthy's arguments, perhaps because he wished to emphasize Ontario's autonomy. But other Liberals did respond. Even though the private dispute may have been the immediate spur for the Act, a public interest in the use of the streams was not hard to demonstrate. Mowat and his ministers had invoked the public interest in the logging industry when the Act was introduced, and the Act was only the most recent declaration of a long-standing legislative policy of giving loggers rights to use the streams. In addition it was argued that the tolls constituted adequate compensation, although this response was more problematic.[15] This question was not the crux of the difference between them, however, nor was it the crux of the difference between Canadian and American lawyers.

More fundamental was the second question: Who should make the decision about McLaren's rights? Even though he believed that the legislature was constitutionally obligated to respect rights, McCarthy looked to some external institution for supervision, either the Dominion, through disallowance (which soon ceased to be a major possibility), or the courts. For Blake, the provincial legislature itself was solely responsible; the provincial community assembled in the legislature should determine its own needs. The recourse for a minority was not to invoke some external power, but to involve itself in politics. Blake put the position squarely in the course of an election speech in 1885, in which he returned to the Rivers and Streams question:

> I care not whether the Act is just or unjust, whether it is right or wrong, whether it is good or bad, whether it is robbery or not. I inquire as to this only, is it a law passed by the Local Legislature ... I admit and I rejoice that there is an appeal from the power that made that law. But I will state to you where that appeal lies: THAT APPEAL IS FROM THE LEGISLATURE WHICH PASSED THE LAW TO THE PEOPLE WHO ELECTED THAT LEGISLATURE, and who can elect another to their minds.[16]

Blake's arguments were echoed by his colleague David Mills, one of the most important and underrated constitutional figures in late-nineteenth-century Canada. Having studied law at Michigan, where he took constitutional law from Thomas Cooley, Mills returned to Canada, where he served variously as practising lawyer, Liberal member of Parliament, newspaper editor, professor of constitutional law, minister of justice, and, ultimately, a judge of the Supreme Court. For him, federalism meant the division of legislative responsibility between mutually exclusive spheres. Each government was supreme in its sphere and powerless beyond. Disallowance of legislation made by a province within its sphere was fundamentally opposed to these basic principles. In the Rivers and Streams debate, he believed that the Ontario Act was perfectly acceptable on the merits. Like Blake, Mills made the institutional questions paramount: 'It is not simply a matter of rivers and streams. It is not, as the Conservatives would fondly have the people believe, a matter of private rights or the compensation to be given therefor. It is something above and beyond both. It is the right of the province to enjoy the inestimable privilege of local self-government.'[17]

The issues at stake can be seen from two perspectives: federalism and rights. From the perspective of federalism, for McCarthy, the provinces were subordinate, to be supervised and regulated by the Dominion. For Blake and Mills, they were autonomous and coordinate governments. This difference encapsulated the struggle about 'provincial rights,' and Blake's vision emerged triumphant. From the perspective of rights, for McCarthy, legislatures could not be trusted with the final say. Disallowance was a legitimate means of supervising the provincial legislatures and protecting individual rights, and imperial disallowance played the same supervisory role for the Dominion legislature. And courts might perform the same function. For Blake and Mills, the determination of the legislatures should be final.

McCarthy's beliefs more closely resemble the dominant beliefs now, more than a century later, but Blake's were dominant in their time. Our evidence for this conclusion is the remaining episodes, the work of the courts, and the outcome of the struggle for 'provincial rights.' Before proceeding to the next group of episodes, we can usefully consider what the courts said about the quarrel between the two loggers. In *McLaren v. Caldwell*[18] the issue was one of statutory interpretation. An Ontario statute enacted in 1849 provided that loggers could use 'all streams ... during the spring, summer, and autumn freshets.' The question was, did 'all streams' include streams that had been made usable by riparian owners? In 1853 the Court of Appeal had held that it did not, and Vice-Chancellor Proudfoot relied on this holding in granting McLaren's claim for an injunction.

Caldwell appealed, and in July 1882, a few months after the debate in Parliament, a divided Ontario Court of Appeal reversed. The majority, Spragge and Morrison J.J., invoked a policy of encouraging the logging industry, which they saw expressed in the early-nineteenth-century statutes. Burton J., dissenting, argued that a statute should not be interpreted to impair McLaren's private property unless its language was clear. In November 1883, a unanimous Supreme Court allowed an appeal by McLaren, primarily on the ground that Burton J. had used in the Court of Appeal: the presumption in favour of private rights. The Privy Council reversed this decision in April 1884, with reasoning that was little more than an assertion about the plain meaning of the words.

What attitudes toward rights are expressed in the Canadian judgments? Perhaps the choice can be seen as simply between the apparent public interest in logging and the private right. From this perspective, the majority of the Court of Appeal preferred the public interest, and the Supreme Court and Burton J. preferred the private right. We prefer, though, another interpretation, which sees the court as more concerned about the appropriate functions of institutions. The preference for the private right was a declaration that only the legislature should make a decision that impaired a private right.[19]

The Rivers and Streams episode was a major victory for the provinces. Ontario reenacted the Act and reenacted it again after it was disallowed again. Eventually, after the Privy Council seemed to support Ontario's position, the Dominion acquiesced.

Sundays and Prohibition

The next two episodes were both crusades, one to make Sunday a day of rest and the other to prohibit drink. Because the major political figures did not often participate in these debates, the opinions of some minor figures emerge, although their thoughts did not differ substantially from those of their leaders. In both episodes rights were not a large element of the discussion, but when they were, lawyers (and everyone else) agreed explicitly that rights could be limited for the good of the public, and implicitly that the legislature was the proper institution to make the decisions about the appropriate limits.

The prohibition crusade began early in the nineteenth century. By late century both the Dominion and the provinces had enacted legislation enabling local governments to prohibit sales of liquor. The basis of the arguments for prohibition was the physical and moral health of the community, supported by statistics about costs of drink. The most common arguments to the contrary were that the restraints simply would not work, that violations would breed disrespect for the law, and (fearing the political costs of being pushed by a powerful single-interest group) that the legislature should not proceed in advance of public opinion.[20] The liberty of the individual to choose was asserted, although not often and not by a wide range of speakers. Whenever it was asserted, the response, explicit or implicit, was that liberty could be limited for the good of the community. Emerson Coatsworth, a lawyer from East York, recalling his reading of Blackstone, expressed this principle best: 'If I remember Blackstone aright – it is some years since I read it – it states that liberty is not unlicensed freedom, not that every man may do exactly as he pleases, but that every man may have the measure of liberty which is consistent with the state of society in which we live.'[21]

The second crusade, to make Sunday a day of rest, was not as successful. The crusaders, primarily a small group of Protestant members from Ontario, made an essentially religious argument during the late 1870s and early 1880s: mortals had a duty to God to respect the Lord's Day.[22] Opposing arguments were made by members who feared that uniform, national, and compulsory sabbatarian restrictions would violate the religious liberty of those who interpreted the Fourth Commandment less strictly than the crusaders, and who believed that one did no dishonour to the Sabbath by picking up mail on the way home from mass.

These responses were based on individual freedoms, but they were transformed into a claim about federalism: Protestant Ontario was attempting to force its religious and cultural habits on Catholic Quebec. A Liberal member from Quebec, Guillaume Amyot, who endeared himself to us for his wit, passion, and perceptiveness, captured an entire vision of Confederation: 'When we joined Confederation, we joined it as a commercial partnership, and not as a salvation army.'[23] As in the Rivers and Streams case, what began as an argument about individual rights ended as a claim for provincial rights.

During the late 1880s secular justifications emerged,[24] in particular, a claim that a day of rest for workers must be secured. The crux of this claim was the need to limit the economic power of employers – and their liberty of contract – for the benefit of workers.[25]

Regulating Factories and Railroads

The next two episodes concern what would now be called economic regulation: regulation of conditions of work in factories, and regulation of railway rates and contracts. Struggles by elite labour groups for better working conditions began in the mid-nineteenth century. In 1879 Dr Darby Bergin began a campaign to persuade Parliament to enact factory legislation. Lack of political will, together with uncertainties about the division of power, frustrated both his efforts and the efforts of labour organizations for the next few years. In the mid-1880s the initiative shifted to Ontario, which enacted a *Factories Act* in 1884. It regulated hours of work for women and children and specified safety requirements for machinery, although political manoeuvring and continuing uncertainties about the division of powers delayed proclamation until late in 1886.[26] No significant claim was made that the legislature was not the appropriate institution to determine the limits on rights, even though there was some doubt about which legislature had jurisdiction, the Dominion or the provincial.[27]

The railways embodied the first massive concentration of corporate power in Canada. Complaints both about high rates for shipping goods and about unfair terms appeared as early as the mid-nineteenth century. Dalton McCarthy, who plays so many different roles in our story, appears here as a champion of regulation. He introduced bills to create a commission to regulate rates several times during the 1880s. Each time his bills were blocked, largely by opposition from the railways and divisions among shippers. The government imposed a faint, ineffective measure in 1886, but no substantial regulation came until 1903.[28] The railways argued that regulation would frighten British investors, diminish revenues that were already inadequate, and curb their ability to respond to competition from carriers in the United States. But there was no serious argument that the legislature was not the appropriate institution to make the determination, and, in particular, there was no substantial proposal to give the courts the job of setting or reviewing railway rates,[29] a requirement that the United States Supreme Court imposed in 1890.[30]

Contracts for carriage of goods were another target of regulation. In response to the notoriously unfair terms that railways had imposed on shippers by using their overwhelming bargaining power, legislation was enacted in 1871 to prohibit contracting out of liability for negligence.[31] Its interpretation was often a problem for the courts. Their record was uneven, but they tended to respect its objective and interpret it liberally. For example, in *Grand Trunk Rwy v. Vogel*, William Ritchie, CJC, said, 'To limit the clause ... would ... entirely frustrate the intention of the legislature, or enable the companies to do so with impunity.'[32]

Some Conclusions about Rights and Legislatures

The crucial question is, who should make the determinations about limits on rights? The dominant answer given by the lawyers of this generation was the legislature, particularly the provincial legislature. In this they differed from lawyers in the United States and England. Furthermore the answer makes a contrast to the Charter of Rights and Freedoms. Section 1 permits 'reasonable' limits on rights, and it is the courts that determine the question of reasonableness. The courts are at the centre of the constitution and have the kind of role that McCarthy conceived, although section 33(1) (the 'notwithstanding' power) enables legislatures to have the final word about some rights.

Several considerations illuminate and explain this difference: the principle of legislative supremacy and loyalty to the British constitution, a fear of executive power, the memory of the searing struggle for responsible government, the absence of the threat of redistribution, and federalism.

Legislative supremacy and loyalty to the British constitution afford much of the explanation; Canada could hardly have established any different constitutional structure. Indeed, the Canadian lawyers had read the great exposition of the late-nineteenth-century British constitution, Dicey's *Law of the Constitution*.[33] Here the reader may interject that this is the sole explanation and, if we do not stop here, we are in danger of making far too much fuss over a relatively simple issue. But the Canadians spoke with a distinctive voice. After all, Dicey celebrated courts, and the rule of law was for him very much rule by courts. Moreover, he said almost nothing about how rights might be related to federalism.

What distinguished Canadian and American approaches to rights in the late nineteenth century was less a commitment to individual rights than a difference in perspective concerning the threat to rights. For Canadian lawyers, the principal threat to individual liberty seemed to come not from tyrannical legislatures but from the arbitrary actions of unaccountable executive authority. Steeped in the British tradition, the lawyers took their lessons not from the democratic excesses associated with debt-relieving, paper-money-producing state legislatures, but from the executive abuses associated with the Stuart kings. The difference is crucial. In the United States, protecting liberty required placing limits on the power of legislatures. In Canada, protecting liberty meant fostering robust legislatures that would be able to constrain executive power. As Blake stated, 'In free Constitutions the Executive power must be guarded, limited and restrained, and must not be permitted to encroach on the rights of the people and the representatives. Executive power it is which has at all times been the great foe of liberty.'[34]

As long as executive power was understood to pose the greatest threat to individual liberty, legislative supremacy and responsible government were viewed as a crucial part of the liberal constitutional solution. Only legislatures could be trusted to protect individual liberty, for only there were decisions made by representatives 'whom you elect and whom you can reject, whose proceedings take place in the light of day, whose speeches and votes you have the opportunity of judging.'[35] Indeed, for Blake and others, individual and political liberty were mutually reinforcing. Making representative legislatures, rather than executives, responsible for all aspects of policy-making would ensure that individual liberty was respected. Conversely, making citizens alive to the responsibilities and opportunities of public deliberation would bring out the best in individuals and nurture 'public virtue.'[36]

For the Canadians, the United States Constitution precisely demonstrated the dangers to liberty posed by executive dominance. As Blake said, '[T]he name under which this power is exercised is wholly immaterial. Whether it be King, President or Cabinet which wields the executive power, the constant tendency of those possessed of such power, is to invade the domain of other branches of the Government and enlarge their own jurisdiction.'[37] David Mills was typically more circuitous, but he reached the same conclusion. 'Under the American Constitution,' Mills argued, 'there has been an attempt made to protect the liberties of the people by making action of any kind, on the part of the state, as difficult as possible.'[38] The problem was that power was thereby so fragmented that the public lost confidence in the ability of Congress to legislate at all. This opened the door to 'demagogues,' which since the time of the Confederation debates had served as a code word for ambitious presidential power.

But why did the Canadian lawyers remember the threat of tyrannical executives so long and so well? Why did they not reorient their thinking to respond to threats from tyrannical legislatures? To find the answer, we turn to three remaining considerations: the memory of the searing struggle for responsible government, the absence of the threat of redistribution, and the preoccupation with issues of federalism.

Much of what was distinctive about the Canadians had been forged in light of the mythologized memory of the struggle for responsible government, which had convulsed the Canadian colonies in the 1830s and 1840s. Blake spoke rhapsodically about his 'earliest recollection,' as a young boy, of watching women make bullets for use in the Rebellion of 1837. Typically cautious, Blake argued that the insurrection was probably 'ill advised,' but he maintained strongly that no one could doubt 'the substantial justice of the principles' at stake.[39] In retellings of the struggle, the people were perceived as a community represented in the legislature, fighting for liberty. And in Ontario, at least, this story became part of a larger story of the battle against a series of external oppressors, Britain, Quebec, and last, the Dominion.[40]

The absence of a threat of redistribution is illuminated by a comparison to the United States. During the second half of the nineteenth century, the central problem of constitutional law in the United States involved the limits of state power to regulate economic activity. The general formulation was the same as it was in England and Canada: rights could be limited in the public interest. It was for the courts, though, to determine these limits, and their judgments provide a famous battleground for competing interpretations.

The traditional explanations, originating in Progressive histories, are that the courts expressed laissez-faire ideology and supported the expansion of industrial capitalism. During the past fifteen or so years, this interpretation has been challenged, and continuity of thought throughout the nineteenth century has been stressed: the courts expressed not laissez-faire ideology but a fear of faction and private interest that was deeply embedded in the American constitutional tradition. Nonetheless, running through all the interpretations is the horror of redistribution by legislatures.[41]

This horror provides the context for the Americans' fear of legislatures and faith in courts. The gulf between their fear and Blake's embrace was not so much that they gave different answers to the same questions as that they lived in a different world, asking different questions. In Canada, economic regulation was not a major issue. More important, the regulation that was debated was not perceived as class conflict or as threatening redistribution. After all, the quarrel between McLaren and Caldwell may have been a quarrel about property, but it was also between two entrepreneurs.

The contrast is illustrated by noting that the courts in the United States had already permitted the sorts of regulation contemplated in the Canadian debates about Sunday, prohibition, railways, and factories. Prohibiting work on Sundays, even to protect workers from the economic power of employers, was justified on public health grounds, not as a preference for labour over capital; and regulation of the railroads was justified because they had been granted a public franchise.

A sweeping conclusion is tempting: the Canadian lawyers were willing to entrust their property to the legislatures because they did not fear deep social and political divisions and assumed that the legislatures would reflect their values about the proper limitations. A corollary, which we can call the 'childhood thesis,' is just as sweeping and just as tempting: as industrialization developed in Canada, more substantial social and political cleavages were perceived, together with threats of redistribution. A heightened concern for judicial protection of individual rights was the result. Canadians eventually came to accept American ideas of rights and rights protection (witness the Charter of Rights and Freedoms). It just took longer for them to grow up.

Caution is needed in the face of temptation. The conclusion can obscure as well as illuminate, because the distinctive beliefs we have described continued to prevail even in episodes that were deeply divisive, notably religion and language, and where passions and fears reached the same pitch as in the Americans' debates about property. The absence of political and social divisions alone was not the crucial reason for the differences in beliefs about rights. Nonetheless, the absence of the threat of redistribution is significant for explaining attitudes toward property at least. Canadians had never viewed rights-bearing individuals as vulnerable to the 'ill humours' of an overbearing majority. Whereas the protection of property rights had been one of the triggers for constitutional reform in the United States, the debates surrounding the Confederation proposal in Canada (1864–67) were virtually silent on this question.[42] Property rights in late-nineteenth-century Canada lacked much of the symbolism they possessed in the United States. The ability (or right) to acquire property was, in the United States, a crucial badge of freedom; as Judith Shklar has observed, it was a way of defining the difference between slavery and freedom.[43] But in Canada, property rights lacked much of this ideological baggage.

The 'childhood thesis' is misleading in an additional way, because by concentrating on what was missing from the Canadian democratic

experience and from Canadian rights consciousness, it fails to understand these lawyers on their own terms. The Canadian lawyers did not
view the rights questions in terms of what they lacked or might become. For them, the legislative protection of rights was desirable because, in their view, this was the only way to realize liberty – in all its
complexity. For them the legislative protection of rights was not a
second-best alternative; it was best suited to Canada and superior to
American judicial review.

We come now to the last and most complex consideration, federalism. We begin by returning to the struggle for responsible government
and introducing the principle of local control over local affairs. These
two concerns were so closely allied that they became almost impossible
to disentangle. The lesson of the 1830s and 1840s was that there were
two great threats to liberty: arbitrary executive rule and rule by outsiders. Frequently the two were combined. Indeed, one of the reasons the
veto power of disallowance became a huge constitutional issue is precisely because it fused these two evils. From the perspective of Blake,
Mills, and others, disallowance was a constitutional evil both because
the federal veto was a potentially limitless and arbitrary executive
power and because it undermined the integrity of local legislatures.
Just as an aristocratic elite had joined forces with the colonial office to
stifle local democratic rule in the 1830s and 1840s, so in the 1880s Prime
Minister John A. Macdonald and his 'Star Chamber' in Ottawa had
exercised the veto power to undermine the integrity of the legislature
(and thereby the people) of Ontario.

The experience of local control over local affairs made the claims for
the provincial legislatures more than an empty demand for power.
They were the appropriate legislatures to determine limits on rights
because their members would be closer to people and more sensitive to
the rights of individuals than would a 'foreign' official. Different groups
that might clash and seek to oppress each other in a larger state were
separated, remaining as communities that shared understandings of
their needs and 'good sense and right feeling.'[44] Here, as well, was the
justification for saying that the protection for a minority was to involve
itself in politics – to participate in the debate within the community.
This understanding of federalism as a way of protecting individual
rights and minorities differed from beliefs of American lawyers, who
expected federalism to increase the range of opportunities and institutions and create checks and balances that would prevent the formation
of an oppressive majority.[45]

Implicit in these beliefs, although rarely discussed, was the possibility that rights might vary among the provinces. In contrast, the rights established by the Charter of Rights and Freedoms are uniform across the nation and support unity, although the override power preserves the possibility of variations, and the debate about Quebec's distinct society has recreated the tension between autonomy and rights.

These ideals about the ways federalism protected individual rights were complicated at best, and opposed at worst, by a tendency for the struggles over provincial autonomy to obscure or pre-empt rights. We have already seen how the debate about Ontario's autonomy obscured McLaren's right. The dominant question was, shall the Dominion or Ontario make the determination? The question of whether the limitation was justified was obscured by, or conflated with, the issue of jurisdiction. Blake's claim about the provincial legislatures had enormous rhetorical power, but it was also deeply ambiguous. Through it the protection of local self-government (or political liberty) tended to become a surrogate for the protection of individual rights.

The debates about language in the Northwest Territories and the Manitoba Schools Crisis illustrate this complication. In both, Canadians were beset by the conflict and the passion that the Americans poured into questions about property. In Canada, Confederation separated the French and the English, the Roman Catholics and the Protestants, into separate provinces, to diminish the opportunities they would have to oppress each other. Yet differences of religion, language, and culture existed in each province. What protection was there for the minority? Some constitutional guarantees were offered, such as section 93 of the BNA Act, but they were limited, as both episodes demonstrate.

Language in the Northwest

At Confederation, Canada had extended only halfway across the continent, to the edge of Ontario, but it soon expanded to the west. In 1869 it acquired from the Hudson's Bay Company a large area containing much of what are now the provinces of Manitoba, Saskatchewan, and Alberta. The Dominion, which had the responsibility of administering this new area, created a structure of local government with the expectation that it would evolve into provincial government. At the outset only a few of the small handful of inhabitants spoke English, and in 1877 Parliament enacted legislation permitting the use of French in the records and proceedings of the legislative council and in the courts.

The numbers and proportion of English-speaking settlers increased greatly, especially during the 1880s. In 1890 McCarthy, acting as anything but the loyal Conservative he had been in the Rivers and Streams debate, introduced a bill terminating the use of French permitted by the 1877 Act and beginning with an inflammatory preamble that declared the desirability of its disappearance throughout Canada. In the ensuing debate, fundamental questions about Canada were at stake: local autonomy, and the accommodation of religious and cultural divisions.[46]

McCarthy's opening speech, designed to demonstrate that there was no constitutional right to use the French language in the Northwest, exemplifies the prevailing beliefs about sources of rights. He declared that the statute of 1877 could not be the source of a right because it was based simply on the will of Parliament. It was, that is, a matter of policy, which had been determined by Parliament, and it could be considered again and determined differently. He then turned to the major constitutional landmarks: the *Treaty of Paris* in 1763, the *Quebec Act* in 1774, the *Constitutional Act* of 1791, the *Act of Union* in 1840, and the *British North America Act* in 1867. None granted rights to use French, except section 133 of the *BNA Act*, which did grant a right, but one limited to Parliament and Quebec, a right he pledged to respect. McCarthy did not mention the common law, presumably because it did not seem to him to be a possible source of the right, and no common law lawyer would have disagreed. Although freedom of speech was a common law right, it did not include choice of language in public discourse.[47]

This framework for determining the existence of rights was shared by all Canadian common law lawyers. The common law and a 'written constitution' or an 'organic constitutional document' were the sole sources, and by 'written constitution' they meant a British statute intended by Parliament to be a constitution, or foundation, for the colony. This definition explains why McCarthy discussed the earlier documents. The authority of the British Parliament made them binding on the Canadian Parliament. Other sources, natural law in particular, were simply not permitted. The possibility that the Canadian community might make rights by some solemn agreement or declaration was considered only once, in the Manitoba schools crisis.

Having established that there were no rights, the choice of language for McCarthy became simply a matter of policy, to be determined for the benefit of the nation. He expressed immense faith in British history and institutions and argued that language was crucial to the character of a people. If Canada was to be a great nation, and if racial and regional enmity was to be avoided, there must be one language, and it must be English.

McCarthy gathered only a few supporters for the principle of his bill, most of them from Ontario. The majority of the opposition, including the major figures from both parties and members from both Quebec and the English-speaking provinces, argued that the exclusive use of English denied the fundamental nature of Canada as a nation of two races; it was unjust to the minority; and it was unworkable – French language and culture would persist.[48] None of them discussed individual rights in any significant way, and their arguments strongly implied that the French speakers had none. It is important to note that this debate about the nature of Canada and the relation between a majority and a minority was cast in terms of good faith and provincial autonomy, not rights.

A smaller group of opponents to McCarthy was composed almost entirely of members from Quebec, who argued that no change should be contemplated and that Parliament should reject the bill outright. They claimed that the French speakers in the Northwest had a constitutional right, which must be respected. They referred to a wide range of foundations for this right: the terms of the cesssion of Quebec to Britain in the 1763 Treaty of Paris, the *British North America Act*, 'British fair play,' and natural law in several different forms.[49] But these references, which expressed different understandings of rights, were scattered and brief.

The Manitoba Schools Crisis

The Manitoba schools crisis is another installment of struggles over race, religion, and culture. Before 1870, when the province of Manitoba was carved out of the territory acquired from the Hudson's Bay Company, there was no legislation about education. The only schools were private and denominational. Roman Catholics and Protestants established and supported their own schools for their own children. In 1871 Manitoba established a provincial board divided into two sections, Protestant and Roman Catholic. Denominational schools could be founded on the initiative of residents and were supported by the residents and by provincial grants.

In 1890 this arrangement was terminated by the *Department of Education Act*, which transferred the existing schools to the government, and by the *Public Schools Act*, which established public schools supported by municipal and provincial taxes. These schools were avowedly nonsectarian, although some religious instruction about 'basic Christianity' was to be given. They were, of course, entirely opposed to Roman Catholic beliefs about education. Because attendance was not compulsory, Roman Catholics could establish different schools for their own children, but supporting these schools did not excuse payment of taxes for public schools.

Historians have debated the causes of this dramatic change. Factors include a provincial government struggling with political troubles, militant anti-Catholic fervour in Ontario, allegations about the inefficiency of the Roman Catholic schools, and massive shifts in population and schools, from rough equality in the early 1870s to overwhelming numbers of English speakers and Protestant schools by the late 1880s. The immediate spark may have been a speech by Dalton McCarthy in 1889 at Portage La Prairie, in which he declared the goal 'to make this a British country in fact as it is in name.'

The struggle that followed seared the nation for almost a decade. So far as it was a constitutional issue, the fundamental text was section 22 of the *Manitoba Act*, which had the same purpose as section 93 of the *BNA Act*: to protect schools established by minority religions. It gave the province authority to legislate about education, but subsection (1) protected any 'right or privilege with respect to denominational schools' existing 'by law or practice' at the Union. Subsection (2) permitted a Protestant or Roman Catholic minority to appeal to the Dominion cabinet if any 'right or privilege' was affected by provincial authority, and subsection (3) provided that if a province violated subsection (1) or did not comply with an order made by the cabinet under subsection (2), Parliament could enact 'remedial' legislation.

Roman Catholics turned first to the courts, seeking to quash municipal bylaws that imposed school taxes, on the ground that the 1890 legislation violated the right or privilege given by subsection (1). In *City of Winnipeg v. Barrett*[50] the claim was dismissed by the trial court and the Manitoba Court of Appeal. The Supreme Court allowed an appeal, but in mid-1892 the Privy Council reversed and restored the judgment of the Manitoba courts: the legislation was valid. Next the Roman Catholics sought relief under subsection (2), launching an appeal to the Dominion cabinet against the 1894 legislation. The government postponed a decision by making a reference to determine its jurisdiction. Thus the courts continued to be the primary focus of the struggle. In early 1894, in *Brophy v. A.G. Manitoba*,[51] the Supreme Court held that the cabinet could not hear the appeal, but a year later the Privy Council reversed it again. A government that was already floundering was obligated to hear the appeal.

The cabinet heard the appeal in March 1895, a month after the Privy Council gave its decision, and ordered Manitoba to restore the Roman Catholic schools. After Manitoba refused, a remedial bill was introduced early in 1896, debated during the late winter, and withdrawn by an exhausted and frustrated government in April. The schools crisis was a major issue in the general election in June that brought the Conservative government to an end and the Liberals and Wilfrid Laurier to power. The debate in Parliament on the remedial bill and especially the debates about the sources of rights and the relation between federalism and minorities are a rich source of the beliefs about rights and their role in politics.[52]

The Conservative government's justification for the bill was that a wrong had been done to the Roman Catholics in Manitoba, which the Parliament had a duty to remedy. Most of the Conservative members accepted this argument and supported the bill. They were joined by a few Liberals, primarily from Quebec. Most of these supporters argued or assumed that the Roman Catholics had a right to maintain their schools and not pay taxes to support the public school system.

The Liberals opposed the bill. Their response, unveiled by Laurier early in the debate, was complex and subtle. Faced by a government in disarray and the prospect of election in the near future, Laurier sought to accommodate a tension between his commitment to provincial autonomy and his own belief that a right had been violated. He also wanted to satisfy the outcry from Roman Catholics in Manitoba and Quebec. Laurier argued that the appeal permitted by the *Manitoba Act* was a means for redress given to a minority: while redress was surely needed, respect for provincial autonomy demanded delicacy and diplomacy. The bill should be opposed not so much for its content but because the government, in its dealings with Manitoba, had failed miserably to give this respect.[53] Most of the Liberals supported Laurier. They were joined by a few renegade Conservatives, most of them from Ontario, driven to opposition by their antipathy toward separate schools.

In the words of one frustrated Conservative leader, Laurier's strategy made a 'vast umbrella' for the opposition, 'under which they all gather and are protected from the pelting rain of criticism ... but beneath which they all quarrel like cats and dogs.'[54] His frustration was understandable. The umbrella accommodated fundamental differences about the existence of the right. Some of the opponents argued or assumed that there was no right. But others, including Laurier himself, disagreed and used the argument about diplomacy to combine opposition to the bill and their belief in the right.[55]

This tangle of alignments and loyalties contains a crucial pattern: the line that divided the members about the fate of the Bill was not the same as the line that divided them about the existence of the right. We will consider the implications of this pattern later and turn to the debate about the existence of the right.

Speakers who supported the right met a large obstacle at the threshold in *Barrett* because the decision of the Privy Council flatly denied that it was given by the *Manitoba Act*. Even though most lawyers believed that this holding was at least surprising, if not wrong, virtually all accepted it as an authoritative interpretation. Deprived of a textual source for the right, proponents claimed that during the discussions preceding the *Manitoba Act* and the entry of Manitoba into Confederation, there was a commitment from the Canadian government, or a compact, that the Roman Catholic schools in Manitoba were to have constitutional protection from a Protestant majority. This compact created a moral right, which would also have been a legal right if the *Manitoba Act* had been properly drafted (or properly interpreted). It was nonetheless a right that Parliament was obligated to enforce. In addition, some speakers derived the same right from the *BNA Act*, or claimed that a commitment to respect the two cultures was made at Confederation.

The most thoughtful expression of these arguments was made by David Mills. He claimed that a compact was made at Confederation and expressed in section 93 of the *BNA Act*, which protected separate schools, not only in the original provinces, but in provinces joining in the future. Another compact, conferring the crucial right, was made during the making of the *Manitoba Act* and given meaning by the original one. The means of protecting this right was the appeal under section 22(3). In considering this appeal, Parliament was obligated to respect a 'simple trust to guard the rights and privileges bestowed upon the minority ... and to restore them if they have been impaired or taken away,' although Mills did contemplate the possibility that 'higher reasons of state' might qualify the duty. Parliamentary supremacy made Parliament free, but only in the sense that there was 'no power of compulsion' to enforce its duty. Here he elegantly articulated the faith, expressed by Blake and McCarthy in the Rivers and Streams debate, that legislative supremacy did not exclude constitutional obligation and that Parliament had a duty to respect the rule of law. At the end of the speech, though, he followed Laurier, opposing the bill and calling for sensitivity and negotiation.[56]

The arguments against the existence of a right, made by some Liberals and by the renegade Conservatives, began with the claim that there had been no compact about separate schools made at Union and none at Confederation, or, at least, none that reached to Manitoba. In addition there was no general commitment to respect two cultures. As well as being an argument about facts, the debate about compact concerned the sources of rights. The claim for the right was essentially that a community could make a solemn commitment about its conduct in the future – that it could create a right. But the identity of the community and the conditions of the commitment were never clearly defined. Could the government of the day make the commitment? And what distinguished a compact from ordinary legislation? The impact of these questions was softened because the alleged compact was part of the making of Manitoba's constitution, but the constitution was made by the British Parliament, and *Barrett* held that it did not include the right. The compact was fundamentally at odds with Parliamentary government. Although there was no clear resolution in this debate, the idea did not reappear. The sources of rights were, in the end, the common law and constitutional text, and the British Parliament was the maker of the text.[57]

Shifting to texts, the opponents argued that the terms of the *BNA Act* and the *Manitoba Act* simply did not give the right. They claimed that the texts were authoritative and that context and moral rights were irrelevant. Here they invoked powerful doctrine about statutory interpretation: the meaning of a text must be determined from its words.[58] This argument was supported by an analysis of the function of Parliament: the assignment of the appeal to a legislature, not a court, implied that the function was to be political, that is, it was to consider the public interest and the good of the country.[59]

The reasoning of the Canadian courts is another source of beliefs about rights. In *Barrett*, the crux was the phrases 'prejudicially affect' and 'in practice' in subsection 22(1) of the *Manitoba Act*. Did the *Public Schools Act* 'prejudicially affect' a right or privilege that the Roman Catholics had 'in practice' before Union? The reasoning of the Canadian courts, both the Manitoba Court of Appeal and the Supreme Court, was marked by a strong willingness to consider the context, especially the schools in Manitoba before Union and the politics at the time of the writing of the *Manitoba Act*. Relying on these contexts, they shared a consensus that a privilege existed 'in practice.' The dividing issue was whether the obligation to pay municipal taxes 'prejudicially affected' the protected privilege. The Manitoba Court of Appeal concluded that it did not, and the Supreme Court reversed. The contrast suggests that the Manitoba court was determined to protect the power of the community to determine its own affairs. The Supreme Court was more sensitive to the plight of the minority and to the vision of Canada as a community of two cultures.

Brophy dealt with subsection 22(2), which gave the 'Roman Catholic minority' an appeal to the cabinet from 'any Act or decision of the legislature of the province or of any provincial authority.' The major issue was jurisdiction: did the section permit an appeal about legislation enacted after Union? A divided Supreme Court held that the appeal was limited to legislation enacted before Union, denying the minority the opportunity to present its appeal. Yet the significance of this result is modest. The problem was much more difficult than that presented in *Barrett*, especially considering the waning of disallowance in the 1890s, a fact that Canadian judges must have known.

Federalism, the Nature of Canada, and Courts

The Northwest language debate and the Manitoba schools crisis continue the demonstration of the belief that limitations on rights should be imposed by legislatures, especially provincial legislatures. They also show how claims about provincial autonomy obscured or preempted the argument that rights and minorities would be better protected by local governments. Another conclusion becomes clear: they show that individual rights were relatively unimportant in posing and resolving public issues and in defining the nature and values of the young nation. In the Northwest language debate, the claim to a right was tenuous at best. In the Manitoba schools crisis, the claim was stronger but problematic, and, more important, was displaced by political tactics. Moreover, in both episodes the resolutions embraced compromises, not the enforcement of rights. In the debates about factory legislation, railway regulation, prohibition, and Sunday, rights were not perceived as a substantial limitation on legislative policy. Throughout, claims about rights were overridden by claims about provincial autonomy.

The courts played only a small part in determining rights and in declaring the values and visions of the nation. They played no part in the Northwest language debate and in the Manitoba schools crisis. Instead their primary role was to focus issues, to determine which side should initiate the political process, and to limit the possibilities of strategy and debate, although never substantially and comprehensively. They performed the same role, even more modestly, in the Rivers and Streams episode; in the other episodes they played virtually no role.

Earlier we posed two questions about limits on rights: where should limits be drawn, and who should have the power to make this determination? Having put aside the first one to pursue the second, we can consider it here, albeit briefly. Do the answers of our Canadian lawyers express any distinctive attitude towards the strength of individual rights, especially in contrast to the United States? Our conclusion is that they did not; Blake and his generation did not have to answer the questions that Americans did. Perhaps, after all, any distinctive attitudes towards rights emerged in the twentieth century.

A supplementary question is, what attitudes did the courts display towards rights? The pile of cases is small and varied: *McLaren v. Caldwell*, the cases about the railway legislation, *Barrett*, and *Brophy*. The patterns are far from clear, and the most useful assessment we can make is a negative one – the courts did not demonstrate any firm tendency to prefer rights to legislative policy.

The Legal Scholars

Nineteenth-century Canadian lawyers wrote a handful of books and about a hundred articles concerning the constitution. Federalism was the dominant topic. What little was said about rights was typically no more than a few pages expressing a faith in the British constitution, especially a faith that rights were adequately protected by Parliamentary government. Conversely these writers disdained the United States constitution and the enterprise of protecting rights by judicial review and limitations on legislative powers.

The first text was *A Manual of Government in Canada; or, The Principles and Institutions of our Federal and Provincial Constitutions*, written in 1879 by D.A. O'Sullivan.[60] He described some of the rights, especially those ensuring good government, such as representation and petitions, but offered no discussion of the nature, source, or strength of rights, no account of legislative supremacy, and no explanation of why these rights were considered and not the traditional individual rights. *The Law of the Canadian Constitution*, written by William Clement, appeared in 1892.[61] He asserted that the struggle between individual and state had been finally settled by the Glorious Revolution in 1688. Clement did not develop the idea except to say that discretion, the antithesis of government by law, had been restrained, and that individuals were both protected by and subject only to the law of the land. In his discussion of contrasts to the United States, he dwelt on federalism and responsible government, without even mentioning constitutional protections. In 1898 A.F.H. Lefroy wrote *The Law of Legislative Power in Canada*, the first text about the division of powers. In his introduction he compared Canada and the United States, stressing legislative supremacy and saying, '[T]he principle of the British constitution seems to be that good servants ought to be trusted ... [The British Constitution] guards the liberty of the subject without destroying the freedom of action of the legislature.'[62] None of these authors considered in any sustained way how rights were threatened. But the emphasis on the history of British liberty and the rule of law suggests an integrated set of assumptions (or constraints on vision): rights were threatened primarily by the Crown and protected by responsible government. In sum, the ideal constitution was the Whig constitution as described by eighteenth- and early-nineteenth-century British writers such as Paley, Hallam, and Macaulay.

The articles, occasional papers, and lectures voiced the same views. In an unpublished 1894 lecture about the United States and British constitutions, David Mills lauded the long history of British liberty. He preferred legislative supremacy and parliamentary government to sovereignty of the people and separation of powers, without mentioning limitations on legislative powers to protect rights. Only in his conclusion did he turn to rights, stressing the need for moral restraint and decency, an appeal that others often made.[63] Notes of lectures given by Mills at the University of Toronto and Richard Weldon at Dalhousie are much the same.[64] Law journals rarely mentioned rights, apart from vague celebrations of liberty.[65]

This scholarly neglect of rights is partially explained by a preoccupation with federalism, especially the perception that Canada's constitution was distinguished by the coupling of federalism and the well-known British constitution. In addition, the struggle between the Dominion and the provinces dominated politics throughout this period, creating a pressing need to articulate the visions of Canada and to synthesize doctrines that made them workable. Another part of the explanation is faith in the British constitution, a few words summoning up the lessons of centuries, that may have made a discussion of rights seem unnecessary. A strong tendency to look for ideas and authority to England was closely related to this faith. Finally, perhaps religion and language seemed to be (and had been made) public issues for politicians and legislatures, not for lawyers and courts.[66] Or, at least, they were not material for late-nineteenth-century legal writing.

During the twentieth century, the regulatory and welfare state emerged and flourished. Redistribution became established social policy and a threat to private property.[67] Disciplined political parties and the power of the cabinet eroded any faith in the legislature as a place for discussion that might change minds. The myth of the community of Ontario lost its hold on the public. In retrospect, much of what was distinctive about the late-nineteenth-century beliefs would soon vanish, and Blake's world came to an end even before he died in 1912.

NOTES

1 Canada, House of Commons, *Debates*, 14 April 1882 at 915.

2 198 U.S. 45 (1905).

3 H. Gillman, *The Constitution Besieged: The Rise and Demise of Lochner Era Police Powers Jurisprudence* (Durham: Duke University Press, 1993).

4 C. Sunstein, 'Lochner's Legacy' (1987) 87 *Columbia L.R.* 873 at 875.

5 Blake spoke on 14 April 1882, and the Charter was established on 17 April 1982.

6 For accounts of this story see C. Armstrong, *The Politics of Federalism: Ontario's Relations with the Federal Government 1867–1941* (Toronto: University of Toronto Press, 1981) at 22–7; J. Benidickson, 'Private Rights and Public Purposes in the Lakes, Rivers, and Streams of Ontario 1870–1930,' in D.H. Flaherty, ed., *Essays in the History of Canadian Law: Volume Two* (Toronto: Osgoode Society for Canadian Legal History and University of Toronto Press, 1983) 365 at 368–75; J. Morrison, 'Oliver Mowat and the Development of Provincial Rights in Ontario: A Study in Dominion Provincial Relations 1867–1896,' in *Three History Theses* (Toronto: Ontario Department of Public Records and Archives, 1961) at 206–23; C. Stychin, 'The Rivers and Streams Dispute: A Challenge to the Public/Private Distinction in Nineteenth-Century Canada' (1988) 46 *U. of Toronto Faculty of L.R.* 341; and R.C. Vipond, *Liberty and Community: Canadian Federalism and the Failure of the Constitution* (Albany: SUNY Press, 1991) at 125–31.

7 Canada, House of Commons, *Debates*, 14 April 1882 at 893, 889, 891, 894,

890, and 891. McCarthy was supported by other Conservatives, especially Macdonald, who mingled appeals to both rights and the national interest. He invoked the 'laws which bind civilized society together, which distinguish civilization from barbarism, which protect life, reputation and property.' These laws were 'the common law of all civilized countries' and must be uniform throughout the country. 'We are not half a dozen Provinces. We are one great Dominion.' Disallowance was necessary to enforce these fundamental laws, thereby to prevent a 'great wrong' and protect the national interest. If this 'great wrong' were permitted, 'What property would be safe? What man would make an investment in this country.' Canada, House of Commons, *Debates*, 14 April 1882 at 924. Among the other supporters, some stressed private property and some the national interest; see, for example, the speeches by John Haggart and William McDougall, Canada, House of Commons, *Debates*, 14 April 1882 at 924. William Meredith, the leader of the Conservative opposition in the Ontario legislature, made the same claims as McCarthy.

8 Canada, House of Commons, *Debates*, 14 April 1882 at 913, 912, and 915. Other Liberals supported Blake, speaking in much the same way. See, for example, the speeches by Wilfrid Laurier and Charles Weldon, Canada, House of Commons, *Debates*, 14 April 1882. Most emphasized provincial autonomy rather than McLaren's rights; Laurier, for example, said, [T]he Provinces are supreme in their sphere, and ... their judgment should not be superseded by the judgment of another power.' Ibid. at 907.

9 McCarthy's reference to the American constitution was not a rejection of the faith in the British constitution. The American example was useful only because 'the same spirit which regulates the written law on the other side has governed and always governs British legislation.' He condemned the Act because it was contrary to 'the history of British legislation.' Canada, House of Commons, *Debates*, 14 April 1882 at 890.

10 'Constitutional' and 'individual' are not the terms they would usually have used, but they are expressive now. See J. Gunn, *Beyond Liberty and Property: The Process of Self-Recognition in Eighteenth-Century Political Thought* (Montreal and Kingston: McGill-Queen's University Press, 1983) at 229–59; J.P. Reid, *The Concept of Liberty in the Age of the American Revolution* (Chicago: University of Chicago Press, 1988); and R.C.B. Risk, 'Blake and Liberty,' in this volume.

11 The classic expression of this faith is Dicey's account of the rule of law; see A.V. Dicey, *An Introduction to the Law of the Constitution* (London: Macmillan, 1885) at 167–216.

12 W. Blackstone, *Commentaries on the Laws of England* (1765; reprint, Chicago: University of Chicago Press, 1979) at 121.
13 Book 6, chapter 5.
14 Supra note 11 at 36.
15 See A.H.F. Lefroy, 'Dominion Control over Provincial Legislation' (1881) 17 *Can. L.J.* 217, 234; and 'Editorial Note: Retroactive Legislation' (1882) 18 *Can. L.J.* 201.
16 Blake's papers are stored in the Public Archives of Ontario. Election Speeches, 1886, no. 4 (env. 19, box 110, B-15-d). See also a speech given on 16 September 1884 at a banquet for Mowat (env. 3, box 110, B-15-a).
17 Mills' papers are stored in the Regional Collection of the Weldon Library, University of Western Ontario. Because their organisation is rudimentary, we refer simply to the collection.
18 *Caldwell v. McClaren*, (1884) 9 H.L. 392; rev'g (1883) 8 S.C.R. 435; rev'g (1881) 6 O.A.R. 456. The vice-chancellor did not give written reasons at trial; the Court of Appeal dismissed an application for an interlocutory injunction, (1880) 5 O.A.R. 363.
19 William Ritchie, CJC, said, 'If the development of the public domain, the exigencies of the public, or the business of the country, is of such importance in comparison with individual loss or inconvenience as to require that private rights should give way to the public necessity, the remedy must be sought at the hands of the legislature through the instrumentality of expropriation, with suitable and full compensation under and by virtue of the right of eminent domain': Ibid. S.C.R. at 444. Note here the thought that 'balancing' is a function for legislatures. The judgments of Burton J.A. and the Supreme Court express no dislike of interference with property.
20 In 1883 Macdonald, concerned about vested rights, said that they should not be denied if there was any way they could be fairly protected. But he also said (a year after the Rivers and Streams debate!) that 'individual rights must yield to the public good.' Canada, House of Commons, *Debates*, 21 May 1883 at 1353.
21 Ibid. 20 May 1891 at 289. Coatsworth's memory was correct – and if he really had not read Blackstone for years, his recollection is impressive indeed.
22 See, for example, speeches in Parliament by Thomas Christie on 4 March 1878, and 27 February 1879.
23 Canada, House of Commons, *Debates*, 30 May 1894 at 3404. For other comments about freedom of conscience, see, for example, speeches in Parliament by John McLennan on 27 February 1879; by Joseph Chapleau

on 26 February 1885; by James Armstrong on 6 April 1892; and by Amyot on 6 June 1892.

24 See, for example, the shift in the speeches in Parliament by John Charlton on 26 February 1885, 27 February 1889, 5 May 1890, and 4 June 1891.

25 This perception was not widely discussed, but it was strongly supported by a few lawyers. The most articulate was Henry O'Brien, a lawyer from Barrie, Ontario, a supporter of McCarthy's campaign for an English Canada, and later editor of the *Canadian Law Times*: see his speech in Parliament (Canada, House of Commons, *Debates*, 9 May 1892 at 2301). See also speeches by Coatsworth on 30 May and 6 June 1892, and Armstrong on 6 April and 6 June 1892. The justifications for this sort of regulation were the public franchise of the railroads and the vulnerability of their employees. O'Brien also argued strongly that prohibition improperly limited liberty (ibid. 20 May 1891), but he would have had no difficulty demonstrating that his two positions were consistent. Prohibition did not involve a public franchise or a vulnerable group.

26 See E. Tucker, *Administering Danger in the Workplace: The Law and Politics of Occupational Health and Safety Regulation in Ontario, 1850–1914* (Toronto: University of Toronto Press, 1990), c. 4–6.

27 See the debates in the Commons on 6 December 1880; 23 February 1881; 9 March 1882; 26 April and 23 May 1883; 17, 31 January, 26 February 1884; 1 April 1885; 21 May 1888; and in the Senate on 18, 19, 21 April 1882.

28 See K. Cruikshank, *Close Ties: Railways, Government and the Board of Railway Commissioners, 1851–1933* (Montreal and Kingston: McGill-Queen's University Press, 1991) at 46–64.

29 See the debates in the Commons on 25 February 1880; 2 March 1882; 11 April 1883; 14 March and 8 April 1886; and the 'Report of the Select Standing Committee on Railways and Canals,' Canada, House of Commons, *Journals*, 1883, Appendix I.

30 See S. Siegel, 'Understanding the Lochner Era: Lessons from the Controversy over Railroad and Utility Rate Regulation' (1984) 70 *Virginia L.R.* 187.

31 *An Act ... to Amend the Railway Act*, 34 Vict. (1871) c. 43, s. 5. This Act was amended several times, but the differences among its various forms are not relevant here. In addition, there was no cry about freedom of contract: see the debates in the Commons, 18 May 1868; 9 February, 1 April 1875; 16 February, 13, 28 March, and 4 April 1883.

32 (1886) 11 S.C.R. 612 at 622. The conspicuous exception to this tendency was Henry Strong J., who combined a faith in freedom with congenital crankiness.

33 Supra note 11.

34 Blake papers, supra note 16; speech at Bowmanville, 26 August 1873 (env. 10, box 110, B-15-a).

35 Blake papers, supra note 16, speech in Bruce County, 1887 [?] (env. 4, box 110, B-15-a).

36 In a speech about the Pacific Scandal, he said, 'Unless there exists in the people a high degree of public virtue, they will be unequal to the grave responsibility of self-government.' Blake papers, supra note 16, speech at Bowmanville, v. supra note 34.

37 Blake papers, supra note 16; speech at Bowmanville, supra note 34.

38 'The Presidential and Cabinet Systems of Government Compared,' Mills Papers, n.d., 21.

39 Blake papers, supra note 16; speech entitled 'The Irish Movement,' 11 January 1896 (env. 58, box 114, B-15-d).

40 Paul Romney has explored this topic, especially in 'From the Rule of Law to Responsible Government: Ontario Political Culture and the Origins of Statism' [1988] Can. Hist. Assoc. Papers 86; and 'From Constitutionalism to Legalism: Trial by Jury, Responsible Government, and the Rule of Law in the Canadian Political Culture' (1989) 7 Law and Hist. R. 120.

41 Morton Horwitz emphasizes this fear in his recent book, The Transformation of American Law, 1870–1960: The Crisis of Legal Orthodoxy (New York: Oxford University Press, 1992) at 9–31. For a sampling of the recent literature, see M. Benedict, 'Laissez-Faire and Liberty: A Re-evaluation of the Meaning and Origins of Laissez-Faire Constitutionalism' (1985) 3 Law and Hist. R. 293; C. Chomsky, 'Progressive Judges in a Progressive Age: Regulatory Legislation in the Minnesota Supreme Court, 1880–1925' (1993) 11 Law and Hist. R. 387; Gillman, The Constitution Besieged, supra note 3; L. Halper, 'Christopher G. Tiedernan, "Laissez-Faire Constitutionalism" and the Dilemmas of Small-Scale Property in the Gilded Age' (1990) 51 Ohio State L.J. 1283; A. Jones, 'Thomas M. Cooley and "Laissez-Faire Constitutionalism": A Reconsideration' (1996) 53 J. American Hist. 751; S. Siegel, 'Lochner Era Jurisprudence and the American Constitutional Tradition' (1991) 70 North Carolina L.R. 1; and A. Soifer, 'The Paradox of Paternalism and Laissez-Faire Constitutionalism: United States Supreme Court, 1888–1921' (1987) 5 Law and Hist. R. 249.

42 One of the few comments about rights was Macdonald's well-known statement that the Senate would protect property.

43 J. Shklar, American Citizenship: The Quest for Inclusion (Cambridge, MA: Harvard University Press, 1991) at 63–101.

44 Ultimately this belief depended upon an assumption that the division of powers in the BNA Act gave the provinces extensive powers to legislate

about individual rights. No one expressed this assumption clearly, let alone considered it carefully, except perhaps David Mills. Throughout his speeches in Parliament he gave an expansive reading to the power of the provinces to legislate about 'property and civil rights' and equated it to the 'police power,' which he derived from American sources, especially Cooley. For example, in arguing that Parliament did not have power to enact legislation about conditions of work in factories, he said, 'All those regulations which a community find it necessary to make in order to prevent one man from interfering with the comfort and well-being of another in the use of that freedom which the law allows him are police regulations, and are a part of that department of jurisprudence embraced with the division, designated – "Property and Civil Rights"': Canada, House of Commons, *Debates*, 1 April 1885.

45 See B. Ackerman, *We the People* (Cambridge, MA: Harvard University Press, 1991) vol. 1 at 186–95; S. Beer, *To Make a Nation: The Rediscovery of American Federalism* (Cambridge, MA: Harvard University Press, 1993) at 256–61, 372–7; and G. Wood, *The Creation of the American Republic, 1775–1787* (Chapel Hill: University of North Carolina Press, 1969) at 499–506.

46 The eventual resolution was an avowed compromise proposed by John Thompson, the Minister of Justice, building on an agreement between Blake and Macdonald. It condemned the spirit of McCarthy's preamble and preserved the right to use French in the courts while permitting the territorial assembly itself to make the choice about the language of its own proceedings, after an election.

47 Canada, House of Commons, *Debates*, 22 January 1890 at 38–55.

48 Three major representatives of this group were Blake, Laurier, and Macdonald. For Blake, the diversity of race, language, and creed was both a danger and a challenge for Canada. He hoped that it might inspire 'still higher and deeper and broader feelings of justice and liberality and tolerance than are permitted to a wholly homogeneous people.' What was needed was 'recognition of the provincial and covenanted rights ... [and] a generous and liberal consideration for those minorities which are under our [the provinces'] control': Ibid. 14 February 1840 at 682 and 679. Laurier celebrated the cherished values of British liberty and claimed, powerfully and at length, that what McCarthy proposed was profoundly un-British. He urged that the duality of language and race be accommodated by mutual forbearance and respect, and local autonomy: Ibid. 1 February 1882 at 725–45. Last, Macdonald called for compromise; any attempt to oppress the French would be 'impossible if it were tried, and it would be foolish and wicked if it were possible': Ibid. at 745. These three and their support-

ers all argued that the choice of language for the Northwest should be made by the local government, and that the outcome should depend upon the patterns of settlement.

49 See speeches in Parliament by Cleophas Beausoleil on 12 February 1890; George Gigault and Hector Langevin on 13 February 1890; James Masson on 20 February 1840; and Amyot and Alphonse LaRiviere on 21 February 1890.

50 [1892] A.C. 445 (P.C.), rev'g 19 S.C.R. 374, aff'g 7 *Man. L.R.* 273.

51 [1895] A.C. 242 (P.C.), rev'g 22 S.C.R 577. See G. Bale, 'Law, Politics and the Manitoba School Question' (1985) 63 *Can. Bar R.* 461 for a thorough discussion of these two cases.

52 The most detailed account of the episode is P. Crunican, *Priests and Politicians: Manitoba Schools and the Election of 1896* (Toronto: University of Toronto Press, 1974).

53 Canada, House of Commons, *Debates*, 3 March 1896 at 2736–59. During this speech Laurier made a comment about rights that parallels Blake's speeches about the *Rivers and Streams Act*: 'Under popular government, the majority must rule … It may be that the majority will … do wrong to the minority. What is the remedy of the minority under these circumstances? The remedy of a minority under a free government is to agitate and endeavour to bring over the majority to their way of thinking.' Canada, House of Commons, *Debates*, 3 March 1896 at 2742–3.

54 George Foster, ibid. 13 March 1896 at 3502.

55 Laurier did not say much about rights in his speech about the Remedial Bill, but he had argued earlier that rights to separate schools were art given by both the *BNA Act* and by section 22. In 1893 he derived rights from section 22 and from the spirit of section 93: '[W]hatever privileges are guaranteed to one minority in a province, I claim in the name of justice and fairness for all minorities in all of the provinces.' Ibid. 8 March 1896 at 1995.

56 Ibid. 18 March 1896 at 3824–5, 3835, 3838, and 3861. In addition to stating the general arguments so powerfully, Mills offered a unique solution to the obstacle of *Barrett* and the awkward division between legal and moral rights. He made a distinction between denominational schools and separate schools, which limited *Barrett* to subsection (1). This argument was typical of the worst parts of Mills' speeches. It was probably utterly confusing to all of his listeners, but it is rigorous and impressive, so long as it can be read and reread. Other typical speeches arguing for the existence of the right were given by Charles Dickey on 5 March, Ezekiel McLeod on 11 March, and Foster on 12 March. The Quebeckers' claims

about rights, like their claims about language, tended to be brief and vague, and based on a wider range of sources.

57 In 1895 the question whether a right given by a community (a 'constitutional right') could be modified or withdrawn was debated by William Caven, a professor of biblical studies at Knox College in Toronto, and John Skirving Ewart, known to Canadian historians as an early advocate of Canadian independence and a brilliant lawyer, who represented the Roman Catholics. Newspaper clippings of the debate are in the Ewart papers, Library of the Legislature of Manitoba, Winnipeg. Whatever a persuasive or comprehensive answer to the question might be, Ewart seems to have got the better of Caven.

58 The first sentence of Maxwell, one of the standard texts, declared, 'Statute law is the will of the Legislature; and the object of all judicial interpretation is to determine what intention is either expressly or by implication conveyed by the language used': P.B. Maxwell, *On the Interpretation of Statutes* (London: William Maxwell, 1875) at 1.

59 Typical speeches arguing against the existence of the right were given by two Liberals, Joseph Martin on 6 March and Louis Davies on 13 March, and by three Conservatives, McCarthy on 17 March and Richard Weldon and Alexander McNeill on 19 March.

60 Toronto: J.C. Stuart, 1874; 2nd ed., *Government in Canada: The Principles and Institutions of Our Federal and Provincial Constitution* (Toronto: Carswell, 1887).

   Editors' Note: O'Sullivan's and other authors' writings about the federalism aspects of constitutional thought in this period are surveyed in R.C.B. Risk, 'Constitutional Scholarship,' in this volume.

61 Toronto: Carswell, 1892 at 1–25.

62 Toronto: Law Book and Publishing, 1897–8 at xlv.

63 Mills papers, supra note 17. There is no indication of where and when this lecture was given. A pamphlet written by J.S. Ewart, representing the Roman Catholics in the Manitoba schools crisis, exemplifies the call for decency: 'Arguments, I have supplied. Sympathy and kindness, tenderness and good-will, are, alas, beyond my power to bestow': *The Manitoba School Question: A Reply to Mr Wade*, pamphlet, 1895, Ewart Papers. Ewart expressed the same thought in a debate with Armour where he spoke of a 'spirit of fairness and sympathy' and a moral obligation: *Week*, 11 July 1892.

64 Mills gave a course on federalism; his notes for part of it are in his papers, supra note 17, and a student's notes for another part are in the Archives of the University of Toronto. Weldon gave a course on Canadian constitu-

tional law. A student's notes for the entire course are available in the Library of the Faculty of Law, Dalhousie University, although the student's attention seems often to have wavered.

65 Rights were occasionally discussed in the non-legal journals. One debate in 1877–8 between R.K. Allen and 'Fidelis' (Agnes Machar, already well known to students of Canadian literature) needs special mention. Allen defended mid-nineteenth-century liberal beliefs, and Machar espoused the cause of the new liberalism, both in a thoughtful and scholarly manner. (Is it suggestive that neither one was a lawyer?) See (1877) 1 *Can. Monthly* 369 (1878) 12 *Can. Monthly* 24, 183, 282, 369. Fidelis also wrote about rights a decade later in the *Week*, 16 February 1888. Also in the *Week* are a series of editorials expressing loss of faith in Spencer (31 January, 24 April, and 22 May 1884) and a good debate between the editor and Ewart about freedom of religion (25 March to 13 May 1892).

66 Articles in the *Canadian Law Times* during the 1890s sought to make this distinction in writing about the Manitoba schools crisis – and in avoiding it.

67 See B. Ferguson, *Remaking Liberalism: The Intellectual Legacy of Adam Shortt, O.D. Skelton, W.C. Clark, and W.A. Mackintosh, 1890–1925* (Montreal and Kingston: McGill-Queen's University Press, 1993).

4

Blake and Liberty

Introduction

This paper seeks to reconstruct Edward Blake's understanding and use of the word 'liberty' and I hope it will illuminate not only his own thought, but constitutional thought generally in Canada in the late nineteenth century, especially the understandings of rights, federalism, and legislatures. Because liberty was a pervasive and powerful strand of Blake's thought, my reconstruction leads into many different corners of his mind, and into many different incidents and issues in the world around him. My undertaking is like tracing a strand in a web – a strand that is both meandering and crucial to the structure and strength of the web (if webs do have such strands).

Edward Blake was a major figure in law and politics in Canada in the second half of the nineteenth century, but despite his stature, historians and lawyers have not written much about him. He appears from the little they have written as a 'noble failure': moody, prickly and aloof, and erratic in politics, but deeply principled, although the principles have not been fully explicated. He was the son of William Hume Blake, who emigrated from Ireland in 1832 and, after a brief try at farming, became a lawyer, a reform member of Parliament, a member of Baldwin's government, and the first Chancellor of Ontario. Edward, his first son, was born in 1833, and educated at home and at Trinity College, where he received a BA in 1853 and an MA in 1858. He became a lawyer in

1856, and was soon a leading counsel. He was elected to both the Ontario Parliament and the House of Commons in 1867, although he soon gave up his Ontario seat. A Liberal, he was a member of Mackenzie's cabinet in the 1870s, became leader of the party in 1884, and lost the general elections of 1882 and 1887 to Sir John A. Macdonald. Throughout the 1870s and 1880s, he was involved in most of the major constitutional issues: provincial rights, the Rivers and Streams Bill, the CPR contracts, the franchise, the incorporation of the Orange Lodge, the execution of Louis Riel, and language in the North West. He resigned as leader in 1888, and left the House of Commons and Canada in 1892, when he went to Britain, to become a member of Parliament from Ireland and plead the cause of Irish Home Rule. He returned to Canada in 1947, and died in Toronto 1912.[1]

During his political career, he continued his legal practice, founding a firm that continues today and arguing some of the major constitutional cases of the late nineteenth century, including *Re Goodhue*,[2] *St Catharines Milling*,[3] the *Executive Power* case,[4] the *Insolvency Reference*,[5] and the *Local Prohibition Reference*.[6] As well, he found time to be Treasurer of the Law Society from 1879 to 1893, and Chancellor of the University of Toronto from 1873 to 1900.[7]

Liberty was the dominant element of his constitutional thought and a symbol that he regularly invoked on public occasions. For example, his best-known speech is probably his 'Aurora' speech, given in 1874, in which he called for a 'national spirit' for Canada. In its conclusion, he described himself as 'one who prefers to be a private in the advanced guard in the army of freedom to a commanding place in the main body.' He continued by speaking of 'the true liberty of a free utterance,' and ended by reciting Tennyson's tribute to freedom in Britain, adding the hope that it might also become applicable to Canada.[8] Whatever else he may have meant, he meant that the national spirit of Canada must be an expression of liberty. Throughout his long career, his faith remained essentially unaltered.

Constitutional Liberty

My reconstruction of Blake's understanding of liberty can best begin by describing a distinction between political and civil liberties. Political liberties were the rights of the people to influence their government, especially the right to make government responsible to them, and civil liberties were the rights of individuals about their own conduct, especially their rights to liberty from restraint by government. This distinction appeared in England during the eighteenth century, and was pervasive by the early nineteenth century. It was not a sharp, firm divide. Both kinds of liberty shared a sense of liberty as liberty from arbitrary and unjustifiable government, and some liberties could be found on both sides of the division. Liberty of speech was both an individual liberty and a crucial safeguard for constitutional liberty; and, more generally, the flourishing of each was understood to depend upon the flourishing of the other. Nonetheless, the distinction was a central one, and Blake assumed it, even though he never made it explicit. The terms 'political' and 'civil' were not the only ones used; 'constitutional' and 'individual' were also used, especially during the nineteenth century, and they are more useful for my undertaking.

Blake spoke more often about the constitutional liberties; his language was powerful and passionate, and the occasions that evoked it were often pressing political issues. His most expansive version was set out in a speech about Ireland given in 1902: 'Liberty is not license. Freedom consists in living under a reign of law, which law is made by the consent of the people who are ruled by it and administered by officials responsible to and appointed by the people who are ruled by it … The essence of freedom is that the law should be made practically by the people who are ruled and administered by persons who are responsible to those people.'[9]

This passage expressed a basic faith for Blake's generation, but it needs much explanation for ours. Two meanings of liberty were implicated; the first was 'natural liberty,' which was the liberty of all persons to do whatever they wished. If this form of liberty were permitted, people's aggressive and selfish instincts would lead quickly to anarchy. Therefore, this liberty could not be permitted, and restraints imposed by laws were necessary for social life. True liberty, 'civil liberty,' was the liberty to act within restraints.

The appropriate restraints for this purpose were Blake's 'reign of law,' which had two requirements: the laws must be made by a responsible government, and they must be general and applied indifferently to all individuals. These characteristics can best be illustrated by considering the antithesis of liberty, arbitrariness, which was unrestrained and irresponsible government – the rule of the Stuart kings. Liberty required restraints on government. Earlier, the restraint had been the law itself, but this understanding had faded during the eighteenth century at the latest, as law came to be understood as the expression of the will of the sovereign. From the late eighteenth century onwards, restraint became responsibility to those who were governed, and particularly to the people assembled in Parliament. Closely related to this requirement of responsibility was the requirement that the law be general and apply indifferently to all individuals, for a law that singled out an individual without justification was the law of an arbitrary despot.[10]

Blake's beliefs about constitutional liberty were demonstrated in his speeches about four major topics: control of the executive, provincial rights, independence for Canada, and Home Rule for Ireland. For the first of these topics, the control of the executive, the general principle of responsible government was manifested in the responsibility of the executive to the Commons, which was for Blake the central feature of parliamentary government. The function of the cabinet was to propose policy and legislation, and the function of the Commons was to debate these proposals and assent – or withdraw its confidence. To permit the executive to have legislative power was to permit despotic and arbitrary government. Over and over again Blake condemned John A. Macdonald's government for violating this principle. No delegation of any significant discretion could be permitted. Throughout, Blake demonstrated great faith in balanced government, the ability of Commons to undertake substantial and independent debate, and the separation of legislature and executive powers.[11]

His two best speeches about the responsibility of the executive were made in August 1873, about the investigation of the Pacific Scandal, which erupted when Macdonald was accused of taking a bribe from a railway promoter. In the first he stated,

> In free Constitutions the Executive power must be guarded, limited, and restrained, and must not be permitted to encroach on the rights of the people and the representatives. Executive power it is which has at all times been the great foe of liberty. The name under which this power is exercised is wholly immaterial. Whether it be a King, President or Cabinet which wields the Executive power, the constant tendency of those possessed of such power, is to invade the domain of the other branches of the Government and enlarge their own jurisdiction. In the great struggle which subsisted for so many years in England, out of which the liberties you now hold gradually evolved, this was the main subject of contention.[12]

The British constitution continued to be his inspiration in the second speech, delivered two days later. 'It is one of the greatest securities for liberty that the people's representatives, responsible directly to them, and liable to be by them dismissed in case they fail in their duty, should have this exclusive right.' The corruption of Sir John's efforts to derail the investigation were demonstrated by making him into a Stuart despot. Nothing as corrupt could be found in history, except, perhaps, in 'the evil days which preceded the great rebellion.'[13]

The second example of Blake's use of the word 'liberty' – the campaign for provincial rights – was the richest and most complex of the four. It was a set of claims about the nature of the provincial legislatures and about legislative and executive powers, expressed by Blake and other Liberal politicians, such as Oliver Mowat and David Mills, as claims for liberty and responsible government, and was made in both the courts and the political arenas.

In the courts, the issues were contests about the interpretation of the *British North America Act (BNA Act)*, especially the nature of the provincial legislatures, the extent of their prerogative and executive powers, and scope of sections 91 and 92. Blake's most important argument was in the *Executive Power* case, which was part of the battle with the Dominion and Macdonald to expand the provincial executive powers. In a magisterial way, he argued that the fundamental principle of the *BNA Act* was responsible government, the cherished reward of the struggle for constitutional liberty, and that it required that the executive powers of the province be co-extensive with its legislative powers and independent of the Dominion; if they were not, the executive would not be responsible to the provincial legislature.[14]

In the political arena, the major issue was disallowance. Throughout the 1880s, Blake argued that the Dominion power to disallow provincial legislation was inconsistent with responsible government – with liberty and the rights of 'British freemen.'[15] The best examples of this argument were in his speeches about the disallowance of Ontario's *Rivers and Streams Act*, which permitted loggers use of streams that had been improved by riparian owners, and imposed an obligation to pay reasonable tolls. The Dominion disallowed the act, and the ensuing debate in Parliament in April 1881 was an intense examination of constitutional principles.[16]

Blake spoke about 'the spirit of the British constitution,' and its slow and peaceful progress towards 'the principles of freedom' and 'popular rule' towards responsible government. As he spoke about this liberty, his terms shifted – and the liberty of the British people to determine their affairs free from despotic monarchs became the liberty of people of Ontario to determine its affairs free from a despotic Dominion. And near the end of this passage, this liberty became the 'right as a state which each of us has as a man – the right to go wrong.' History, the spirit of the British constitution, and the powerful language of liberalism, were all used as powerful support for his attack on disallowance.

The third and fourth examples of Blake's language about constitutional liberty, independence for Canada, and Irish Home Rule, were, like the language about provincial rights, claims that a people – a political community – should have liberty from arbitrary government. His vision of independence for Canada appeared in many different contexts, throughout which he expressed a belief that Canada should control its own affairs and its own destiny. One manifestation was his campaign for abolition of appeals to the Privy Council. Another was his belief that Canada should have liberty to make its own commercial treaties. His speech in Parliament in 1882 was an expression not only of this belief, but of much of his general understanding of liberty. He began by talking about the values of an unwritten constitution, especially its capacity for 'beneficial change, for development, for progress,' and continued,

> The underlying principle and spirit of the constitution has been the development of the popular principle of government; and this has been continuously enforced and realized, to a greater and greater extent, as there existed and were made apparent, greater capacity in the people to exercise the powers of self-government; greater knowledge, greater information, greater training on the part of the people to take a larger share in their own government; and what applies to the constitution as it exists with reference to the internal organization of the United Kingdom, applies in quite as marked a manner, in later years, to the relations of the Empire to the colonies and to the political condition of the various dependencies of the Empire ... in regard to the relations of the Empire to the colonies ... you perceive a principle of growth, of vitality, of development, and of progress.

The progress was towards liberty. The empire resembled a federation, and the 'exact range of subjects committed to the charge of the local community ... are questions which you cannot answer precisely. The answer varies from year to year and from generation to generation.'[17] Considering its population, its experience with self-government, its territory, and its economy, Canada had reached a stage at which it should have responsibility for determining its own commercial affairs. Only this 'local freedom' could preserve loyalty to the empire.

The campaign for Home Rule for Ireland had deep roots in his family's past. He made a few appeals in Parliament during the 1880s,[18] and many more after he returned to England.[19] Again, the plea was for constitutional liberty – responsible government and the rule of law. Canada was the model for the future of Ireland.[20]

Blake said little about the authority or source of the constitutional rights, but what he did say suggests that the major source was the constitution itself – the British constitution that was both timeless and embedded in every age of the history of the nation. He never invoked natural law as a source, and never suggested that the rights were positive rights or granted by the Crown or the state. He did invoke rights expressed in the *BNA Act*, but in a way that linked them to this timeless constitution; for example, by speaking of it as an 'organic' document, or by expanding on the phrase in the preamble that invoked the British constitution.

Blake was not a profound thinker, and none of this structure was original. His understanding of liberty was drawn from British constitutional history, especially the whig interpretation of the first half of the nineteenth century. Here, the central story of British history was the struggle for constitutional liberty. Beginning in the early medieval times, the basic principles – the limited monarchy, the role of Parliament, and liberty – were continually refined and defended through the centuries, especially in the Glorious Revolution.[21] Among the writers who expressed this vision, Blake seems to have read Hallem more than others. Over and over, his speeches invoked this story, and his faith in progress towards liberty and the unwritten constitution.[22] He saw the story continuing in Canada, where the people had wrested their liberty, first from Britain, and then from local oppressors, and usually he spoke expressly or implicitly of the people of Ontario.

He did not, however, adopt the whole whig constitution. Most important, he did not believe that governing was the responsibility of a privileged few, and he did not make the link between property and liberty, which made private property crucial to the protection of constitutional liberty and the protection of property the central purpose of liberty. Instead, he had faith in democracy; liberty was the liberty of the people to govern themselves. Speaking in London about the Pacific Scandal, he said 'the rights of Parliament are the rights of the people ... [W]e are not separate from you; from you we spring, to you we return.'[23] In 1885, he told the Young Men's Liberal Club that they should not forget that 'we live in a democratic age,' and that the 'reign of the common people' was approaching.[24] He said several times that Parliament ought to be the 'mirror' of the opinions of the people of the country;[25] he looked to a society with few distinctions among classes; and he called for 'a true aristocracy of energy, learning, ability, and integrity.'[26]

The vote was fundamental to this liberty: it was 'the crowning badge' and the 'flower' of freedom.[27] His faith in democracy meant a preference for a wide franchise, although his campaign for provincial rights imposed the overriding principle that the franchise should be settled by the provinces. 'The true tests to my mind are citizenship and intelligence.'[28] There were, though, limits: faced with the question of giving the franchise to women, he took refuge behind the principle of provincial choice, but waffled long enough to seem to be unwilling; most native persons were not free enough or educated enough to be worthy; and Chinese were beyond consideration.[29]

Entangled with his faith in the whig constitution and responsible government was a call for virtue. The liberty of self-government demanded virtuous citizens – and virtuous politicians. Speaking about the Pacific Scandal, he said:

> We recalled, sir, in anticipation of this great contest, the fundamental principles of liberty. We were not forgetful of the maxim that public virtue is the foundation of popular Government; we were not forgetful of the great truth that unless there exists in the people a high degree of public virtue, they will be unequal to the grave responsibility of self-government. We remember that whatever tends to the destruction of popular Government, which is endangered by the introduction of motives conflicting with that principle, and must, the moment such motives become prevalent inevitably fall. When that high sense off public virtue has been so far weakened as to leave the country practically at the mercy of men who, by money or influence, control the exercise of the suffrage, they have succeeded in converting that which has been regarded as the shield of liberty into an instrument of tyranny.[30]

Here were echoes of the tradition of civic virtue, its fear of corruption, and its core belief that individuals realized themselves through participation in the public life of their community.[31] This sense of virtue and responsibility illuminated Blake's vision for Canada. Its proper destiny and the measure of its maturity was its virtue – the practice of liberty.

The major parts of Blake's vision were shared by other powerful Liberals, especially Oliver Mowat and David Mills, and gave them a language for making political and legal claims. To make Macdonald into a Stuart despot, or to claim capacity and powers for a provincial legislature by reference to the liberal individual invoked powerful images. Their vision had deep roots in the Ontario political experience, in a reform tradition which stretched back through Blake's father and the Baldwins, and which perceived Ontario's politics as dominated by its struggle for the liberty of the community against a series of oppressors.[32]

Individual Liberty

Constitutional liberties were one kind of liberties in the implicit framework of Blake's understandings; individual liberties were the other. Speaking to the Young Men's Liberal Club in 1885, he said, 'I want you to remember that there are three great freedoms that have been wrestled from unwilling rulers in olden time ... freedom of opinion, freedom of person and freedom of property.'[33] The form of this list of freedoms varied on different occasions, but the substance remained the same.[34] Like the constitutional liberties, their major source was English history and ultimately the constitution itself. Freedom of opinion embraced freedoms of conscience, speech and religion. Speaking about the C.P.R, scandal, he said, 'who is there that does not know that freedom of speech is liberty? Not the greatest security for liberty – it is liberty itself. Freedom of speech! Give me freedom of speech for a people and I will undertake that this freedom shall secure for them every other freedom, freedom of life, freedom of person and freedom of property.'[35]

A closely related issue was presented by the bill to impose the use of English in the Northwest, introduced by Dalton McCarthy in 1890. Blake spoke eloquently about the fears and sensitivities of minorities and about the conflagration that might occur if their fears drove them to unite race and creed in one party. Twice he asked the majority of English-speakers to 'put themselves in the French-Canadian's place,' and pleaded for understanding and toleration of 'rights and sensitivities.' Diversity was a challenge for Canada, and respect for minorities was a measure of her progress towards maturity. He proposed an amendment that declared Parliament's firm rejection of the principle of community of language, and left the question to be determined after the Northwest had developed.[36]

Blake believed in a fundamental separation of religion from politics. In speaking about the incorporation of the Orange Order, he declared, 'our religious opinions should be held entirely separate from our political leanings,' and he gave the warning he gave in the Northwest debate: 'No greater calamity can befall a community than when the cleavage of political parties is coincident with the cleavage of religious bodies ... Our political differences are bitter enough, without introducing into them religious differences.'[37]

Blake's beliefs about the third of the individual liberties on his list, property, were different. His most expansive statement came in 1881: 'amongst the most valuable liberties in connection with property is freedom to sell or exchange it to the best advantage, freedom to dispose of it where you will, to whom you will upon the best terms you can ... We think that a free and voluntary exchange is to the mutual benefit of both parties who effect the exchange, and we believe that that position is established by the mere fact that it is a voluntary exchange, because if it had not been suitable to both parties it would not have taken place at all.'[38]

Here liberty was liberty from regulation by the state to participate in a private market, not the liberty to participate in the public life of the community. Blake's speeches about this liberty were, however, tinged by the hope that the 'class distinctions of the old world' would be diminished, and he judged the health of a society, not by the riches of a few and 'a false scale of civilization, which I am disposed to call luxury' but by the state of 'the many' or 'the lowest class.' He hoped that they could gain independence, through their own 'self-denial, energy and intelligence.'[39] He often expressed a belief in competition, but occasionally spoke in a way that suggested a competition among equals. He also often expressed fears of monopolies, especially private monopolies,[40] and he was enthusiastic about industrial partnership and cooperation as solutions to the gulf between labour and capital, although they depended upon a 'practical and felt community of interest.'[41]

The Majority and the Minority: The Strength of Rights

Much of the protection for these liberties was the responsibility of the courts, and enshrined in great constitutional documents and principles – Magna Carta, habeas corpus, and the rule of law. These protections were a large and secure part of Blake's faith, but they did not occupy an especially distinctive or substantial part of his legal or political lives. His thoughts about legislatures were much more interesting, especially their role in limiting and protecting rights.

Individual liberties are claims against the state, but they are not absolute. Thinking about limits presents two questions : i) What are the limits that can properly be imposed? Another way of asking this question is to ask, what is the strength of the right – what sorts of considerations, policies, or principles can overcome it? ii) How should these limits be imposed – through what process and by whom? Blake's answers to these questions suggest understandings that are in some ways deeply different from ours.

In his speech about disallowance of the Rivers and Streams Bill, after claiming autonomy for Ontario, Blake invoked the 'spirit of the constitution,' and said, 'I am a friend to the preservation of the rights of property ... but I believe in the subordination of those rights to the public good ... I deny that the people of my Province are insensible to or careless about the true principles of legislation. I believe they are thoroughly alive to them, and I am content that my rights of property, humble though they are, and those of my children, shall belong to the Legislature of my country – to be disposed of subject to the good sense and right feeling of the people of that Province.'[42]

On the hustings in 1886, he spoke even more strongly:

I said in Parliament that I care not whether the Act is just or unjust, whether it is right or wrong, whether it is good or bad, whether it is robbery or not. I inquire as to this only, is it a law passed by the Local Legislature, within the exclusive competence of that Legislature, and, not substantially affecting Dominion interests? If so, you have no right to touch it ... I admit and I rejoice that there is an appeal from the pottier WORD that made that law. But I will state to you where that appeal lies: THAT APPEAL IS FROM THE LEGISLATURE WHICH PASSED THE LAW TO THE PEOPLE WHO ELECTED THAT LEGISLATURE, and who can elect another to their minds ... Are you not satisfied to live under the rule of your own people. Are you not equal to self-government? Are you not content to rely upon the sense of fairness and right, of honesty and expediency of your fellow-citizens of Ontario in reference to their and your own affairs? Do you feel so doubtful as to your own knowledge of what is just, expedient, honest and right, that you must allow governors to set themselves up over you to determine for you whether your laws are good or bad?[43]

These comments beg to be explained; they are provocative and represent statements about rights that were widespread among lawyers in the late nineteenth century. Civil liberties, and rights generally, were limited by the needs of the community, and the community assembled in the legislature would determine its needs and the strength of rights, according to its own 'good sense and right feeling.' The legislature was a place where persuasive debate could occur and the various interests in the community could be represented. The protection for the minority was the opportunity to persuade the majority in the legislature, and ultimately to appeal to the people. In the end, the majority would – and should – prevail, but it had an obligation to be sensitive to the rights and feelings of the minority, and to respect the 'spirit of the constitution,' and 'the true principles of legislation.' These should shape its 'good sense and right feeling.'

Blake did not face many difficult choices about the strength of individual rights, probably because he sat in the Dominion legislature and had a strong sense that the provinces should have responsibility for 'property and civil rights.' Clearly, he gave some rights great strength. Freedom of speech was crucial to constitutional liberty, and he would not have permitted any significant limits on political speech, but the course of politics did not push him to declare whether he would have permitted different limits for other kinds of unpopular speech. He seemed to accord freedom of religion the same strength as well, although he never had an opportunity of speaking about a specific and substantial restriction of an individual's choice of worship. Perhaps he was more willing to countenance limitation of liberty of property than liberty of speech or religion, but the evidence is only suggestive.

What, then, was the nature of the protection that rights gave, especially against a majority? Blake could have had no doubts about parliamentary supremacy, and could have had no sense that liberty, rights, law or the 'spirit of the constitution' were restraints on legislative power. And yet his understanding was not simply a confused hope for protection for rights in a world of unrestrained legislative power located from our perspective – between the eighteenth century and the Charter. The obligation of the majority was a constitutional one, and rights were constitutional rights. Blake did not make the distinction between law and politics and values that leads the twentieth century to separate the powers of the legislature from the values of the majority, and that has contributed to the dissolution of compulsion in Blake's constitution. Rights were to be limited by public discourse of the community about shared values. This discourse made the rights more than hopes that might be ignored by the politics of a majority, but less than rights protected by entrenchment against politics and the legislature.

These understandings about limitations on rights and the power of a majority were grounded in the mainstream of nineteenth-century English constitutional thought. In the background were the waning of natural rights,[44] the power of utilitarianism, and positivist understandings of sovereignty.[45] In the realm of constitutional thought itself during first half of the nineteenth century, the dominant faith was that the best possible protection of individual rights was given by the existing constitution – the matchless constitution of the late eighteenth century, with its mixed forms and its balances, which slowly became the Parliamentary government of the nineteenth century.[46] Whatever else this meant, it meant that the legislature had a substantial role in the protection of the rights; constitutional liberty was a protection of individual liberty. In 1823, Lord John Russell said, 'as long ... as the supreme power of the state is placed in the hands of one or many, over whom the people have no control, the tenure of civil and personal liberty must be frail and uncertain. The only efficient remedy against oppression is for the people to retain a share of that supreme power in their possession.'

I can offer two specific landmarks to support my suggestion that Blake's understandings were grounded in mainstream English constitutional thought. The first is Paley's *Moral And Political Philosophy*, which was a dominant text for university students in England in the late eighteenth century and first part of the nineteenth. It was used even longer in Ontario, and Blake read it at Trinity College – or at least he should have read it.[47] In his analysis of civil liberty, Paley said, 'Civil liberty is the not being restrained by any law, but what conduces in a greater degree to the public welfare. To do what we will is natural liberty; to do what we will, consistently with the interest of the community to which we belong, is civil liberty.' And in speaking of toleration, he said, 'the jurisdiction of the magistrate is limited by no consideration but that of general utility ... There is nothing in the nature of religion as such which exempts it from the authority of the legislature, when the safety or welfare of the community requires his interposition.' The legislature could justly take away life, liberty and property, 'for any reason which in the judgment of the legislature renders such a measure necessary to the common welfare.' This structure did not, however, necessarily provide meagre rights; from this foundation, Paley built a powerful argument for religious toleration. As well, Paley expounded the ways the composition and processes of the legislature encouraged 'expedient and wintery' laws and avoided the 'formation of a junto.'[48]

My second landmark is Mill's *Considerations on Representative Government*, published in 1861, just after Blake graduated from Trinity. For Mill, one of the great dangers of representative government was that a majority might prefer its own 'sinister' or 'class' interests to the 'general good of the community,' and unfairly oppress a minority. His responses to this danger were to ensure that all interests be represented proportionally (the Hare scheme) and plural voting. A legislature so composed was a forum for deliberation and persuasion. 'I know not how a representative assembly can more usefully employ itself than in talk ... A place where every interest and shade of opinion in the country can have its cause even passionately pleaded, in the face of the government and of all other interests and opinions, can compel them to listen, and either comply, or state clearly why they do not, is in itself, if it answered no other purpose, one of the most important political institutions that can exist anywhere and one of the foremost benefits of a free government.'[49]

But in the end, the majority must prevail: 'In a representative body actually deliberating, the minority must of course be overruled.'[50] Blake often spoke, implicitly or expressly, about the need for deliberation in Parliament, and proposed the Hare scheme, saying, 'Our principle of Government is that the majority must decide ... But if the minority must bow to the voice of the majority, the majority is all the more bound to see that the minority has its fair share of representation, its fair weight in the councils of the country. The majority must remember that it may become the minority one day.'[51]

At this point, I can finally try to answer an examination question that Blake might have thought about. It appeared on the final examination at Trinity, in a course called 'Civil Polity,' in 1856. Some evidence of the difficulty of reconstructing the thoughts of another generation is that even after knowing the question and cramming for several years, not only do I fear I may not get an A, I don't have any firm idea of the kind of mark I deserve.

a) Shew that a person confined to a quarantine station by due course of law cannot justly complain of any infringement of his civil liberty.
b) What kind of liberty is infringed by it?
c) Shew in what manner the liberty of individuals is secured by the British Constitution.
d) What kind of constitution makes the best provision for the liberty of a community?[52]

Parts a) and b) are easy, and require only remembering a couple of pages from Paley, which contain the definitions and the very example of the quarantine station: the confinement is imposed 'consistently with the interest of the community,' and therefore civil liberty is not infringed; it is 'natural liberty' that is limited.

Parts c) and d) separate civil and political liberties. I think that part c) calls for a lot of writing about Magna Carta, habeas corpus, the rule of law, the courts, and the protection of civil liberties by political liberty. Part d) worries me, though. The basic principle is responsible government – at least, I'm certain Blake would have thought it was – but I'm not sure what version the examiner expects me to present. This is 1856; does he (and whoever he was, he was a male) want me to talk about the debate about the franchise? Or about the cabinet? I'd like to have taken the course before answering at any length.

These individual liberties – liberty of the person, conscience, speech, religion, and property, and the ways of protecting them – were derived from English experience, but in Canada, Blake considered them in distinctive contexts and, perhaps, adjusted them in small but distinctive ways. Most of the major political episodes entangled rights with federalism. The first and most obvious thread in this tangle was that the campaign for provincial autonomy implied that individual liberty might be left to the mercy of unsympathetic provinces. The excerpts from the Rivers and Streams speeches demonstrate that Blake realized this implication full well, and he proclaimed the autonomy of Ontario – its right to be wrong. But again, the *Rivers and Streams Act* could reasonably have seemed to be a modest imposition. He was not pushed to make a firm, clear choice between autonomy and liberty in a situation where provincial legislation was a vital restriction of liberty.[53] The second thread suggested that federalism was a way of protecting rights. Each of the provinces shared a distinctive history and a distinctive culture, and therefore tended to share a common 'good sense and right feeling.' Oppression of a minority was less likely than in a more heterogeneous state. Closely related is his understanding of groups. Many of the major episodes involved claims about the rights of a group, especially the Roman Catholics. He did not, though, make any significant effort to think how the rights of a group might be different from the rights of an individual. Instead, the rights of groups tended to be represented by the autonomy of the provinces.

Federalism apart, Blake may have been more willing than his English texts to permit limitations for the benefit of the community. The texts tended to rejoice in the way the constitution protected individual rights, but, in contrast, Blake said, 'I am content that my rights of property, shall belong to the Legislature ... to be disposed of subject to the good sense and right feeling of the people.'[54] Is there a suggestion here of responsibility to the community, contrasted to protection of individual rights; or was he carried away by the political moment? One short passage is not enough to support more than a suggestion. If, though, there is a distinctive sense of community here, it may have been shaped by the history of Ontario's struggles for liberty – for responsible government. This experience, which was so important to Blake, may have made a sense of community – a community assembled in Parliament.

Perspective

After Blake died, J. Clark Murray wrote in the *Week*, 'The work that has been done by the retired leader forms a significant episode in the history of Canada. For it is not difficult, if one will look with earnest eyes at the struggles of these years, to see in Mr Blake's work the old task of liberalism – a struggle against the old foes of constitutional government in a new form. The foundation and security of constitutional government consist in the minute and perpetual control of the Executive by the people.'[55]

Murray was correct in seeing the struggle for constitutional liberty at the centre of Blake's life, and in seeing that his ideas were rooted in the past. But his struggle was not limited to the control of the executive, and, more important, he glimpsed a vision of social and political life that the tribute did not suggest. His beliefs about public virtue, social structure, the economy, and the destiny of Canada all illuminated his understanding of liberty, and combined to suggest a vision of a society based on liberty – a society based on equality, wide dispersal of economic power, and participation in public life.

Today, our thinking about rights and liberty are dominated by the *Charter of Rights and Freedoms*: section 7 gives each of us a right to 'life, liberty, and security of the person,' which is subject, in section 1, to 'such reasonable limits prescribed by law as can be demonstrably be justified in a free and democratic society,' and subject, in section 33(2), to the 'override' power. What illumination can a reconstruction of Blake's understandings about liberty yield for us?

My story suggests that section 1 and section 33(2) have firmer grounding in our history than we might have thought. The express acknowlegment in section 1 of the needs of the 'free and democratic society' resembles Blake's belief that individual liberty must be limited by the needs of the community. The crucial difference is that the decision under section 1 of the Charter is made by courts, not the community assembled in Parliament. Liberty has become a right to be protected from the community – by courts and a written Charter, and not a right entrusted to the community. The story of how this happened is complex, but one of the strands is a transformation in legal thought during the late nineteenth century. Courts became central to the constitution, and a radical gulf was imposed between law and politics – and community – a gulf that Blake did not perceive.

The power given in section 33(2) resembles Blake's belief that the majority of the community should in the end prevail, and may suggest to us that a passionate belief in rights is not as profoundly inconsistent with legislative supremacy as looking at American constitutional faiths might suggest. The question for us is whether we have the sense of community, respect, and toleration that is needed for Blake's vision.

But what about section 7, and the word 'liberty' itself? Can Blake's experience help us find meanings? We share his principled faith in democratic government, rational discourse, the rule of law, and the dignity of the individual – and liberty, and his passion can be an exemplar for us. But his age is not ours, and his particular meanings cannot be ours. Consider some of our pressing questions; What kind and degree of limitation of the discretion of an administrative agency will meet the requirement of 'prescribed by law'? What sorts of liberty should we have to chose our occupations in a state that is so intensely regulated and upon which we are so profoundly dependent? And should our liberty include some decent minimum liberty from want? These questions are ours, not Blake's. There is no still point, in Blake's mind or anywhere else in our past, that will give us interpretations of the word 'liberty.' We must make our own, thinking about the basic principles that we share with him.

NOTES

1 F.H. Underhill, 'Edward Blake,' in C. Bissell, ed., *Our Living Tradition: Seven Canadians* (Toronto: University of Toronto Press, 1957) 3. I wish to thank Louise Collinson for her wonderful research help, which has greatly enriched not only this paper but other work of mine, and Rob Vipond, for

three years of conversations about constitutional thought. This paper shares some of its subject and interests with his book, *Liberty and Community: Canadian Federalism and the Failure of the Constitution* (Albany, NY: SUNY Press, 1991).

2 (1872), 19 Grant Ch. 366.

3 (1888), 14 A.C. 46 (P.C.), aff'g (1886), 13 S.C.R. 57, aff'g (1886), 13 O.A.R. 148, aff'g (1885), 10 O.R. 196.

4 *A.G. Canada v. A.G. Ontario* (1892), 19 O.A.R. 31, aff'd (1893), 23 S.C.R. 458.

5 *A.G. Ontario v. A.G. Canada* (1894), A.C. 189 (P.C.), rev'g (1894), 20 O.A.R. 489.

6 *A.G. Ontario v. A.G. Canada* (1896), A.C. 348 (P.C.), rev'g (1894), 24 S.C.R. 170.

7 For accounts of his life, see M.A. Banks, *Edward Blake, Irish Nationalist: A Canadian Statesman in Irish Politics* (Toronto: University of Toronto Press , 1957) 3; J.D. Livermore, 'The Personal Agonies of Edward Blake' (1975) 56 *Can. Hist. R.* 45; J.D. Livermore, 'Towards a Union of Hearts' (PhD thesis, Queen's University, 1975); J. Schull, *Edward Blake*, 2 vols. (Toronto: MacMillan, 1975 and 1976); F.H. Underhill, 'Edward Blake and Canadian Liberal Nationalism,' in R. Flenley, ed., *Essays in Canadian History in Honour of G.M. Wrong* (Toronto: MacMillan, 1939) 132; F.H. Underhill, 'Edward Blake, the Supreme Court Act, and the Appeal to the Privy Council, 1875– 76' (1938) 19 *Can. Hist. R.* 245.

8 Speeches, 30 October 1874. The speeches used in this paper are all in the Blake Papers in the Public Archives of Ontario in five boxes, 110–14. They will be referred to by date, except for 'Election Speeches,' which will be referred to by date and number assigned by the publisher.

9 Speeches, 21 October 1902; see also Canada, House of Commons, *Debates*, 12 May 1890, and Speeches, 13 March 1902.

10 See J.A. Gunn, 'A Measure of Liberty,' in J.A. Gunn, ed., *Beyond Liberty and Property: The Process of Self-Recognition in Eighteenth-Century Political Thought* (Montreal and Kingston: McGill-Queen's University Press, 1983); M. Kammen, *Spheres of Liberty: Changing Perceptions of Liberty in American Culture* (Madison: University of Wisconsin Press, 1986); and J.P. Reid, *The Concept of Liberty in the Age of American Revolution* (Chicago: University of Chicago Press, 1988).

11 For example, Speeches, January 1875, 29 March 1881; Canada, House of Commons, *Debates*, 29 April 1880, 21 April 1882, 16 May 1882, 24 April 1883, 23 February 1885, 21 May 1885, 1 July 1885, 29 April 1886, 2 May 1886, 4 May 1886, 6 May 1886, 1 June 1886, and 2 June 1886.

12 Speeches, 26 August 1873.

13 Speeches, 28 August 1873.

14 Blake's argument was printed privately and is in the Blake papers in the Public Archives of Ontario.

15 Canada, House of Commons, *Debates*, 23 June 1885. Some of his speeches about provincial rights were ibid. 17 April 1885; Speeches 2 June 1875, 15 September 1884, 7 October 1884, 17 October 1884, 5 January 1885; Election Speeches 1886, nos. 2 and 13.

16 The best account of this episode is J. Benidickson, 'Private Rights and Public Purposes in the Lakes, Rivers, and Streams of Ontario,' in D.H. Flaherty, ed., *Essays in the History of Canadian Law: Volume Two* (Toronto: Osgoode Society for Canadian Legal History and University of Toronto Press, 1983) 364 at 371–5. See also C. Armstrong, *The Politics of Federalism: Ontario's Relations with the Federal Government, 1867–1942* (Toronto: University of Toronto Press, 1981) 25–7; J.C. Morrison, 'Oliver Mowat and the Development of Provincial Rights in Ontario,' in *Three History Theses* (Toronto: Ontario Department of Public Archives and Records, 1961) 206–16; C. Stychin, 'The Rivers and Streams Dispute: A Challenge to the Public–Private Distinction in Canada' (1988) 46 *U of Toronto Faculty of L.R.* 341; and Vipond, *Liberty and Community*, supra note 1, 76–82. For the experience in the United States, see J.W. Hurst, *Law and Economic Growth: The Legal History of the Lumber Industry in Wisconsin, 1836–1915* (Cambridge, MA: Harvard University Press, 1964) 143–270.

17 Canada, House of Commons, *Debates*, 21 April 1882.

18 See, for example, ibid. 4 May 1886, 6 May 1886, 15 April 1887, and 22 April 1887.

19 Examples of speeches he gave outside of Great Britain after leaving Parliament are Speeches, 4 August 1892, 31 January 1894, and 21 October 1902. See also Speeches, 11 January 1896.

20 For example, 'I am arguing from Canada, once discontented and rebellious, but which Home Rule has made peaceful, contented and law-abiding, to Ireland, which has been for want of Home rule agitated, alienated, and lawless, but which from my soul I believe will, under Home Rule, become peaceful, contented, and law-abiding': Speeches, 4 August 1892.

21 See J.W. Burrow, *A Liberal Descent* (Cambridge: Cambridge University Press, 1981); H.T. Dickinson, *Liberty and Property: Political Ideology in Eighteenth-Century Britain* (London: Methuen, 1979); and A. Kriegel, 'Liberty and Whiggery in Early Nineteenth-Century England' (1980) 52 *J. Modern History* 253.

22 Canada, House of Commons, *Debates*, 21 April 1882. See also Speeches 26

August 1873, 28 August 1873, 29 March 1881; Canada, House of Commons, *Debates*, 22 February 1877, 14 April 1882, 21 April 1882, 28 February 1884, and 17 April 1885.

23 Speeches, 28 August 1873.

24 Speeches, 15 January 1885

25 For example, Canada, House of Commons, *Debates*, 12 February 1883, and Election Speeches, 1886, no. 2.

26 Election Speeches, 1886, no. 5. He believed this aristocracy had an obligation to participate in public life; about this obligation, see also Speeches, 21 August 1880, and 15 January 1885.

27 Canada, House of Commons, *Debates*, 5 May 1885.

28 Speeches, 9 September 1877. See also Canada, House of Commons, *Debates*, 12 February 1883, and 17 April 1885, and Speeches, 2 June, and Election Speeches 1886, nos. 2, 5, and 9.

29 Canada, House of Commons, *Debates*, 14 March 1881, 18 April 1882, 12 February 1883, 17 April 1885, 30 April 1885, 2 May 1885, and 26 May 1885, and Election Speeches, 1886, nos. 5 and 9.

30 Speeches, 26 August 1873.

31 This brief reference does not, I hope, require a full account of the literature about virtue and commerce; the various meanings of liberty are set out in J.O. Appleby, *Capitalism and the New Social Order: The Republican Vision of the 1790s* (New York: New York University Press, 1984) at 15–23, and J.H. Hexter, 'Republic, Virtue, Liberty, and the Political Universe of J.G.A. Pocock,' in J.H. Hexter, ed., *On Historians* (Cambridge, MA: Harvard University Press, 1979) 255 at 293–303.

32 See Paul Romney's writing about the reform tradition, especially 'From the Rule of Law to Responsible Government: Ontario Political Culture and the Origins of Canadian Statism' (1986) *Can. Hist. Assoc. Historical Papers*, 86.

33 Speeches, 15 January 1885.

34 Freedom of the person was essentially the freedoms and protections of the criminal process, for example, habeas corpus, and the right to a trial by jury.

35 Speeches, 28 August 1873.

36 Canada, House of Commons, *Debates*, 13 February 1890.

37 Ibid. 17 March 1884. See also Speeches, 24 September 1877, and 21 February 1887.

38 Speeches, 29 March 1881. See also Speeches, 15 January 1885.

39 Ibid. 15 January 1885, and Election Speeches, 1886, no. 5.

40 Canada, House of Commons, *Debates*, 15 December 1880 (railways), 17 January 1881 (railways), 27 March 1882 (public lands), 27 March 1882

(timberlands), 14 May 1882 (telegraphs), 4 May 1883 (railways), 11 June 1885 (railways), 30 June 1885 (beet sugar), and 16 July 1885 (liquor).

41 Speeches, n.d.

42 Canada, House of Commons, *Debates*, 14 April 1882.

43 Election Speeches, 1886, no. 4. See also Speeches, 16 September 1884.

44 J. Waldron, ed., *'Nonsense upon Stilts': Bentham, Burke and Marx on the Rights of Man* (London: Methuen, 1987).

45 M. Francis, 'The Nineteenth-Century Theory of Sovereignty and Thomas Hobbes' (1980) 1 *Hist. Pol. Thought* 517: 'Sovereignty had become the graveyard of political philosophy instead of its summit. Authority, obligation, consent, right, and many others disappeared in it, and never seemed to have much meaning afterwards.' Another figure in the background is Locke, although I think the influence here is distant. Blake's justification of majority rule and the ultimate authority of the good sense of the community echoes the *Two Treatises of Government* and the influence may have come through Story, whose discussion of the majority referred to Locke and used a construction and language that is very similar to the language Blake used in his speeches about the *Rivers and Streams Act*: J. Story, *Commentaries on the Constitution of the United States*, 1st ed. (1833, reprinted New York: Da Capo Press, 1970) bk. 3, c. 3, ss. 327, 334, and 337.

46 See M.J.C. Vile, *Constitutionalism and the Separation of Powers* (Oxford: Clarendon Press, 1967), c. 8.

47 I have not found a reading list from Trinity College for 1853, the year Blake graduated, but in 1854 Paley was specified for the course in 'Civil Polity' and included in the general reading list for the final examinations for candidates for medals. (Fisher Rare Book Library, University of Toronto Archives). Considering the widespread use of Paley, it seems a reasonable assumption that his works were on Blake's reading lists as well. See A.B. McKillop, *A Disciplined Intelligence: Critical Inquiry and Canadian Thought in the Victorian Era* (Montreal and Kingston: McGill-Queen's University Press, 1979) at 62–5 for an account of the importance of Paley's natural theology in Canadian education.

48 Paley clearly specified that the legislature (the sovereign) was to determine whether the public welfare outweighed private interest.

49 J.S. Mill, *Considerations on Representative Government* (New York: Harper, 1862) 117.

50 Ibid. at 145–6.

51 Speeches, 3 October 1884. See also Speeches 2 June 1875, in which he justified the Hare scheme by saying, 'By such a system, minorities who do

not agree with me in my views would get their fair share of representation in the country.'

Editors' Note: For a fuller analysis of Blake's and others' views about the relationship between democracy and rights, see R. Risk and R.C. Vipond, 'Rights Talk in Canada in the Late Nineteenth Century,' in this volume.

52 Civil Polity, Arts, Annual Examinations, 1866, University of Toronto Archives.

53 The New Brunswick schools issue and the debate about language in the North West should be considered. In short, Blake's speeches gave the provinces great autonomy, but whether this autonomy would always have trumped liberty isn't clear.

54 Canada, House of Commons, Debates, 14 April 1882.

55 Week, 7 July 1887, 511–12.

5

John Skirving Ewart:
The Legal Thought

John Skirving Ewart is well known to Canadian historians as a minor figure in the story of independence and as a lawyer who wrote some books with peculiar titles. He is almost unknown to Canadian lawyers, including legal scholars. Such is the state of our knowledge of our legal history. My objectives in this paper are to describe his legal writing and to reconstruct his understandings about law and legal reasoning. My hopes are to demonstrate that he was a more accomplished and complex person than historians have believed and that he was a formidable legal scholar. More generally, I hope to contribute to an understanding of Canadian common law thought in the late nineteenth and early twentieth centuries.

Ewart was born in Ontario in 1849 and articled with his uncle, Oliver Mowat. After practising in Toronto for 10 years, he moved to Winnipeg in 1881 and became one of the leading counsel in the West. He acquired a small measure of fame by representing the Roman Catholics in the litigation about the Manitoba schools and in the public controversy that followed. In 1904 he moved to Ottawa and continued to be a leading counsel, but he gradually terminated his practice and shifted his efforts to political journalism, especially a campaign for Canadian independence. Until his death in 1933 he poured out a steady stream of letters, pamphlets, and books proclaiming the Kingdom of Canada.[1]

He began his legal writing during his years in Toronto, publishing an index of statutes and texts on procedure and costs.[2] He was also one of the founders of the Osgoode Hall Legal and Literary Society. Soon after he arrived in Winnipeg, he founded and edited the *Manitoba Law Journal*, which was designed to accompany a new series of provincial law reports, and wrote much of its contents until it expired two years later. He wrote a few other articles about narrow issues of doctrine,[3] but all these efforts hardly justify writing this paper a century later. The late nineteenth and early twentieth centuries were his most productive period, and the results are impressive indeed. In 1896 he began a series of articles about estoppel[4] that preceded his major book, *An Exposition of the Principles of Estoppel*,[5] which appeared in 1900. During the next five years he fought debates about his analysis of estoppel and wrote an insightful paper about waiver that anticipated most of what he would say in a book he wrote twelve years later, in 1917. As well as this legal writing, he wrote his first paper about the Kingdom of Canada,[6] which contained most of what he would say during the next three decades, and gave a handful of public speeches, most of them about social and political issues. He also managed to continue his work as counsel and take a trip around the world. After 1905 and his move to Ottawa, his writing tended to become repetitive and often superficial and shrill. He wrote little more about law, except the book about waiver. All that was new was an uncompleted constitutional history of Canada and a study of the causes of war.

I shall analyse the writing on estoppel at length and almost exclusively. It is the best part of his legal writing and is among the best legal scholarship done in Canada between Confederation and the 1920s. It offers an opportunity to understand his assumptions and understandings about the common law and the assumptions and understandings of the legal community of which he was a part. Ewart was a powerful and insightful thinker, but he was not radical, and most of his ways of thinking were shared by his contemporaries.

Estoppel: The General Principles

'Estoppel' is a word that may baffle most historians, because it has no apparent meaning for them, and bemuse most lawyers, because they may know it only as a jumble of odds and ends of doctrine and wonder why anyone would have chosen to write a book about it. The essence of the doctrine is that an individual may be prohibited ('estopped') from asserting some proposition about facts or law, even though it may be true, if he or she has made an inconsistent representation that has been

relied upon. For example, a corporation may issue shares to me (perhaps by mistake) even though I am not a shareholder, and I may use
them as security for a loan. If I default, the corporation may be estopped
from denying that I was the owner of the shares, because they are a
representation (that I am the owner) that the lender relied on.

The notion that one individual may rely on a representation made by
another may seem simple and sensible, but it is not – at least not for the
common law. In the late nineteenth century, the doctrine was composed of inconsistent and incomplete fragments, and the texts essentially replicated this tangle. Ewart sought to construct a coherent and
unified structure from this jumble, and his undertaking was part of a
grand vision that dominated legal scholarship in the second half of the
nineteenth century. The common law seemed to scholars to be in chaos,
especially after the abolition of the forms of action, and legal education
seemed to have languished for centuries. A small group of scholars,
including Anson, Dicey, Holland, and Pollock, sought to reconstitute
the doctrine and to revitalize legal education. Their major undertaking
was writing expository texts, in which they sought to make the doctrine
unified, coherent, and internally consistent; for example, Anson's *Contracts*,[7] Dicey's *Law of the Constitution*,[8] and Pollock's *Torts*.[9] Some of
these texts, including these three, were great scholarship and continue
to be among the standard literature in edition after edition.[10]

Ewart declared his method in the preface to his book. He proposed to
begin by stating general principles, and then to apply them to a wide
range of different contexts. He demonstrated great confidence, and an
affection – passion, or even obsession might be a better word – for
definitions and classification, a characteristic that pervaded his writing
throughout his life.

The presentation of the general principles was remarkably short.
Eleven short principles were stated in less than a page, in a chapter that
was less than two pages long, and they can be summarized in a couple
of sentences. For an estoppel to be imposed, a representation must have
been made by the person who is to be estopped, or by someone whose
representation he or she has made possible. It must have been about
fact or law (that is, it must not be a promise about the future), and it
must have been material (that is, its contents must justify the reliance).
There must have been some duty to the person who is claiming the
estoppel, who must be the person to whom it was made and who must
have changed position as a consequence of the representation in some
prejudicial and reasonably foreseeable way. Fraud or bad faith in mak-

ing the representation is not an element of the claim, but carelessness is necessary – sometimes.

These principles dominated the book, and Ewart's understanding and use of them demonstrate much of his understanding of the common law. All common law lawyers believed that the common law was – or should be – composed of principles, and they all believed that good lawyers thought in terms of principles, but the contents and implications of this belief were complex. The word 'principle' seems to have had two meanings or families of meanings. One meaning was propositions of doctrine, that is, propositions that could and should be used to determine the outcome of particular cases. The other was ethical propositions that were not doctrine but ideals, sources of doctrine, or standards for its application. These two meanings were often blurred and tangled together, and often merged in a vague faith that the common law was rational, orderly, and 'principled.'

Ewart shared this faith in principles and these meanings. He usually used the word to mean propositions of doctrine, and he distinguished expressly and sharply between propositions that were the established doctrine and propositions that he believed should be the doctrine. He acknowledged that some parts of his basic principles were not the established doctrine and offered them as preferable alternatives. Text writers usually professed to do no more than state the established doctrine, albeit in an orderly and 'scientific' way, and Ewart was distinctive among the English and Canadian writers in his expressed ambition to propose reform.

A faith in principles was accompanied, and often overlapped, by a faith that the common law was scientific, and here Ewart was typical. In his preface, he claimed to have made a 'scientific' synthesis, and he used the word often throughout the book and in his other writing. 'Scientific' usually meant orderly, rigorous, and internally consistent. For example, Ewart said that a set of rules about apparent authority in which one overlapped the others was not 'framed according to scientific ideal.'[11] It also suggested a faith, which paralleled the dominant understandings about the natural and social sciences, that the common law was or should be composed of objective rules that could be discovered by its practitioners.

Where did principles come from and what justified them? In the sense that they were propositions of doctrine, the dominant faith was that they were made by courts through induction from decided cases, and their authority was derived from doctrine about precedent. In the sense that they were ethical propositions, the sources and justifications were rarely discussed. Ewart was characteristically much more rigorous and self-revealing about those questions than most lawyers, and perhaps more defiant. He fashioned his basic principles himself, and the accomplishment was impressive. The primary material was the decided cases and the existing stock of ideas, which he generalized and unified. He borrowed much from the established doctrine about estoppel and from the structure of torts, especially as it was presented in Pollock's *Torts*, although the understanding that liability for representations could be arranged in much the same way as liability for physical harm was a powerful insight. Yet he would have protested against the conclusion that these principles were no more than either generalizations from the cases or a product of his own will or political beliefs. His understanding was that they were ultimately an elaboration of the basic concept of estoppel, which was itself a product of the requirements of the 'best form of society' (a phrase he used in an unpublished paper that will be discussed later). Each individual was both an individual and a member of society and as a member owed duties – both social and legal – to the other members. Each owed others a duty to avoid causing harm, and the extent of this duty could be measured along a scale from egoism to altruism. Ewart had faith that the course of society had been, and would continue to be, towards altruism:

That the duties thus imposed are not absolute but relative to the conditions which may obtain from time to time is but to say that social rules are not yet finally codified; that advancement and progress and improvement have not yet ceased. Indeed, as we observe the rapid development of the law of estoppel, and the increasing list of duties which is ever being lengthened by the necessities of later activities, we see that not only are the relations of life still widening out into greater complexities, but that the laws of altruism and mutual aid are making rapid head as against those of mere individualism.[12]

The opposition of egoism and altruism, the faith in an evolutionary progress towards altruism, and the sense of increasing complexity and differentiation were all elements of his political and social thought, which will be considered later. His belief that the liability in estoppel was ultimately justified by altruism was a belief about the relation between values and law. He had no doubt that values should shape the common law. Altruism should prevail because it was the heart of 'the best form of society,' and evolution would ensure that it did prevail.

This structure resolved a crucial tension that pervaded late-nineteenth-century thought about the common law. One fundamental article of faith was that the common law was and should be objective and apolitical. Its principles and its reasoning were not the exercise of the will of the judges, and they were fundamentally different from lawmaking by legislatures. This faith existed in tension and potential conflict with two other elements of the thought. The first was the belief that the common law did and should express values, and the second was the observation that the common law was made by judges and changed by judges. How could the common law be both objective and apolitical, and also be an ethical statement made by judges? Most writers resolved this conflict through a vague faith in the flexibility and adaptability of the common law, and the ambiguity of the word 'principle' was often apparent in descriptions of this flexibility.[13] For Ewart, altruism and evolution were the means to a resolution. The doctrine about estoppel should be determined by evolution towards 'the best form of society.' The function of a scholar or a court was to discover the principles implicit in altruism and to reason from these principles to particular results.

What was a judge or a scholar to do if the dictates of altruism conflicted with the existing doctrine? This unhappy conflict was entirely possible, and it was evident to Ewart throughout much of the domain of estoppel. He was entirely aware that principles could be incomplete and inconsistent, and that the decisions in specific cases were not always determined by reasoning from principles. The dominant faith, established in the rules about precedent, was that a court must follow the existing authority and that a single decision was an authority, even though it might seem unfair or inconsistent with other cases.[14] Ewart never doubted this obligation and never sought to resolve the conflict. He could do no more than suggest ways of reformulating the doctrine to avoid conflict or say that he believed the doctrine was wrong.

Most of the principles either presented no substantial and distinctive difficulty or could be analysed by using settled ideas and doctrine from other fields of law, especially torts. Three issues presented peculiar difficulty: the requirement of a duty, the liability for representations made by others, and the significance of fraud and negligence. The first, the requirement of a duty, was the cornerstone, and its analysis was his most extensive presentation of the ethical beliefs that justified his structure. His conception of this duty was similar to the requirement of a duty for tort liability, and he expressly invoked the analysis from Pollock's *Torts*, especially one passage: 'The whole modern law of negligence, with its many developments, enforces the duty of fellow-citizens to observe, in varying circumstances, an appropriate measure of prudence to avoid causing harm to each other.'[15]

Ewart's use of the duty concept was a creative undertaking. Duty had not been established as a secure and discrete element of tort doctrine until the 1880s, and even in Pollock's text it was only discussed in a few general paragraphs and not clearly separated from standard of care or foreseeability.[16] The cornerstone was not, however, precisely cut, and it supported less of the weight of the structure than Ewart claimed it did. As an element of doctrine, duty made sense only as a relationship between a plaintiff and defendant that justified imposing an obligation to take reasonable care to avoid causing harm, but Ewart's discussion did not define or explore different kinds of relationships. Instead, it was essentially a general justification of liability: the obligations of altruism imposed on all of us a duty to live up to our representations. But this limitation can be seen only with the benefit of hindsight. His analysis, especially his understanding that duty should be conceived as a separate and major element of the doctrine and that it was a battleground of competing values, was at least as perceptive as the best of the current torts scholarship.

Ewart's discussion of the other two topics, the liability for representations made by others and the significance of fraud and negligence, seemed to be more technical than the discussion of duty, but, like the rest of the book, both were illuminated by the belief in progress towards altruism. The liability for representations made by others depended upon a distinction between personal representations, which were made by the person who was to be estopped, and assisted representations, which were made by someone else with the assistance of the person to be estopped. This distinction, especially the concept of assisted representations, was his own creation, and another example of his passion for definitions and classification. The existing doctrine dealt only with personal representations (albeit not by name). Ewart claimed that estoppel was being imposed by the courts – and should be imposed for assisted representations, but under different and misleading labels.[17]

This perception demonstrates his analytical powers and his determination to establish large general principles. It extended the scope of the principles of estoppel in a coherent way, because if liability was based on the consequences of conduct, there could be no fundamental difference between making a misrepresentation and enabling someone else to make one. The major expansion was the inclusion of the principle declared in *Lickbarrow v. Mason*:[18] '[W]henever one of two innocent persons must suffer by the acts of a third, he who enables such person to occasion the loss must sustain it.'[19]

This principle had been established for more than a century, but it had never been fully integrated with other principles.[20] Nothing in the existing literature suggested that it could be considered as part of a general doctrine of estoppel, and there were some firm dicta to the contrary, but Ewart's analysis was effective. Given his definition of assisted estoppel, *Lickbarrow* is included, and the general principles of estoppel serve to analyse its problems far better than the confusing tangle of doctrine and dicta that surrounded it.[21]

The distinction was also useful in the analysis of the third issue – the significance of fraud and negligence. Should it, and did it, make any difference if the representation was made fraudulently, in bad faith, or carelessly?[22] The cases were confusing and inconsistent, but 'reconciliation of the conflicting dicta is accomplished by classification,' and 'a little care in distinction and classification is all that is necessary.' The basic proposition was that fraud, bad faith, or carelessness in making the representation was not required for liability. 'Consideration of "how the representation came to be made" – whether through carelessness or intention – is ... immaterial,'[23] and 'the general rule regards merely the act done, and is entirely indifferent to the motive or reason for it, or the carelessness or diligence that may be in it.' But in the course of the analysis of carelessness, the analysis took an abrupt and unannounced turn, which eventually led to confusion and perhaps to inconsistency. Ewart claimed that the courts had imposed estoppel for assisted representations (masked under different words) because the person estopped had been careless in enabling the representation to be made. He approved this 'estoppel by carelessness,' but he did not consider the relation between this approval and his original claim that carelessness should be 'immaterial.' The entire structure of his analysis suggests that approval of liability for carelessness could only have been approval for this liability as an element of a larger liability for representations made regardless of 'how the representation came to be made,' but the context and the passage itself suggest approval for an expansion of a narrower liability – perhaps a liability limited to fraud or bad faith. This uncertainty affected the analysis of the requirement of a duty; for example, in the discussion of documents mistakenly signed, he made the duty a standard of care: '[H]e is or is not estopped ... according as his conduct may or may not exhibit "an appropriate measure of prudence to avoid causing harm to others."'[24]

The reason for this confusion may have been conflicting conceptions of the basis for liability. The bulk of his analysis made liability a strict liability. It was essentially a product of the reliance on a representation made by the defendant, regardless of the reasons for making the representation and the attitude of the defendant. In contrast, the 'estoppel by carelessness' seems to be derived from torts doctrine, and to be essentially a liability for harm caused by negligence. The choice between strict liability and negligence was debated often in the late nineteenth century, especially in the United States, but Ewart does not seem to have drawn on this experience. He did not clearly perceive or resolve the difference between the two grounds, and what answer altruism would have led him to is debatable. But both strands of his tangle anticipated important changes. His emphasis on reliance anticipated the expansion of reliance as a ground for liability in the twentieth century,[25] and his approval of negligence as a ground for liability for a representation came long before liability for damages for carelessly made representations appeared in the tort doctrine.

Estoppel: The Application of the Principles

The exposition of the general principles occupied about half the book. In the second half, Ewart considered a series of topics – land, goods, documents of title, negotiable instruments, mistakenly executed documents, agency, and partnership. The pattern of these chapters tended to be the same: a demonstration of confusion in the reasoning of the cases, coupled with an argument that estoppel would provide either a more comprehensible and coherent means of analysis of the results or different and better results.[26] Throughout, the principles were dominant. Ewart had faith that they could be the starting points for reasoning, and that all his conclusions were drawn from them and from nowhere else. Three topics are useful illustrations of this undertaking: documents of title, negotiable instruments, and agency.

The first, 'documents of title,' was not an established term. It was his own invention and, like much of his thinking, it was an effort to gather together subjects that had previously not seemed to be the same. It included transfers of goods, bills of lading, dock warrants, and transfers and certificates of shares.[27] These documents all had these characteristics: they dealt in one way or another with title to goods, they were ordinarily used as proof of ownership, and they were 'ambulatory.' This was another of Ewart's terms, which he defined as 'intended to be transferable free from equities,'[28] that is, free from any claims not apparent from the documents themselves. Given these common characteristics, the effect of the making and transfer of these documents should be governed by the general principles of estoppel: persons who sign or transfer such a document 'ought to be estopped, as against persons who change their position on the faith of it, from denying the truthfulness of its contents.'[29] He claimed that the courts had perceived this principle in the early nineteenth century, especially in *Lickbarrow v. Mason*, but had then lost sight of it and wandered into inconsistency and confusion. Attempts to approach the problems by attributing negotiability to the documents or considering them as symbols of the goods had led to some unfortunate decisions and had obscured the proper analysis. Legislation had modified much of this common law, and much of it was consistent with the principles of estoppel, but it was fragmentary and particular and had been given 'literal and narrow interpretation.'[30]

In his discussion of the second example, negotiable instruments, Ewart began by sweeping away much of the traditional discourse in a way that can be seen as either bold or imaginative or idiosyncratic and perverse. He challenged the traditional understanding that negotiability was a product of the law merchant and inconsistent with general common law principles: 'What then is this law merchant which opposes itself to the common law and dominates it? and whence does it come? As a matter of fact, and not merely of phrase, may we not even ask whether there is a law of financiers or a law of tailors?'[31]

The practices and needs of merchants had been the stuff from which this law had been made, but it had been made by judges, and it was part of the general law, and not outside it and inconsistent. The law about negotiability had been 'derived from the usages and customs of people; from whence also are derived the main part of the whole body of law ... Judge-made law (not merchant-made), with Lord Mansfield as chief builder, is what we have here.'[32] His next target was the concept of negotiable instruments itself. The traditional conception was that they had a set of distinctive characteristics, especially that a transferee could sue in his or her own name, and took free from defences of the maker and claims of prior holders. Ewart had no difficulty demonstrating that sometimes they did not have all these characteristics, and that other kinds of documents sometimes had one or the other.

Having disposed of the concept of negotiability, to his own satisfaction, at least, he did not challenge the results of the cases.[33] Instead, he sought to demonstrate that they could be understood better by using the principles of estoppel. His analysis was based on his distinction between 'ambulatory' and 'non-ambulatory' claims. If an ambulatory claim was transferred to a remote holder, the maker was estopped from asserting defences that could have been asserted against the person to whom it was originally given, and an intermediate holder was estopped from asserting claims about the way in which the claim had been acquired by the remote holder.

This analysis was not limited to claims that were traditionally 'negotiable instruments.' The distinction between ambulatory and non-ambulatory claims and the general principles of estoppel could and should apply to any kind of claim, and Ewart showed how they could govern claims such as bonds, scrip, and shares. Throughout, the crucial notion was the ambulatory claim, which was a package of consequences invoked by intention. Ewart did little to illuminate it, and in his analysis of the question as to what kinds of documents were ambulatory, he said only, '[C]ustom must always supply the answer ... The difficulty in this connection is one largely of fact.'[34]

Agency is the third of the examples of the application of the principles of estoppel. Here again the results suggested by the principles were generally the same as the results the courts had reached, and Ewart's primary purpose was to show that the principles were a better explanation than the existing doctrine, which was complex at best and often either inconsistent or incoherent. His explanation can be summarized in two propositions. First, principals were bound by acts of an agent that they had authorized. Second, principals were estopped from denying the authority of an agent if they represented its existence or extent, or assisted a representation by the agent, and the representation was relied on. The representation might be made expressly or, more likely in the difficult problems, by implication from contexts. The crucial element in the theory was the difference between 'being estopped' and 'being bound.' Ewart did not explain the nature of 'being bound,' but presumably it was a contractual liability that depended upon the will of the principal. The difference between the two may seem unimportant, but it later led Ewart into an important quarrel, which will be described later.

Ewart's undertaking in the second part of the book was ambitious and imperialistic. Estoppel was given a sweeping scope and introduced into unexpected contexts, all of which were encrusted with decades or centuries of assumptions and doctrine. His performance was impressive, and sometimes even brilliant. Hundreds of cases, from Canada, England, and the United States, were considered. Much of the analysis was convincing, and all of it was provocative. He had a remarkable ability to perceive both inconsistencies in the reasoning and patterns of similarity and difference, and also the power to order the perceptions into effective arguments. These are characteristic abilities of a lawyer, and doubtless one of the reasons why Ewart was a leading counsel.

The book was reviewed and debated in journals in England, the United States, and Canada, and it was highly praised in most of the reviews.[35] The praise was justified. The book was an ambitious synthesis of a neglected and tangled corner of doctrine. It was, though, far from being a landmark. It did not present any insights into the nature of law and legal reasoning, and the reasoning was occasionally inconsistent, oversimplified, or idiosyncratic. Much of the analysis of the cases was the result of powerful thought and did not depend upon or even illustrate the principles, and the monolithic devotion to estoppel, especially liability for representations, obscured competing interests and considerations, especially in complex commercial problems. Yet fate might have been kinder to Ewart. Both *Estoppel* and all the rest of his writing had no effect on common law doctrine and have rarely been used as references. The major reasons are probably the great respect the Canadian legal community gave to English texts as opposed to Canadian writing and the fate of estoppel itself, which has never emerged from the shadows of other bodies of doctrine.

The book was, though, among the best legal scholarship done in Canada between Confederation and the 1920s, and arguably the best. Most of the contemporary texts and writing in the journals consisted of exposition of doctrine that contained little or no imagination and synthesis. Many of the texts were standard English texts adapted by adding Canadian statutes and cases, and the discussions in the journals about doubtful issues were generally composed of narrow assertions supported by descriptions of individual cases. There are almost no attempts to speculate or to explore beyond the doctrine, and only a very few writers were as ambitious or as insightful as Ewart.[36]

Estoppel: The Quarrels

His writing about estoppel led Ewart into three debates that were, like the writing, interesting in themselves and useful illustrations of his thought and the thought of his generation.

The first of these debates began with a challenge from the editor of the *Canadian Law Times* aimed at an article entitled 'Deceit and Estoppel,' which appeared a few years before the book and was designed to be a preliminary version of a chapter.[37] In it, Ewart analysed the kinds of claims in which misrepresentations created civil liability, and especially the differences among them respecting a requirement of fraud. He claimed that the lack of 'harmony' was 'anomalous,' and also that the requirement of fraud in actions for damages was undesirable. The editor attacked him, not for his claim, which is the striking part of the article in retrospect, but for his definition of negligence, one of the kinds of claims. The attack was entirely justified, and Ewart corrected his analysis – without comment – in the book. The useful parts of the debate are not its substance but the premises about common law reasoning, which the two shared despite their difference about the doctrine. The editor said that 'jurisprudence ought to approach as nearly as possible to an exact science ... [A]ll agree in the desirability of defining as accurately as possible the various legal conceptions with which the science deals.'[38] Ewart of all lawyers could hardly protest. The editor also shared his faith in differentiation and evolutionary progress, although Ewart might have squirmed when he read this about his analysis: 'Such a doctrine savours of the infancy of metaphysics and jurisprudence, and is entirely out of harmony with the tendencies of that evolutionary process which, by the introduction of more and more minute differentiations, is constantly imparting increased clearness and definiteness to the fundamental conceptions of every science.'[39]

The other two debates were waged in the *Columbia Law Review*. First, Ewart's questions about the nature and existence of the law merchant were challenged by Francis Burdick, a professor at Michigan law school.[40] He mocked Ewart's questions and sought to demonstrate that the law merchant was indeed a body of law, setting out its history at great length. Ewart's replies were even more mocking, but they were not as clear as he seemed to believe. He quarrelled with Burdick's account of the historical facts and, more important, claimed that even on Burdick's own account the law merchant was not consistent and precise enough to be considered a separate body of law rather than a collection of ideas and practices that had influenced the making of the common law. This led him to question the existence of all sorts of .'laws' – the law of nature, the law of nations, and the common law itself. The display was based on an assumption about the meaning of 'law,' which he never stated clearly, but which seems to have been thoroughly positivist: law was no more than a body of rules or decisions sufficiently concrete and dense to determine outcomes of particular disputes: 'If you say the Common law was, or is, a true body of law, with an existence separate from the decisions ... I venture to disagree and to protest ... [W]as there "a true body of law in England known as the common law"; a body of law which not merely furnished enlightenment for the courts, but which, being a *true* body of law, was binding upon the courts?'[41]

Values shaped law, but they were not part of law. This thought may be fundamentally inconsistent with the basic undertaking in *Estoppel*, in which the duty of altruism seemed to be inherent in the doctrine, but Ewart wrote only a few paragraphs about these questions and seems not to have thought about them carefully. He continued his attack with a powerful comment on the influences that shaped judicial decisions:

> The courts have been examining lately some very modern developments in social relations, and adding 'Boycott' and 'Strikes' to the digests as additional headings. Now from what source are the judges getting the law upon these subjects? Is it out of that gaseous Common Law which if one may surmise has existed from all eternity (for no one has ever heard of its creation or other genesis)? ... [T]he idea of judges laboriously delving into nothing, nowhere, and pretending that they are unearthing primeval aphorisms, axioms and principles, placed there by omnipotence or by nature (by behemoths, just as likely) for use in these later stages – well, for one, I don't believe it ... [E]ach judge is consulting, not any body of law, 'true,' 'common,' or otherwise, but is declaring what to him with all his personal idiosyncracies, his dreads, his antipathies, his sympathies, his forecasts, his characteristics and mental climate – what to his particular brain, appears to be best.[42]

Most scholars agreed that judges made law, but they either ignored the problems about process and influences or described a process of making the law from distant and unproblematic sources.[43] Ewart often expressed a realization that judges made law, but this particular comment had a distinctive edge. It suggested a process that was personal and subjective.[44] This perception challenged the faith in an autonomous and objective process, and it anticipated the much more sustained and thorough challenges made later in the twentieth century. The perception is now commonplace (even though it is also contested), and it may seem crude, but it is only commonplace and crude because of developments in legal scholarship during the twentieth century. In Ewart's time it was unusual and radical, especially among English and Canadian lawyers. But, again, it seems inconsistent with the bulk of his thought, and it seems especially inconsistent with the faith he expressed in *Estoppel* in evolutionary progress, his apparently objective determination of the implications of altruism, and his reasoning from his principles.

The third debate was the most important. Walter Wheeler Cook, then a young professor at Yale and later one of the major realists, attacked Ewart's claim that estoppel was the explanation of the liability in agency, and especially the liability of a principal for a contract made by an agent without authority but within apparent authority. Cook claimed that the liability was instead 'a true contractual liability ... [T]he principal is bound because according to all sound principles he has entered into a contact with the third party.'[45] Ewart's response was based on the principles of estoppel and a denial that the principal and the third party had come to an agreement. Each one sought to demonstrate the consistency and the power of his reasoning from his basic principles, and each one sought to reveal inconsistencies in the other's reasoning. They each acknowledged some ultimate justification beyond consistency. For Ewart, altruism was the justification of liability for estoppel, even though he did not mention it in this debate, and Cook asserted that 'a man is bound by his manifested intention because it is only fair that he should be.' But neither one sought to show how his ultimate justification led to his position in the debate; and neither claimed that his reasoning would lead to better results.

Neither managed to make an entirely consistent or persuasive case, even within the terms of the debate. Cook's will theory of contract did not accommodate agency comfortably, because an agent's conduct might be entirely inconsistent with the will of the principal. Ewart was, as usual, confident and witty, but he was unable or unwilling to understand some fairly straightforward propositions about appearances and intention, and, more telling, he was unable to demonstrate persuasively how a person who did no more than make an agreement with an agent had 'changed his position prejudicially' (which was one of the requirements of his own principles).

This debate may seem to be arid and hopelessly unimportant. What difference could it make what explanation was used for a liability that both protagonists agreed existed and should exist? Ultimately it was a debate about justification of liability, and it reflected important changes in early-twentieth-century legal thought. In Cook's argument, the use of intention and agreement seemed to depend upon nineteenth-century conceptions of contract, especially liability based on will, but the exist-ence and content of the agreement were determined by appearances, especially the appearances created by the conduct of the agent. This dominance of appearances threatened to make will a ghost and to undermine the distinction between contract and tort. Ewart's denial that an agreement had been made only made this threat more apparent. Ewart's justification for the liability was reliance: the third party had relied on a representation made by the principal, and here too he anticipated the expansion of liability based on reliance in the twentieth century. The two protagonists shared more than they acknowledged, because for both the appearances created by the principal were crucial.

Waiver

Ewart's writing about estoppel ended in 1905 with the end of this quarrel with Cook, and in the same year he wrote his first article about waiver, which was the other topic to which he made a significant contribution.[46] Here his efforts were different in an amusing way: he had sought to create a coherent and unified structure for estoppel and to establish it as an important common law doctrine, but he sought to eliminate waiver entirely from the legal vocabulary. In the 1905 article he wrote about waiver in insurance cases, its most common and impor-tant context, and especially about the analysis of a term that made a policy void upon breach of a condition. According to Ewart the usual analysis was that breach caused a 'forfeiture' of the policy, and the insured could not recover without proving a waiver of the breach by the insurer. He claimed that this analysis was fundamentally wrong. The breach of the condition did not make the policy void but instead gave the insurer a power to terminate if it wished. Given this founda-tion, he argued that unless the insurer exercised this power, the policy remained enforceable, and election, not waiver, was the proper analy-sis. He claimed that this approach would be 'of great assistance to the courts in their struggles with some of the insurance companies.'[47] For example, it would require an insurer to demonstrate an election rather than relying on the argument that a waiver could not be inferred from its silence, and it would put the difficult burden of proof on the insurer. Again the reasoning was powerful and conceptual; consequences were deduced from fundamental propositions of doctrine. Ewart was pleased with the results of the change he proposed, but he did not explain why, or integrate this preference into the doctrinal analysis.

During the next decade he wrote three articles repeating this analysis,[48] and in 1917 he published his second text, *Waiver Distributed*.[49] Here he continued to claim that waiver was not an independent and significant concept and sought to demonstrate that wherever it was invoked in the cases to justify some result, it masked the operation of some other concept and contributed only confusion: 'All ... that is usually spoken of as "waiver" is, in the judgment of the author, referable to one or another of the well-defined and well-understood departments of the law, Election, Estoppel, Contract, Release.'[50]

The book was well received,[51] but it was not nearly as large an achievement as *Estoppel*. The addition of estoppel, contract, and release to election was essentially an elaboration of the basic insight, which had been amply demonstrated in the 1905 article. Ewart sought interminably to demonstrate confusion and inconsistency in the cases and texts, but the effort lacked the power and unity of his earlier work. The organization was careless, and some of the doctrinal analysis was incomplete, at best, especially the analysis about the requirement of consideration for contracts.

Ewart sent a copy of the book to Williston, the great American contracts scholar, and the two exchanged thirteen letters about waiver between August and October of 1917.[52] Williston began by saying that he was especially interested in waiver because he had 'a book of contracts ... on the stocks ... I ... distribute waiver. I do not, however, give it all away.' He posed a difficult problem of contract doctrine for Ewart: if one party to a contract promised not to require performance of a condition of the other's right to enforce the contract, and if the other relied on the promise, it was enforceable, but why? That is, to use Williston's example, if an insurance policy required proof of loss within sixty days, the insurer promised not to require the proofs to be made in that time, and the insured relied on this promise, it was enforceable, but why? Estoppel could not be used, because it governed only representations about facts and not promises, but the general principle of contract doctrine required consideration for enforcement of a promise. This question is at the beginnings of a story that is now familiar to all contract students: the emergence of promissory estoppel in the United States, and the doctrine that reliance on a promise is justification for enforcement, regardless of consideration.[53] Williston told Ewart that he proposed to use the concept of 'promissory estoppel' to justify enforcement of the promise, and that it was 'bound up' with waiver. He sent a draft of a few pages of the book, in which promissory estoppel was a species of waiver. In a later letter, he seemed to admit that this structure was designed to preserve the general principle of consideration: 'I do insist that there is a category which is now ... spoken of as waiver, which cannot be distributed in other recognized departments of the law without involving what you have truly stated to be objectionable a violation of general rules.'[54]

As the exchange progressed, Ewart often floundered. He seemed occasionally to fail to grasp Williston's basic problem, perhaps because he did not fully understand the doctrine of consideration, but he did make a protest about exceptions to general rules[55] that was a peculiarly appropriate challenge to Williston, who was a paragon of conceptual legal scholars, and he encouraged Williston to make a general proposal for enforcement of promises if they had been relied upon. 'Surely we are not bound to eternalize the anomalies and stupidities of the law.'[56] However, he seemed to fail to realize that this proposal was essentially a return to estoppel and an expansion of his own efforts to make reliance a ground of liability. This failure is ironic, and it demonstrates that his legal thinking became much less insightful after 1905. Williston replied, '[P]ersonally, I should not be dissatisfied with a general rule which regarded promises as binding if the promisee has reasonably relied on them,' but he undertook no more than to 'put more strongly than I have done' the argument for general enforceability.[57]

Williston's *Contracts*, one of the great treatises in Anglo-American legal literature, appeared in 1920,[58] and the analysis of promissory estoppel was substantially the same as it had been in the draft he had sent Ewart: waiver had eight divisions, including promissory estoppel. In 1927 Ewart challenged this analysis in the *Minnesota Law Review*[59] and made his argument that waiver had no 'peculiarly legal significance' and was not a 'legal concept.'[60] About promissory estoppel, he said, 'One's sense of scientific accuracy rebels against the statement that a promise by itself is not sufficient because there is no consideration; and that estoppel by itself is not sufficient because there is no misrepresentation of fact; but that in combination they are sufficient although both defects remain unremoved.'[61]

He proposed that agreement alone should be justification for modification of obligations, without consideration or estoppel, but did not explain what the agreement was, unless it was a simple promise, or why he limited enforceability only to promises that modified obligations. Williston wrote Ewart a gracious note, and their correspondence came to an end. In contrast to Williston's grace, some of Ewart's later letters in the exchange seem crabby, if not rude.[62]

The Patriot and the Privy Council

Ewart's 1904 Kingdom paper was a general plea for Canadian independence, and independence included abolition of appeals to the Privy Council. The result of appeals, he claimed, was that

> Canada is forced to develop according to the ideas of a body of men out of touch and sympathy with Canadian methods and motions, instead of being expanded according to the genius and the wishes of Canadians themselves ... Lacking local knowledge, and all those shades of feeling and points of view which life in Canada alone can give, the Privy Councillors are ... unable to appreciate some of the arguments which, to a Canadian, are full of significance and meaning.[63]

Most lawyers during the late nineteenth and early twentieth centuries defended the Privy Council, usually by invoking its prestige and objectivity, the needs for uniformity and bonds of Empire, and the duties of loyalty. Ewart was the most eloquent and fervent of the minority. He repeated his views several times, and most effectively in a series of articles in 1913, in which he discussed six recent cases in which the Privy Council had reversed the Supreme Court.[64] He claimed that the Privy Council had been paternalistic and careless, that parts of the reasoning were 'absurd,' and that all the results were 'flagrantly and indisputably wrong.' He claimed that the court had been 'unconsciously inclined to accept arguments which support the interests of British bondholders and shareholders, rather than those which appear to militate against them,' and he concluded,

> In Canada we have men capable of building and managing railways on colossal scales; men capable of conducting immense financial undertakings; men capable of directing educational institutions of the highest merit; men capable of originating and making successful vast business enterprises;

men capable as mechanics, inventors, dentists, doctors, statesmen. ARE THE LAWYERS THE ONLY IMBECILES?[65]

What Is the Best Form of Society?

Ewart published very little about the political and economic organization of society. His pleas for the Roman Catholics express ideals about individual civil liberties: the toleration of minorities, the sanctity of the individual conscience, and the distinction between the public and private worlds.[66] He expressed the same beliefs in a debate about Sunday legislation in 1902: church and state should be separated, religious belief and observance should be left to private choice, and the only justification for legislation restricting conduct on Sunday was the public good.[67] His unpublished writings, which are largely notes for speeches, from which the title to this section is taken, repeat these beliefs, but they also demonstrate a much wider range of thought and show that he was not the mid-nineteenth-century liberal that he might otherwise seem to be.[68]

One of the common issues in late-nineteenth-century political discourse was the justification for interference by the state in individual conduct. Ewart argued that interference was justified not only to protect others – a position he attributed to both Mill and Spencer – but both to remedy inequality among individuals and for the general welfare. Each individual was a part of the state and obligated to contribute to its welfare. The limits of the justifiable interference depended upon the preferences of each society, and could be determined only by experience.

More generally, Ewart condemned the exploitation and greed of capitalism and proclaimed a faith in progress from egoism, competition, and inequality towards altruism, co-operation, and equality – in short, towards a Christian socialism. To be altruistic was to 'do unto others.' His faith in progress was pervasive and strong, and evolution was a crucial element. Struggle and the survival of the strongest had run its course and would be replaced by an evolution in which development would be determined by the needs of 'the best form of society,' which was 'sympathetic co-operation.' The immediate sources for this vision seem to have been late-nineteenth-century English political thought, supplemented by Bellamy and the social gospel.[69]

The vision illuminates his analysis of estoppel. The obligation to live up to representations is an expression of altruism, and the common law is ultimately justified by moral principle. But the principle is not the expression of the subjective preferences of the judges. Instead it is objective, and, for Ewart, found in the nature of the best society and the progress of evolution.

Conclusion

Ewart shared the dominant understandings of his generation, especially a faith in the common law, and particularly a common law that was composed of ordered and consistent principles and was both objective and apolitical, and ethical. At the same time, some of his thought was inconsistent with these faiths and tended to undermine it in ways that would not be fully realized for decades, especially his demonstrations of the malleability of generalizations and his perception that the common law might be an expression of the tastes of the judges. Both his accomplishments as a legal scholar and his inconsistencies are the product of a powerful and insightful mind. He deserves to be better remembered.

NOTES

1 S. Cole, 'The Better Patriot: John S. Ewart and the Canadian Nation' (PhD thesis, University of Washington, 1968); J. Dafoe, 'The Views and Influence of John S. Ewart' (1933) 14 *Can. Hist. R.* 136; D. Farr, 'John S. Ewart,' in R.L. McDougall, ed., *Our Living Tradition: Second and Third Series* (Toronto: University of Toronto Press, 1959); R. Stubbs, 'John S. Ewart: A Great Canadian' (1962) 1 *Man. L.J.* 3; F. Underhill, 'The Political Ideas of John S. Ewart' *Can. Hist. Assn. Annual Report*, 1933, 23.
2 J.S. Ewart, *Ewart's Index of the Statutes* (Toronto: Rowsell and Hutchison, 1874); J.S. Ewart, *A Manual of Costs* (Toronto: Rowsell and Hutchison, 1881); and J.S. Ewart and T.W. Taylor, *The Judicature Act and Rules, 1881* (Toronto: Carswell, 1888).
3 J.S. Ewart, 'Of Chattel Mortgages Where the Term of Credit Exceeds a Year' (1881) 1 *Can. L.T.* 71, and 'Injunction and Negative Covenants' (1894) 14 *Can. L.T.* 177. Neither suggests any patterns of thought that are not in the writings about estoppel.
4 J.S. Ewart, 'Estoppel, and Principal and Agent' (1896) 16 *Can. L.T.* 205, 229, 260, 283; J.S. Ewart, 'Estoppel: Purchaser for Value without Notice' (1897) 17 *Can. L.T.* 282; J.S. Ewart, 'Priorities in Relation to Estoppel' (1897) 17

Can. L.T. 229; J.S. Ewart, 'Estoppel by Negligence' (1899) 15 L.Q.R. 383; and
J.S. Ewart, 'Negotiability and Estoppel' (1900) 16 L.Q.R. 135.

5 J.S. Ewart, An Exposition of the Principles of Estoppel by Misrepresentation
   (Toronto: Carswell, 1900) (hereafter Estoppel).

6 J.S. Ewart, 'The Kingdom of Canada' (1904) 3 Can. L.R. 481, 530.

7 W. Anson, Principles of the English Law of Contract and of Agency in Its
   Relation to Contract (London: Frowde, 1880).

8 A.V. Dicey, Introduction to the Study of the Law of the Constitution (London:
   Macmillan, 1885).

9 F. Pollock, The Law of Torts (London: Stevens, 1887).   ·

10 For an excellent study of this undertaking, see D. Sugarman, 'Legal
   Theory, the Common Law Mind, and the Making of the Textbook Tradi-
   tion,' in W. Twinning, ed., Legal Theory and Common Law (Oxford: Basil
   Blackwell, 1986) 26.

11 Estoppel, supra note 5 at 488. There is at least one usage that may not be
   adequately served by this description. In one of his early articles, Ewart,
   'Injunction and Negative Covenants,' supra note 3, he contrasted law as
   'grammar and phrasing' to 'the administration of justice on something like
   a scientific basis.' This passage may seem to promise something more than
   reasoning that is 'orderly, rigorous, and internally consistent,' but the
   argument in the article does not offer any distinctive justifications for its
   conclusions. If anything, the passage and the argument that follows
   suggest only that an element of conceptual reasoning may have been
   connoted by 'scientific.'

12 Estoppel, supra note 5 at 28–9.

13 See R.W. Gordon, 'Historicism in Legal Scholarship' (1981) 90 Yale L.J.
   1017, for a general description of this 'adaptive' strategy. Examples from
   the Canadian literature are W. Alward, 'Volenti non fit injuria' (1907) 41
   Can. L.J. 387; F. Hoyles, 'Implied Warranty of Authority' (1904) 40 Can. L.J.
   685; and F. Hoyles, 'Contracts in Restraint of Trade' (1907) 27 Can. L.T. 672.

14 See J.W. Salmond, 'The Theory of Judicial Precedents' (1900) 16 L.Q.R. 376
   for a statement of the prevailing doctrine.

15 This passage is quoted in Estoppel, supra note 5 at 30.

16 See, for example, Pollock, supra note 8 at 17–34.

17 For example: 'Lack of sufficient classification has produced the impression
   that for estoppel the misrepresentation complained of must have been that
   of the estoppel-denier himself. It is overlooked that much more frequently
   estoppel arises because of the misrepresentation of some third person,
   which has been assisted (usually unwittingly) by the estoppel denier; and
   when cases of that sort do occur, other principles than those of estoppel

are applied to them.' ... 'But hitherto the existence of the class itself has not been sufficiently recognized, nor has it till now received a distinguishing name; and it is therefore not matter for much surprise that that of which we are in search has not been with precision disentangled, nor its true affinities observed.' *Estoppel*, supra note 5 at 178–9, 102.

18 (1787) 2 T.R. 70, 100 E.R. 35.

19 Ibid. at E.R. 39.

20 The link between *Lickbarrow v. Mason* and estoppel had been anticipated by another Canadian, A.H. Marsh, but he did not elaborate the insight. See 'Equitable Estoppel' (1883) 3 *Can. L.T.* 223 at 225.

21 The principle in *Lickbarrow v. Mason* is a good example of the ambiguity and shifts of meaning of the word 'principle.' The proposition cannot be doctrine in the sense of a rule, because it is too vague and open-ended to determine the outcomes of cases.

22 At the outset, Ewart carefully separated negligence as a cause of action and carelessness as a form of conduct, and asserted, sensibly, that carelessness was the appropriate concept in this inquiry.

23 *Estoppel*, supra note 5 at 101.

24 Ibid. at 435.

25 To anticipate a bit, this 'anticipation' may be a product of the past, particularly a distinctive emphasis on community and responsibility.

26 For example, respecting documents mistakenly signed, he said, 'A study of the authorities of this class reveals the greatest confusion; principally, it is thought, because of the almost entire absence from them of conscious reference to the principles of the law of estoppel. Various other principles and various distinctions have been attempted, but without satisfactory result, or with this result only, that they may when closely examined be found to be, in one way or another, unconscious illustrations or adaptations of the principles of estoppel.' *Estoppel*, supra note 5 at 427.

27 Ewart would also have included documents about title to land, such as conveyances, but traditional ways of thinking and authority were too well established.

28 *Estoppel*, supra note 5 at 385.

29 Ibid. at 313. But again, principles had to struggle against confusion and inadequate perceptions: 'And probably apart from profound learning upon the subject, this estoppel view of the matter would evoke little opposition. But the accumulation of precedents involving other principles, the diversity and antagonism of those precedents and principles when applied to different sorts of documents of title, and the existence of statutes which proceed upon no principle at all, render the establishment

of our suggested method of treatment impossible, or nearly so.' Ibid. at 307.

30 Ibid. at 336.
31 Ibid. at 373.
32 Ibid. at 374, 375.
33 At one point, though, Ewart claimed that the doctrine had gone astray. If a claim was overdue when it was transferred, the holder was subject to both the defences of the maker and the claims of intermediate holders. Ewart argued that allowing the defences of the holder was justified, because the maker might have refused payment because of some defences (and therefore, presumably, a representation of regularity did not exist). But the claims of the holder should not be permitted, because the failure to pay was irrelevant to any representation that possession entailed.
34 Ibid. at 75.
35 Book Review (1900) 36 *Can. L.J.* 727: 'Mr Ewart has laid down a scientific and certainly an entirely new arrangement of the doctrine treated of. His treatment of it shows much originality of thought, a clever handling of a very difficult subject, as well as careful research.'
   Book Review (1900) 20 *Can. L.T.* 374: 'This is the most noticeable Canadian law book that has been published for a long time.'
   Book Review (1900) 48 *American L. Register* 746: 'To take a principle of limited application and by patient research and scholarly speculation to widen it into a general and far-reaching theory is to achieve a distinct professional triumph … his axe has fallen in a virgin forest, and when we remember that he must have hewed his way forward, with no blazed path to guide him, his performance seems admirable. The theory he champions may be too inclusive; but that is a fault of all experimental plans, and doubtless it will be moderated in time.'
   Book Review (1901) 17 *L.Q.R.* 98: 'It is a long time since we have met with a legal work at once so original and so convincing as that now before us. Mr Ewart propounds some startling new theories of the foundation of legal liability and supports them with such acute and close reasoning and so much learning that he carries us along with him in spite of our prejudices in favour of the doctrines and authorities on which we have been brought up … The book is well worthy of careful study by all persons interested in the scientific development of law.' (This review is unsigned, and it might have been written by Pollock, who was the editor of the *Law Quarterly Review* at the time.)
   Book Review (1901) 10 *Yale L.J.* 69: 'The treatment of the subject is bold and original; in fact more in conformance with modern scientific thought

than that of most law books. This gives it a peculiar value to the student, while the great number of cases made accessible make it valuable for the practitioner.'

A couple of the reviews gave more qualified praise. Book Review (1901) 1 *Colorado L.R.* 502: 'This is an original and suggestive book. It displays a careful study of leading cases, an unusual ability to analyse decisions, to criticize authorities and to announce broad generalizations. That the author's conclusions are as trustworthy as they are daring is open to question. His own confidence, however, in their absolute accuracy is unbounded.'

Book Review (1901) 14 *Harvard L.R.* 310: '[A] commendable attempt at a thorough treatment of the subject ... [in the discussion of applications of estoppel] it would seem that the author gives to estoppel far too great a scope. Instead of treating it as a doctrine to be resorted to only when the desired result can be attained on no other theory, he makes use of it in every possible case.'

36 Examples that from their nature are likely to represent the prevailing modes of reasoning are J.E. McDougall, *Lectures on Torts and Negligence* (Toronto: J.P. Mabee, 1882) (a lecture given to students at Osgoode Hall; there are a handful of other lectures in the *Canadian Law Times* in the 1890s), and J. Power, 'Actio personalis cum persona moritur' (1899) 19 *Can. L.T.* 129, 166, 201, 215 (a doctoral thesis). One exception to this generalization is A.H.F. Lefroy, who was a professor of Roman and Constitutional Law at the University of Toronto. He is known now, if at all, for texts on constitutional law, but he also wrote two remarkable articles about the common law in the *Law Quarterly Review*: 'Judge-Made Law' (1904) 20 *L.Q.R.* 399, and 'The Basis of Case Law' (1906) 22 *L.Q.R.* 293, 416. These are among the best writings in England about the law-making function of judges. See also Lefroy, 'Jurisprudence' (1911) 27 *L.Q.R.* 18.

Editors' note: For Lefroy's work on common law reasoning, see R.C.B. Risk, 'A.H.F. Lefroy,' in this volume.

37 'Deceit and Estoppel' (1897) 17 *Can. L.T.* 229.

38 'Misrepresentation as Negligence' (1897) 33 *Can. L.J.* 708 at 709.

39 'Will an Action of Negligence Lie for Deceit?' (1898) *Can. L.J.* 59 at 64.

40 F. Burdick, 'What Is the Law Merchant?' (1902) 2 *Colorado L.R.* 470; J.S. Ewart, 'What Is the Law Merchant?' (1903) 3 *Colorado L.R.* 135; and J.S. Ewart, 'What Is the Common Law?' (1904) 4 *Colorado L.R.* 117. Ewart's second article was a response to Burdick's comment, appended by the editors to the first: 'I have laughed heartily at its sallies of wit, and been dazzled, if not enlightened, by its rhetorical pyrotechnics, but I do not see that it calls for a serious reply.'

41 Ewart, 'Common Law,' supra note 40 at 118 (emphasis in original).

42 Ibid. at 120, 124, 125.

43 This process can be and was perceived as discovering, but this word should not be understood to imply that the law grew on trees to be harvested by judges. This inference was made by twentieth-century scholars, who had little sympathy for the generation that preceded them.

44 Note, for example, the repetition of 'his.' Ewart was too good a writer for this to be an accident.

45 W.W. Cook, 'Agency by Estoppel' (1905) 5 *Colorado L.R.* 3. Ewart replied in 'Agency by Estoppel' (1905) 5 *Colorado L.R.* 354, and Cook continued in 'Agency by Estoppel' (1906) 6 *Colorado L.R.* 34. Ewart's analysis was also challenged in a short note, (1901) 15 *Harvard L.R.* 324, and he replied in 'Estoppel: Principal and Agent' (1903) 16 *Harvard L.R. 186.*

46 *Ewart, 'Waiver in Insurance Cases' (1905) 18 Harvard L.R.* 364.

47 Ibid. at 372.

48 J.S. Ewart, 'Election in Insurance Cases' (1912) 12 *Colorado L.R.* 619; J.S. Ewart, 'Waiver or Election' (1916) 29 *Harvard L.R.* 724; and J.S. Ewart, 'Waiver' (1917) 53 *Can. L.J.* 206.

49 *Waiver Distributed among the Departments Election, Estoppel, Contract, Release* (Cambridge, MA: Harvard University Press, 1917). Roscoe Pound contributed an introduction.

50 Ibid. at 5.

51 See Book Review (1917) 66 *U. of Pennsylvania L.R.* 183; Book Review (1918) 54 *Can. L.J.* 75; Book Review (1918) 38 *Can. L.T.* 60; and Book Review (1918) 32 *Harvard L.R.* 499.

52 These letters are in the Ewart papers in the Manitoba Archives.

53 The simplest source is G. Gilmore, *The Death of Contract* (Columbus: Ohio State University Press, 1974) at 55–85. Earlier discussions of promissory estoppel and reliance are P. Boyer, 'Promissory Estoppel: Requirements and Limitations of the Doctrine' (1950) 98 *U. of Pennsylvania L.R.* 459; and 'Promissory Estoppel: Principle from Precedents' (1952) 50 *Michigan L.R.* 639, 873; and R. Shattuck, 'Gratuitous Promises: A New Writ?' (1937) 35 *Michigan L.R.* 908. A good general discussion is A. Feinman, 'Promissory Estoppel and Judicial Method' (1984) 97 *Harvard L.R.* 678.

54 24 September 1917.

55 'To me, a general rule of which there are violations or to which there are exceptions, is a bad rule – or rather no rule at all. Its formulation indicates undeveloped thought. Closer investigation and keener analysis will supply something better.' 12 September 1917.

56 1 October 1917.

57 24 September 1917 and 3 October 1917.

58 S. Williston, *A Treatise on the Law of Contracts* (New York: Lawyers' Cooperative Publishing, 1920)

59 J.S. Ewart, 'Professor Williston's Review of Waiver' (1927) 11 *Minnesota L.R.* 415.

60 Ibid. at 415.

61 Ibid. at 420.

62 Ewart proposed publishing the exchange in the *Harvard Law Review,* a prospect that probably dismayed Williston, who politely declined. Ewart wrote one more article about waiver, but it added nothing. J.S. Ewart, 'Waiver in Insurance Law' (1928) 6 *Can. Bar R.* 257.

63 'The Kingdom of Canada,' supra note 6 at 542, 544.

64 J.S. Ewart, 'The Judicial Committee' (1913) 33 *Can L.T.* 396, 475, 479, 577, 669, 673. See also J.S. Ewart, 'The Canadian Constitution' (1908) 8 *Colorado L.R.* 27; J.S. Ewart, 'The King v. The Royal Bank' (1913) 33 *Can. L.T.* 269; J.S. Ewart, 'The Judicial Committee' (1914) 34 *Can. L.T.* 163; and J.S. Ewart, 'Rex v. The Royal Bank' (1914) 50 *Can. L.J.* 561.

65 Ewart, 'The Judicial Committee,' supra note 64 at 678.

66 His role and writing in the Manitoba schools question are described in S. Shaw, 'The Role of John S. Ewart in the Manitoba School Question' (MA thesis, University of Manitoba, 1959).

67 Ewart gave three lectures, on 26 October and 9 and 23 November 1902, which were published as pamphlets entitled *The Sunday Question.*

68 These notes are in the Ewart papers at the Manitoba Archives. The two most interesting are a review of W. Tiedman, *State and Federal Control of Persons and Property*, and notes for a speech given several times in 1898 entitled 'Spencer, Mill, Bellamy, and George.'

69 The description of the English thought in S. Collini, *Liberalism and Sociology: L.T. Hobhouse and Political Argument in England, 1880–1914* (Cambridge: Cambridge University Press, 1979), is especially useful.

6

Sir William R. Meredith, CJO:
The Search for Authority

Introduction

This paper is a study of the judicial mind of Sir William R. Meredith, especially his beliefs about the common law and statutes. I offer it as a tribute to John Willis, with respect for his humane and restless mind, and with gratitude for all that he taught me. I am especially grateful for so many long talks on Sundays, when I had just begun to teach and he had been acknowledged for decades to be a great teacher, and we were both worried about Monday's classes. I discovered only slowly how much I learned listening to him struggling to rethink grand questions about law, and how much his students learned on Mondays from his struggle. I don't think Meredith struggled much with grand questions, but I do think he was a humane man, and perhaps in this way he is an appropriate subject for my tribute.

The major stages in Meredith's career were typical of the careers of many Canadian judges, and only these stages need to be described for the purposes of this paper. He was born in London in 1840, and became a lawyer, a prominent counsel, and a Bencher of the Law Society of Upper Canada. He entered politics as a Conservative, and was elected to the provincial legislature in 1872. In 1878, he became leader of the party, but the reign of Oliver Mowat doomed him to remain in opposition. He left politics in 1894, and was appointed chief justice of the Court of Common Pleas. He became a member of the Court of Appeal and the chief justice of Ontario in 1913, and died in 1921. His public service included more than his work as a politician and judge: in 1906 he was an important member of a commission that proposed a reorganization of the University of Toronto, and in 1914 he proposed the system of workers' compensation that replaced the common law, a system that today remains substantially as he designed it.[1]

The Judgments

This study of Meredith's mind is based on all of his judgments that are reported in the *Ontario Reports* and the *Ontario Law Reports*, which were the two major series of reports. There are about 750 of these judgments, and they are most of his important judgments.[2] They cover a wide range of topics and doctrine, which can best be described by showing how the first 315 cases are distributed within two different kinds of classifications: the traditional categories of doctrine and the distinction between the common law and statutes.

Considering doctrine, the largest group, by far, consisted of 68 cases about civil procedure. The next two largest groups were cases about municipal law; for example, about the validity of bylaws or elections, and cases about criminal law and procedure, including offences under the liquor legislation. These two groups consisted of 22 cases each. In the traditional areas of private law, there were 15 cases about contracts; 32 about torts, including 6 about employers' liability; and 30 about property, including 8 about landlord and tenant law, 8 about mortgages, and 5 about the sale of land. Closely related to the property cases were 13 about the administration of estates, 19 about the interpretation of wills, and 11 about statutes of limitations, most of which were about land. The last set of cases was composed of three groups: 14 about commercial law, for example, about commercial paper and conditional sales; 22 about debtors and creditors, for example, quarrels among creditors about fraudulent preferences; and 9 about mechanics' liens. These last three groups overlap even more than the others because disputes about the validity of chattel mortgages or conditional sales were usually disputes among creditors, and mechanics' lien problems were a specialized form of these disputes. Beyond these groups, there were a few groups that were more diverse and a wide scattering of adds and ends. In particular, there were seven about insurance, four about corporations, and three about domestic conflicts. These proportions remained essentially the same after 1905, except for the appearance of cases about the emerging administrative agencies, especially the Ontario Railway and Municipal Board, and about constitutional issues, especially the separate schools in Ottawa.

These figures regarding the categories of doctrine might have been expected. However, the figures about the distinction between common law and statutes are surprising, at least to me. Few of the cases involved common law reasoning alone, and, conversely, many were dominated by statutes. Making a distinction between them is difficult, because many of the cases involved statutes that had already been considered by courts. Some of these statutes were thoroughly encrusted with authority, and deciding these cases was, to some varying degree, essentially thinking about this authority, rather than about the statute itself. The most useful figures are about extremes. Among the first 315 cases, less than 75 involved interpretations of statutes essentially unlimited by any judicial authority. However, Meredith's work was still far from the work of courts in the modern regulatory state. Apart from the *Criminal Code* and the legislation about municipalities, most of the statutes were about disputes among individuals, for example, the *Landlord and Tenant Act*, the *Bills of Sale and Chattel Mortgages Act*, and the *Limitations Act*.

The kinds of problems presented by these cases were more diverse than these classifications might suggest. Both the facts and the doctrinal issues tended to differ greatly among themselves and to appear in jumbled orders. Reading them is a chastening experience for anyone accustomed to the narrow range and careful order of case books or specialized practices. Even among the cases in a single area of doctrine, few patterns appeared. Two exceptions were the cases about the interpretation of wills and, more importantly, challenges to the actions of municipalities, especially the effect of breaches of statutory requirements. But apart from these exceptions, Meredith had little opportunity to develop expertise and to elaborate doctrine over a series of cases.

Despite the diversity in the doctrine among these cases, their facts represented only a small part of the complex and changing society that produced them. For example, there were no cases about the timber industry, except for a couple about the use of the rivers for log drives, and there were only a couple about mining. There were none about large corporations or about the development of national commercial transactions. Nor was there any sense of the economic, social, and political changes that were making Canada 'a nation transformed.'[3] In contrast, in the middle of the nineteenth century, important roles and transactions in the economy, and doctrinal issues about them, appeared much more often in the cases.[4]

This absence of representative and important transactions and conflicts from the cases he decided is paralleled by impressions of the importance of the judgments. Meredith himself gave no hint of any belief that his work had any public importance. He did not profess or even hope to be making rules for the conduct of a society or to be responsible in any way for the legal order itself. Of course, an appearance of this kind may be a mask, but my impression is that it was not. Surprisingly few of the cases, taken alone or together, seem to me to have been of great and continuing public importance. Only a very few contained any coherent statement of values or made a significant contribution to the content of the law or its processes.

Meredith made virtually no general comments about law, his functions as a judge, or the common law and statutes. His judgments consisted of the facts, the doctrine he thought was relevant, and, occasionally, a few lines of comment about the doctrine or the parties, but no more. He wrote a handful of occasional speeches and reports, but both these and his speeches in the legislature were limited to the merits of specific issues. However, despite their particularity, his judgments suggest intelligible and consistent patterns of belief about his functions, the nature of the common law, and how to think about both the common law and statutes.

His implicit understanding of his proper function as judge was that he was simply to find the facts (or, on appeal, to consider whether evidence was adequate to support findings of fact), and to find and apply the appropriate law. If asked, he probably would have been satisfied with this description and would have been unable to say much more. The description may seem appropriate for most judges at most times, and if it is especially appropriate for Meredith, it is so more because of what it does not include than because of what it does. The process of finding facts was an important part of this function and was probably the most important part for most litigants, but it is not included in the scope of this study. The process of finding and applying the law can be described by making a distinction between the common law and legislation.

The Common Law

The process of finding and applying the common law was essentially a search – a search for authority – and the nature of this search is crucial to Meredith's thinking. The dominant and most apparent element of this search was that the typical authority he searched for was a single case. Throughout his judgments, he determined questions of law by invoking single cases, or groups of cases that were considered individually, as though they were substantially independent of each other. This process reflected the prevailing rules about precedent and the authority of single cases; if a court was obliged to decide an issue of law, a single decision by another court from the same or a higher level in the judicial hierarchy was a sufficient and compelling authority, unless it was inconsistent with a case from a higher court or a settled pattern of authority, even though the court believed it was unjust and wrongly decided.[5] Meredith often expressly acknowledged these rules, and made such comments as these: '[W]hatever doubt there may be as to whether, if the point there decided were now open for determination, the same conclusion would be reached ... I am bound to accept that decision,'[6] and, 'I must, however, no matter how strong my own opinion on this point may be, bow to the authority of any decided case in which the contrary view has been adjudged to be the correct one.'[7] This doctrine of strict precedent had emerged primarily during the nineteenth century,[8] and was settled for Meredith beyond any doubt and beyond any realization that there might be some alternative.

The concept of the ratio of a case was an important element of these rules, because formally the ratio was the only governing authority. Meredith never expressed any general thoughts about this concept and how the ratio was to be determined, and he only rarely undertook any careful and sustained analysis of the facts and reasons of cases for the purpose of deciding whether one should be an authority for another. He simply asserted that particular cases did or did not govern an issue, and occasionally supplemented these assertions with vague references to the principle of the precedents.[9]

The role of single cases in Meredith's reasoning was not only conformity to the rules about precedent. It was part of his working assumptions about the substance and process of the common law. Whatever he might have said if he had given a speech, in his work he seemed to assume that the common law was composed essentially of single cases, and that its substance and working reality was the content of these cases and the principles derived from and tested by them. He must have realized, of course, that principles had been made for centuries by English courts and text writers, and his entire legal world had been shaped by Blackstone. But when he decided individual cases, these principles were essentially a set of rules for deciding the easy issues and, more important, a map for determining and locating the harder issues and for assembling and considering possible precedents.

The process of determining the law in the difficult cases – the search for authority – was not essentially reasoning from these principles and sub-principles or making implications from cases. Instead, it was rummaging in a jumbled cupboard full of cases to find one that looked like the issue to be decided. For some issues, the map of principles led him quickly to one that seemed to be adequate. For others, it did not, and for these the search consisted of describing the possible authorities as though he were taking them out of the cupboard in the order in which he found them and holding them up to the light to see if they might fit. This process took several slightly different forms. Sometimes he seemed simply to be groping for authority; sometimes he seemed to be determining whether an idea or possibility could be justified; and sometimes he seemed to be determining whether a case or dictum was consistent with other cases. An example of rummaging in the cupboard is *Morris v. Cairncross*.[10] The major issue was whether a tenant for years was liable for permissive waste. Meredith described all the English cases he could find, and concluded that they were inconsistent. The result was determined by the weight of numbers, and he undertook no analysis of the cases beyond description and considered no standards for making the decision beyond counting.

He did not believe that the contents of the cupboard of common law were ordered in any rational way or were internally consistent. If the cases he found were inconsistent and if none of them seemed binding according to the hierarchy of authority, his job was to attempt to determine the 'weight of authority' – a phrase he often used – and the weight was typically determined by numbers. The cases were made into piles, and the largest pile prevailed. More generally, he did not believe expressly or implicitly that the common law was a science – in any of the meanings that lawyers and scientists have ascribed to this word.

He seemed generally to believe that this common law and the process of finding and applying it were apolitical and neutral, even though some other beliefs and practices were ultimately inconsistent. Again, whatever he might have said in a speech, the legitimacy or justification of the common law was the authority of the hierarchy of courts, and not, for example, its age, some higher law, or its utility. The law simply existed in the cupboard, to be found and applied, and the reasons for its existence and its content were irrelevant. He often claimed that he was 'bound', 'compelled', 'obligated,' or 'required' to reach the results he did.

The cupboard of cases held much more than the cases that were binding on him according to the rules about precedent and the hierar-chy of courts. He often followed English cases that were not binding on him; for example, decisions of trial courts.[11] He used decisions from other provinces only rarely, but, in contrast, he used American cases often. During his first 20 years, he discussed American cases in about 20 per cent of his judgments. This figure is probably high compared to the figures for Canadian judges in different periods, but it alone does not demonstrate the extent of his respect, because courts often discuss cases perfunctorily, and distinguish or reject them. My impression is that Meredith respected and relied on these cases extensively, and did so more than the judges in the mid-nineteenth century or judges today. Most often, he used them as a support or adornment for a conclusion that he reached independently, usually because the conclusion seemed to him to be governed by English or Canadian authorities. At the other extreme, he occasionally used them as illustrations of possible reason-ings and results that he did not use because he felt bound by authority.

More importantly, he sometimes used them to decide issues for which he could find no authority. For example, in *Wilson Lumber v. Simpson*,[12] the issue was the meaning of the phrase 'more or less' in a description of land. Meredith said, 'I was not referred to nor have I found any reported English or Canadian case ... There are, however, American cases in which the question has been considered and de-cided.' He described them, and announced his conclusion by saying simply, 'I entirely agree.'[13] He did not use these cases for their ideas or reasonings, which were simple and obvious. Usually he merely de-scribed them without exploring their reasoning. My impression is that he used them primarily for their results. Knowing that someone else had reached a conclusion made it more appealing, and the appeal was enhanced by the judicial form – the form of the authority that he could not find from England or Canada.

The contents of the cupboard and the doctrine of strict precedent did not control the outcome of all the cases (if precedents can ever control any outcomes). Meredith clearly believed that cases could be and were binding, but he did not believe the common law was comprehensive, and that he would find an authority in the cupboard for every issue. He also seemed to realize, without any acknowledgment, that the applica-tion of general doctrine often required discretion. Most of the choices he made were unexplained and masked by assertions; for example, assertions about the principles to be applied or the results of their application, the authority of individual cases, the intention of parties to agreements, or the proximate causes of events.[14] However, he did occasionally acknowledge the need to make choices, and the usual form of acknowledgments reflected his assumptions about the common law: he was unable to find an authority – the cupboard was bare.

It is difficult to determine the attitudes he expressed in the results of the choices because so many of them were masked and because the cases were so widely dispersed. However, there were some tendencies. In disputes about commercial transactions, especially contracts, he attempted to protect reasonable expectations and to make exchanges fair between the parties.[15] In torts claims, he tended to avoid imposing liability on landowners,[16] but he tended to favour plaintiffs in claims against insurers and large utilities – for example, railways and street railways – and to favour workers in claims against employers for injuries suffered at work.[17]

More important for the purposes of this paper is the way he made and expressed his choices. Those that were not masked were usually simply announced with little or no attempt to justify them, although he occasionally made a vague appeal to 'the reason of the thing,' a phrase he used often, or 'fairness.' He rarely described or analysed social needs and interests or the merits of possible results by any standard beyond authority, and he usually put any discussion of this kind that he did undertake at the end of his judgments, after a conclusion had been announced, ostensibly on the basis of authority.[18] Ultimately, Meredith's beliefs about the common law were incoherent. The cupboard contained only the apolitical law, but it was not complete. His process of reasoning could not integrate its contents with the world outside, and his choices could not have any claim to legitimacy that the contents of the cupboard itself did not have.

For most of his choices, an unarticulated conventional morality gave results that seemed fair and acceptable, at least to Meredith and those who shared his general attitudes. The lack of analysis was most apparent in complex commercial cases. For example, in *Re Mitchell and Union Bank of Canada*,[19] he decided that a 'lien-note' was negotiable, simply by asserting, without any discussion of the complex commercial considerations at stake, that provisions for acceleration of payment did not make the obligation conditional. Another example is *Meredith v. Peer*,[20] which involved the difficult problem of the liability of the owner of a house for damage to a neighbour's house caused by ice sliding from the roof. Meredith said that he had been 'unable to find any reported English or Canadian case,' and described some American cases, which were conflicting, and some Ontario cases about comparable problems. Then he simply announced that 'after giving the question for decision my best consideration, my conclusion is ... that negligence, and not strict liability, should be the basis of liability.' Neither the doctrinal difficulties of the tangle of negligence, nuisance, and property, nor the policies that might inform the choice were discussed.

Meredith was aware, and openly acknowledged, that common law doctrine had changed and that it continued to change, but he demonstrated no responsibility for making change himself, not even when he was a member of the Court of Appeal. The changes had been made by the English courts or the Supreme Court, or in some other more heroic age. Few, if any, of his cases suggest that he made any significant efforts to change the law silently, by distinguishing and rearranging cases. Several times he stopped short when the authorities seemed to permit working towards changes that came later, although in each case he probably did not have a strong conviction that the change was desirable. For example, he was unwilling to expand recovery of damages for nervous shock,[21] or the liability of landowners to child trespassers.[22] Even apart from change, he demonstrated no responsibility to declare or synthesize doctrine for the sake of simplicity and certainty.

These attitudes about his functions were significantly different from the attitudes of the judges in Ontario half a century before, who revealed more of their attitudes (although they were far from being entirely open), and who felt an obligation to consider the distinctive Canadian conditions and to settle and declare doctrine. Two cases about instalment agreements make a remarkable contrast. The first is *O'Keefe v. Taylor*,[23] decided by Chancellor Blake in 1851. A purchaser agreed to buy one hundred acres of uncleared land under an agreement that provided for a deposit, possession, and three annual instalments. The purchaser paid the deposit, took possession, and cleared the land, but made no payments. The vendor agreed to sell the land to another purchaser (who had notice) without making a demand for payment. The purchaser brought an action for specific performance, and succeeded. The doctrine seemed to Blake to be confused by some recent cases, but the dominant pattern was that a failure to pay on time was a default, but not necessarily a substantial default, which would deprive the purchaser of an equitable remedy. Time was not of the essence unless the agreement provided that it was, and this agreement did not. After the default, the purchaser had a reasonable time to pay, and without a demand from the vendor, a reasonable time could be a long time indeed. Blake discussed this doctrine and also made some general comments that were clearly a crucial part of his reasoning. He posed the 'great magnitude and importance' of the issue and the need to consider the distinctive Canadian conditions to achieve 'justice in particular cases' and the 'general welfare,' which was settlement and progress. 'We are about to define the position of multitudes by whom a country is being peopled – by whose enterprise and labour the wastes of this vast province are rendered subservient to the purposes of civilization with unexampled rapidity.' Blake's determination to consider Canadian conditions was distinctive, but the other judges in the mid-nineteenth century often shared much of the belief in a need to settle and declare the law, and to encourage economic activity.

Fifty-seven years later, Meredith decided *Labelle v. O'Connor*.[24] Here the agreement provided that 'time is to be considered the essence ... and unless the payments are punctually made [the vendors] are to be at liberty to resell.' The purchaser took possession and failed to pay the second instalment. He asked the vendors for an extension, and did not receive a reply. Two months passed, and the purchaser offered to pay the entire balance. Two more months passed without a reply, and then the vendors announced that the agreement was at an end and that they would keep both the land and the payments. The purchaser brought an action for specific performance and failed, but Meredith dissented. He described English cases without significant analysis, and said, 'I am of opinion that the parties did not intend that the mere failure of the respondent to pay an instalment on the day fixed for payment ... should cause the loss of his rights under the agreement.' The only explanation of this interpretation was the association in the agreement of the provision that time was of the essence and the power to resell that was given to the vendor. This explanation could only demonstrate that the interpretation was possible, but it was strained and other interpretations were possible. The assertion about intention masked a choice. Meredith gave no reasons for his choice but it suggests a preference for fairness between the parties. The vendors delay suggested that time was not important to them and a windfall would be avoided.

The contrasts to *O'Keefe v. Taylor* are illuminating. Meredith's judgment lacks the openness, the attempt to justify the result by reasoning that went beyond doctrine, and the consideration of Canadian conditions, the economic context, and the general public interest. Of course, conditions had changed and the rights of purchasers under instalment agreements were not as important to the economy in 1908 as they were in 1851, but Meredith only very rarely considered distinctive Canadian needs or economic function.[25]

Meredith's reluctance to take responsibility for the common law doctrine was not a product of contentment with the law as it stood or a general unwillingness to accept change. He often expressed disapproval of doctrine at the same time that he said he was bound by it,[26] and any simple assertion that he did not believe what he said – or that the accumulation of authority does not affect results trivializes the powerful effect of lawyers' beliefs and habits. More importantly, as a participant in the legislative process, he was willing to propose changes without any suggestions that the mere existence of the common law imposed any restraint. For example, his judgments about employers' liability to workers for injuries suffered at work contain virtually no general comments about the doctrine, but during the hearings of his commission about workers' compensation he condemned the common law as 'entirely inadequate' and 'unfair and unequitable?'[27] Nor did he demonstrate any hostility towards changes in the world outside the law when he was applying general standards. He did not, for example, demonstrate any reluctance to accept the automobile in determining tort liability.[28]

The Statutes

The kinds of statutes he worked with varied greatly. The two he considered most often, by far, were the *Municipal Act*, which presented a wide range of about 100 problems, and the *Railway Act*, which was involved in about 75 cases regarding, for example, expropriations and accidents. There were three other significant groups of statutes, each of which was considered in about 30 cases. The first group was composed of statutes about property, which included the *Landlord and Tenant Act*, the *Mechanics' Lien Act*, and the *Limitations Act*; the second was composed of statutes about criminal law, including the *Criminal Code* and the legislation about prohibition; and the third was composed of statutes about commercial transactions, including the *Bills of Sale and Chattel Mortgages Act*, the *Bills of Exchange Act*, and the *Conditional Sales Act*. The *Workmen's Compensation Act* was considered in about 15 cases and the *Corporations Act* in about 10. Cases involving the powers of administrative agencies appeared only late in his tenure, and almost all of them were appeals from the Ontario Railway and Municipal Board.

Meredith assumed that his ultimate obligation was to be faithful to the legislation, and this obligation usually included more than a formal acknowledgement of legislative supremacy. It was usually an unexpressed understanding of an institutional relationship that required from him respect and a willingness to elaborate and implement the purpose of legislation. This obligation and its performance were often masked behind an assertion that the results he reached were intended by the legislature, even where the issues, let alone the results, could not imaginably have been contemplated by its members.[29] This assertion depended either upon an unusual and sophisticated meaning of the word 'intention' or, more likely, a habitual inability or unwillingness to reflect and generalize about what he was doing.

The primary source, and usually the only source, of information about the purpose of a statute was the words of the statute itself, although he occasionally looked at background documents such as reports by royal commissions, without any hesitation or discussion of the authority of using this kind of material. This authority imposed sharp limits on the ways it could be used, which he usually exceeded.[30]

The words of the statutes were also the ultimate sources and limits of their meaning, but Meredith demonstrated little faith in 'plain meanings.' He was aware that meanings were often not plain and often did not make themselves apparent without careful thought. Occasionally he asserted that a meaning was plain, but usually in these cases the problems were relatively simple, and the meanings he asserted were reasonable and either ones that he preferred or ones that were apparently inescapable (if words alone can ever control meanings).[31] In only a very few cases did he assert that a meaning was plain when it was debatable. The most interesting and provocative of these cases was *Queen v. Simpson*,[32] which required interpretation of a prohibition in the *Pharmacy Act* against keeping an 'open shop' for selling drugs without being a registered pharmacist. Simpson owned a large department store in which he established a drugstore that was entirely under the supervision of a registered pharmacist. Counsel for Simpson argued that the purpose of the Act was to protect the public. Meredith affirmed the conviction and said simply, 'I have no doubt the defendant did keep an open shop ... I do not think one gains much by searching for the spirit of the legislation: when the language is plain it is better to follow it ... It may be as a matter of policy that a case such as this should not be within the Act, but that is for the Legislature.' The judgment is not persuasive, because the argument about purpose was cogent and was ignored. Perhaps his years in the legislature had taught him an understanding, which he was unwilling to declare, that the argument was wrong, and that part of the purpose of the legislation was to give pharmacists protection against competition.[33] In contrast to these few judgments, in which he seemed to take unjustified refuge behind an unreasoned assertion of plain meaning, there were at least as many in which he was willing to reach results that were not included in the reasonably possible meanings of the words. An example is *Meehan v. Peers*.[34] The *Assessment Act* provided that if a tenant paid taxes that could be recovered from another person, the tenant could deduct the amount paid from the rent. Peers and two relatives were assessed as owners, and Peers paid the taxes, even though the assessment against him was a mistake. Later, Meehan became the owner and made a lease to Peers, who then sought to deduct the payment from the rent. Meredith denied the deduction and said that 'it can never have been intended' that the deduction could be made for taxes for which the tenant was primarily liable, and that 'the section must be read accordingly.' The result was fair, but it was not a reasonably possible meaning of the words. However, these cases, in which plain meanings were asserted or denied, were unusual. Most of the cases required interpretation of vague, imprecise, or ambiguous words.

The most impressive aspect of Meredith's use of sources of meaning was his consideration of a statute as a whole or its history. Both are traditions and common techniques, but he used them often and well. In *Re Robertson and City of Chatham*,[35] a municipality assessed the cost of local improvements against the land benefited in proportion to the frontage of the parcels. An owner appealed to a county court judge, and the issue was whether the judge had authority to make the assessment proportional to the extent of the benefit received. The legislation was 'complicated, cumbrous, and contradictory,' and the sections giving the right to appeal were vague, but Meredith concluded that both the overall pattern and the earlier versions demonstrated that assessment proportional to frontage was a basic principle.[36] Also, in contrast to his decisions about common law, he was also often willing openly to consider and assess the consequences of possible decisions.[37] Much of the form of his reasoning was similar to his reasoning about common law. His preferences and choices were often stated more openly, but he generally failed to describe and analyse any of the competing needs or interests.[38] Many of the statutes had already been considered by courts and some were thoroughly encrusted with authority. Again, Meredith considered this authority as a series of single cases,[39] and often displayed the possible precedents in lists, with no analysis and little comment. He was faithful to English authority,[40] but he also had a great respect for American experience.[41]

The most important conclusion about Meredith's general attitudes towards statutes is that he demonstrated no general tendency to interpret statutes narrowly to preserve common law rights or to restrict the powers of the expanding administrative state. This conclusion needs a lengthy justification, which can best begin with his attitude towards statutes that modified the common law. A few statutes imposed restraints on the conduct of bargaining and on permitted terms for the purpose of what would now be called consumer protection, and Meredith interpreted them liberally.

The most interesting one, and perhaps the most interesting of all his cases, was *Cobban v. Canadian Pacific Railway*.[42] Section 226 of the *Railway Act* gave the governor-in-council power to prescribe uniform classifications of freight; section 227 required approval of bylaws setting rates; section 246(1) required shippers to pay the rates 'lawfully payable'; and section 246(2) prohibited contracting out of liability for negligence. The Canadian Pacific had two sets of rates for glass, which were traded according to approved classifications. One rate was 'double first class,' and the other was 'third class,' which was lower and applied when the glass was 'shipped at owner's risk, shippers signing special plate glass release form.' Cobban shipped glass and signed a form that released the railway from liability for loss or damage caused in any way, including negligence. The glass was lost, and Cobban claimed damages. Doubtless, the release would have been effective apart from statute, because one of the basic principles of nineteenth- and early-twentieth-century common law was that the courts would not supervise the fairness of bargains. Meredith held that the release did not preclude liability for negligence, essentially because approval under section 226 should be subject to the limitation imposed by section 246. The railway argued that section 246 should not apply if it charged less than its maximum rate, and, in effect, that it should be permitted to offer different grades of service for different rates. Meredith responded that the rates 'lawfully payable' were any rates 'within the maximum fixed by the by-law,' and that the railway's construction 'would entirely defeat the object which the statute was designed to accomplish and leave persons dealing with a railway company ... in the same position in which they were before the Act was passed.' *Cobban* was part of a long series of cases about the continuing efforts of the railways to escape liability, and Meredith's judgment stands as an impressive effort to protect shippers from the power of the railways. He said,

> I am not impressed by the argument that such legislation interferes with freedom of contract, and ought, therefore, to be strictly construed. The corporations with which the Act deals are intended to perform important duties towards the public in return for which they receive valuable privileges; and ... it is in the highest degree important and perhaps necessary to the efficient discharge of those duties that corporations entrusted with such powers ought not, on grounds of public policy, to be allowed so to contract that their operations may be carried on without any liability attaching to them for negligence ... Giving to the Act ... the construction which I think ought to be givers to it, is not calculated to interfere with freedom of contract, but rather to put the shipper, who is to a great extent at the mercy of the carrier by rail, the latter having, as he has in a large measure, a monopoly ... in a position in some degree of equality with the carrier, and to enable the parties to stand in such relation to one another that there may be real freedom of contract on both sides.

A useful contrast to *Cobban* is *Harpelle v. Carroll*,[43] in which Meredith considered the effect of an addition to the *Landlord and Tenant Act* made in 1845, which provided that 'the relation of landlord and tenant shall be deemed to be founded on the express or implied contract of the parties, and not upon tenure or service, and a reversion shall not be necessary to such relation.' A lease was made that did not expressly give a right to distrain. The tenant defaulted, and the landlord sought to distrain against chattels that the tenant had mortgaged. The mortgagee claimed that the amendment made the relation entirely contractual, and therefore no right to distrain could exist that was not created by contract because the right to distrain, inherent in the relation between landlord and tenant, depended upon tenure and the reversion. Meredith considered the nature and history of the landlord and tenant relation and concluded that the effect of the amendment was only to permit the relation to be created, even though the landlord did not hold the reversion. He said, 'I ought not, I think, without a much clearer expression of the will of the Legislature, to give to its enactment such a construction as would practically sweep away the whole body of the law (common and statutes) affecting the relation of landlord and tenant ... without substituting for it anything but the bald provisions of this section.'

In *Cobban*, the common law was supplanted by Meredith's interpretation, and in *Harpelle*, it was preserved, but the interpretations are consistent and persuasive. In *Cobban*, the terms and the history of the statute made the purpose of protecting shippers clear. Its effect in the particular context was not clear, and Meredith's judgment is a sensible effort to achieve the purpose by considering possible consequences. In *Harpelle*, the purpose was not clear, and might reasonably have been understood to be much less than the abandonment of a large body of common law that was well settled and not unfair or irrational.[44]

Another example of Meredith's general willingness to implement statutory modifications of common law is found in three cases about liability for automobile accidents. The *Motor Vehicles Act* provided, in section 19, that 'the owner of a motor vehicle shall be responsible for any violation of this Act,' and Meredith agreed without hesitation that this responsibility included civil liability. In *Wynne v. Dalby*,[45] a claim was made against a conditional vendor. Meredith said that 'the word "owner" is an elastic term, and the meaning which must be given to it in a statutory enactment depends very much upon the object the enactment is designed to serve.' He proceeded to describe several English cases in a search for authority, and concluded that 'I see no reason why [the purchaser], while he was in the exclusive possession of and had complete dominion over the car ... was not the owner of it ... The purpose of sec. 19 was, I think, to avoid any question being raised as to whether a servant of the owner who was driving a motor vehicle ... was acting within the scope of his employment.' In *Parlov v. Lozina and Raolovich*,[46] he held that a joint owner was liable and said that section 19 was 'passed for the protection of the public.' A year later a much more difficult problem was presented by *LeBar v. Barber and Clarke*.[47] Section 19 had been amended by adding the phrase 'unless at the time of such violation the motor vehicle was in the possession of a person not being in the employ of the owner, who had stolen it from the owner.' An owner stored his car in a garage with instructions to put it on jacks and maintain the batteries. The garage owner or an employee drove the car in violation of these instructions, and caused an accident. A majority of the Court of Appeal held that the owner was not liable. Meredith dissented, and said the object of section 19 was 'to make the owner careful of the person to whom he entrusted the possession of his motor vehicle in other words, to treat the vehicle as a dangerous article, the possession of which the owner must not entrust to another except with the consequent responsibility.' The liability of an owner under section 19 was a substantial expansion of common law liability. Meredith was willing to interpret 'owner' liberally in order to implement what he perceived to be its purpose.

Meredith decided only about a dozen reported cases involving review of administrative agencies, and almost all were appeals from the Ontario Railway and Municipal Board. Most were appeals about assessments of property for municipal taxes, and do not demonstrate any significant attitudes, except, perhaps, some respect for the board – all the appeals were dismissed – and one blunt assertion that taxing statutes were not to be interpreted narrowly.[48] The other cases, especially two of them, are much more interesting and useful. In *Re Toronto and Suburban Railway*,[49] the board ordered the railway to pave two streets for 18 inches on both sides of its tracks, and the railway appealed. The city and the railway had made an agreement in which the railway had committed itself to 'keep in proper repair' this part of the streets, but when this agreement was made, both the streets were mud roads, and the railway argued that its obligation was only to keep them as mud roads. Meredith's response, which demonstrates both his willingness to accept change and his use of cases from the United States, was that:

Having regard in the proximity of the roads to a large and rapidly growing city, the duration of the franchise ... the right of the public to use for the purpose of travel that part of the highways on which the railway should be constructed ... I am of opinion that the covenant should be construed as the Court of Appeals of the State of New York ... construed a similar obligation.

In the alternative and apart from contractual obligation, he concluded that the board had the power to order the paving. It had power to order 'repairs or improvements to ... any tracks,' and 'tracks should be interpreted widely, to include the space beside the tracks,' because the major purpose of the provision was to protect the public and employees.

In *Re Consolidated Telephone, and Caledon and Erin*,[50] the board refused to approve a sale by a telephone company of part of its system to two townships, and the company appealed. The legislation required approval and a hearing, and permitted the board to authorize a member to 'report to the Board' and adopt the report as its order. The chairman of the board held a hearing and reported that the sale should not be

approved because it was improvident and would impose an unreasonable burden on the subscribers. The board adopted this report as its
order and the company appealed on two grounds. It claimed that the
board had not given a hearing, but Meredith held that considering the
report from the chairman was adequate. Today this issue would be
debatable: an argument that the report should have been much more
extensive than it was to serve as a hearing would be opposed by an
argument that authority to adopt the report as an order was implicit
approval of a report that was merely a conclusion. The second ground
of appeal was that the board had exercised its discretion improperly.
Both counsel and Meredith floundered in analysing the limits of discretion, but Meredith's attitude was clear. 'The Board does not, in my
opinion, act judicially, but acts as the delegate of the Legislature,' and
could properly consider whatever the legislature could consider. 'The
discretion of the Board is absolute.'

The cases about municipalities were also review of government, but
municipalities and this review function had been established for centuries in England and since the mid-nineteenth century in Ontario, and
most of the cases did not present any issues involving the changes in the
contemporary society. The results of most of the cases and some general comments suggest that Meredith tended to attempt both to ensure
that the process of making decisions in municipalities worked fairly
and efficiently, and to respect its results.[51] Only a few of these cases
raised difficult issues about the expansion of regulation. In *Re Halladay
and Ottawa*,[52] he quashed a bylaw requiring early closing of grocery
stores because the function of determining the adequacy of a petition
had been delegated to the clerk. Meredith said that the bylaw 'is a
rather violent interference with the rights of a body of persons carrying
on a legitimate trade, and strict compliance ... should be required
before there is forced upon a minority ... the will of the majority.' In *Re
Hassard and Toronto*,[53] he quashed a bylaw limiting the number of liquor
licences, and asserted again that strict compliance was needed, because
the bylaw would deprive some licence holders of the right to continue
their business and would reduce the value of their property. In contrast, he seemed willing to give generous support to zoning bylaws,
even though they also meant restriction by a majority of the use of
property.[54] Perhaps he felt there was a difference between earning
a living and the enjoyment of property, or had greater sympathy
with the protection of property values than he did with restrictions on
competition.

The attitudes towards particular interests Meredith expressed in interpretation were substantially the same as the attitudes he expressed in working with the common law.[55] In particular, he tended to avoid imposing liability on landowners, to favour plaintiffs in claims against insurers and railways,[56] and to favour workers in claims against employers for injuries suffered at work. The claims by workers were the most interesting. Most of them were made under the *Workmen's Compensation Act*, which restricted the scope of the fellow servant rule. In *McLaughlin v. Ontario Iron and Steel*,[57] he held that a crane that ran on tracks above the floor of a factory was a 'locomotive, engine, machine or train upon a railway, tramway or street railway' and therefore the employer was liable for the negligence of the operator that injured a fellow worker. In *Norman v. Hamilton Bridge Works*,[58] an employee injured in a construction accident made a claim under a municipal bylaw that set standards for construction. Meredith held that the bylaw governed any contractor 'engaged in a large part of the work,' that breach gave a cause of action, and that a particular requirement of temporary flooring extended to all floors, even though its provisions, read 'literally,' would have applied only to the ground floor. He acknowledged that this reading 'practically eliminated' the word 'said' from the bylaw.

Meredith's attitudes towards the common law and legislation were different, but not inconsistent. I have sought to show that he demonstrated no responsibility for the fabric of the common law, not even for small incremental changes. Knowing only this much, it might be tempting to predict that he would have interpreted legislation narrowly, especially if it might bring change. I have sought to show that the prediction would be wrong.

Explanations of this difference in his attitudes to the common law and legislation must be tentative until we know much more about our legal history, but for Meredith I suggest two overlapping possibilities. The first is an assumption about the appropriate functions of institutions. He seems to have assumed that change in the law should be made by the legislature, not the courts, and that courts had a responsibility to interpret the legislation faithfully and to implement the change it seemed to require. The second reason for his attitudes begins with the realization that little of the legislation he considered threatened the interests of his class or the established social order. Consider, for example, the relations between capital and labour, and the *Workmen's Compensation Act*. Most of the judges interpreted the act liberally, and Meredith interpreted it at least as liberally as most, but neither the act nor these decisions threatened the power of capital or the existing economic order. The decisions were applications of general doctrine that was unfavourable to workers, and which made recovery for most injuries suffered at work unlikely. The decisions are difficult to explain, but the distinction between the general doctrine and its application is probably crucial to any effective explanation. The general doctrine may have seemed to be firmly established by authority and to express basic beliefs about freedom of contract and individual responsibility, and the applications may have been responses to pressing and apparent individual needs, which may have been both an expression of sympathy and a support of control through the exercise of mercy. The basic beliefs were being eroded, and by 1912, at least, Meredith believed that the general doctrine should be changed. But his assumptions about his function as judge forbade changing or even questioning the general doctrine, and the compensation scheme he proposed also did not threaten the established order. Meredith did not have to make any interpretations affecting the interests of organized labour, in which such a threat might have seemed to be at stake.[59]

The interpretations of the regulatory legislation are more difficult to analyse because there are only a few cases and because the purposes and effects of the legislation itself were complex and have not been thoroughly explored. However, the general thesis is tempting. Perhaps Meredith was interpreting the statutes of a legislature controlled by groups whose interests he shared, and perhaps these interests and his assumptions about the functions of legal institutions supported each other.[60]

Conclusion

During the hearings of his commission on workers' compensation, Meredith made a rare and revealing comment about law and judges. A worker spoke about the class struggle, and said that 'when we get into law, we always know who comes out best. We know the man with the money and the man with the influence comes out on top, and we know the District judge ... is not a member of the working class, but a member of the wealthy class himself.' Meredith replied:

I venture to say that as a whole the sympathies, as far as a judge is permitted to have sympathies, have been with the working man, and where they have had to determine against him in hard cases it is because they have been compelled by the law to do so ... [Y]ou think a court is entitled to do natural justice, but the court has no such power. The court is confined to administering justice according to the law, and a judge sitting would have no more right in determining a case contrary to the law than he would have to go to you and take out of your pocket your money. The fault is not in the administration of justice; you must change your law. It is the law that is at fault.[61]

The law he was talking about was common law, especially the law about negligence and the fellow servant rule, ameliorated slightly by legislation. Yet Meredith asserted that judges had no responsibility for its content or its change. He clearly believed that this law was unjust and should be changed, but he believed the change should be made by the legislature, not the courts: 'you' – not the judges – 'must change your law.' The law existed independently of the judges, and their function was to administer it 'according to law' in an impersonal and autonomous way. There was some room for 'sympathy,' but he had no coherent sense of its limits or justification or of how it should be integrated with the law or autonomous administration.

But, ultimately, a study based on judgments, especially judgments as restrained as Meredith's, must be limited, and we don't yet know enough about our legal history to be able to escape the limits. We don't even know the questions that must be asked. Much good writing has appeared lately about legal history in the United States and England. This writing can be provocative and can enable useful comparisons to be made, but we must not assume that questions that have been appropriate for the United States or England are appropriate for Canada, or that our judges have been just like English judges, only duller and more deferential.

For example, the term 'formalism' has often been used to describe the distinctive way judges in the United States reasoned during the second half of the nineteenth century and the early part of the twentieth. There are some reservations about the utility of the concept and some differences about the identity of all its characteristics, but a useful and widely shared understanding is that formalism was a belief that the law was, or should be, a science, and a set of apolitical and objective rules which established mutually exclusive and exhaustive divisions and which could be applied without discretion in an impersonal and autonomous way. In England, the ways of reasoning also changed during the nineteenth century, but a faith in strict precedent seems to have been the dominant element, and formalism seems to have been a much less useful concept.[62]

Considering this recent writing, it may be tempting to ask whether Meredith was a formalist. Given this meaning, the answer is that he demonstrated some but not all of its characteristics, and a more precise answer requires a more precise definition. But the answer alone is uninteresting, and, more importantly, the question may be useless and may mask more appropriate ones. Formalism in the United States – whatever it was – was a product of changes in politics, economics, and the legal profession that appeared in the mid-nineteenth century. Many of the changes in England and Canada were the same, but the differences in content and timing were substantial. The attitudes of the judges and the ways they reasoned changed – Meredith and the other judges at the turn of the century were different from the judges in the mid-nineteenth century, but the differences and their causes were not entirely the same as they were in England and the United States.

Understanding of these changes must be based on the Canadian context, including geography, political traditions, and economic development. This study of Meredith's mind is a small and preliminary part of an attempt to study the law and lawyers from about 1880 to 1930, and to gain this understanding. It cannot be an appropriate tribute to John Willis unless I promise him to try to do the work that needs to be done to finish it. I do, but I wish I could still talk to him about it on Sundays.

NOTES

1 See R. Dembski, 'A Matter of Conscience' (1983) 73 *Ont. Hist.* 131, and 'William Ralph Meredith: Leader of the Conservative Opposition in Ontario' (PhD thesis, University of Guelph, 1977); and F. Mahood, 'William Ralph Meredith and the Ontario Progressive Party: Social Policy and the Politics of Failure, 1879–1894' (MA thesis, Queen's University, 1980).

2 There were three major series of reports during the time Meredith was a judge. The first two were the *Ontario Reports* (O.R.) and the *Ontario Appeal Reports* (O.A.R.), and both were replaced in 1900 by the *Ontario Law Reports* (O.L.R.). Two other series began in 1901: the *Ontario Weekly Reporter* (O.W.R.) and the *Ontario Weekly Notes* (O.W.N.). The purpose of both was

to report a large number of judgments quickly, and they included the judgments reported in the *Ontario Law Reports* and many more, although they often edited them substantially. The propositions in the text about Meredith's judgments are based on a survey of both these series, and the qualifications are added because some significant judgments may have been missed.

3 C. Brown and R. Cook, *Canada 1896–1921: A Nation Transformed* (Toronto: McClelland and Stewart, 1974).

4 See R.C.B. Risk, 'The Law and the Economy in Mid-Nineteenth-Century Ontario: A Perspective' (1977) 27 *U.T.L.J.* 403.

5 There was some uncertainty and division of opinion about the authority of decisions of the House of Lords and the English Court of Appeal, especially about decisions that were contrary to those made by the Supreme Court of Canada: see B. Laskin, *The British Tradition in Canadian Law* (London: Stevens, 1969), and B. Hodgins, 'The Authority of English Decisions' (1923) 1 *Can. Bar R.* 470. Meredith clearly believed he was bound by decisions of the Supreme Court. In *Slater v. Laboree* (1905) 10 O.L.R. 648, decisions of English courts, including the House of Lords, about the liability of an endorser were inconsistent with a later Supreme Court judgment, and Meredith said, '[I]t was not for the learned Judge nor is it for us to question whether a decision of the Highest Court in Canada is in accordance with the previous cases. It is our duty, as it was his, to follow it.' However, he also believed that he was bound by decisions of the House of Lords and the English Court of Appeal if they were not inconsistent with the Canadian decisions; see for example, *Hanes v. Burnham* (1895) 26 O.R. 528.

6 *Kinsey v. Kinsey* (1894) 26 O.R. 99.

7 *Eckhardt v. Lancashire Insurance* (1898) 29 O.R. 695. See also *In re Reid v. Graham Brothers* (1894) 26 O.R. 126; *Hewitt v. Cane* (1894) 20 O.R. 133; *Trusts Corporation of Ontario v. Hood* (1896) 27 O.R. 135; *Re Soules* (1898) 30 O.R. 140; *Stirton v. Gummer* (1899) 31 O.R. 227; *Whitelock v. Cook* (1900) 31 O.R. 463; *Carswell v. Langley* (1902) 3 O.L.R. 261; and *Chandler and Massey Ltd. v. Grand Trunk Railway* (1903) 5 O.L.R. 589.

8 See C.K. Allen, *Law in the Making*, 6th ed. (Oxford: Clarendon Press, 1958) at 206–30; R. Cross, *Precedent in English Law* (Oxford: Clarendon Press, 1961) at 17–30; and J.P. Dawson, *The Oracles of the Law* (Ann Arbor: University of Michigan Law School, 1968) at 77–99.

9 He used the term 'principle' often, but his meaning was not consistent or clear. Sometimes principles were the settled and familiar generalizations, or the map; sometimes they were basic propositions upon which particular

doctrine was based; and sometimes they were simply his preferences about results. See, for example, *Stirton v. Gummer* supra note 7; *Davey v. Christoff* (1916) 36 O.L.R. 123 (C.A.); and *Quartier v. Farah* (1921) 49 O.L.R. 186 (C.A.). In some judgments, different meanings are used in different passages; for example, in *R. v. Steele* (1895) 26 O.R. 540, he described a series of cases and said that 'the principle to be deduced from these cases is.' Later, after having come to his conclusion, he justified it by invoking 'the fundamental principles upon which our law is and must be administered.' In *Carter v. Canadian Northern Railway* (1914) 23 O.L.R. 140, he stated the general 'principle' that parol evidence was admissible to show that a written agreement was subject to a condition precedent, but worried because he could not find any reported case in which the particular issue before him had been decided, and concluded that the result he reached seemed justified 'upon principle.' See also *Light v. Hawley* (1891) 29 O.R. 25; *Bain v. Anderson* (1896) 27 O.R. 369; *Building and Loan Association v. McKenzie* (1897) 28 O.R. 316; *Douglas v. Stephenson* (1898) 29 O.R. 616; *Tomkins v. Brockville Rink* (1899) 31 O.R. 124; *Provident Chemical Works v. Canada Chemical* (1901) 2 O.L.R. 182; *Sharp v. Grand Trunk Railway* (1901) 1 O.L.R. 200; *Hopkinson v. Perdue* (1904) 8 O.L.R. 228; and *Carter v. Canadian Northern Railway* (1910) 23 O.L.R. 140.

10 (1907) 14 O.L.R. 544. See also *Re Cockburn* (1896) 27 O.R. 450; *Fitchett v. Mellow* (1897) 29 O.R. 6; *Smith v. Hayes* (1898) 29 O.R. 283; *Smith v. Rogers* (1899) 30 O.R. 256; *Stirton v. Gummer*, supra note 7; and *Davey v. Christoff*, supra note 9.

11 See, for example, *Maisonneuve v. Township of Roxborough* (1899) 30 O.R. 127. In *Quartier v. Farah*, supra note 9, Meredith postponed giving judgment on a difficult issue 'in the hope that the law might be authoritatively declared by the English Courts.'

12 (1910) 22 O.L.R. 452.

13 In *Hopkinson v. Perdue*, supra note 9, a husband and wife brought an action for an assault upon the wife which, if it occurred, was either a rape or an indecent assault. Both gave evidence of complaints made by the wife to the husband shortly after the assault occurred, and the major issue was the admissibility of this evidence. General rules of evidence made it inadmissible, but English cases had made an exception for criminal cases. Again, Meredith could not find any English or Canadian cases. He said, '[W]e have therefore to decide on principle and ... unfettered by authority,' but having suggested that he was about to undertake some kind of reasoning, he simply adopted 'entirely' the reasoning in American cases, which asserted that the justification for the exception applied to civil cases as well

as criminal cases. See also *Re the Ontario Insurance Act and the Supreme Legion Select Knights of Canada* (1899) 31 O.R. 154; *Huffman v. Rush* (1904) 7 O.L.R. 346; *McKeown v. Toronto Railway* (1909) 19 O.L.R. 361 ('with this statement of the law I entirely agree'); *Squires v. Toronto Railway* (1920) 47 O.L.R. 613 (C.A.) ('I adopt the reasoning of the Court and its statement of the law'); and *Garside v. Grand Trunk Railway* (1925) 33 O.L.R. 388 (C.A.).

14 See, for example, *Light v. Hawley,* supra note 9; *Bain v. Anderson* (1896) 27 O.R. 369; *Smith v. Rogers,* supra note 10; *Bailey v. Gillies* (1901) 4 O.L.R. 182; *City of Ottawa v. Ottawa Electric Railway* (1901) 1 O.L.R. 377; *McPherson v. Trustees S.S. No. 7 Usborne* (1902) 1 O.L.R. 261; and *Davidson v. Grand Trunk Railway* (1903) 5 O.L.R. 574.

15 See, for example, *Townsend v. Toronto, Hamilton and Buffalo Railway* (1896) 38 O.R. 195; *Building and Loan Association v. McKenzie,* supra note 9; *Munro v. Waller* (1897) 28 O.R. 574; *Bailey v. Gillies,* supra note 14; *Mendels v. Gibson* (1903) 9 O.L.R. 94; *Labelle v. O'Connor* (1908) 15 O.L.R. 519; *Davey v. Christoff,* supra note 9.

16 See, for example, *Fitchett v. Mellow* and *Smith v. Hayes,* both supra note 10.

17 Examples of claims against railways are *Davidson v. Grand Trunk Railway* (1903) 5 O.L.R. 574; *Gowland v. Hamilton, Grimsby, and Beamsville Electric Railway* (1914) 33 O.L.R. 372 (C.A.); *Squires v. Toronto Railway,* supra note 13; *Garside v. Grand Trunk Railway,* supra note 13. Examples of claims against employers are *Billing v. Semmens* (1904) 7 O.L.R. 340; *Brown v. Waterous Engine Works* (1904) 8 O.L.R. 37; *Markle v. Donaldson* (1904) 7 O.L.R. 376.

18 See, for example, *Smith v. Rogers,* supra note 10; *R. v. Steele,* supra note 9; *Wilson Lumber v. Simpson,* supra note 12; *Davey v. Christoff,* supra note 9; and *Village of Merritton v. County of Lincoln* (1917) 41 O.L.R. 6.

19 (1922) 52 O.L.R. 523 (C.A.).

20 (1917) 39 O.L.R. 271.

21 *Geiger v. Grand Trunk Railway* (1905) 10 O.L.R. 511.

22 *Smith v. Hayes,* supra note 10.

23 (1851) 2 Ch. 95.

24 (1908) 15 O.L.R. 519.

25 One of the few cases in which he considered Canadian conditions was *R. v. Steele,* supra note 9, in which the issue was the standard for finding an apprehension of bias of a magistrate.

26 See, for example, *Bagshaw v. Bagshaw* (1920) 48 O.L.R. 52.

27 See, for example, Sir William Ralph Meredith C.J.O., *Interim Report on Laws Relating to the Liability of Employers to Make Compensation to Their Employees for Injuries Received in the Course of Their Employment Which Are in Force in*

Other Countries (1912), Minutes of Evidence 424, and Sir William Ralph Meredith, C.J.O., *Final Report* ... (1913) xi, xii.

28 See, for example, McIntyre *v.* Coote (1909) 19 O.L.R. 9.

29 See, for example, *Union School Section v. Lockhart* (1895) 26 O.R. 662; *Challoner v. Township of Lobo* (1900) 32 O.R. 247; and *Wicke v. Township of Ellice* (1906) 11 O.L.R. 422.

30 See, for example, *R. v. Patterson* (1895) 26 O.R. 656; *R. v. Toronto Railway* (1915) 34 O.L.R. 589 (C.A.); and *Re Ontario and Minnesota Power and Town of Fort Frances* (1916) 35 O.L.R. 459 (C.A.).

31 See, for example, *Re Lazier* (1899) 30 O.R. 419; *Bacon v. Grand Trunk Railway* (1906) 12 O.L.R. 196; *R. v. Letherby* (1908) 17 O.L.R. 304; and *R. v. Wing* (1913) 29 O.L.R. 553.

32 (1896) 27 O.R. 603; see also *Heaton v. Flood* (1897) 29 O.R. 87, which involved an awkward gap in the *Bills of Sale and Chattel Mortgages Act, 1894,* and demonstrates Meredith's lack of analysis in commercial problems.

33 See, for example, M. Bliss, *A Living Profit: Studies in the Social History of Canadian Business, 1883–1911* (Toronto: McClelland and Stewart, 1974), c. 2, and L.M. Friedman, 'Freedom of Contract and Occupational Licensing, 1890–1910: A Legal and Social Study' (1965) 53 *California L.R.* 487.

34 (1917) 39 O.L.R. 271; see also *Township of Morris v. County of Huron* (1895) 26 O.R. 689.

35 (1895) 30 O.R. 158.

36 For other readings of statutes as a whole, see *Union School Section v. Lockhart,* supra note 29; *Challoner v. Township of Lobo,* supra note 29; *Larkin v. Larkin* (1900) 32 O.R. 80; *R. v. Walsh* (1903) 5 O.L.R. 268; *R. v. Pierce* (1904) 9 O.L.R. 375; *Re Lumbers and Howard* (1905) 9 O.L.R. 684; and *Village of Merrittown v. County of Lincoln,* supra note 18. For other uses of the history of statutes, see *Hargrare v. Elliot* (1896) 28 O.R. 152; *Re Medland and City of Toronto* (1899) 31 O.R. 243; *R. v. Duering* (1901) 2 O.L.R. 593; *Re School Section 5 of the Township of Cartwright and Township of Cartwright* (1902) 4 O.L.R. 272; *James v. Rathbun* (1905) 2 D.L.R. 271; *McMurray v. East Nissouri (Section 3) Public School Board* (1910) 21 O.L.R. 46; *R. v. Cohen* (1915) 33 O.L.R. 340; and *Abell v. Village of Woodbridge* (1919) 45 O.L.R. 79 (C.A.).

37 See, for example, *Maisonneuve v. Township of Roxborough,* supra note 11; *Wicke v. Township of Ellice,* supra note 29; *Re Rowland and McCallum* (1910) 22 O.L.R 418; and *Re Toronto Public School Board and City of Toronto* (1941) 2 O.L.R. 727.

38 See, for example, *Patrick v. Walbourne* (1896) 27 O.R. 221; *Heaton v. Flood,* supra note 32; *Greer v. Canadian Pacific Railway* (1914) 32 O.L.R. 104 (C.A.);

Little v. Smith (1914) 32 O.L.R. 518 (C.A.); *Bellamy v. Williams* (1917) 41
O.L.R. 244 (C.A.); *Stock v. Myers and Cook* (1919) 46 O.L.R. 420 (C.A.); and
Mason v. Lindsay (1942) 4 O.L.R. 365. As in the common law reasoning, this
lack of analysis was most apparent in complex commercial cases.

39 See, for example, *Union School Section v. Lockhart*, supra note 29; *Eckhardt v.
Lancashire Insurance*, supra note 7; *Challoner v. Township of Lobo*, supra note
29; *Town of Arnprior v. United States Fidelity and Guaranty* (1913) 30 O.L.R.
618 (C.A.): and *Fuller v. City of Niagara Falls* (1920) 48 O.L.R. 332 (C.A.). In
Smith v. Darling, 36 O.L.R. 587 (C.A.), he felt obliged to follow a holding of
the Court of Appeal, despite his contrary preferences, even though it had
been reversed on different grounds by the Supreme Court, and two judges
of the Supreme Court had gone out of their way to disapprove the
holding.

40 See, for example, *Maisonneuve v. Township of Roxborough*, supra note 11;
Pennington v. Morley (1902) 3 O.L.R. 514; and *McMurray v. East Nissouri
(Section 3) Public School Board*, supra note 36. In *Greenwood v. Rae* (1916) 36
O.L.R. 367 (C.A.), he followed an English trial judgment, despite a
difference in the legislation, and without doing the thinking he seemed to
feel needed to be done, relying in part on its adoption by English texts.

41 The best example is *Deihl v. Zanger* (1914) 31 O.L.R. 340 (C.A.). See also
Patrick v. Walbourne, supra note 38; *R. v. Simpson*, supra note 32; *Tomkins v.
Brockville Rink*, supra note 9; *Re Ontario Insurance Act* (1899) 31 O.R. 154; *Re
Williams and Town of Brampton*, infra note 51; *Re City of Ottawa and Grey
Nuns* (1913) 29 O.L.R. 568 (C.A.); *Little v. Smith*, supra note 38; *Smith v.
Cambellford Board of Education* (1917) 39 O.L.R. 323 (C.A.); and *Bellamy v.
Williams* (1918) 41 O.L.R. 244 (C.A.).

42 (1895) 26 O.R. 732; see also *Sheppard v. Canadian Pacific Railway* (1908) 16
O.L.R. 259, and see also *R. v. T. Eaton Co.* (1899) 31 O.R. 276 and *R. v. James*
(1902) 4 O.L.R. 537.

43 (1896) 27 O.R. 240.

44 In *Hendrie v. Toronto, Hamilton and Buffalo Railway* (1895) 26 O.R. 667, the
railway asserted that a municipal bylaw confirmed by statute gave it
power to take Hendrie's land, without having paid or tendered compensation as required by the *Railway Act*. Meredith said, 'it would … require a
very clear expression of the intention of the Legislature … to give to its
enactments such a construction as would take away from the plaintiff the
rights … under … the *Dominion Railway Act* … and full effect can be given
to the by-law and the Act of the legislature without giving to them an
effect that would work so manifest an injustice and make the legislation
contravene the principle that no one's property shall be taken from him

even for the public good without just compensation.' In *R. v. Hendershott and Wetter* (1895) 26 O.R. 678 and *R. v. Coleman* (1898) 30 O.R. 93, he accepted, without hesitation, statutory changes to the common law of evidence because the intention to make the changes was clear.

45 (1913) 30 O.L.R. 67 (C.A.).

46 (1921) 44 O.L.R. 299 (C.A.).

47 (1922) 52 O.L.R. 299 (C.A.). Meredith was born in 1840 and was willing to accept the automobile and to implement changes in the common law at the age of 82. The possibility that these cases can be explained by a hostility to the car and a desire to punish its owners is denied by some of his other decisions; see, for example, *McIntyre v. Coote*, supra note 28.

48 *Re Hiram Walker & Sons and Walkerville* (1917) 40 O.L.R. 154 (C.A.); see also *Re Ottawa and Grey Nuns*, supra note 41; *Ottawa Young Men's Christian Association v. Ottawa* (1913) 29 O.L.R. 574 (C.A.); *Re Ontario and Minnesota Power v. Fort Frances*, supra note 30; and *Re McIntyre Porcupine Mines and Morgan* (1921).

49 (1913) 39 O.L.R. I05 (C.A.).

50 (1920) 48 O.L.R. 140 (C.A.). In *Re Toronto Railway and Toronto* (1918) 44 O.L.R. 381 (C.A.), the railway argued that the board was a superior court for the purposes of section 96 of the *British North America Act*; Meredith rejected the argument for two reasons. First, an attack under section 96 could not be made in collateral proceedings, and for this proposition he relied on cases from the United States; second, the functions of the board were 'administrative, not judicial,' although he did not explain the difference. See also *Brant v. Canadian Pacific Railway* (1916) 36 O.L.R. 619 (C.A.).

51 See, for example, *Maisonneuve v. Roxborough*, supra note 11; *Re Toronto Public School Board and Toronto* (1901) 2 O.L.R. 727; *R. v. Walsh* (1903) 5 O.L.R. 263; *Re Wentworth Election* (1905) 9 O.L.R. 201; *Re Hickey and Town of Orillia, Re Williams and Town of Brampton* (1908) 17 O.L.R. 317; and *Norfolk v. Roberts* (1912) 28 O.L.R. 593 (C.A.). The last of these cases was the most difficult. The town of Brampton made a reasonable agreement with a large business about charges for water that involved a fixed rate in return for a substantial contribution towards the construction of a new main. The general rates increased, but a change in legislation made such a differential illegal without the approval of a majority of electors. The council nevertheless agreed not to collect the increase, and a ratepayer brought an action for a declaration and mandamus to enforce payment, which Meredith dismissed, saying, '[T]he trend of modern decisions is ... to recognize the right of such bodies, while acting bona fide and within the limit of the

powers conferred upon them by the Legislature, to transact their business without interference by the Courts.'

52 (1907) 15 O.L.R. 65; see also *R. v. Woollatt* (1906) 11 O.L.R. 544.

53 (1908) 16 O.L.R. 500.

54 *City of Toronto v. Solway* (1919) 46 O.L.R. 24 (C.A.).

55 See, for example, attitudes about payment of obligations in *Eckhardt v. Lancashire Insurance*, supra note 7; *Lees v. Ottawa and New York Railway* (1900) 31 O.R. 567; and *Re Kay v. Story* (1904) 8 O.L.R. 45.

56 For examples of claims against railways, see *Plester v. Grand Trunk Railway* (1900) 32 O.R. 55; *Toronto v. Toronto Railway* (1905) 10 O.L.R. 730; *Re Armstrong and James Bay Railway* (1906) 12 O.L.R. 137; *Bacon v. Grand Trunk Railway*, supra note 31; and *Greer v. Canadian Pacific Railway*, supra note 38.

57 (1910) 20 O.L.R. 335.

58 (1907) 15 O.L.R. 457. Meredith's judgment was reversed on appeal. For a general discussion of employers' liability, see R.C.B. Risk, 'This Nuisance of Litigation: The Origins of Workers' Compensation in Ontario,' in D.H. Flaherty, ed., *Essays in the History of Canadian Law: Volume Two* (Toronto: Osgoode Society for Canadian Legal History and University of Toronto Press, 1983) 418.

59 In *Metallic Roofing Company of Canada v. Local Union No. 30, Amalgamated Sheet Metal Workers' International Association* (1903) 5 O.L.R 424, Meredith held that an action could not be brought against a local union because it was neither an individual nor a corporation, but the authority strongly supported this result and made a different result difficult to reach.

60 Meredith decided only a handful of constitutional cases. They are among the few cases he decided that had some general political importance, but the facts are too limited for them to be useful in a study of his ways of reasoning. The most interesting were three cases about the power of the provincial government to require English to be used exclusively as the language of instruction in the public schools, especially the Roman Catholic separate schools in Ottawa. This issue of language in the separate schools had been a political issue for decades, and Meredith had a clear record as a politician with a strong preference for the use of English only. In 1912, the government made a regulation: 'regulation 17.' It permitted the use of French only when it was necessary for the education of French-speaking students, and only in the lower grades, and required that French-speaking students learn English. This regulation was immediately the centre of conflict. In *Mackell v. Ottawa Separate School Trustees* (1915) 34 O.L.R. 335 (C.A.), he decided that a slightly revised version was *intra vires*. This result obviously coincided with his personal and political convictions,

but it was also firmly supported by the terms of the *British North America Act*, and a different decision would have been difficult to justify. This decision was affirmed by the Privy Council. The second and third of these three cases were about the constitutionality of a provincial statute that permitted the government to appoint a commission to manage the schools if they failed to comply. In *Ottawa Separate School Trustees v. City of Ottawa* (1916) 36 O.L.R. 485 (C.A.), Meredith decided that it was *intra vires*; his decision was reversed by the Privy Council, but on a narrow and technical ground that may not have been argued before the Court of Appeal. The government amended the statute to avoid this ground, and Meredith decided that this version was *intra vires* in *Re Ottawa Separate Schools* (1917) 41 O.L.R. 259 (C.A.).

61 *Interim Report*, supra note 27 at 187–8.

62 See, for example, C.C. Goetsch, 'The Future of Legal Formalism' (1980) 24 *Am. J. of Legal History* 221; M.J. Horwitz, *The Transformation of American Law, 1780–1860* (Cambridge, MA: Harvard University Press, 1977) c. 7; D. Kennedy, 'Form and Substance in Private Law Adjudication' (1967) 89 *Harvard L.R.* 1685; W.E. Nelson, 'The Impact of the Antislavery Movement upon Styles of Judicial Reasoning in Nineteenth-Century America' (1974) 87 *Harvard L.R.* 513; and L.S. Paine, 'Instrumentalism v. Formalism: Dissolving the Dichotomy' [1978] *Wisconsin L.R.* 997.

PART TWO

The Challenge of Modernity: Canadian Legal Thought in the 1930s

7

Volume One of the Journal: A Tribute and a Belated Review

The *University of Toronto Law Journal* was founded in 1935 and has thus just completed a half-century of publication. This does not make it old as law journals go, and compared with a few others it is a mere stripling. Its birthday does, though, justify some small celebration. I can hardly praise it, at least not for its past 15 years, during which I have been the editor, but I do wish to pay tribute to its ideal. My tribute is this study of the first volume – a belated review. It was a remarkable volume indeed: it was the beginning of the first scholarly legal journal in Canada; it contained articles that continue to be illuminating and stimulating; and it introduced into Canada ways of thinking about law that continue to be among the major elements of our thought.

All I know about the origins of the journal is that it was a child of the law school at the University of Toronto, and especially of W.P.M. Kennedy, the school's dean and the first editor. During the early 1930s Kennedy sought to establish a distinctive vision of legal education and scholarship. He argued that the traditional professional legal education omitted 'the social meaning of it all ... [and] law in relation to life,' whereas

> we have no professional ends to serve ... [W]e study law as a social science, a great creative process of social engineering, in which a deep and intensive inquiry is made into the social value of legal rules and principles, and a search is pursued in every field of law to find out how far it

is in truth serving the true ends of society. We relate law to life, not life to law.[1]

The journal was conceived as an expression of this vision of law and legal education. In his introduction, Kennedy declared that the journal

is the natural outcome of a new vigour in legal studies in the University of Toronto ... We aim to produce a journal, learned and scientific, with high standards of scholarship and research which will be of interest to teachers and students of law, to members of the profession, to jurists, and to men of affairs ... We venture specially to hope that we may be able to do something to encourage legal scholarship in Canada, to foster a knowledge of the comparative laws of the British Empire, not merely as substantive or adjectival systems, but as expressions of organized community life, of ordered progress, and of social justice.[2]

This declaration of objectives was a departure from what Canadian lawyers might have expected. Other Canadian law journals had tended to treat law as an autonomous process and were dominated by the needs and interests of practising lawyers. In contrast, Kennedy's objectives stressed scholarship, not utility for practice, and suggested a substantially different way of thinking about law.

The contents of the first volume contained a wide range of kinds of writing, authors, topics, and approaches. There were nine articles. Percy Corbett, dean of the school at McGill, explored the source of authority of international law. Cecil ('Caesar') Wright, who taught at Osgoode Hall Law School and was the editor of the *Canadian Bar Review*, assessed the *Restatements of Contracts and Agency*, and A. Berriedale Keith did the same for the *Restatement of Conflicts of Laws*. J.A. Corry, then at the law school at Saskatchewan but about to leave law teaching to become a political scientist at Queen's University, made proposals for interpretation of statutes in the common law world, and the Hon. P.B. Mignault discussed interpretation of the civil code. John Willis, from the law school at Dalhousie University, considered ways of thinking about administrative agencies, and Jacob Finkelman, from the law school at the University of Toronto, wrote about the separation of powers in the common law. F.C. Auld, also from the law school at Toronto, sought inspiration for reform of the criminal procedure in comparisons with procedure on the European Continent, and Vincent C. MacDonald, dean of the law school at Dalhousie University, surveyed trends and approaches in the interpretation of sections 91 and 92 of the *British North America Act*.3

These articles occupied a little more than half the volume – about 245 pages out of 450. The remainder consisted of notes and documents, surveys of Canadian legislation, case comments, and book reviews. The notes and documents were odds and ends: for example, descriptions or reproductions of documents about Commonwealth and international issues and short descriptions of the New York Law Revision Commission and the Industrial Law Research Council, which was a small group based at the University of Toronto Law School established to study industrial law and make proposals for reform. The surveys of legislation were short and straightforward summaries of the important legislation in the federal government and four groups of provinces – the Maritime provinces, Quebec, Ontario, and the western provinces. They demonstrated a sense of the importance of legislation and a determination to make it a substantial and legitimate part of the materials for legal scholarship, but the reason for the choice of this particular form – a general descriptive survey – is not apparent. The surveys were not scholarly accomplishments in any sense at all, let alone the ambitious sense declared in the introduction, and they could not have been of much, if any, use to practising lawyers. They were probably designed to be no more than a record that might be useful to non-lawyers and readers in other countries.

The case comments were almost all written by students at the law school, some of whom later became outstanding scholars or practitioners – including Moffat Hancock, William Howland, and G. Arthur Martin. The choice of the cases does not make any obvious pattern, and they seem to be simply cases that particular students or teachers found interesting in 1935. The analysis in the comments displayed little of the expansive vision proclaimed for the law school. They stressed the internal coherence and consistency of the doctrine, and the only ventures beyond the doctrine were short statements about policy or values that were assumed to be axiomatic or widely shared.

The reviews were astonishing, at least in their number. All told, 126 books were reviewed, and although some of the reviews consisted of only a handful of sentences, there were still over 50 that were at least a page long. The reviewers spanned a wide range of interests and qualifications and included some outstanding lawyers and scholars. Among the Canadians were Brooke Claxton, Percy Corbett, George deT. Glazebrook, John D. Falconbridge, Norman MacKenzie, Arthur Plumptre,

Frank Scott, and John Robinette. Among the others were Edward Borchard, Erwin Corwin, William Holdsworth, Ivor Jennings, Philip Jessup, Lord Macmillan, Samuel Thorne, and Edward Wade. Most of the reviews simply described the books and assessed their substance. Only a few ventured to express general thoughts, and both these and all the implicit assumptions can best be subsumed in a discussion of the articles.

I have three general impressions about all this writing, especially the articles. The first is that the promise made by Kennedy in his introduction was kept: the journal was a scholarly journal, and it did seek to study law as more than doctrine and the domain of practising lawyers. The second is that the quality was remarkably high. Even though much of the writing was no more than competent or even mediocre, most of it was good work, and some of it still sparkles and stimulates. As an editor, I admire and envy. The accomplishment was more than Kennedy or I might reasonably hope for. The third impression is for me the most important: it is that the volume was pervaded by a strong sense of excitement, which was composed of three elements. The first was a sense of change – change in the social and economic context of law, and change in the ways of thinking about law. The second was a sense of a need for reform of law and a faith that reform was possible. And the third was a belief that legal scholars, legal scholarship, and legal education had a distinctive and necessary role in making reform. These impressions need to be elaborated, and this job can be most usefully done in a discussion of the articles. Four of them are especially useful – those by Wright, Corry, Willis, and MacDonald.

Caesar Wright was born in London, Ontario, in 1907 and attended the University of Western Ontario and Osgoode Hall Law School, when the curriculum combined articling and a few lectures given by a tiny faculty. He did graduate work at Harvard Law School for a year, and in 1927 he returned to become a lecturer at Osgoode. During the 1930s and 1940s he emerged as a major torts scholar and a powerful missionary for a full-time professional law school on the Harvard model. The Benchers of the Law Society rejected his vision of a law school, and after a series of battles he resigned in 1949, together with Stanley Edwards, Bora Laskin, and John Willis. Immediately afterwards, all of them but Edwards (who went into practice) were hired to teach at Toronto and Wright was appointed dean to replace Kennedy, who was retiring. Within a few years he had erased whatever remained of Kennedy's vision and established his vision of a professional law school.

Wright's article about the *Restatement of Contracts and Agency*[4] began with a general essay on the common law. He perceived it as essentially composed of principles, which were made by induction from decisions made by courts, and which could be made into consistent and coherent patterns, 'the accumulated wisdom of the past.'[5] He often described it as rational and scientific, by which he seems to have meant internally coherent and consistent. Bits and pieces of the pattern of principle could be filled in by implication, although there was a limit at which this process became legislating. Deciding individual cases was usually a process of deduction from the principles, but in some cases judges made choices that were not determined by the principles alone. Wright did not explain which kinds of cases required these choices or how they should be made, nor did he relate making them to the process of making deductions from principles.[6]

The crucial question for Wright was, who had the responsibility to formulate the principles. In England this job had been done exclusively by the courts, and, 'since ... the courts have led legal thought so long and so successfully there has undoubtedly developed an "attitude of fatalism" – that all must be left to the courts. The functions of a law teacher have been confined to speaking *after* the court has spoken, and to fit into the legal mosaic as neatly as possible this new piece of the pattern.'[7]

In the United States, a large number of independent jurisdictions and a rapid commercial expansion created a substantially different context: 'No longer was a unified group working with a unified legal language and tradition. Diversified groups with different mental approaches were at work on a body of law that had to be adapted to solve problems under entirely different conditions of political, social, and economic life.'[8]

Doctrine became diverse and uncertain, and the law schools did much of the job of synthesizing the tangle and making and teaching 'a fundamental common law.'[9] The law teacher 'has gradually encroached upon the function of the "judge" as the sole analyst and synthesist of the law. In addition, the necessity of evaluating different lines of reasoning has led to a development of a critical sense that has, up to the present, been sadly lacking in England.'[10]

Canada suffered from the disadvantages of both England and the United States. The federal system produced a large volume of diverse authority; the courts failed to contribute to 'ascertaining fundamental principles,'[11] largely because they were mindlessly faithful to English authority; and legal education was designed merely to teach a trade.

Wright next described the purpose and form of the *Restatements*, the process of making them, and their limitations and usefulness. The limitations were a product of the form that had been adopted – they were statements of 'black-letter' rules. Moreover, these rules were not simply a consolidation of what courts had said. Choices had been made, either among conflicting authorities or where little or no authority existed. The lack of references and discussion deprived 'outsiders' of a 'critical diversity,' and of knowing when choices of this kind had been made and when the rules were simply a consolidation of what the courts had said. Also, there were some issues that could not be reduced to rules. Wright's example was vicarious liability. 'The problem is really an economic one ... What is needed here is discussion of the theory, conscious or unconscious, on which the decisions have proceeded.'[12] Presumably these were some, at least, of the issues for which courts made choices, but Wright did not describe them or explain why they could not be reduced to rules. The limitations of the *Restatements* were for Wright far outweighed by the advantages, particularly the advantages for reform of Canadian common law. They offered new approaches, analysis and doctrine, a challenge to the existing assumptions and doctrine, and a useful terminology.

His review concluded with an analysis of two examples. The first was section 90 of the *Restatement* and enforcement of promises made without consideration but relied upon by the promisee. Here Wright demonstrated that the courts were enforcing many of these promises even though the doctrine seemed to make them unenforceable, and he claimed that failure to enforce them would be 'manifest injustice.'[13] The second example was agency, and particularly the liability of a principal to a third party in both contract and tort. Here the argument was much the same: the doctrine, especially the nineteenth-century doctrine about fault and will, was inadequate to explain the results of the cases, and reform was needed.

Throughout, Wright demonstrated a powerful belief that the common law was essentially coherent and legitimate, but that it needed to be reformed. The reforms to be made involved more than correcting mistakes in prior reasoning and elaborating the pattern of principle. They included changes in ways of reasoning and the substance of the established doctrine. Wright made an ambitious claim for the role of law teachers and their scholarship. 'The function of the law teacher and writer is to show the way.'[14] One important source of material for reform was the experience of other jurisdictions, and this was the perspective for his scholarly interest in the *Restatements*.

Wright's article about the *Restatements* was in sharp contrast to Keith's article about the *Restatement of Conflicts*,[15] which was much more traditional and simply described the proposed doctrine and how it resembled and differed from the established English doctrine. But the mood of Wright's article was the dominant mood of the volume. Some of the themes he expressed were echoed by Auld in his discussion of the criminal law, especially perceptions of change, the need for reform, and the use of comparative material. For example:

> [T]he common lawyer ... is a worshipper at the shrine of tradition, and is singularly averse to the idea of change ... Events of recent years have, however, tended to disturb our ancient faith ... [Crime is a social disease which] needs to be studied and corrected and repressed by new methods that shall be in touch with, and shall correspond to, the aims and methods of a scientific sociology ... [T]he duty of the law reformer is plain. He must analyse the evils of his system of laws with a view to their correction; and a dependable step in any thoroughgoing analysis is that of comparison. He must see how other systems of laws have dealt with these common problems ... [Reform is] 'in the air' ... a 'new deal,' in these matters, is called for ... [Comparative law can give] added light upon the perplexing problems that confront us.[16]

J.A. Corry, the author of the next article to be considered, is now known as a political scientist, but he wrote 'Administrative Law and the Interpretation of Statutes'[17] after having taught law for almost a decade. He studied law at Saskatchewan and Oxford, and began to teach at Saskatchewan in 1927. In 1934–5 he studied law at Columbia, and in 1936 he went to Queen's to begin his career in political science. His major interest in the 1930s was the administrative state, and his article began by describing the crucial role of the courts. 'All statutes must be interpreted; and we learn the meaning of the powers and duties of administration through the common-law judges expounding statutes as applied to particular cases.' This role was being challenged, for example by proposals for administrative courts, privative clauses, and grants to agencies of extensive powers to make detailed rules, 'because efficient administration is being embarrassed by judicial interpretation ... What we must secure is intelligent judicial co-operation in the fulfilment of the aims and objects of parliament.'[18]

The prevailing approach of the courts was literal interpretation – words had inherent meanings, which must govern interpretation. Corry claimed that, wherever philosophic analysis might lead, words simply did not have meanings that could be sufficiently precise. 'Even where careful use of them gives relative precision, the infinite variety of factual combinations is bound to cause doubt as to their meaning in relation to particular cases.' Nor could the meaning of words be found in the intention of the user – the legislature. A body as numerous and diverse as a modern legislature could not have a single intention. 'The intention of the legislature is a fiction.' Corry did believe that words did have inherent meanings and could set limits, but these limits were 'surprisingly wide,' and within them the court had a choice. 'In many cases, there is no logical compulsion on the judge to accept a single meaning ... In making his choice he makes law, in spite of his protests to the contrary.'[19]

This choice might be, and too often was, an expression of the personal values of the judge, but such choices were undesirable because '[t]he democratic method requires that policy should be determined by discussion and vote.' Instead, the judge should seek to respect and implement the purpose or object of the legislature. 'Though the intention of the legislature is a fiction, the purpose or object of the legislation is very real ... The statute must be treated as a means to an end; the end should be determined by the social forces which brought it about and not by private choice of the judge.' For Corry, this search for the purpose gave objectivity and legitimacy that the personal choices of judges lacked. The work of the judge was creative, but '[t]his does not ... make him a despot.'[20]

Corry concluded with a long study of the history of interpretation, especially the literal rule. A combination of legislative supremacy, prolixity of statutes, and the Lockean constitution and its respect for individual liberty and property had made the literal rule dominant by the early nineteenth century. Corry analysed a handful of nineteenth-and early-twentieth-century cases to demonstrate that words did not control outcomes, and that judges talked about plain meanings but imposed their own beliefs. 'In so far as the policy of legislation deviates from the judges' personal view of what ought to be, the doctrine of literal interpretation frequently results in strict interpretation.' Yet abandoning the rule would not deny legislative supremacy and make the judges into legislators.[21]

Corry's proposals were an elegant and persuasive synthesis of approaches to interpretation that had developed during the twentieth century, especially in the American periodicals of the 1920s and early 1930s, which he might have studied during the preceding year while he was at Columbia. These approaches shared a rejection of a faith, attributed to the nineteenth century, that judges could discover meaning or intention in words alone, and a belief that interpretation should seek the object or purpose of a statute and social policy.[22]

John Willis' 'Three Approaches to Administrative Law'[23] was one of the first articles written in Canada about the administrative process. Willis was born in England and educated at Winchester and Oxford, then went to Harvard Law School in 1930 to study under Felix Frankfurter. He came to Dalhousie Law School in 1933, expecting to stay for only a year, but stayed and taught in Canada until his retirement in 1970. His article was about regulatory agencies: the attitudes of the courts towards them, appropriate ways of designing them, and a review of their work. It began with a perceptive account of the rise of government in the twentieth century, especially the regulatory agency – 'the government in miniature' – and then posed the crucial question:

> The practical problem is how to fit into our constitutional structure these new institutions whose growth seems inevitable. Its solution, however, depends upon the answer to a more fundamental question – what shall be the approach of legislatures to government by department and commission? Shall it be that of the judiciary, frankly hostile? Or shall it be conceptual … ? Or shall it be functional, asking always the questions: (i) who is best fitted to exercise a discretion upon a question of this nature? and (ii) to what extent and by what type of persons shall the exercise of the discretion be supervised?[24]

The judicial approach had been hostile because the judges had been hostile to each of the three crucial characteristics of the agencies. First, the courts had been loyal to the common law and hostile to statutes as a form of law and to the institutions and standards they created: '[T]he common law is regarded as standard law, and statutes as an interference with its ordinary course.' Second, they had been loyal to the 'uncompromisingly individualistic' values of the common law and hostile to 'a social philosophy which sets public welfare above private right.' The power of their values, especially as expressed in presumptions, 'goes far to nullify the effect of statutes which emphasize not the rights of the subject but the claims of the state upon him.' Third, the courts had been opposed to the exercise of powers by the executive, especially discretionary powers. Willis demonstrated this hostility by analysing the course of cases during the past 50 years and demonstrating an increasing willingness on the part of the courts to review decisions of agencies.[25]

Willis' discussion of the 'conceptual' approach was vague and incomplete, but it was nevertheless provocative and insightful. He began by asserting that concepts were necessary for legal reasoning, although he did not define clearly what concepts and conceptual reasoning were. By 'concepts' he seems to have meant principles or general propositions, and he gave as examples trust, bailment, and the distinction between judicial and administrative powers. They were to be used by courts to decide particular disputes, but sometimes more than one concept seemed to apply and the choice among competing concepts was 'really a question not of law but of political science.'[26] The thought that more than one general principle might govern a dispute was the beginning of a fundamental challenge to late-nineteenth-century common law thought, but Willis did not pursue its implications. Instead, he turned to argue that concepts tended to acquire fixed and particular meanings that obscured their original significance. This modest thought was an introduction to an attack on the established English thought about law and government, as declared by Dicey and Lord Hewart, which Willis sought to show was inappropriate for modern government. Much of this discussion was a demonstration of how ideas shape perceptions and understanding, and in particular how lawyers carry two inconsistent sets of thought in their heads: the traditional faith and an understanding of the needs of modern government.

Willis clearly preferred the functional approach:

> The problem put is, how shall the powers of government be divided up? The problem is neither one of law nor of formal logic, but of expediency. The functional approach examines, first, the existing functions of existing governmental bodies in order to discover what kind of work each has in the past done best, and assigns the new work to the body which experience has shown best fitted to perform work of that type. If there is no such body, a new one is created *ad hoc*.[27]

Willis used this functional approach to explain the creation of agencies, giving licensing agencies as an example. Their work involved both policy-making and fact-finding. The legislatures were appropriate bodies for policy-making but not for fact-finding: '[A] court, although skilled in the ascertainment of facts and in the weighing of arguments, is unskilled in the consistent determination of policy,' and the executive could not appear to be free from 'the exigencies of party politics.'28 In short, 'All three existing arms of government being found inadequate to achieve the social purpose aimed at, a new type of body, called a commission, a government in miniature, is set up.'29

Willis also used this approach to design arrangements for review of the agencies. Some form of review was needed because 'no body ... should be empowered to decide the limits of its own jurisdiction,' but '[b]y whom? Not by the ordinary courts, for they have no experience of administrative policy.' The answer was a specialized and independent body, 'composed of persons trained in the practice of the whole law pertaining to administration.' This discussion emphasized a great faith in experience and expertise, which pervaded the entire article and most of Willis' writing in the 1930s.30

Willis shared much with Wright and Corry, especially the mood of excitement and change, the rejection of late-nineteenth-century judicial reasoning and values, and the plea to make law respond to its social context. Yet he also differed from them, in that he seemed to be more enthusiastic about the new and threatening world of administrative agencies, and, more important, in that his challenge to the rule of law was deeper and more dangerous. He proposed that judicial review, which was crucial to the preservation of the rule of law in the administrative state, should be replaced by review by a specialized administrative agency. And he occasionally seemed to suggest that the judge might inescapably be the despot that Wright and Corry struggled to escape, and that the objective reasoning of the rule of law was merely a mask. This dark streak was a minor element in his thought, which was never fully developed and which was entangled throughout with the more optimistic resort to the social context and policy he shared with Wright and Corry.31 In this way, Willis' thought resembled that of the Realists in the United States, although it was not merely derivative. Much of it was distinctive, especially the use of the functional approach in the design of administrative agencies. The inconsistent strands in his thought were never reconciled. The dark streak was simply covered over, but the inconsistency was the product of the efforts of a fertile and powerful mind.

One of the other articles was also about government and the agencies: 'Separation of Powers: A Study in Administrative Law,' by Jacob

Finkelman.[32] It was an analysis of the principle of the separation of powers, and especially its significance in the work of the courts in review of agencies and interpretation of the *BNA Act*. Its ideal was an eloquent general statement of the emerging ways of thinking. Law must serve 'practical ends ... the ends of society,' and must be measured by experience and not the 'test of logical principles out of tune with life.'[33] The bulk of the analysis was of the cases about review – the availability of the prerogative writs, the right to a hearing, and the liability of public officials, from which the conclusion was that the principle of separation of powers played no part in the doctrine or in the results. The analysis was based on a belief that the doctrine had not determined the outcome of the cases; it presented the uncertainties, inconsistencies, and trends in the cases but did not display any of the imagination or scope that Willis did.

One thinker in the volume who seems to have shared some of Willis' insights was Corbett. His article on international law shared the sense of change and reform and the emphasis on facts and perceptions of reality that pervaded the entire volume, and in a review, he said,

> Among all the fictions for which the legal profession is justly famous, none has been more persistent than that the rule of law for every conflict exists and can be discovered as the sole and inevitable conclusion of a process of logical thought. In one compartment of his brain [the lawyer] keeps his shrewd knowledge of forensic life, in another the congratulatory clap-trap of his calling, and rarely do these twain meet.[34]

The last of the four authors I want to consider extensively is Vincent MacDonald. He graduated from Dalhousie in 1925 and practised for 10 years before returning there as Dean. He was the only one who had not done graduate study of law in the United States. 'Judicial Interpretation of the Canadian Constitution'[35] was a comprehensive study of the interpretation of the *BNA Act*, including 'the meaning which the act has in the eyes of the courts today and, secondly, the doctrines and processes where-by that meaning has been ascertained.'[36]

It began with the blunt assertion that the *BNA Act* 'is not aptly framed to enable Canadian governments properly to grapple with current problems at all or in the way which a changed political philosophy requires.' Implicit in this assertion was the pervasive faith that the crucial standard for measuring law was its social context. MacDonald made the familiar claim that the dominant intention at Confederation had been to make a 'strong central government' and sought to demonstrate that the terms of the *BNA Act* expressed this intention faithfully. The study of the work of the courts began with 'lines of approach' and canons, essentially a list of propositions about interpretation taken from the leading cases from the late nineteenth century onwards, faithfully reproduced without any integration or critical analysis. He then turned to a description of trends and saw a simple, powerful trend in the cases. Up to 1925 and *Toronto Electric Commissioners v. Snider*[37] the courts narrowed the Dominion power and expanded the provincial powers. After that case they reversed this direction and established 'a flowing tide of returning vitality which, if sustained, may yet give Canada the constitution which it was intended to have.' Parallel to this trend was a shift from a 'literalistic ... technical' style to a liberal and purposeful approach.[38]

MacDonald's discussion of trends was based on the assumption, which ran throughout the article, that the terms of the *BNA Act* did not determine the outcomes of cases. But he did not integrate this assumption with his apparent faith in the 'lines of approach' and canons. Nor did he consider what the effect of the terms might be or what the other reasons for the results might be, and some of his other comments demonstrated some uncertainty. At the outset he said about the Privy Council that 'facts which relate to the history, personnel, and mental attitudes of that body up to now are extremely relevant to questions as to how we got the constitution which we have to-day.' Near his conclusion, in his discussion of the time for determining meaning, he said, '[T]he chief element of predictability of legal decision inheres in a known and uniform technique.'[39]

The consideration of change led MacDonald to consider the problem presented by changing contexts and preferences. Should meanings that words had in 1867 and the intention of the framers control the division of powers decades later? MacDonald gave this familiar problem a peculiar twist:

> Another way of putting this is to say that the act is to be construed in the light of the intention of its framers or in the light of the meaning which their words may have from time to time – To seek the intention from the words, or 'what has been said' merely, must result in attributing an intention as wide and as varying as the words themselves, which obviously change their connotation with time. Construction by intention limits the words to their accepted meaning in 1867 and allows the horizon of that year to restrict the measures of the future.[40]

He implied a preference for the changing meanings, but he did not give any justification for departures from the intention of the framers or choices among possible meanings, except, by implication from the entire structure of the article, the current economic and technological context and political preferences. Nor did he reconcile this preference with his apparent disapproval of the frustration of the original intentions.

In the conclusion MacDonald restated his belief that the prevailing division of powers was inappropriate. Canada's growing international independence, the vastly increased scale of economic and social organization, and the need for national economic regulation and social programs made amendment necessary. He could not, though, imagine a feasible way in which the amendments might be made. There could be no hope that they would be made by the courts, for even if the courts chose to respond, they could not act quickly enough and the scale of the changes that were needed was beyond their powers, but legislative change was frustrated by the lack of any effective procedure for making amendments.

At the very end of the article, MacDonald returned to his major theme – judicial construction. The terms of the Constitution depended upon the interpretations of the courts, and much of Canada's inadequate Constitution had been made by the Privy Council, 'and, inevitably, the question must arise as to whether it shall continue to be entrusted with the ultimate power of interpretation.'[41] The question had no express answer, although the discussion of the considerations left little doubt about his preference for the abolition of appeals.[42]

The claims that the BNA Act was inadequate for Canada's needs, especially in the depression, and that the courts had frustrated the original intention had been openly made by Canadian scholars since the late 1920s, but MacDonald's analysis was the most elaborate.[43] The scope of his article was ambitious, especially considering the sparse and crabbed writing about the Constitution since the late nineteenth century, but it was occasionally confused and inconsistent and did not demonstrate any significant originality or imagination.

These four scholars – Wright, Corry, Willis, and MacDonald – were distinctive individuals, and their assumptions, beliefs, and interests were far from identical, but they shared much, and what they shared pervaded most of the rest of the volume. Their most obvious characteristic was a rejection of nineteenth-century thought, or at least their understanding of it.

The thought that they rejected had emerged in England during the second half of the nineteenth century, and it can usefully be called 'the rule of law.' Its essential elements were the equality and autonomy of individuals, a division between the public and private realms, and the paramountcy of common law and courts. The common law was composed of general principles that were internally coherent and consistent. These principles were made by induction from the decided cases, and they were used to decide other cases through deductive reasoning, although most thinkers, especially by the end of the century, did not believe that the stock of settled principles would govern all cases. If none existed, the court made law in making its decision. These principles were understood to be expressions of values, generally Victorian and liberal values about the individual and society, but the process of forming them, making new ones, and applying them was objective and autonomous from its political and social context.[44]

This 'rule of law' was imported into Canada primarily from England and was firmly established by the early twentieth century. It erased most of an earlier tradition (in Ontario, at least), which was expressed most comprehensively in the writing of its major figure, Chief Justice John Beverley Robinson. This tradition stressed community, hierarchy, the responsibility of individuals to each other and to the community, respect for the legislature, and a faith that the common law was a visible expression of some fundamental purpose or power.

The thinkers in the 1930s rejected the reasoning and the values they perceived in the rule of law thought, although their perceptions of it were greatly oversimplified, largely because they were influenced by the descriptions by critics in the United States, especially Pound. They perceived and rejected the dominance of abstract logic and the reasoning that made a gulf between law and its context. They rejected the paramountcy of the courts and the common law, separation of law from life, devotion to the internal coherence and consistency of doctrine, and the faith that doctrine and logic could and should determine the outcome of cases. They usually had no precise and consistent understanding of what they meant by 'logic,' although they usually seem to have meant syllogistic logic – the deduction of results from a general principle and particular facts or, more vaguely, thinking divorced from social context and need. Instead, they proclaimed that law must not be an end in itself but must be measured by society and its purposes.

They also proclaimed that judges must often make choices. These choices were constrained by the common law and the terms of statutes, although none of them considered the nature of the limits or the ways in which the doctrine might influence results. These choices were expressions of values, but the values must not be the personal values of the judges. They rejected values they saw expressed in the structure and principles of the common law and in particular cases. These discussions of values tended to be much less extensive and powerful than the rejection of the rule of law reasoning, and much less powerful than the discussions by the critics in the United States. They tended to be brief and vague assertions, without any coherent account of the values that were at stake, and Willis was the only one who talked bluntly about a conflict between different political ideologies.

They believed that judges and scholars should study facts – 'what really happens' – and the social context of law, instead of abstract principles. Finkelman said, 'If law is to serve social ends, the legal scientist must approach his task with an open mind, must seek to ascertain the facts of social life as they are.'[45] This attitude was most often expressed about the work of the courts. For example, Corry said, 'We must look much more closely at what the judges do than at what they say,'[46] and Wright, invoking Pound, distinguished between the 'law in books' and the 'law in action.'[47] All four of the articles sought to reveal patterns in cases that were not apparent in the doctrine, although none of them stopped to consider what the effect of the doctrine might be, and none went further and called upon scholars to study the social effects of the decisions. The values and needs that should shape reform and the choices to be made by the courts seemed to be inherent in the social record, and to be discoverable by careful study of context and facts. Wright looked to 'commercial expediency' and 'business experience' for reform of the common law about agency,[48] and Corry looked to the 'purpose or object of the legislation ... and the social forces that brought it about' for statutory interpretation.[49] Willis would have designed agencies according to function, experience, and expertise, and MacDonald would have remade the Constitution to respond to 'our present social and economic organization and needs, and to prevailing political theories.'[50] None of the four made an extensive appeal to the social sciences, but implicit in their faith in research was a faith that it could be carried out objectively and free from the choices and values of the researcher. This faith is best captured by Corry's assertion that the purpose of a statute is 'very real.'[51] And for Willis the expertise of the administrators was as objective as the social record.

The last major characteristic of these thinkers was their belief that legislation and administrative agencies were important parts of the legal universe and lawyers' thought. The strength of this belief was not so much a few express proclamations as it was a matter-of-fact awareness that pervaded the entire issue. However, courts continued to be the primary focus. The major shift was from a preoccupation with common law reasoning to writing about statutory interpretation, review, and constitutional adjudication. Only Willis chose to consider the agencies themselves as a primary topic.

The scholars had a distinctive role in this vision, as critics and proponents of reform. For Wright, Corry, Willis, and MacDonald and for many of the others who wrote in the volume, this role dominated their efforts; their writing was inspired and pervaded by a passion to assess the law and to reform it. Their rejection of late-nineteenth-century thought and their proposals for common law reasoning would have seemed revolutionary to any lawyer educated in the rule of law thought, but they were not radical critics of their society and its politics. In their writing they all seemed to accept the established social order and allocations of power, although generally from a perspective that seems somewhat to the left of the centre of the political spectrum.

The role they proposed for scholars did not have a secure base. In England, in the late nineteenth century, legal scholars carved a narrow ledge for themselves within the hierarchical structure of the profession and were (or appeared to be) faithful handmaidens, whose primary role was the exposition and synthesis of doctrine.[52] Succeeding generations consolidated this ledge. In the United States scholars were much less shaped by a professional hierarchy, perhaps because they were more firmly established in universities and because the profession itself was much less structured. They were also much more willing to criticize and propose reforms. The Canadian scholars adopted the role of the scholars in the United States, but their profession was not likely to give them even a narrow ledge for this role and they were not yet firmly established in universities. They were doomed to struggle for at least a couple of decades until they found a ledge in the universities, although until recently this ledge was a narrow one that was a far cry from Kennedy's dream.

The new ways of thought and scholarship appeared surprisingly suddenly. There are only a few traces before they were revealed in 1932, in a short manifesto written by Caesar Wright in the *Canadian Bar Review* entitled 'An Extra-Legal Approach to Law.'[53] In it Wright rejected nineteenth-century thought and declared that 'the end of the law

228 The Challenge of Modernity

must always be found outside the law itself.'[54] Law should serve social purposes, and lawyers and legal scholars must study its social context. This issue of the *U.T.L.J.* three years later was the first substantial collection of the work of the revolutionaries. They were unorganized and isolated in their world of scholarship, but excited and with their future before them.

There were strong parallels between the work of this group and work in the other social sciences in Canada,[55] but they had little or no contact with other scholars and derived little of their understanding from them.[56] The major influence that shaped their understandings of law and the role of the scholar was twentieth-century scholarship in the United States. The similarities and parallels are pervasive, and some of the particular influences can be traced reasonably plausibly. Wright was greatly influenced by Pound during his graduate work, and Corry seems to have been influenced by his year at Columbia and the literature on interpretation. It is remarkable, though, that throughout the volume there are very few references to the Realists, and only Willis among all the writers during the 1930s expressed distinctively Realist thought.

This thought had appeared in the United States in the late nineteenth and early twentieth centuries, long before its appearance in Canada. The major reasons for this difference in timing are massive differences in the professional and intellectual contexts. In the United States the context included a group of law teachers established in universities, pragmatism, the Progressive movement, and suggestive developments in the social sciences. In Canada, the rule of law tradition was much stronger and the law teachers were much more dominated by the professional hierarchy; idealism, not pragmatism, was the dominant philosophical tradition until after the First World War; and the social sciences were barely beginning.

The scholars in Canada were not as successful in reshaping legal thought as were their counterparts in the United States. Their thought became powerful in the scholarly community, but they failed to destroy the rule of law tradition, and it continued to be the dominant discourse of lawyers for decades. The rule of law tradition continues much stronger in Canada than in the United States, and the competing vision proclaimed in the first volume of the *U.T.L.J.* appeared earlier in Canada than in England and continues to be stronger. Both modes of thought continue in uneasy tension, modified by the course of thought in the following years. Law school common rooms are full of debate and misunderstanding about the purposes of discourse, and first-year students are often not sure when to talk about 'law' and when to talk about 'policy.' This tension can be seen as the product of the transfer of the allegiance of an intellectual colony. The adoption of the 'rule of law' in the late nineteenth century was a declaration of allegiance to a model imported primarily from England. In the 1930s the revolutionaries sought to replace it with a model made in the United States. For decades afterwards Canadian graduate students were sent to American schools, and we faithfully studied neutral principles, the legal processes, law and economics, and now Critical Legal Studies. And more law teachers have read Rawls on justice than have read George Grant. Yet this perspective alone is too bleak. The tension can also be seen as an expression of a distinctive Canadian accommodation. But if it is, we have failed to think enough to understand it and to develop its riches.

I began with a faintly masked pride about the first volume, and I end with a hope. I hope simply that the *U.T.L J.* will continue to contribute to shaping Canadian legal thought for the next 50 years.

NOTES

1 W.P.M. Kennedy, 'Law as a Social Science' [1934] *South African L.T.* 100, at 100, 101, and 103; this article was one of a regular series that Kennedy wrote in the *South Africa Law Times* about Canadian law.

Editor's Note: For an extended discussion of Kennedy's view of law and his ambitions for a law school, see R.C.B. Risk, 'The Many Minds of W.P.M. Kennedy,' in this volume. For the general context of scholarship in the 1930s, see R.C.B. Risk, 'Canadian Law Teachers,' in this volume.

2 W.P.M. Kennedy, 'Foreword' (1935) 1 *U.T.LJ.* 1, 2.

3 F.C. Auld, 'The Comparative Jurisprudence of Criminal Process' (1935) 1 *U.T.L.J.* 82; P.E. Corbett, 'Fundamentals of a New Law of Nations' (1935) 1 *U.T.LJ.* 3; J.A. Corry, 'Administrative Law and the Interpretation of Statutes' (1936) 1 *U.T.L.J.* 286; J. Finkelman, 'Separation of Powers: A Study in Administrative Law' (1936) 1 *U.T.L J.* 313; A.B. Keith, 'The American Law Institute's Restatement of the Conflict of Laws' (1936) 1 *U.T.L.J.* 233; V. MacDonald, 'Judicial Interpretation of the Canadian Constitution' (1936) 1 *U.T.L.J.* 260; P.B. Mignault, 'Le Code civil de la Province de Quebec et son interpretation' (1935) 1 *U.T.L J.* 104; J. Willis, 'Three Approaches to Administrative Law: The Judicial, the Conceptual and the

Functional' (1935) 1 *U.T.L.J.* 53; and C.A. Wright, 'The American Law Institute's Restatement of Contracts and Agency' (1935) 1 *U.T.LJ.* 17.

4 Wright, supra note 3.
5 Ibid. 18.
6 For example, he did not expressly say whether the choices were the product of the incompleteness or internal inconsistency of the particular pattern, the nature of elaborating or reasoning from general principles, or some inherent and pervasive indeterminacy. However, his enthusiasm for the whole enterprise demonstrated that he would have denied any pervasive indeterminacy.
7 Ibid. 20–1.
8 Ibid. 19.
9 Ibid. 21.
10 Ibid. 20.
11 Ibid. 26.
12 Ibid. 34–5.
13 Ibid. 38.
14 Ibid. 22. He wrote at length about the role of the scholar and reform later in the 1930s, in 'Law and the Law Schools' (1938) 16 *Can. Bar R.* 579. Here education is limited to the training of lawyers, in contrast to Kennedy's vision of law as a social science. So far as understanding the common law thought generally goes, there are three themes: i) an emphasis on 'change, criticism and reform,' and the obligation to consider the 'is' as well as the 'ought'; ii) the need for research ('What shall be our standard?'), especially research into comparative law, and the context of social fact and need; and iii) an understanding that law reflects economic philosophy.
15 Keith, supra note 3.
16 Ibid. 82, 83, 102, 103.
17 Corry, supra note 3.
18 Ibid. 288–9.
19 Ibid. 290, 291, 292.
20 Ibid. 291, 292.
21 Ibid. 289, 309.
22 Two of the major articles were M. Radin, 'Statutory Interpretation' (1930) 43 *Harvard L.R.* 863, and J.M. Landis, 'A Note on Statutory Interpretation' (1930) 43 *Harvard L.R.* 886. In his autobiography Corry says little about approaches to legal thought, but in describing the year at Columbia he refers to 'an intellectual ferment' and says that 'new movements of thought were looking at law from philosophical and sociological points of view.' J.A. Corry, *My Life and Work, A Happy Partnership: The Memoirs of*

J.A. Corry (Montreal and Kingston: McGill-Queen's University Press, 1981).

23 Willis, supra note 3. The phrase 'administrative process' would have seemed odd to Willis, but it is more useful to describe the article than any that is familiar to contemporary readers. See R.C.B. Risk, 'John Willis: A Tribute,' in this volume.

24 Ibid. 59.

25 Ibid. 59, 60. The cases he analysed were English; the Canadian record is different.

26 Ibid. 70.

27 Ibid. 75.

28 Ibid. 77.

29 Ibid. 78.

30 Ibid. 78, 80. Proposals for review by a specialized agency had been made in the late 1920s and early 1930s by a few scholars in England, especially W.A. Robson, and had been summarily rejected by the Donoughmore Committee; see *Report of the Committee on Minister's Powers* Cmd 4060 (1932) 110.

31 The dark streak and the essential inconsistency between it and the dominant optimistic faith is most apparent in his great article, 'Statute Interpretation is a Nutshell' (1938) 16 *Can. Bar. Rev.* 1

32 Finkelman, supra note 3.

33 33. Ibid. 313, 341, 342. Finkelman expressed the same attitudes in a review of a set of books about the administrative process: J. Finkelman, 'Review' (1936) 1 *U.T.L.J.* 196.

34 P.E. Corbett, 'Review' (1936) 1 *U.T.L.J.* 410, at 410.

35 MacDonald, supra note 3.

36 Ibid. 260.

37 [1925] A.C. 306 (P.C.).

38 MacDonald, supra note 3, 260, 276, 277. MacDonald based his perception of the shift in the trend on *Proprietary Articles Trade Association v. Attorney General Canada for Canada* [1931] A.C. 310 (P.C.); *In re Regulation and Control of Aeronautics in Canada* [1932] A.C. 54 (P.C.); *In re Regulation and Control of Radio Communications in Canada* [1932] A.C. 304 (P.C.); and *British Coal Corporation v. The King* [1935] A.C. 500 (P.C.).

39 MacDonald, supra note 3 at 261, 281.

40 Ibid. 280.

41 Ibid. 284.

42 The fate of the New Deal legislation provoked an express and angry claim for abolition of appeals from MacDonald and several other constitutional

scholars in a symposium arranged by Caesar Wright. See W.P.M. Kennedy, 'The British North America Act: Past and Future' (1937) 15 *Can. Bar R.* 391; V. MacDonald, 'The Canadian Constitution – Seventy Years After' (1937) 15 *Can. Bar R.* 401; and F.R. Scott, 'The Consequences of the Privy Council Decisions' (1937) 15 *Can. Bar R.* 485.

43 See, for example, W.P.M. Kennedy, *Essays in Constitutional Law* (London: Oxford University Press, 1934); F.R. Scott, 'The Development of Canadian Federalism' (1931) 3 *Procs. Can. Political Science Assoc.* 231; and H. Smith, 'The Residue of Power in Canada' (1926) 4 *Can. Bar R.* 432.

44 Finkelman, 'Review,' supra note 33 at 196.

45 Ibid.
Editors' Note: From here on the notes are numbered in a way different from that of the original article, because in the original this note was omitted and subsequent notes were placed in the wrong place in the text.

46 Corry, supra note 3 at 289.

47 Wright, supra note 3 at 47.

48 Ibid. 43, 47.

49 Corry, supra note 3 at 292.

50 MacDonald, supra note 3, 282.

51 Corry, supra note 3 at 292.

52 D. Sugarman, 'Legal Theory, the Common Law Mind, and the Making of the Textbook Tradition,' in W. Twining, ed., *Legal Theory and Common Law* (Oxford: Basil Blackwell, 1986) 26.

53 C.A. Wright, 'An Extra-Legal Approach to Law' (1932) 10 *Can. Bar R.* 1.

54 Ibid. 2.

55 See C. Berger, *The Writing of Canadian History: Aspects of English Canadian Historical Writing since 1900* (Toronto: University of Toronto Press, 1976); C. Ferguson, 'The New Political Economy and Canadian Liberal Democratic Thought: Queen's University 1890–1925' (PhD thesis, York University, 1982); and D. Owram, *The Government Generation: Canadian Intellectuals and the State, 1900–1945* (Toronto: University of Toronto Press, 1986); and. See also L. Armour and E. Trott, *The Faces of Reason: An Essay on Philosophy and Culture in England Canada, 1850–1950* (Waterloo: Wilfrid Laurier University Press, 1981); and A.B. McKillop, *A Disciplined Intelligence: Critical Inquiry and Canadian Thought in the Victorian Era* (Montreal and Kingston: McGill-Queen's University Press, 1979).

56 *Editors' Note*: For a more extended discussion of Canadian legal scholarship in the 1930s, see R.C.B. Risk, 'Canadian Law Teachers,' in this volume.

8

The Scholars and the Constitution: POGG and the Privy Council

Canadian lawyers, historians, and political scientists have written count-less pages about the judgments of the Judicial Committee of the Privy Council that interpreted the division of legislative powers made by sections 91 and 92 of the *British North America Act* of 1867 (*BNA Act*).[1] They have named heroes and villains, and successive generations have had different understandings about how to analyse the judgments and about what standards define a hero or a villain. This essay does not attempt to add more pages to this pile. Instead, it is about the writers themselves and their ways of writing. It is, though, limited to the writers who were also lawyers, particularly common lawyers, because they have distinctive and important ways of thinking that need to be studied. My argument is hardly startling: their writing reflected their beliefs about legal reasoning and legal scholarship, as well as their visions of Canada. The story and the argument can best be presented chronologically, in four parts, although the dates do no more than mark convenient separations.

First, a description of sections 91 and 92 is needed. Section 92 gave the provinces power to legislate 'exclusively … in relation to matters coming within' a list of 16 subjects, including, for example, 'direct taxation within the province' (s. 92(2)), 'property and civil rights in the province' (s. 92(13)), and 'all matters of a merely local or private nature' in the province (s. 92(16)). Section 91 opened by giving the Dominion power to legislate for 'the Peace, Order and Good Government' (POGG)

of Canada, in relation to all matters not assigned to the provinces. It
continued, 'for greater certainty,' with a declaration that the exclusive
power of the Dominion included all matters coming within a list of 29
subjects, including, for example, the regulation of trade and commerce
(s. 91(2)), taxation by any means (s. 91(3)), and the criminal law (s.
91(27)). Section 91 then concluded by saying that any matter coming
within any of the subjects in this list 'shall not be deemed to come
within the class of matters of a local or private nature' assigned to the
provinces. After lawyers had read and reread these sections for a century and more the assumption suggested by the phrase 'for greater
certainty' had become wonderfully ironic.

From Confederation to 1900: Lefroy

The early decisions by the Supreme Court of Canada tended to favour
the Dominion,[2] but in the early 1880s, the results were mixed. In 1881,
in *Citizen's Insurance v. Parsons*,[3] the Privy Council dismissed a challenge to Ontario legislation regulating the terms of insurance policies,
and Sir Montague Smith limited section 91(2) to regulation of interprovincial and international trade, and, 'it may be ... general regulation
of trade throughout the whole Dominion.' A year later, in *Russell v. R.*[4]
both the Supreme Court of Canada and the Privy Council upheld the
Dominion's *Canada Temperance Act*, which permitted prohibition of
liquor by local option. A majority of the Supreme Court put the Act
squarely within section 91(2), but the Privy Council chose a different
ground. Because prohibition was a matter of 'public order, safety, or
morals,' it was not within any of the enumerated powers in section 92,
and there was no need to decide whether it came within section 91(2) or
the general power to legislate for the peace, order, and good government of Canada. Later generations saw *Russell* as the high-water mark
of Dominion power.

The trend of the cases shifted decisively a year later in *R. v. Hodge*,[5] in
which the Privy Council upheld an Ontario statute regulating taverns,
as a matter of 'good government, ... peace, and public decency.' A few
years later, in 1885, a Dominion statute much like the Ontario statute
affirmed in *Hodge* was declared *ultra vires* in the *McCarthy Act Reference*,[6] and the triumphs of the provinces continued through the next
decade. The climax came in 1896, in the Privy Council's decision in the
Local Prohibition Reference,[7] upholding Ontario's local option legislation,
which permitted prohibition of liquor in substantially the same way as

the Dominion's *Canada Temperance Act*. The result was hardly startling, because the crusade against drink was just the sort of local matter assigned to the provinces at Confederation, and from this perspective, *Russell* was the problematic holding. It was Lord Watson's reasons that were significant. He began with an essay on the structure of sections 91 and 92, which was dominated by a fear that POGG was a threat to the autonomy of the provinces. This fear led him to read it as secondary to the powers enumerated in section 92, and also to declare that it should be 'strictly confined' to matters of 'national concern.' This declaration was central to the analysis of sections 91 and 92 during the next four decades: was it a declaration that POGG was a robust power to deal with matters of a general or national nature, or a warning that POGG would be narrowly interpreted? Next, Watson announced that the result in *Russell* itself could not have been based on section 91(2), justifying this assertion by asserting that the word 'regulation' did not include prohibition. Turning to the provincial powers, he said that the prohibition legislation was valid under either section 92(13) or section 92(16), launching section 92(13) on its path to becoming the dominant section during the 1920s and 1930s.

Writings by lawyers about constitutional law began in the late 1870s, and by 1900 a small pile of texts, articles, and lectures had appeared, all written by practitioners.[8] Loyal to Great Britain, they saw Canada's Constitution as a distinctive combination of federalism and the glorious British Constitution, especially parliamentary sovereignty, responsible government, and liberty. Federalism was their major topic, almost the exclusive topic, probably because it marked Canada's distinctiveness and it created the most pressing doctrinal issues.

The most useful example of this writing was *The Law of Legislative Power in Canada*, written by A.H.F. Lefroy while he was a practitioner in Toronto, which appeared in 1898. In its preface, Lefroy announced that his objective was to 'extract' from the cases on the *BNA Act* the doctrine that was of 'general application upon the law governing the distribution of power ... [and] to formulate the results so arrived at in general Propositions.' The introduction was a long hymn to the British constitution and liberty, and to the accomplishment of combining responsible government and federalism. The main body of the text was just what Lefroy promised in the preface. It was composed of 68 numbered propositions, derived from the cases and each followed by extensive commentary. *Russell*, *Hodge*, the *Local Prohibition Reference*, and the other Privy Council judgments were analysed and synthesized at length.

Many of the propositions were taken directly from the language of the judgments; the commentary was mostly quotations or paraphrases of judgments; and there was a large amount of uncritical overlapping and duplication. Nonetheless, the result was a major accomplishment. By the mid-1890s, the cases had become a jumble, which Lefroy ordered in ways that now seem simple, and much of what seemed simple after he wrote had not seemed simple before. Throughout, he was respectful to the courts, offering no criticism except an occasional suggestion that the cases might not be entirely consistent.[9]

For Lefroy, the powers of the Dominion and the provinces were mutually exclusive spheres of absolute power, defined and separated by sharp boundaries. The duty of the courts was to determine the limits of these spheres. Their function was ultimately statutory interpretation, which was generally understood to be the determination of the will of the legislature as expressed in the words of the statute. Only the words of statutes were to be considered, unless they were unclear, and if they were, the interpretation was to be guided by 'legal principles,' typically the common law presumptions.[10] Lefroy perceived this task as an objective and apolitical one, and the only standard for assessing decisions was their consistency with the terms of the BNA Act and the 'legal principles.' Once made, decisions became precedents, which subsequent courts were obliged to follow.

Throughout, the text and its doctrine seemed to be separate from time, context, and values. The very form of the text contributed to this perception: the propositions were put in heavy type and set off by spacing from the commentary, which thereby became secondary. Both propositions and commentary were virtually all doctrinal analysis, unrelated to any historical, social, or political context, and there was little or no acknowledgment that the doctrine had changed. There was no significant discussion of Confederation and its understandings, or of the provincial rights movement: a struggle for power between the provinces, led by Ontario, and the Dominion, waged on many battlegrounds, and ending in triumph for the provinces. Nor was there any sense that the doctrine might be assessed by an inquiry into the nature of Canada, its federalism, and its needs.

A few months after the text appeared, Lefroy wrote a short comment about the Local Prohibition Reference, expressing a fear that the inquiry into whether a matter had become a matter of 'national concern' might 'bring before the courts very difficult questions and questions of a very political character.'[11] His fear was that questions about division of powers might become questions of degree, not of bright lines, and might involve judgments about the nature and needs of the nation. As we shall see later, this fear was a crucial contrast to beliefs about interpretation almost a hundred years later.

Lefroy's text manifested understandings of legal reasoning and scholarship that became dominant among scholars in England and the United States during the second half of the nineteenth century. The basic elements of this thought were the equality and autonomy of individuals and legal entities generally, a division between the public and private realms, a conception of rights as spheres of absolute power, the paramountcy of the common law and the courts, and a belief that legal reasoning was sharply separated from politics and context.[12] Canadian lawyers embraced English thought; Lefroy had studied at Oxford, where much of the formative scholarship was done, and he was one of its exemplars in Canada. In contrast, he and his generation of the Canadian legal community did not often look to the United States, except to proclaim the superiority of the British Constitution.

Lawyers learned during this period to separate talk about jurisdiction and power sharply from the nature and needs of Canada and its citizens, a lesson that shaped their thinking for much of the twentieth century. Yet their writings were not entirely divorced from the fray of late-nineteenth-century politics. The language of separate and autonomous spheres of power was also the language of the campaign for provincial rights. This link between scholarship, constitutional doctrine, and politics was clearly displayed in a set of lectures on constitutional law given at the University of Toronto in the 1890s by David Mills, a lawyer and one of the major provincial rights politicians. The point is not that Lefroy and Mills bent their scholarship to a political purpose. Instead, the language of absolute rights and spheres of powers was a pervasive one, and one that could give powerful symbols to the political campaign.[13]

From 1900 to the Late 1920s: Ewart, Labatt, Smith

In the early twentieth century, Lord Haldane replaced Lord Watson as the dominant figure in the Privy Council, and a new generation of judges, led by Sir Lyman Poore Duff, appeared on the Supreme Court of Canada. By the late 1920s, the Dominion's powers seemed to many Canadians to be a pale image of what had been contemplated at Confederation and what the *BNA Act* had given it: POGG was a minor, supplementary power, to be used only in emergencies; section 91(2) was severely restricted; and section 92(13) seemed to be the dominant power. How was this departure to be understood? Was it essentially a product of the cases decided before 1900, especially the *Local Prohibition Reference*? Or, instead, was it a product of the twentieth-century cases? Was the villain, or the saviour, Watson or Haldane? These have been tempting questions for half a century, but an attempt to fashion yet another answer here would stray from the topic. Instead, for studying the writers and their writings, the judgments can be ink blots, in the manner of a Rorschach test, for the writers to interpret.

Although several judgments between 1910 and 1920 suggested trends and doctrines, the major cases were decided in the early 1920s. The first was the *Board of Commerce Reference*. Here, Haldane limited section 91(2) by saying that it did not permit regulation of 'a particular trade in which Canadians would otherwise be free to engage in the provinces,' thereby extending the doctrine in *Parsons* about regulating terms of contracts of a trade to regulating an entire trade. As well, he added a comment that could be read as making section 91(2) no more than a supplement to POGG, and said that section 91(27) was confined to matters that were, in their 'very nature,' criminal. Coming to POGG itself, he announced the limitation for which he became notorious in Canada: if legislation also affected property and civil rights, POGG could be used only in 'exceptional' or 'special circumstances such as a great war.'[14]

A little less than two years later, in *Fort Frances Pulp and Power v. Manitoba Free Press*, he added the phrases 'sudden danger to the social order' and 'emergency,'[15] and in *Toronto Electric Commissioners v. Snider*, he spoke of 'some extra-ordinary peril to the national life of Canada.'[16] As well, Haldane explained *Russell*, which he had been at pains to narrow throughout, by saying that drink had been a 'menace to the national life of Canada,' and the Dominion prohibition had been designed 'to protect the nation from disaster.' The 'national concern' was either forgotten or collapsed into an emergency.

Early in this period, the Supreme Court of Canada was divided; but at the end Duff dominated, and some of his decisions, rather than being entirely determined by the authority of the Privy Council, anticipated some of its more extreme holdings. Both Duff and Haldane seemed unwilling to contemplate the possibility that a particular episode or a collection of particular episodes could have some general or national dimensions. The capacity of the provinces to legislate, typically through section 92(13), was alone sufficient to exclude the Dominion.[17]

From 1900 until the mid 1920s, almost all the writings continued to be done by practising lawyers, the only conspicuous academic being Lefroy, who had become a professor at the University of Toronto in 1900. Almost all of it took the form of articles in legal periodicals, analysing particular decisions of the Supreme Court or the Privy Council.[18] The understandings of legal reasoning and the job of a scholar continued to be the understandings that were dominant in the late nineteenth century, and a wonderful example was a debate about *Royal Bank of Canada v. The King*.[19] The problem was, who was entitled to the proceeds of bonds issued by a railway under construction in Alberta. They had been sold in England under an agreement providing that the proceeds were to be paid into an account of the Royal Bank in Edmonton, to be disbursed as construction proceeded, but the railway floundered. The bondholders were doubtless entitled to recover the proceeds from the railway, because the purpose of the bonds had ceased to exist, but Alberta enacted a statute expropriating the proceeds. In response, the bondholders brought an action claiming that the statute was invalid, and that they, not Alberta, were entitled to recover the proceeds. The validity depended upon the location of the proceeds: were they property 'in the province'? Reversing the Supreme Court, the Privy Council held that the locus was Montreal, the head office of the Bank, and not Alberta, and therefore the claim of the bondholders to recover the proceeds was 'a civil right outside the province,' and the legislation was invalid.

The debate, waged from 1913 to 1915 in 12 articles, involved three of the major writers of the period and a couple of minor supporters. The first to enter the fray was Lefroy. He defined a civil right as a power to 'invoke the aid of the courts of the province by way of action or by way of defence.' Because the bondholders had a right to sue the Royal Bank in Alberta, the Treasurer had the same right. Therefore, the claim was a civil right in the province, and the legislation came within section 92 (13). He argued as well that bondholders also had a right to sue the Bank at its head office in Quebec, implying that Quebec could have enacted similar legislation.[20] Next came J.S. Ewart from Winnipeg, well known to Canadian historians as a passionate advocate of independence for Canada, a leading counsel, and a remarkably powerful thinker, albeit cranky and erratic. He argued that the money was in the province, and therefore 'property' within section 92 (13), or an asset of the company that could be expropriated under section 92 (10).[21]

The last of the three principal protagonists was C.B. Labatt, who defended the Privy Council. He was not as learned as Lefroy or as imaginative as Ewart, but he was an editor of the *Canadian Law Journal* and the most prolific writer of the period. He argued that the definition of a civil right should be derived from private international law: a substantive right incident to property. According to this principle, the proceeds were in Quebec, not Alberta, and the legislation was therefore *ultra vires*.[22]

Despite heated disagreements, all three scholars shared understandings about legal reasoning and interpretation, and basic principles about division of powers issues. Outcomes should be determined by using these principles, and subsidiary doctrines appropriate for particular cases, such as the common law doctrine about the location of a debt. In applying these principles, the nature of federalism, the historical understandings that might illuminate the *BNA Act* and the contemporary context were simply not permitted or even contemplated. For example, Labatt and Lefroy did not justify their definitions of civil rights, except for a vague reference to the autonomy of the provinces made by Lefroy, and none of the three considered the vulnerability of non-resident bondholders, or the effectiveness of democratic responsibility as a limit on provincial legislatures, even when considering whether Alberta or Quebec, or both, could legislate about the proceeds. Considerations of this sort were not simply irrelevant; instead, they were embedded in the general principles. Certainly outcomes might sometimes be affected by this kind of influence in the application of the principles, but this possibility was no more than the possibility of human error and fallibility. Their understandings about legal reasoning illuminated the gulf between law, and politics and context. In his reply to Labatt, Lefroy challenged a claim, made by one of Labatt's supporters, that no one could doubt the 'perfect justice or wisdom' of the Privy Council's decision:

> All I can assume to discuss is law, not perfect justice or wisdom. Law may be, and ought to be, just and wise. But whether it is or not, is a matter with which a lawyer, as such, has nothing to do. That is what the old philosopher Hobbes meant when he laid down the dictum so shocking to weak minds – that 'no law can be unjust.'[23]

Labatt agreed. After Ewart had suggested that the Privy Council had been influenced by a desire to protect property and British investors, and that such influence was not only improper but a reason for abolishing appeals, Labatt rushed to its defence. Its ignorance of Canadian conditions, which Ewart saw as a disqualification, was really a blessing:

> A controversy determined by jurists of ample practical experience, who consider the law and the facts with the intellectual detachment of College professors forming an opinion in regard to the soundness of abstract doctrines may well be said to have been determined under ideal conditions.[24]

Before 1925, POGG was rarely considered, although in a few articles it was perceived as a substantial power, albeit an unsettled or undefined one, and the possibility that matters might have national dimensions or importance seemed to be a real one. In 1909, for example, A.C. Heighington claimed that it might support the Dominion's *Industrial Disputes Investigation Act*, prohibiting strikes at railways and public works before arbitration,[25] a claim denied 15 years later in *Snider*. Section 91(2), which was discussed more often, also seemed to most authors to be a substantial power even though they were clearly aware of *Parsons*. Lefroy and Z.A Lash, for example, both claimed that it gave the Dominion extensive powers to regulate the national economy.[26] Cases decided before 1900 were not perceived as raising discrete topics or problems, and there was little criticism of the judgments or the fate of the *BNA Act*.[27] Whether this absence of criticism was a product of beliefs about scholarship or an assessment of the cases is difficult to determine, although the debate about the *Royal Bank* case shows that criticism was not utterly unthinkable.

Beliefs about legal reasoning and scholarship changed drastically in the mid-1920s, and the occasion for declaring the change was the *Snider* case, especially Haldane's comments about *Russell*. In 1926, H.A. Smith, a young Englishman teaching at McGill, wrote two articles that presented both a sustained criticism of the Privy Council and a different mode of reasoning.[28] He agreed that the object of interpretation was to discover the intent of the legislature as expressed in the words of the statute, but he argued that words alone did not have fixed meanings. Instead, their meanings depended upon purposes and contexts. Therefore, evidence about the making of a statute, such as parliamentary debates and public speeches, should be considered. Yet the English courts had deprived themselves of this information by an 'arbitrary and unreasonable rule,' with the result that Canada had been given 'a Constitution substantially different from that which her founders intended that she should have.' Smith undertook a long account of the debates at Confederation to show that 'the Dominion was endowed with a general power to pass all legislation that it might deem to be for the general interest of Canada.' The early decisions of the Privy Council had been faithful to this vision: the 'national concern' limitation in the *Local Prohibition Reference* was 'a clear recognition of the true test of jurisdiction'; but after Haldane, and the *Board of Commerce Reference* and *Snider*, section 92 (13) was 'the real residuary power ... in normal times,' and 'this result is the precise opposite of that which our fathers hoped and endeavoured to attain.' This set of ideas – his reading of the *BNA Act*, the claim that its meaning (as demonstrated by the context) had been betrayed, and the criticism of approaches to interpretation – set the stage for the next 50 years of constitutional arguments.[29] Smith's attack on excluding evidence of context was much more than an attack on a small corner of doctrine. Ultimately it was a challenge to the distinction between law and politics, for to admit the evidence was to diminish the authority of 'legal principles,' and to perceive interpretation as grounded in a particular time and place.[30]

The 1930s: Kennedy, MacDonald, Scott

The Privy Council decided three cases, early in the 1930s, all involving challenges to Dominion legislation, that seemed to Canadian observers to signal a shift, both in results and in the manner of reasoning, in cases about the division of legislative powers.[31] In the first, *Proprietary Articles Trade Association v. A.G.Canada*,[32] Lord Atkin gave section 91(27) an expansive reading,[33] asserting that Haldane could not have meant what he said in the *Board of Commerce Reference* about acts in 'their very nature' criminal. As well, he went out of his way to disavow Haldane's suggestion that section 91(2) was merely a supplementary power. Two more cases, the *Aeronautics Reference*[34] and the *Radio Communication Reference*[35] involved, for the first time in any substantial way, the Dominion's power to implement treaty obligations. Section 132, which gave the Dominion power to implement 'Empire treaties,' seemed to be limited to treaties binding Canada as part of the British Empire; but Lord Sankey suggested that it also gave the Dominion power to make legislation to implement treaties that it made as an independent nation. As well, he made some comments that seemed to give general support to the Dominion. He spoke of its 'high functions and almost sovereign powers,'[36] and seemed to suggest that the 'national concern' could support legislation to implement treaties.

Smith returned to England in 1929, and three other writers were dominant during the 1930s. The most prolific was W.P.M. Kennedy, dean of the Honour School of Law at the University of Toronto, who had been a distinguished historian of Elizabethan England before shifting his interests to Canada and law. After writing a 'whiggish' constitutional history of Canada in the early 1920s, his approach changed dramatically.[37] The second was Vincent MacDonald, who joined the Faculty of Law at Dalhousie University after 10 years of varied practice, and became dean there in 1934.[38]

The third was Frank Scott, a member of the Faculty of Law at McGill, a major Canadian poet, a founder of the Co-operative Commonwealth Federation (CCF), and a crusader for civil liberties.[39] All three were obviously academics, and from this time onwards practitioners contributed a smaller and smaller portion of the writings.

For these three Canada had become an independent nation and her economy and social structure, and the appropriate role of government, had all changed. They believed passionately that only a strong Dominion government could respond adequately to the Depression. Even though they were encouraged by the suggestions of change in the early 1930s, they feared that the BNA Act, especially as interpreted by the Privy Council, was inadequate, and called for reform. All these beliefs were shared with a larger group of intellectuals, especially economists, political scientists, and social workers, that had emerged since 1900.[40]

The most useful example of their work is a comprehensive article written by MacDonald in 1935 for the first volume of the University of Toronto Law Journal, itself a mark of the emergence of new attitudes towards legal thought and scholarship.[41] He began with an account of Confederation, claiming that the dominant objective had been to create a strong Dominion. Turning to the work of the courts, he set out a list of the principles and canons used in interpretation, taken from the leading cases: the same sort of list that formed Lefroy's text. He described trends in the results and reasonings in the cases, beginning with the betrayal of the BNA Act and the erosion of the Dominion's powers from the late nineteenth century to the late 1920s. Macdonald did not stop to give details or designate villains, saying that the story was trite. He described the signs of a shift in the early 1930s, and then turned to a discussion of interpretation generally, struggling to accommodate both the changing needs of Canada and the authority of the original text of the BNA Act. He concluded that the BNA Act, as interpreted by the Privy Council, was inappropriate for the needs of the nation that Canada had become. Amendment was needed, and even appeals to the Privy Council might be reconsidered. Kennedy and Scott would have agreed with virtually every word. These three shared beliefs about interpretation that were substantially the same as Smith's, although they rarely expressed them at any length. The obligation of the courts continued to be to determine the intent of the legislature, although 'purpose' came to be the more common term. The words of a text alone were not reliable, but purpose could be gathered from history and context.[42] As well, they shared with Smith a belief about the general design of Confederation and the BNA Act: it gave the provinces specific powers to legislate about local matters, with the residue to the Dominion. POGG was the sole grant of power to the Dominion, and the enumerations in section 91 were examples. Their efforts to articulate and justify this interpretation, which differed from much of the scholarship in the late nineteenth and early twentieth centuries, was a major part of the making of a vision of Confederation that dominated Canadian thought about the Constitution for decades.

In the late 1920s and early 1930s, they berated the Privy Council for both its approach to interpretation and its betrayal of the BNA Act. Its claim that interpretation should be limited to words alone was founded on the unrealistic faith that words alone could have meaning, and had led it to ignore clear evidence about the objective of Confederation. In 1929, Kennedy made both Watson and Haldane villains by saying that the path of deviation began with Hodge. 'Words could scarcely be clearer,' but nonetheless the results were 'diametrically opposed.'

Seldom have statesmen more deliberately striven to write their purpose into law, and seldom have these more signally failed before the judicial technique of statutory interpretation.[43]

In 1931, Scott also located the beginnings of deviation in the late nineteenth century, but assigned most of the blame to Haldane, for his fictitious limitations on POGG, chiefly the 'extraordinary' emergency doctrine, which were a 'flat contradiction of the agreement of 1867,' and which had obscured Watson's 'sensible' inquiry into national concern. Scott was the first scholar to assert specifically that section 91 had been divided, and POGG had been separated from the eruunerations. He clearly believed that the BNA Act, especially POGG, properly interpreted, would have been appropriate for the country Canada had become, but, like Kennedy, he called for fundamental reform.[44]

The only sustained discussion of interpretation and the most radical proposal came from MacDonald. Accepting that interpretation must be based ultimately on the text of the *BNA Act*, he argued in his 1935 article that courts should not seek the original intention of the framers or the meaning of true words in 1867, as the Privy Council had done in most of its judgments about the division of powers: 'Construction by intention limits the words to their accepted meaning in 1867, and allows the horizon of that year to restrict the measures of the future.' Instead, the guide should be the meaning of the words 'from time to time,' which 'gives flexibility and power of adaptation.'[45] He made the same argument in writing about treaties, arguing in 1933 that section 132, if interpreted 'progressively and liberally,' would alone give the Dominion adequate power to legislate to implement treaties,[46] and in 1935 he illuminated his understanding of interpretation of words 'from time to time,' by adding 'against the background of recent legal and political facts,' and considering 'the purposes' of the *BNA Act*.[47] This proposal was an attempt to grapple with change, a theme that pervaded the writings of this period. It contained a tension between respect for the understandings at Confederation and the needs of a different time, a tension that MacDonald and the others avoided discussing, perhaps because for them, a strong national government was both what had been intended and what was needed in the depths of the Depression.

Smith, Kennedy, Scott, and MacDonald were representatives of new approaches to legal reasoning and scholarship, which had begun around the turn of the century in law schools in the United States, under the banners of 'sociological jurisprudence,' and 'legal realism,' and in England a few decades afterwards. Although these new approaches did not constitute a unified school, they shared a few dominant themes. This new generation rejected the late-nineteenth-century beliefs or, more accurately, their own version of their ancestors' beliefs. Instead, they believed that judicial decisions were shaped, not by the play of formal logic on common law doctrine and statutory texts, but by values, choices, and contexts. They attacked the distinction between law and politics and the vision of legal reasoning as objective and autonomous. Law should be assessed, not by its internal elegance, but by its social effects and by new values. Faith in absolute individual rights and a *laissez-faire* market must be replaced by balancing interests, collective responsibility, and a greater role for the state in regulating the economy and providing minimum support for individual life.

The function of scholarship included criticism and proposing reform, and was not limited to faithful syntheses of the cases. In the United States, the changes wrought by these approaches were profound, but in

England they were modest and limited largely to public law scholarship and a relatively few individuals.[48] In Canada, during the late 1920s and the 1930s these ideas appeared in writings by a handful of academics, including these four, whose roles and abilities made them conspicuous in the literature. Sometimes, though, these new approaches were found together with the old ones, as in Macdonald's 1935 article where the list of principles and canons that Lefroy might have written appeared together with the newer criticism and approaches to interpretation. They seemed to have read much of the writings from the United States, especially Roscoe Pound's early articles; but very few of them studied law abroad, and their writings did not simply duplicate the American models. Much of their concerns and their ideas seem to have been their own, developed for the problems they perceived in Canada, in the context of the general changes in twentieth-century culture and thought.

During the mid 1930s, the central constitutional issue was the fate of Prime Minister R.B. Bennett's New Deal. Early in 1935, he promised Canadians a grand legislative program to escape from the Depression, to rescue the capitalist economic order, and to save his floundering government. A few months later, Parliament enacted his program in six statutes, which fell far short of his promises and failed to save him from the electors. Mackenzie King and the Liberals came to power in the general election of 1935, and King quickly referred all six statutes to the Supreme Court of Canada, together with two others enacted by Borden's government in 1934. After the courts had pronounced most of them invalid, some scholars said that the outcomes had been predictable or inevitable,[49] but during 1935 and 1936 the outcome was not so clear. In 1936, several competent writers made sustained arguments for validity, relying on either POGG or 91(2),[50] and MacDonald, who was probably the most competent to make a prediction, gave his cautious opinion that there was a 'reasonable possibility' of validity.[51]

The Supreme Court pronounced most of the program invalid and so did the Privy Council, although the results for a few of the statutes differed.[52] There were two major issues or groups of cases. One concerned treaties: three of the statutes were enacted to fulfill treaty obligations about working conditions undertaken by the Dominion for Canada as an independent nation. Because they seemed clearly to regulate subjects within section 92, they could be valid only if the Dominion had a distinctive power to implement treaties. The Supreme Court divided three to three, and the Privy Council concluded that they were invalid. Atkin said that section 132 was limited to treaties binding Canada as part of the British Empire, and that there was no other power to legislate about treaties. He rejected the appeal to the *Aeronautics Reference* and the *Radio Reference* by limiting them to their narrowest grounds or, less charitably, by misreading them.

The other major issue was economic regulation and the fate of the *Natural Products Marketing Act,* enacted in 1934. It was designed to support producers of natural products, and expressly limited to products for which the principal market was outside the province that produced them, and products that were, in some part, exported. Speaking through Duff, the Supreme Court unanimously held it *ultra vires,* and the Privy Council affirmed, saying that it was 'unnecessary to add anything.' It was hardly surprising that the Privy Council was so magnanimous; Duff's judgment sought to do no more than synthesize its decisions thoroughly and faithfully, although his readings tended to be ungenerous to the Dominion at every turn, contrasted; for example, to some of the scholarly writings in the mid-1930s. For section 91(2), he was unwilling to contemplate the possibility of a general regulation of trade or an expansive use of the necessarily incidental doctrine. For POGG he began with a narrow analysis of Watson's language in the *Local Prohibition Reference:* not all matters that affected 'the body politic of the Dominion' or that were of 'national content' were within the Dominion's reach, only 'some' of them. After a thorough account of the cases, he offered little to determine what these 'some' were, except to repeat the warning that 'great caution' was needed for such a 'delicate and difficult task.' Atkin was pleased enough to hope that this would become 'the *locus classicus* of the law on this point.'[53]

These decisions seemed to deny the hopes of the early 1930s and to condemn Canada to constitutional paralysis. The reaction was outrage, which can be illustrated by two examples. The first was a symposium in the *Canadian Bar Review,* which gathered comment from leading scholars. Kennedy, the editor of the symposium, said,

> The federal power is gone with the winds. It can be relied on at the best when the nation is intoxicated with alcohol, to worst when the nation is intoxicated with war, but in times of sober poverty, sober financial chaos, sober unemployment, sober exploitation, it cannot be used.[54]

Scott was just as passionate:

> This straining at technicalities will do little to enhance the prestige of the
> courts ... Canada has suffered a national set-back of grievous proportions.
> A federal government that cannot concern itself with questions of wages
> and hours and unemployment in industry, whose attempts at the regula-
> tion of trade and commerce are consistently thwarted, which has no power
> to join its sister nations in the establishment of world living standards ... is
> a government wholly unable to direct and to control our economic devel-
> opment.[55]

The second example of outrage was the O'Connor Report, made in
1934 to the Senate by W.F. O'Connor.[56] At the time, he was the Senate's
clerk and counsel, but earlier he had been a member of the Board of
Commerce and had represented it before the Supreme Court and the
Privy Council. Throughout almost 150 pages of his report, he vented
anger and frustration. After quoting extensively from the discussions
preceding Confederation, he turned to an analysis of the structure of
sections 91 and 92. The basic principle was a division between general
and local matters: section 91 assigned power to the Dominion to legislate about general matters, and section 92 assigned power to the provinces to legislate about local matters. This interpretation was supported
by a thorough analysis of the various components of sections 91 and 92:
the enumerated subjects in section 92, the opening words of section 91,
the enumerated subjects in section 91, the 'notwithstanding' clause, the
'deeming' clause, and section 92(16).

O'Connor claimed that the careful design of the BNA Act had been
'repealed by judicial legislation.' The Privy Council had been guilty of
'demonstrable error' and 'serious and persistent deviation,' and it had
'tortured' crucial words in the Act 'in violation of their clear grammatical sense as well as their purpose.' Its path of error began as early as
Parsons, and a stray comment about the concluding words of section 91.
Russell v. The Queen represented a proper understanding of this structure, but error returned in the 1890s and continued in Watson's 'extraordinary' decision in the Local Prohibition Reference, which struck
section 91 'the deadliest blow it has received.' The opening grant of
power in section 91, its sole grant of power, was divided from the
enumerations and limited to 'extraordinary circumstances only, and
without exclusiveness or paramountcy.' This interpretation 'paralyzed
many essential law-making activities of the Dominion ... If only this

fatal error in construction could be undone, nothing much need be done in order to restore the *BNA Act* to that state of reasonable satisfactoriness in which it was before the fatal error was committed.' Instead, the result was 'an undeniable partial breakdown of the general scheme of Confederation.' During the twentieth century, Haldane's decisions 'exceeded those of Watson in their emasculatory assault upon the Dominion's authority.'[57] 'Villains' may be too mild a word to capture O'Connor's opinion of Watson and Haldane.[58]

Earlier, writers in the late nineteenth century had also undertaken analyses of the structure of sections 91 and 92, although not at nearly such length. Some of them, like O'Connor, believed that the central principle was the division between general and local matters, although they did not share his belief that the division was an expression of a design for a strong Dominion, and they supported the claims of the provinces instead.[59] O'Connor's analysis shaped debate for two or three decades. Even though he had demonstrated a faith in words, grammar, and punctuation that was deeply at odds with the new ideas about interpretation, scholars tended to make their arguments in his terms, perhaps because his conclusions were so appealing to most of them.

From 1940 to the Early 1970s: Laskin, Lederman, Labrie

This story ends around 1974 and includes only the trends in scholarship that continued or began in the 1950s and early 1960s. There are two reasons for these limits. First, major changes in Canadian legal scholarship and education began in the 1970s and still continue. Bundles of ideas such as law and society, law and economics, critical legal studies, feminist legal analysis, debates about interpretation, and legal history, have made law schools more exciting places than I remember them being in the 1950s and 1960s. They have created a new world of scholarship for which a manageable perspective would be difficult to find. Second, my topic is writings about the decisions of the Privy Council. After it ceased to be Canada's final court of appeal in 1949, its decisions became less important to current doctrine and had less power to arouse passion and dissent. By the 1970s, they were no longer a battleground of constitutional scholarship, having been relegated to legal historians.

The protagonists who dominated the 1930s, Kennedy, MacDonald, and Scott, continued to write in the 1940s and 1950s, in substantially the same way and with substantially the same conclusions, although all of them incorporated O'Connor's analysis of the cases and therefore tended to see Watson as the villain even more than they had in the 1930s.[60] They were followed by younger scholars, who shared their beliefs about Canada and their strong criticisms of the Privy Council.[61] The best-known was Bora Laskin, and his 1947 article about POGG is probably the most famous in this literature.[62]

Laskin began by taking it as settled and uncontroversial that POGG was the sole grant of power to the Dominion, that the enumerations were merely examples and that the Privy Council had severed them and made POGG into a residuary clause with a trivial scope. The bulk of the article was a comprehensive and searing indictment of its judgments, especially of the work of Duff and Haldane. Laskin spared Watson from the brunt of the indictment, arguing that even though the decision in the *Local Prohibition Reference* was muddled, it did permit accommodation of the 'social economic development of Canada,' through recognition of different and changing aspects. But Haldane's creation of the emergency doctrine was the work of a constitutional Houdini whose magic was 'strong enough to make [POGG] disappear altogether and to make it reappear as a spirit.' The judgment in *Snider* was 'almost shocking in its casualness,' and a product of 'inflexible concepts that are often the product of a neat mind, often unwilling in the interests of some sort of formal logic to discourage thought patterns that had been nicely fitted together.'

Duff's judgment in the *Natural Products Marketing Act Reference* failed to understand the *Local Prohibition Reference*, and amounted to no more than a '*circulus inexatricabilis.*' Again and again, as he went through the cases, Laskin demonstrated the series of woeful errors: inconsistencies, failures to explain, sheer inventions of doctrine, departures from the meaning of the *BNA Act* apparent to 'any careful reading,' and a preoccupation with subjects of legislation, not aspects. He did not discuss the understandings at Confederation, the changes in the social and economic contexts, or the nature of contemporary Canada and its needs; but throughout, there ran a strong feeling that these decisions were not only poorly crafted but inappropriate for Canada. He concluded with a hope for change and for better work from an independent Supreme Court of Canada.[63]

A few years later, in 1951, writing about the Court as the final court of appeal, Laskin undertook the first substantial discussion of its work since Lefroy's text in the late nineteenth century.[64] Here, he saw the early cases as faithful to the *BNA Act*, the contributions of Duff to the eventual catastrophe, and the slow loss of independence and initiative to the Privy Council. Ten years later, much the same story as Laskin told for POGG was told by Alexander Smith for the trade and commerce power, in his book, *The Commerce Power in Canada and the United States*.[65] He traced its erosion from *Parsons* to the *Natural Products Marketing Reference* with less passion than Laskin, but thoroughly and with great care. He, too, included the Supreme Court decisions at length.[66]

Competing assessments of the Privy Council began to appear in the 1950s, first in Quebec among civilians,[67] and then in a younger generation of common law scholars, of whom the first was William Lederman. In a series of articles beginning in 1965, he argued that at the heart of Canada was a balanced federalism: a balance between unity and diversity, and between a strong Dominion and autonomous provinces.[68] The 'equilibrium points' of this balanced federalism had been developed painstakingly by the courts, especially the Privy Council, using two techniques. First, the larger and more expansive powers in the *BNA Act*, especially POGG, had been integrated with each other and limited. Lederman accepted the reading of section 91 that made its enumerations independent grants of powers and POGG a residue of the powers not enumerated in either section 92 or section 91, arguing that this reading was as consistent with the text as any other reading (presumably the readings that saw a grant of two powers, over general and local matters) and more appropriate for Canada. The crucial question was when should new functions of government be recognized as new aspects? For Lederman, the best answer had been given by Watson, 'the greatest of the Privy Council judges concerned with the Canadian constitution,' in his speech in the *Local Prohibition Reference*. The villain of the 1930s was now a hero, and even Haldane was given modest approval.[69]

The second way the courts had made a balanced federalism was based on Lederman's perception that the powers in sections 91 and 92 overlapped extensively and pervasively. This perception was not, by then, unusual; most modern scholars had either proclaimed it or would have accepted it, but Lederman made it a central theme. The courts chose between the overlapping powers through determination of pith and substance or they recognized concurrent powers, and Lederman saw a tendency to more and more consistency as well as balance.[70] His reading of the cases, especially his perception of balance, paralleled shifts in federalism that emerged during the 1950s and 1960s: the need for coordination resulting from expansion of governmental programs, and decentralization resulting from the ambitions of the provinces.[71]

In 1977, Peter Hogg published *Constitutional Law of Canada*,[72] which I wish to consider even though it is beyond my time limit, because it was the first significant text about the doctrine since Lefroy's. Like Lefroy, he synthesized the doctrine in an orderly and coherent way, and the text deservedly became a standard and respected reference. He demonstrated more faith than Laskin and Lederman in the meanings of the *BNA Act* and the coherence of doctrine, although he perceived much more change and inconsistency in these cases than Lefroy did, and described much more context. Like Lederman, Hogg also accepted the reading of section 91 that made the enumerations independent grants of powers, and POGG a residue, relying both on the text and reasoning in the decisions. *Russell*, the shining example of POGG as the sole grant of power and a strong Dominion, was deemed incorrect, albeit in retrospect, and POGG was limited to emergencies and national concern. 'One can debate a *fait accompli* for only so long.'[73]A textbook may be an inappropriate place to declare heroes, but here Watson was granted what he might have preferred anyway, orthodoxy.

Most scholars in the 1950s and 1960s shared beliefs about legal reasoning, especially interpretation, which were essentially a continuation of the approaches that emerged in the late 1920s and 1930s: statutory and constitutional texts alone did not determine outcomes, at least not in hard cases. Because the meanings of words were, at least at the edges, indefinite, judges made choices. To pretend otherwise was to mask the choices with barren 'logic' and 'abstract reasoning.' Yet the choices were not personal or political; instead, interpretation was a distinctive, rational process. The judge must be faithful to the purpose of the text, taking into account its context and the values and needs of the contemporary society.[74]

The beliefs were rarely elaborated in any rigorous or sustained way, and varied from scholar to scholar, but Laskin and Lederman were good examples of both the common ground and the diversity. In his reconsideration of POGG Laskin condemned the Privy Council's 'cold abstract logic' and 'rigid abstractions,' and its failure to take account of 'the social and factual considerations' in the New Deal legislation, and the future of 'our society and its contemporary problems.'[75] For Laskin critical analysis of doctrine was central, and his criticisms of true reasonings of the past were not expanded into explanations of how judges might do their work better. He did not, for example, explain the tension between respect for the *BNA Act*, implicit in the argument that some Privy Council interpretations were contrary to 'any careful reading,' and the need to take account of current needs and problems, nor did he explain how judges should determine current values.

Even though Lederman's assessment of the results of the cases was different, he shared much of Laskin's beliefs about interpretation, especially the responsibility of judges to respond to current social conditions and needs. He claimed that the *BNA Act* was 'ambiguous or incomplete' and therefore any debate about whether the Privy Council had betrayed its terms was meaningless. 'I do not think the Judicial Committee should be disparaged for having failed to find answers in the text of the *BNA Act* that were not there to be found.' The real issue was the need to escape from literal interpretation – the futile faith in the meanings of words that the Privy Council had too often displayed, and to undertake 'sociological' interpretation – a care for the 'ongoing life of the country.' Because the words of a text alone could not give answers, they must be 'related to the cultural, social and economic realities of the society for which they were and are intended.' In making their choices among overlapping powers, judges should weigh 'the relative values of uniformity and regional diversity, ... the relative merits of local versus central administration, and the justice of minority claims,' and seek to implement 'widely prevailing beliefs.' The crucial question was 'is it better for the people that this thing be done on a national level or on a provincial level?'[76]

The contrast to Lefroy's beliefs about interpretation and the structure of powers was large and obvious. One illustration was embedded in Lederman's word 'balance.' His vision of federalism as a balance between the Dominion and the provinces merged with balancing as a way of reasoning. Lefroy's belief that courts determined the sharp, bright lines between mutually exclusive spheres of absolute power, without consideration of context or need, was replaced by a belief that courts balanced overlapping and competing claims.[77] Here again is the jurisprudence of cooperative federalism. And Lefroy's fear of the implications of the inquiry into 'national concern' turned out to be prescient. In explaining why aeronautics was justifiably a 'national concern,' Lederman said that it did not 'imply large scale trespass' on provincial powers, and did not take over 'great portions.'[78] Such questions of degree were just the kinds of questions that Lefroy had feared.[79]

A contrast to the scholars in the 1920s and 1930s was not as obvious or great as the contrast to Lefroy, but it existed nonetheless. Scholars in the 1950s and 1960s seemed to be more distant from the issues swirling about them, than had scholars in the 1920s and 1930s, and to be less passionate or, to be more precise, less openly so about the outcomes. For example, Laskin's article on POGG was powerful and passionate, but despite his personal belief in the need for a strong Dominion, the power and the passion seemed directed at the inadequacies of legal reasoning and not at a betrayal of Canada. Neither he nor Lederman sought expressly to explain the decisions of the Privy Council by invoking social, economic, or political beliefs in any sustained way, or to talk much about contemporary conditions and issues. Instead, they emphasized judicial techniques, especially approaches to interpretation.

This contrast may reflect differences in legal education and scholarship. In the few decades after World War II, law schools in Canada contained two approaches to teaching and thinking, which mingled but which were never synthesized. The first was a modified continuation of the way of thinking established in the late nineteenth century which, unlike its fate in the United States, continued to be powerful in Canada. It was not, though, the approach of Laskin and Lederman. The second was a tamed version of the ferment of the 1920s and 1930s. The dangerous political edges were shorn away, and lawyers and legal scholars were perceived as professionals, skilled in the workings of the legal processes and in implementing society's preferences, which were typically perceived to be unproblematic and widely shared. This approach originated in the United States, and Canadian legal scholars in the 1950s and 1960s were much more shaped by thinking there than their predecessors were in the 1930s. Perhaps the difference between the 1930s and the 1950s and 1960s is best expressed in the word 'tamed': the political passions of Kennedy, MacDonald, and Scott had been tamed, or muffled.[80]

The dominant moods of the 1950s and 1960s can be illuminated by looking at a remarkable glimpse of bleaker beliefs about interpretation. F.E. Labrie, writing in 1949, bluntly declared, '[C]onstitutional interpretation exists as a legislative process,' and, '[T]he BNA Act will have whatever meaning the courts choose to ascribe to it.' The rules made by courts, which Lefroy so carefully extracted, were 'meaningless' and precedents 'can have but little room for application.' The choices of reasoning in cases were inconsistent, and the results all might have been different. The crucial function was the determination of the aspects, or pith and substance, and for the 'newer fields and problems of government ... the courts' discretion is virtually unfettered.' Labrie gave examples from all the major cases, although he did not offer any rigorous theory of interpretation that linked them to his general claim.[81]

Mainstream scholars would cheerfully have agreed that texts alone did not determine outcomes, but most would have hastened to affirm the duty of courts to make 'policy,' derived from the purposes of the Constitution, or from the needs and values of Canadian society and its federalism. Intentionally or not, LaBrie did not. Instead he stressed uncertainty and contingency. When he wrote this article, he had been teaching for a only few years and had never studied outside Canada. He made few references to literature beyond the cases, and the only clue to the sources of his interests and ideas was a footnote to John Willis' article, 'Statute Interpretation in a Nutshell.'[82] His article was read by contemporaries but soon disappeared from the literature.

The Explanations

Historians, political scientists, and legal scholars have offered a multitude of explanations for the decisions of the Privy Council.[83] Parts of this literature are hobbled by a few pervasive and overlapping tendencies. Some writers offered an explanation without specifying the period or the cases that they were explaining, even though the range of issues and complexity of events made it unlikely that one factor could be an effective explanation even at one brief time, let alone over the long span of time between 1880 and 1940. Some writers confused the doctrinal issues at stake in the cases, or assumed that they were essentially the same; but the division of legislative powers, the nature of the provincial legislatures, and the powers of provincial executives were all different issues, even though a holding about one might have suggested appropriate holdings for another. Other writers provided little of the evidence that would usually satisfy historians; and still others made a sharp and simplistic distinction between law and the rest of life, and between 'legal' and 'political' or 'sociological' explanations that reduced law to an extreme and unrealistic positivism and excluded any serious consideration of legal thought. Last, almost all of the writers accepted a vision of Confederation and the *BNA Act* in which the Dominion government was intended to be powerful and dominant, and assumed that their task was to explain departures and betrayals.[84]

Among the more substantial explanations,[85] the most particular one was by F. Murray Greenwood, who argued in 1974 that the decisions of the Privy Council in the late nineteenth century were a product of its own interest in preserving its role.[86] Perceiving agitation in Canada to abolish appeals and make its Supreme Court the final court of appeal, it sought to preserve its role by making decisions that were both distinctive and responsive to the predominant opinion in Canada. Greenwood's argument was grounded in the results of the cases, but it seemed too particular to be the entire story.[87]

Next came explanations based on economic attitudes of the judges. In 1937, in the symposium about the New Deal cases, Frank Scott briefly suggested that the decisions made by the Privy Council during the 1930s were influenced by an aversion to economic regulation,[88] and in 1961 James Mallory made the same argument at length,[89] using cases from the late nineteenth century to the 1930s as examples. The results of the cases, some comments throughout the judgments, and the general political and economic beliefs of the legal profession made the idea a powerful one for the 1920s and 1930s. For cases decided before the 1920s, however, it was at odds with the results and, for the decisions of the Canadian courts it was also at odds with armchair speculation about kinds of governmental involvement in the economy and Canadian attitudes towards the state.[90] Much later, in 1991, Bruce Ryder made a fruitful modification by suggesting that the courts have been tolerant of legislation that seemed 'necessary to the preservation of morality and the social order,' and much less tolerant of legislation that seemed to be 'an interference with market relations.'[91]

Other explanations were based on beliefs about federalism, and they can be divided into two sharply different groups. The first began with the observation, first briefly made by Kennedy in 1930, that even though the decisions departed from the text of the BNA Act and the understandings at Confederation, they were appropriate for the pluralism of Canada.[92] He also suggested that a continuation of the tendency towards decentralization would be dangerous, but even with this qualification, his attitude was more benign than it was a few years later. Alan Cairns made the same observation a major theme of a widely known and respected article written in 1971, in which he argued that the criticism in the 1930s was misplaced, and that the appropriateness of its results justified the Privy Council.[93] The observation alone was not an explanation, but Cairns also said that Watson and Haldane acted deliberately; that is, presumably, they interpreted the Constitution in response to their perceptions of change and need. This claim could point to a famous comment by Haldane about Watson and his experience as counsel before he became Lord Chancellor;[94] but it raised large and difficult questions about their perceptions of their function and, especially for the cases in the late nineteenth century, as to how they gathered their knowledge of Canada.

The other use of beliefs about federalism involved, not the distinctive nature, real or imagined, of Canada, but the influence of ideas about the nature of federalism. It appeared first in LaBrie's 1949 article. Having argued that text, rules, precedent did not determine aspects and outcomes, he turned to ask what did, and his answer began with the claim that the major factor was a model of federalism: the courts had imposed a federalism of 'complete equality ... a sort of opposed interest and continuing rivalry between provincial and federal sovereign legislatures.' In implementing this model of federalism, the courts had undertaken the 'maintenance of a delicate balance.'[95] LaBrie also suggested other influences, especially comparisons to the past, the intent of the legislature, and the effect of the legislation; but here his arguments were much less powerful; as well, he never sought to link the influences to the economic and political faiths he claimed were fundamental. LaBrie argued that this undertaking explained a reluctance to find new aspects, and therefore the withering of POGG and the narrowing of section 91(2).[96]

LaBrie did not develop this brief flash, and historians and politicial scientists have been unwilling to take lawyers' ideas and doctrines seriously in seeking explanation. Nonetheless, the path is a promising one. Consider the Privy Council's judgments in the late nineteenth century about the nature of Canadian federalism; the provincial legislatures were 'supreme' within their spheres, and the provincial executives were entirely independent of the Dominion's executives. These judgments made what has been called 'coordinate federalism,' although the phrase 'model of autonomy' may be more expressive. The crucial point in considering the influence of ideas is that this model was the dominant understanding of English and Canadian lawyers from the 1860s onwards. It was best expressed for English lawyers by Dicey in his classic text, *The Law of the Constitution*, written in 1885, where he spoke of 'co-ordinate and independent authorities,' and said that the central government should not have any power of 'encroaching upon the rights retained by the states.'[97] In Canada, it appeared first around 1874 in speeches by David Mills, a lawyer, journalist, and Liberal member of Parliament. By the late 1880s, it was firmly established and the stuff of texts. My suggestion is that the Privy Council's decisions about the nature of Canadian federalism were in large part expressions of their beliefs about the proper nature of federalism.

The difficult question is, though, was there a relation between this model of federalism and the decisions about the division of powers? Perhaps the independence in the model seemed to entail some measure of equality, and this thought might have been supported by the strong and pervasive belief in liberty; each of the governments must have liberty, perhaps, as well, to consider other elements of the lawyers' ideas, the understanding of powers as defined and separated by sharp lines contributed to the withering of POGG and the narrowing of section 91(2), a possibility Scott saw in 1932.[98]

Conclusion

My argument has been that writings about the Canadian Constitution have reflected differing beliefs about legal reasoning and legal scholarship, and about visions of Canada. That is, as I said, hardly startling. In retrospect, I wish to recall the way in which the beliefs about legal reasoning were shaped first by models from England and then the United States. One can only hope that our current constitutional ferment will encourage thinking that is distinctively Canadian, about Canada as a distinctive country.

NOTES

1 The *BNA Act* was a statute of the imperial British parliament, enacted in 1867 to create the Dominion of Canada: 30–31 Vic., c. 3 (U.K.). In 1982, the name '*BNA Act*' was replaced by a new one: the *Constitution Act*, as part of the constitutional rearrangements that included establishing the *Charter of Rights and Freedoms* and formally patriating the Constitution. However, convenience justifies using the name that was used throughout the period covered in this paper.

2 The major cases were *Severn v. R.* (1878) 2 S.C.R. 70, and *Fredericton v. R.* (1880) 3 S.C.R. 505. For a discussion of the cases from Confederation to 1900, see R.C.B. Risk, 'Canadian Courts under the Influence' (1990) 40 *U.T.L.J.* 687.

3 (1881) 4 S.C. R. 215, aff'd 7 A.C. 195 (P.C.).

4 (1882) 7 A.C. 829 (P.C.). This case was essentially the same as *Fredericton*, supra note 2, which was not appealed; the result was the same, but the reasoning was different.

5 (1883) 9 A.C. 117 (P.C.).

6 In keeping with the prevailing practice for references, neither court gave a judgment. The arguments were reprinted in Canada, House of Commons, *Sessional Papers*, 1885, no. 85.

7 *A.G. Ontario v. A.G. Dominion and the Distillers and Brewers Association of Canada* (1896) A.C. 348 (P.C.), rev'g (1894) 24 S.C R. 170.

8 The major texts were: W.H.P. Clement, *The Law of the Canadian Constitution* (1st ed. Toronto: Carswell, 1892; 2nd ed., Toronto: Carswell, 1904; 3rd ed., Toronto: Carswell, 1916); A.H.F. Lefroy, *The Law of Legislative Power in Canada* (Toronto: Law Book and Publishing, 189798); T.J.J. Loranger, *Letters upon the Interpretation of the Federal Constitution* (Quebec: Morning Chronicle Office, 1884); D.A. O'Sullivan, *A Manual of Government in Canada* (1st ed., Toronto: J.C. Smart, 1879; 2nd ed., Toronto: Carswell, 1887); and J. Travis, *A Law Treatise on the Constitutional Powers of Parliament and of the Local Legislatures under the British North America Act, 1867* (St John: Sun Publishing, 1884). Articles about constitutional law began to appear in law journals in significant numbers during the 1880s, and virtually all of them were doctrinal analyses of particular issues of the division of powers. *Editors' Note*: For more on the writing of the late nineteenth century see R.C.B. Risk, 'Constitutional Scholarship in the Late Nineteenth Century,' in this volume.

9 Ibid. at note 8. For a longer account of Lefroy, see R. Risk, 'A.H.F. Lefroy,' in this volume.

10 See P.B. Maxwell, *The Interpretation of Statutes* (London: W. Maxwell & Son, 1875); and H.J. Powell, 'The Original Understanding of the Original Intent' (1985) 99 *Harvard L.R.* 885.

11 A.H.F Lefroy, 'Prohibition: The Late Privy Council Decision' (1896) 16 *Can. L.T.* 125 at 133.

12 Of course this description is a model, and even as a model, it is greatly simplified, but Lefroy was one of the paradigms. See G.B. Baker, 'The Reconstitution of Upper Canadian Legal Thought in the Late Victorian Empire' (1985) 3 *Law and Hist. Rev.* 219; R. Gordon, 'Legal Thought and Legal Practice in the Age of American Enterprise,' in G. Geison, ed., *Professions and Professional Ideologies in America* (Chapel Hill: University of North Carolina Press, 1983) 70; D. Kennedy, 'Towards an Historical Understanding of Legal Consciousness: The Case of Classical Legal Thought in America, 1850–1940' (1980) 3 *Research in L. & Soc.* 3; and D. Sugarman, 'Legal Theory, the Common Law Mind, and the Making of the Textbook Tradition,' in W. Twining, ed., *Legal Theory and Common Law* (Oxford: Basil Blackwell, 1985) 26.

13 Mills' typescript lectures are in the David Mills Papers, University of

Western Ontario Library. For an illuminating study of the language of the provincial rights' politicians, and its links to legal thought, see R.C. Vipond, *Liberty and Community: Canadian Federalism and the Failure of the Constitution* (Albany: SUNY Press, 1991).

14 [1922] 1 A.C. 191 at 197–8 (P.C.).

15 [1923] A.C. 696 at 703 and 704 (P.C.).

16 [1925] A.C. 396 at 412 (P.C.).

17 A few months after *Snider*, in *The King v. Eastern Terminal Elevator* [1924] Ex.C.R. 167 [1925] S.C.R. 434, the Supreme Court considered the *Canada Grain Act*, which was designed to impose comprehensive control on the grain trade, largely for the benefit of exporters. Duff, who was now dominant, would have held the entire Act invalid.

18 Lefroy published three more books, all of which were derived from *The Law of Legislative Power in Canada*, and Clement's text appeared in a second and third edition, but there was no new effort to write a comprehensive text about the division of powers. W.R. Riddell, a judge in Ontario, wrote two books on the Constitution: *The Constitution of Canada in Its History and Practical Working* (New Haven: Yale University Press, 1917), and *The Canadian Constitution in Form and Fact* (New York: Columbia University Press, 1923), but he did not consider the division of powers.

19 [1913] A.C. 283 (P.C.).

20 A.H.F. Lefroy, 'The Alberta and Great Waterways Railway Case' (1913) 29 L.Q.R. 285, and (1913) 49 *Can. L J.* 561; and 'Royal Bank of Canada v. The King' (1914) 50 *Can. L.J.* 622. At the outset, in 'The Alberta and Great Waterways Railway Case,' he announced (at 288) that the Privy Council had finally made a mistake: having studied every one of its reported judgments carefully, he had 'never seen the smallest loophole for criticism or for doubt as to the correctness of any one of them before this last judgment.' The quotation in the text is taken from 'The Alberta and Great Waterways Railway Case' at 289.

21 J.S. Ewart, 'The King v. The Royal Bank' (1913) 33 *Can. L.T.* 269, and 'The Judicial Committee: *Rex v. The Royal Bank*' (1914) 50 *Can. L.J.* 560. His first article was one of a series in which he sought to demonstrate that appeals to the Privy Council should be abolished: it had been not only ignorant of vital Canadian context, but erratic and sloppy as well. For accounts of Ewart's life and legal writings, see D. Farr, 'John S. Ewart,' in R.L. McDougall, ed., *Our Living Tradition: Second and Third Series* (Toronto: University of Toronto Press, 1959), and R.C.B. Risk, 'John Skirving Ewart,' in this volume.

22 C.B. Labatt, 'Power of Provincial Legislatures to Enact Statutes Affecting

the Rights of Non-Resident Shareholders in Provincial Companies' (1914) 50 *Can. L.J.* 41 and 473; 'Government Impairment of a Concession Granted by the Government: A Rejoinder to a Critic' (1914) 50 *Can. L.J.* 204; 'Power of Provincial Legislatures to Enact Statutes Affecting the Rights of Non-Residents: A Reply to Some of My Critics' (1915) 51 *Can. L.J.* 265. He argued that Lefroy's claim (that there was a civil right in Alberta) depended upon circular reasoning and upon the existence of an effective claim in Alberta; but the condition of payment, construction of the railroad, had not been fulfilled. In reply to Ewart, Labatt made the same argument that the claim was incomplete and, more fundamentally, pointed out that Ewart had simply assumed, incorrectly and without justification, that the proceeds of the bonds were in Alberta. Two Toronto lawyers supported Labatt: G.S.H. [Heighington?], 'The Royal Bank v. The King' (1914) 50 *Can. L.J.* 583, and 'Royal Bank Case' (1915) 51 *Can. L.J.* 60; and C.H. Masters, 'Legislative Powers' (1914) 50 *Can. L.J.* 208.

23 Lefroy, 'Royal Bank,' supra note 20 at 624.
24 Labatt, 'A Reply,' supra note 22 at 287.
25 A.C. Heighington, 'The Jurisdiction of the Parliament of Canada in Regard to the Prevention and Settlement of Labour Strikes' (1909) 29 *Can. L.T.* 929.
26 Z.A. Lash, 'The Working of Federal Institutions in Canada' (1917) 37 *Can. L.T.* 275; A.H.F. Lefroy, 'Points of Special Interest in Canada's Federal Constitution' (1913) 33 *Can. L.T.* 898;and A.H.F. Lefroy, 'The John Deere Plow Company Case' (1915) 35 *Can. L.T.* 148. In a comment about the *Insurance Reference*, H.A. Garrett demonstrated more concern about the scope of s. 91(2), saying that it was unsettled and unilluminated, and that '[t]he interpretations have been negative rather than positive': 'The Dominion Insurance Act, 1917, and Provincial Rights' (1918) 38 *Can. L.T.* 466 at 476. The difference between his perception and Lefroy's and Lash's may have been the holding in the *Insurance Reference* itself. Four years later, after the *Board of Commerce Reference*, Garrett clearly perceived change: '[I]ts meaning is gradually being interpreted in a negative way': 'Companies and Dominion and Provincial Laws' (1922) 42 *Can. L.T.* 466, 530, and 583 at 533.
27 The provincial rights movement was acknowledged, but not expressly related to the doctrine about division of powers; see Editor, 'Federal and Provincial Jurisdiction as to Companies' (1918) 54 *Can. L.J.* 81; and Editor, 'Company Law: Dominion and Provincial Jurisdiction' (1921) 57 *Can. L.J.* 87. Early in the 1900s, the decisions that made the provincial legislatures autonomous and equal in nature to Parliament were criticised as a misreading of the *BNA Act*, but they too were not related to the doctrine about

division of powers; see M. Rae, 'Some Constitutional Opinions of the Late Mr Justice Gwynne' (1904) 24 *Can. L.T.* 1.

28 H.A. Smith, 'The Residue of Power in Canada' (1926) 4 *Can. Bar R.* 432, and 'Interpretation in English and Continental Law' (1927) *International and Comparative L. Q.* 153. The second article dealt more with interpretation generally and less with the Canadian Constitution, and it presented a more radical claim about meaning. My account mingles the two. Several years before writing these articles, Smith wrote a book comparing the American and Canadian constitutions, *Federalism in North America* (Boston: Chipman, 1923). Here he suggested a vision of Confederation in which the Dominion was dominant, but he did not undertake any analysis of the cases. The influences on Smith are difficult to determine. For accounts of his career, see (1938) *Recueil des Cours* 607; R. St J. Macdonald, 'An Historical Introduction to the Teaching of International Law in Canada' (1974) *Can. Yearbook of Int'l Law* 67 at 72–4; and R.A. Macdonald, 'The National Law Programme at McGill' (1990) 13 *Dal. L.J.* 211 at 256–61. There is a possible connection to Harold Laski, who was one of the central figures in the changes in England. Smith also made challenges to the earlier ideas in his proposals for legal education, in which he called for an independent law school, that would 'serve in the fullest possible manner the legal needs of the Dominion': H.A. Smith, 'The Functions of a Law School' (1921) 41 *Can. L.T.* 27 at 29.

29 'The Residue of Power in Canada,' supra note 28, at 433, 438, 439, 433, and 434. Two articles, written a few months before Smith's articles, described the changes but they were not as precise and did not explain or criticise; see F.E.H., 'Editorial: Judicial Committee Differences' (1925) 3 *Can. Bar R.* 135, and W.E. Raney, 'Another Question of Dominion Jurisdiction Emerges' (1925) 3 *Can. Bar R.* 614.

30 For the orthodox approach, see C.K. Allen, *Law in the Making* (Oxford: Clarendon Press, 1927) 273–89; Allen noted Smith's protest in a footnote in his second edition (1930) at 294, but did not permit it to affect the general approach.

31 In *Edwards v. A.G. Canada* [1930] A.C.124 (P.C.), Lord Sankey spoke of a 'living tree' and the need for a 'large and liberal interpretation,' but he also took pains to point out that the issue was not the division of powers. As well as the three cases considered in the text, there was a fourth, *British Coal Corporation v. R.* [1935] A.C. 500 (P.C.).

32 [1931] A.C. 668 (P.C.).

33 'The criminal quality of an act cannot be discerned by intuition; nor can it be discovered by reference to any standard but one: Is the act prohibited

with penal consequences. Morality and criminality are far from co-extensive': ibid. 681.

34 [1931] A.C. 54 (P.C.).

35 [1932] A.C. 18 (P.C.).

36 *The Aeronautics Reference*, supra note 34.

37 His fast major book about Canada was *The Constitution of Canada* (Toronto: University of Toronto Press, 1922), and a few years later he wrote 'The Disallowance of Provincial Acts in the Dominion of Canada' (1924) 6 *J. Comparative Legislation* (3rd ser.) 81. His principal constitutional writings during the late 1920s and the 1930s were 'Canada: Law and Custom in the Canadian Constitution' (1929) 20 *Round Table* 143; 'Review' (1930) 8 *Can. Bar R.* 703; 'Some Aspects of Canadian and Australian Federal Constitutional Law' (1930) 15 *Cornell L.Q.* 345; 'The Imperial Conferences, 1926–1930: The Statute of Westminster' (1932) 48 *L.Q.R.* 91; *Some Aspects of the Theories and Workings of Constitutional Law* (New York: Macmillan, 1932); 'Crisis in the Canadian Constitution' (1934) 24 *Round Table* 803; 'British Coal Corporation' (1935) 13 *Can. Bar R.* 621; 'The Workings of the British North America Acts, 1867–1931' (1936) 48 *Juridical R.* 57; and 'The British North America Act: Past and Future' (1937) 15 *Can. Bar R.* 393. Kennedy's early book is discussed in C. Berger, *The Writing of Canadian History: Aspects of English-Canadian Historical Writing since 1900* (Toronto: University of Toronto Press, 1976) at 40–2, and there are some good glimpses of his approaches to legal education in C.I. Kyer and J.E. Bickenbach, *The Fiercest Debate: Cecil A. Wright, The Benchers, and Legal Education in Ontario, 1923–1957* (Toronto: Osgoode Society for Canadian Legal History and University of Toronto Press, 1987) at 107–20, but he has been otherwise sadly neglected.

Editors' Note: See also R.C.B. Risk, 'The Many Minds of W.P.M. Kennedy,' in this volume.

38 For an account of MacDonald, see J. Willis, *A History of Dalhousie Law School* (Toronto: University of Toronto Press, 1979) 100, 104–5, and 121–4. His major writings during the 1930s were: 'Canada's Power to Perform Treaty Obligations' (1933) 11 *Can. Bar R.* 581; 'British Coal Corporation v. The King: Three Comments' (1935) 13 *Can. Bar R.* 625; 'Judicial Interpretation of the Canadian Constitution' (1935) 1 *U.T.L.J.* 260; 'The Canadian Constitution Seventy Years After' (1937) 35 *Can. Bar R.* 401; 'Constitutional Interpretation and Extrinsic Evidence' (1939) 17 *Can. Bar R.* 77; 'The Licensing Powers of the Provinces' (1939) 17 *Can. Bar R.* 240; and 'The Constitution and the Courts in 1939' (1940) 38 *Can. Bar R.* 147.

39 See S. Djwa, *The Politics of the Imagination: A Life of F.R. Scott* (Toronto:
McClelland and Stewart, 1987); S. Djwa and R. St J. Macdonald, eds.,
On F.R. Scott: Essays on His Contributions to Law, Literature and Politics
(Montreal and Kingston: McGill-Queen's University Press, 1983), and
M. Horn, 'Frank Scott, the League for Social Reconstruction, and the
Constitution' in J. Ajzenstat, ed., *Canadian Constitutionalism: 1791–*
1991 (Ottawa: Canadian Study of Parliament Group, 1992) 231. The
major pieces of Scott's writing about the Constitution during the
1930s were: 'The Privy Council and Minority Rights' (1930) 37 *Queen's*
Q. 658; 'The Development of Canadian Federalism' (1931) *Proceedings*
of Can Pol. Science Assoc. 231; *Social Reconstruction and the BNA Act*
(Toronto: Thomas Nelson, 1934) – a pamphlet written for the League
for Social Reconstruction; 'Canada's Future in the British Common-
wealth' (1937) *Foreign Affairs* 102; 'The Consequences of the Privy
Council Decisions' (1937) 15 *Can. Bar R.* 485; 'The Privy Council and
Mr Bennett's "New Deal" Legislation' (1937) 3 *Can. J. Economics and*
Political Science 234; 'The Royal Commission on Dominion–Provincial
Relations' (1938) 7 *U. of Toronto Q.* 141; 'The Constitution and the
War' (1939) 19 *Can. Forum* 243; 'Constitutional Problems,' in F.R. Scott,
ed., *Canada Today* (Toronto: Oxford University Press, 1939) at 78–85.
As well, Scott contributed to two important publications by the
League for Social Reconstruction: *Social Planning for Canada* (Toronto:
Thomas Nelson, 1935), and its brief to the Rowell-Sirois Commission
in 1937.
40 See D. Owram, *The Government Generation: Canadian Intellectuals and the*
State, 1900–1945 (Toronto: University of Toronto Press, 1986) at 6, 7,
and 9.
41 Willis, supra note 38. For an account of this volume and its significance for
the 1930s, see R.C.B. Risk, 'Volume One of the Journal,' in this volume.
42 J.A. Corry, 'Administrative Law: Interpretation of Statutes' (1936) 1
U.T.L.J. 286. The general changes in legal thought during this period,
especially in the United States, also included beliefs about interpretation
that were more bleak. Some scholars argued that not only were the choices
made by judges not determined by the words of statutes, but they were
not constrained by context or purpose either. They were essentially political. Some strains of this belief appeared in Canada in 1938, in John
Willis' great article, 'Statute Interpretation in a Nutshell' (1938) 16 *Can. Bar*
R. 1, but it did not appear among the Canadian constitutional scholars
during the 1930s. For this 'dark streak,' see G. Peller, 'The Metaphysics of
American Law,' (1985) 73 *California L.R.* 1151; and for Willis, see R.C.B.
Risk, 'John Willis: A Tribute,' in this volume.

43 Kennedy, 'Canada: Law and Custom,' supra note 37, at 152, and Kennedy, 'The Workings of the British North America Acts,' ibid. at 60.

44 Scott, 'The Development of Canadian Federalism,' supra note 39, especially at 41–8; the quotations are taken from 42 and 46.

45 'Judicial Interpretation of the Canadian Constitution,' supra note 38 at 280.

46 MacDonald, 'Canada's Power to Perform Treaty Obligations,' supra note 38 at 589.

47 MacDonald, 'British Coal Corporation v. The King,' ibid., at 632 and 633. As well, he declared, at 582–3, 'A constitution is intended never to be outgrown ... and to be given a progressive construction which will keep it an apt instrument of government even in its application to circumstances not foreseen by its framers. The words remain as written, but their connotation may be changed if their spirit be left unaltered.'

48 The experience in the United States has been written about extensively; the most useful includes M.J. Horwitz, *The Transformation of American Law, 1870–1960* (New York: Oxford University Press, 1992) c. 6 and 7; N. Hull, 'Some Realism about the Llewellyn–Pound Exchange over Realism' [1987] *Wisconsin L.R.* 921; E.A. Purcell, *The Crisis of Democratic Theory: Scientific Naturalism and the Problem of Value* (Lexington: University of Kentucky Press, 1973); J.H. Schlegel, 'American Legal Realism and Empirical Social Science: From the Yale Experience' (1979) 28 *Buffalo L.R.* 459; J.H. Schlegel, 'American Legal Realism and Empirical Social Science: The Singular Case of Underhill Moore' (1980) 29 *Buffalo L.R.* 195; J. Singer, 'Legal Realism Now' (1985) 76 *California L.R.* 465; and G.E. White, 'From Sociological Jurisprudence to Realism: Jurisprudence and Social Change in Early Twentieth-Century America' (1972) 58 *Virginia L.R.* 999.
   The English experience has not been nearly so well described, but for a recent and illuminating account of the general currents of public law thought, see M. Loughlin, *Public Law and Political Theory* (Oxford: Clarendon Press, 1992) c. 7.

49 F.C. Cronkite, 'The Social Legislation References' (1937) 15 *Can. Bar R.* 475 at 478; I. Jennings, 'Constitutional Interpretation: The Experience of Canada' (1937) 51 *Harvard L.R.* 1 at 38; and B. Keith, 'The Privy Council Decisions: A Comment from Great Britain' (1937) 15 *Can. Bar R.* 428 at 439.

50 B. Claxton, 'Social Reform and the Constitution' (1935) 1 *Can. J. Economics and Pol. Science* 409; and T.G. Norris, 'The Natural Products Marketing Act, 1934' (1935) 1 *Can. J. Economics and Pol. Science* 465. Both these articles are impressive pieces of scholarship, which anticipated some of the trends of the 1980s. Another article on the New Deal statutes was C.W. Jenks, 'The Dominion Jurisdiction in Respect of Criminal Law as a Basis for Social Legislation in Canada' (1935) 13 *Can. Bar R.* 279.

51 MacDonald, 'Judicial Interpretation,' supra note 38, at 283; see also
Kennedy, 'The Workings,' supra note 37, at 64–8.
52 *A.G. B.C. v. A.G. Canada* [1937] A.C. 368 (P.C.), aff'g [1936] S.C.R. 363; *A.G.
B.C. v. A.G. Canada* [1937] A.C. 391 (P.C.), aff'g [1936] S.C.R. 384; *A.G. B.C.
v. A.G. Canada* [1937] A.C. 377 (P.C.), aff'g [1936] S.C.R. 398; *A.G. Canada v.
A.G. Ont.* [1937] A.C. 355 (P.C.), aff'g [1936] S.C.R. 427; *A.G. Canada v. A.G.
Ont.* [1937] A.C. 326 (P.C.), aff'g [1936] S.C.R. 461; and *A.G. Ont. v. A.G.
Canada* [1937] A.C. 405 (P.C.); varying [1936] S.C.R. 379.
See W. McConnell, 'The Judicial Review of Prime Minister Bennett's "New
Deal"' (1968) 6 *Osgoode Hall L.J.* 39, for a description of these cases.
53 *A.G. B.C. v. A.G. Canada* [1937] A.C. 337 (P.C.), aff'g [1935] S.C.R. 398 at
A.C. 387, S.C.R. 638 and 639, and A.C. 205.
54 Kennedy, 'The British North America Act,' supra note 37 at 398–9.
55 Scott, 'The Consequences of the Privy Council Decisions,' supra note 39 at
492.
56 *Report to the Senate of Canada on the British North America Act* (Ottawa:
King's Printer, 1939).
57 Ibid. at 41, 67, 38–40, 41, and 69.
58 In the late 1930s, O'Connor was defended by E. Richar, 'Peace, Order and
Good Government' (1940) 18 *Can. Bar R.* 243, and attacked by V. Gray,
'The O'Connor Report on the British North America Act, 1867' (1939) 17
Can. Bar R. 309.
59 See especially the texts written by Loranger and O'Sullivan, supra note 8.
60 Their major articles were W.P.M. Kennedy, 'The Interpretation of the
British North America Act' (1943) 8 *Cambridge L.J.* 146; V. MacDonald, 'The
Constitution in a Changing World' (1948) 26 *Can. Bar R.* 21; V. MacDonald,
'The Privy Council and the Canadian Constitution' (1951) 29 *Can. Bar R.*
1021; F.R. Scott, 'Political Nationalism and Confederation' (1942) 8 *Can. J.
Economics and Pol. Science* 386; and F.R. Scott, 'Centralisation and Decentralization in Canadian Federalism' (1951) 29 *Can. Bar R.* 1095. Kennedy's article was essentially an elegant summary of O'Connor. Scott made a
more thorough account of Confederation than he did in the 1930s, but
added little by way of new ideas, except for the use of O'Connor. Mac-
Donald not only incorporated O'Connor, but also some ideas about
'functionalism.'
61 The first in this group was R. Tuck, 'Canada and the Judicial Committee of
the Privy Council' (1941) 4 *U.T.L.J.* 33. His article was a thorough study of
the cases, emphasizing throughout the erratic course of the Privy Council
and its failure to adapt the *BNA Act* to the changing conditions and needs
of Canada.

62 B. Laskin, 'Peace, Order and Good Government Re-examined' (1947) 25 *Can. Bar R.* 1054.

63 Ibid. at 1068, 1076, 1079, 1077, 1070, and 1064.

64 B. Laskin, 'The Supreme Court of Canada: A Final Court of and for Canadians' (1951) 29 *Can. Bar R.* 1038.

65 (Toronto: Butterworths, 1963).

66 The same story was told by other scholars: M. MacGuigan, 'The Privy Council and the Supreme Court: A Jurisprudential Analysis' (1964) 4 *Alberta L.R.* 419; and E. McWhinney, *Judicial Review in the English Speaking World* (Toronto: University of Toronto Press, 1956) c. 4.

67 L.P. Pigeon, 'The Meaning of Provincial Autonomy' (1951) 29 *Can. Bar R.* 1126.

68 See W. Lederman, 'The Concurrent Operation of Federal and Provincial Laws in Canada' (1962) 9 *McGill L.J.* 185, as reprinted in W. Lederman, *Continuing Canadian Constitutional Dilemmas* (Toronto: Butterworths, 1981); W. Lederman, 'The Balanced Interpretation of the Federal Distribution of Legislative Powers in Canada,' in P.A. Crepeau and C.B. Macpherson, eds., *The Future of Canadian Federalism* (Toronto: University of Toronto Press, 1965) 91, as reprinted in *Continuing Canadian Constitutional Dilemmas*, 246; W. Lederman, 'Cooperative Federalism: Constitutional Revision and Parliamentary Government in Canada' (1971) *Queen's Q.* 7; and W. Lederman, 'Unity and Diversity in Canadian Federalism: Ideals and Methods of Moderation' (1975) 53 *Can. Bar R.* 597, as reprinted in *Continuing Canadian Constitutional Dilemmas* 285.

69 'Unity and Diversity,' ibid. at 291 and 294.

70 Lederman wrote about overlap, although without the idea of balance in 1953: 'Classification of Laws and the British North America Act,' in J. Corry, F. Cronkite, and E. Whitmore, eds., *Legal Essays in Honour of Arthur Moxon* (Toronto: University of Toronto Press, 1953) 183, as reprinted in *Continuing Canadian Constitutional Dilemmas*, supra note 68, at 243–5, 250–4, 275–8.

71 See R. Simeon and I. Robinson, *State, Society, and the Development of Canadian Federalism* (Toronto: University of Toronto Press, 1990), especially c. 8 and 9, far an account of these developments.

72 (Toronto: Carswell, 1977). The word 'significant' is included to take account of the fact that there were a few other textbooks, which need not be mentioned here.

73 Ibid. at 292.

74 In 1967, the results of the cases were defended by a historian, G.P. Browne, in *The Judicial Committee and the British North America Act* (Toronto:

University of Toronto Press, 1967), who argued that the separation between POGG and the enumerations in section 91 was derived from the text of the *BNA Act*, displaying a remarkable faith in the meaning of the bare text that was scorned by the mainstream scholars.

75 The quotations are from Laskin, supra note 62, at 1059, 1060, 1080, and 1082.

76 W. Lederman, 'Thoughts on Reform of the Supreme Court of Canada' (1970) 8 *Alberta L.R.* 1, at 2 and 3; Lederman, supra note 68; and Lederman, supra note 70, at 241.

77 See T. Aleinikoff, 'Constitutional Law in the Age of Balancing' (1987) 96 *Yale L.J.* 943 for a comprehensive account of the emergence of 'balancing' as the dominant way of reasoning in constitutional cases in the United States.

78 Lederman, supra note 68, at 296.

79 Another example of the contrast was Lefroy's retreat from the proposal by Story that judges consider 'public policy and public welfare, according to the changes of time and circumstances': supra note 8, at 475–6.

80 For stimulating accounts of legal thought in the United States in the 1950s and 1960, see R.W. Gordon, 'New Developments in Legal Theory,' in D. Kairys, ed., *The Politics of Law* (New York: Pantheon Books, 1982); Horwitz, supra note 48, at c. 9; and G. Peller, 'Neutral Principles in the 1950s' (1988) 21 *Michigan J. of Law Reform* 561. Gordon's brief description of legal education in the United States in the 1960s is remarkably perceptive. Some of these contrasts were noted in 1958 by E. McWhinney in 'English Legal Philosophy and Canadian Legal Philosophy' (1958) 4 *McGill L.J.* 213 at 216–17.

81 F.E. Labrie, 'Canadian Constitutional Interpretation and Legislative Review' (1949) 8 *U.T.L.J.* 298 at 298, 312, 343, 342, 318, and 310. In 1953, Lederman made some claims about doctrine and precedent that resembled LaBrie's arguments, in his first constitutional article – Lederman, supra note 70 – although he went on to argue that the judges should make their choices according to a vision of federalism and the needs of the country. In his later articles, he came to express more faith in the accumulated work of the courts and a distinctively 'legal' reasoning, than he had suggested here.

82 Supra note 42.

83 The literature, apart from items I shall refer to later, includes, A.C. Cairns, 'Comment on "Critics of the Judicial Committee: The New Orthodoxy and an Alternative Explanation"' (1986) 19 *Can. J. of Pol. Science* 521; C.O. Johnson, 'Did Judah P. Benjamin Plant the "States' Rights" Doctrine in the

Interpretation of the British North America Act?' (1967) 45 *Can. Bar R.* 454; M. MacGuigan, 'The Privy Council and the Supreme Court: A Jurisprudential Analysis' (1965) 4 *Alberta L.R.* 419; J.G. Morrison, *Oliver Mowat and the Development of Provincial Rights in Ontario: A Study in Dominion–Provincial Relations, 1867–1896* (Toronto: Ontario Department of Public Records and Archives, 1961) 286–95; J. Robinnette, 'Lord Haldane and the British North America Act' (1970) 20 *U.T.L.J.* 55; P. Russell, 'Comment on "Critics of the Judicial Committee: The New Orthodoxy and an Alternative Explanation"' (1956) 19 *Can. J. Pol. Science* 521; F. Vaughan, 'Critics of the Judicial Committee of the Privy Council: The New Orthodoxy and an Alternative Explanation' (1986) 19 *Can. J. Pol. Science* 495; and S. Wexler, 'The Urge to Idealise: Viscount Haldane and the Constitution of Canada' (1984) 29 *McGill L.J.* 609.

84 One recent exception to this tendency is a pair of articles by Paul Romney: 'The Nature and Scope of Provincial Autonomy: Oliver Mowat, the Quebec Resolutions, and the Construction of the British North America Act' (1992) 25 *Can. J. Pol. Science* 3, and 'Why Lord Watson Was Right,' in Ajzenstat, ed., supra note 39 at 193.

85 Here are some even briefer comments about other explanations. Some scholars have observed that some members of the Privy Council were sympathetic to 'home rule' for Ireland. This sympathy alone is not an explanation. Assuming that it was based on a general belief in liberty for distinctive communities, why did the provinces seem to be distinctive communities or how did the provinces resemble Ireland? The answer probably depends upon a study of how the Privy Council acquired its knowledge of Canada, and here this explanation merges with some of the others. Some scholars have invoked Lord Haldane's idealism. (He was an accomplished philosopher, and a Hegelian.) This argument presents much the same question as the arguments based on 'home rule': why was the general will appropriately expressed through Ontario, rather than the Dominion, and why did rational principles tend to favour the provinces? Next, some scholars have argued that the Privy Council believed that its function was political, to undertake statecraft. This argument is at odds with the form of the arguments and the judgments, which are typical lawyers' talk and differ little from the form of arguments and judgments of the Supreme Court. More importantly, it leads to the same sort of question that has already appeared: why would statecraft lead to strong provinces? The simplest explanation is the speculation that Judah Benjamin, who had been a senior official in the American Confederacy and later a leading counsel in England, persuaded the Privy Council to

espouse 'states rights'; but research into his appearances has demonstrated that the facts don't support the speculation. Last, perhaps the Privy Council was influenced by its desire to preserve the Empire; but even assuming such a desire, it is not clear what decisions about federalism it would produce.

86 F.M. Greenwood, 'Lord Watson, Institutional Self-Interest, and the Decentralization of Canadian Federalism in the 1890s' (1974) *U. of British Columbia L.R.* 244. As well as proposing his own explanation, Greenwood also gives a good survey of the competing candidates.

87 Note that one element of the explanation, that of responsiveness to predominant opinion in Canada, alone could be an explanation, and in this way Greenwood's explanation approaches some of the others, but involves some of the same questions, especially about the Privy Council's understanding of its function and its knowledge of Canada.

88 Scott, supra note 39, at 492.

89 J.R. Mallory, *Social Credit and the Federal Power in Canada* (Toronto: University of Toronto Press, 1954) at 25–56; see also J.R. Mallory, 'The Courts and the Sovereignty of the Canadian Parliament' (1944) 10 *Can. J. Pol. Science* 165.

90 See B.J. Hibbitts, '"A Bridle for Leviathan": The Supreme Court and The Board of Commerce' (1989) 21 *Ottawa L.R.* 65.

91 'The Demise and Rise of the Classical Paradigm' (1991) 36 *McGill L.J.* 349.

92 'I often wonder, however, with the inevitable divergencies in our national life due to race, religion, geography and such like, whether after all the way of the Privy Council up to 1929 has not been the better way': Kennedy, 'Review,' supra note 37 at 708; also, *Some Aspects of the Theories and Workings of Constitutional Law*, in supra note 37 at 101–2.

93 A.C. Cairns, 'The Judicial Committee and Its Critics' (1971) 4 *Can. J. Pol. Science* 301.

94 R.B. Haldane, 'Lord Watson' (1899) 11 *Juridical R.* 278; and Lord Haldane, 'The Work for the Empire of the Judicial Committee of the Privy Council' (1921)1 *Cambridge L.J.* 143.

95 LaBrie, supra note 81, at 319–24, 344.

96 *Hodge v. The Queen* (1883) 9 A.C. 117 (P.C.), as well as the *Liquidators* judgment.

97 A.V. Dicey, *The Law of the Constitution* (London: MacMillan, 1885) at 142 and 138.

98 Scott, supra note 39 at 233.

9

John Willis: A Tribute

John Willis has been respected and loved in the Canadian legal community as a teacher, colleague, and scholar for decades, and one of his articles – 'Statute Interpretation in a Nutshell'[1] – is probably the best-known single piece of Canadian legal writing. The law about government was his abiding interest and the subject of most of his writing. This article is a study of this writing, especially the writing done during the 1930s. It is primarily part of an undertaking to understand the minds of Canadian lawyers, but it is also a tribute. My conclusion is that this writing was outstanding scholarship. Canadians do not easily believe that one of us has been outstanding, not only within our community but beyond, but this is my claim and my tribute.

Both his preferences and my tastes and limitations make it a study of his writing and not a biography, but a few dates and places in his life are a useful introduction. He was born in England in 1907, and educated at Winchester and at Oxford, graduating in 1929 with a 'double first' in classics and jurisprudence. After teaching at a public school for a year he went to Harvard Law School for two years, from 1930 to 1932. He then returned to England, taught school for another year, and in 1933 came to Canada and Dalhousie Law School. He spent the next forty-seven years teaching at Dalhousie, Osgoode Hall, the University of Toronto, and the University of British Columbia, except for a year working for the International Monetary Fund, and five years in practice in Halifax. He retired in 1980, and now lives in Annapolis Royal.

Much of his writing was a challenge to the ideals about law that were dominant during the second half of the nineteenth century, and which can conveniently here be called the traditional ideals.[2] In these ideals – at least so far as Willis and his generation understood them – the law was pre-eminently common law, and its primary purpose was to establish rights and boundaries for individual autonomy. To achieve this purpose, a fundamental division was made between the public and private worlds; obligation was conceived as a product of will; and the proper form of the law was general and comprehensive rules that contained little or no discretion and that governed all individuals and the state equally. The courts and the legal profession were crucial institutions in this vision, because they were the custodians who declared and interpreted these rules. The ideals made this function apolitical, and the law, especially the common law, was perceived as a distinctive and autonomous enterprise. These ideals were fundamentally the same in England and the United States, although in England the faith in precedent, especially the authority of single cases, was more powerful, and in the United States there was a greater emphasis on conceptual thinking about systems of rules.

These ideals included ideals about law and government, which were expressed in their best-known form in Dicey's statement of the rule of law, which he first proclaimed in 1885.[3] The rule was expressed in three propositions: first, no person should be subject to the power of the state except for a breach of the law – the common law and statutes – determined by the 'ordinary courts.' 'In this sense the rule of law is contrasted with ... wide, arbitrary, or discretionary powers.' Second, all persons, including all government officials, should be subject to the ordinary law, and their liability should be enforceable in the courts. Third, the rules of the Constitution were established in lawsuits brought by private persons. In a famous article about the *droit administratif* written in 1903, Dicey proclaimed the crucial role of the courts and the common law, and in 1915 he claimed that the continuing grant of powers to government departments, especially powers to make judicial decisions, 'saps the foundations' of the rule of law, although he found its salvation in the judicial supervision of government, through review for *ultra vires* and unfair procedures, and through civil actions.[4]

So far as this rule of law was a description of the current state of English law, much of it was misleading or wrong. It underestimated the extent of governmental functions and discretion, and the significance of other forms of law, and it exaggerated the liability of government – an action in tort against a governmental official was less likely to succeed than an action against a private individual. Yet Dicey's statement of the rule of law was far more important as a statement of ideals than as a description. These ideals became the established creed about law and government. In England they shaped the minds of generations of lawyers – and the legal education Willis received at Oxford.

During the 1920s they were the basis of protests by lawyers against the continuous expansion of the powers of government, which culminated in Lord Hewart's *New Despotism*, published in 1929.[5] Hewart claimed that there was 'a persistent and well-contrived system, intending to produce, and in practice producing, a despotic power which ... places Government departments above the Sovereignty of Parliament and beyond the jurisdiction of the Courts.'[6] Extensive judicial and legislative powers were being given to government departments; Parliament was failing to supervise the use of these legislative powers; statutes often seemed to forbid supervision by the courts; and, more generally, the rule of law was being fundamentally subverted. Throughout, Hewart proclaimed the traditional ideals and Dicey's rule of law.

The book was superficial and shrill, but it was much better journalism than it was sustained thought. In response to the prospect of its publication, the Lord Chancellor appointed a powerful committee, the Donoughmore Committee, to consider the 'legislative, and judicial and quasi-judicial powers of ministers and departments,' and the safeguards needed to 'secure the constitutional principles of the sovereignty of Parliament and the supremacy of the law.' The committee reported in 1932 and firmly denied any threat of injustice or despotism.[7] It assumed and affirmed the traditional ideals; for example, it affirmed the antithesis between law (general rules), and discretion and arbitrariness, and it expressed a fundamental faith in courts, including their apolitical functions and the traditional approaches to interpretation.[8] It declared a need for delegation of powers by Parliament, and made modest proposals to accommodate these powers with the rule of law.

For delegated legislative powers, it proposed limits to the kinds of powers that could be granted, supervision by Parliament through committees, and unrestricted review by the courts for *ultra vires*. For judicial and quasi-judicial powers, it made definitions based on the distinction between law and discretion: both were powers to determine disputes and required presentations by the parties and determination of facts. Judicial decisions were characterized by application of law, and quasi-judicial decisions required the exercise of discretion. Decisions that did

not require presentations by parties or findings of facts were administrative. The principle of separation of powers dictated that judicial
decisions should usually be made by courts, and quasi-judicial and
administrative decisions should be made by ministers or departments.[9]

The traditional ideals, including the ideals about law and government as they were expressed by the Donoughmore Committee, continued to be the dominant faith in England throughout the 1930s, and the
faith was not often examined, or even remembered and displayed. The
lawyers, especially the academics, did remarkably little thinking and
writing about law and government, and the only significant thinking
that was done, and the only challenge to the ideals, was from a few
scholars, especially Robson, Laski, and Jennings.

While the Donoughmore Committee was deliberating, Willis was at
Harvard, on a Commonwealth scholarship, and it was an exciting
time to be there. Two strands of thought are especially significant for
understanding him and his context. The first was thought about the
nature and purpose of law generally. Early in the twentieth century,
Pound proclaimed a need for a 'sociological jurisprudence'; he de-
nounced the 'mechanical jurisprudence' of the nineteenth century and
declared that law must openly serve social purposes. Late in the 1920s
Pound himself was challenged by the realist movement, led by Frank,
Llewellyn, and Cohen, which made an even more radical attack on the
traditional ideals. In 1930, the appearance of Frank's *Law and the
Modern Mind*, and a debate between Pound and Llewellyn[10] must
have made a dramatic contrast for Willis from the world he had left in
Oxford. The second strand was thought about law and government.
In the late nineteenth century, lawyers and political scientists had
begun to study the agencies and judicial review as discrete and important topics, and by 1930 the thought was much more extensive and
rich than it was in England, even apart from the distinctive constitutional issues.[11] At Harvard, Felix Frankfurter was inspiring a generation of colleagues and students in courses in administrative law and
public utilities.

Willis' BA did not entitle him to do a graduate degree, and a three-
year undergraduate program seemed likely to be an unattractive grind,
and therefore he simply took courses he liked. He came under the wing
of Frankfurter, and his first book, *The Parliamentary Powers of English
Government Departments*, published in 1933, was written as a seminar
paper for Frankfurter.[12] It was a response to the dire warnings from
England about despotism, the irresponsible executive, and the passing
of the traditional constitutional ideals, and its introduction took express

aim at *The New Despotism*. The topic was the discretionary powers of government departments that seemed to be insulated by statute from supervision by the courts.[13] These were the powers where 'the constitutional shoe pinches,'[14] and they had been the most common examples of the alleged despotism. Like *The New Despotism*, it was passionate and eloquent, but in contrast it was based on careful research and analysis. It was praised in reviews,[15] but it is little known today, perhaps because it seems so much limited to the particular controversies of its times.

Throughout the book, Willis observed with unusual clarity how government was changing. In the early twentieth century

the State had changed its character, had ceased to be soldier and policeman, and was rapidly becoming protector and nurse ... Again the rights of the community bulk larger than the rights of the individual.[16]

But his observation went far beyond the general changes in function and sheer growth, which were obvious by 1930. He saw subtle changes in the structure and functions of legal institutions, and saw how many of the changes had been made through the accumulation of changes in procedure and administrative powers. The implications of these changes were not realized

until there comes a day when trivial changes of procedure, cumulative in their effect, each precedent going a little further than the one before it, have gnawed their way into the fabric of substance, and the elaborate, supposedly perpetual edifice of a constitutional theory is seen to be tottering to its fall. Then and only then is a cry raised, and as if to compensate for their blind apathy, party leaders open the flood gates of oratory and swamp the issues in swirling rhetoric.[17]

Willis demonstrated through careful and extensive research in the statutes that most of the powers he was considering were narrower and more circumscribed than the attacks on them had suggested. They had an extensive and respectable history, and had not appeared suddenly in the 1920s as a result of some nefarious plot of officials. He argued powerfully and passionately that these powers were necessary for the modern state. Of course, what was necessary and reasonable was debatable, and in making this argument he demonstrated an attitude that would continue throughout his writing – a willingness to accept the modern state, a willingness to give extensive powers to government, and a great faith in expertise:

The widening of the field of government brought to the departments new legislative powers, for who else could deal effectively with matters that required special knowledge of conditions and special skill? ... But it does not follow, as some writers have thought, that power leads to arbitrary methods; at no other time has such an effort been made to take action on the basis of fact rather than conjecture ... The civil service [is] the best informed and most forward looking body of persons in England to-day ... The rationale of ... delegation ... is to give full play to the determinations of the expert.[18]

He was determined to study 'what really happens,' rather than the formal legal doctrine, and he believed that the important reality of government was the daily routine of government business, and not the more dramatic conflicts in courts and Parliament.[19] The major argument of the book was his belief that the test of the existence of the new despotism should be the ways in which powers had actually been used, and not the ways in which they might have been used or the fate of abstract constitutional principles. He asserted that the use of the powers had not impinged unreasonably upon individual rights:

The generality of the words used is not in itself important; the proper question is what has in fact been done under those words ... Questions of government cannot be settled by drawing analogies from the behaviour of a pickpocket when the policeman is off his beat.[20]

This emphasis on facts was one of the distinctive elements of legal thought in the United States in the twentieth century, especially the thought of the realists. Of course, lawyers cannot ignore facts, but the emphasis on generalization and abstraction in the traditional ideals seemed to diminish the significance of particular facts. Willis' concern was intense even by the standards of the realists, and his argument that the test of the existence of a new despotism and infringements of individual rights should depend solely upon what actually happened was distinctive.

Parts of this argument led into statutory interpretation, because the decisions of the courts about the terms that sought to insulate administrative action from review began to change just as he was writing. An early willingness to give the terms a substantial effect gave way to a very narrow reading that made them virtually ineffective. In discussing the recent cases, Willis squarely challenged the traditional ideals about interpretation. He declared that words did not have plain meanings, and that interpretation was not autonomous and apolitical:

> The courts ... purport to deal only with questions of power and not questions of policy; but since their decisions rest mainly on statutory interpretation, and ambiguous words derive their force not from any innate virtue of their own but from what the interpreter puts into them, these decisions are in effect judgments of a court upon what in their opinion should be the scope of executive discretion.[21]

And he left no doubt that he believed the courts had been hostile towards executive powers, especially in the recent past. He did not undertake to analyse in any comprehensive way why this antipathy existed, although he did suggest that common law values were one of the major causes. The courts saw the legislation 'through the fog of the common law, so comes about the doctrine that statutes are to be interpreted strictly, that there is a presumption in favour of the liberty of the subject and the result of the doctrine, that it is not thought *mal propos* to measure modern development by the yardstick of the Case of Proclamations.'[22]

This understanding, coupled with a strong dislike of privilege, led him to comment harshly on some of the recent cases, which had involved attacks by property owners on orders confirming urban housing redevelopment schemes. Willis claimed that the courts delayed 'great improvements' by performing their 'legal acrobatics' for the benefit of 'worthless slum owners.'[23] More generally, he argued that these attitudes made the courts inappropriate to supervise government, and he proposed a system of specialized courts. '[W]hy should our system of government be conceived of as a pyramid with the courts at the ... apex? Who shall be the final interpreters of social legislation and in what spirit shall they approach the task?' The courts had frustrated the objectives of the Parliament, and therefore 'a new system of government must be administered by those who do not draw their inspiration from Common Law analogies.'[24]

His perceptions of the changes in government led to the realization that these changes and the values that inspired them were inconsistent with the traditional ideals and assumptions about the Constitution and law and government. He was especially eloquent and biting about the way in which lawyers managed to carry both the reality and these ideals in their heads at the same time:

[T]he English lawyer, with his strange but quite intelligible aptitude for divorcing life from law ... failed to realize the significant changes going on beneath the trappings of legal theory ... [To] a lawyer a statute does not speak the living language of the day. Lawyers' ears are attuned to the accents of the forgotten past, new commands are faintly apprehended through the fog of the Common Law.[25]

Willis returned to England in 1932 with a promise of a university position, which perished in the depression, and a year later he was offered a job at Dalhousie Law School for a year, as a replacement for a faculty member who was going on leave. He came for want of any other opportunities, and stayed. During the next two years he published two articles – one about the report of the Donoughmore Committee and the other about local government in England – two book reviews, and a case comment.[26] His next important piece of writing, 'Three Approaches to Administrative Law,'[27] appeared in 1935, and it is the piece of his writing I admire most, because it has the most impressive combination of insight, wit, and passion, and an orderly framework for analysis. He began by describing the expansion of government and its institutions. The most common framework in the legal literature for description and analysis of government had been the distinction between judicial and legislative powers, but Willis saw that this framework was inadequate to accommodate the diversity of powers and functions, and especially inappropriate for the independent regulatory agency, which was becoming common in Canada and which he called a 'government in miniature.'[28] He then stated his theme: 'The practical problem is how to get into our constitutional structure these new institutions whose growth seems inevitable.' The answer depended, 'as will the solution of most problems of administrative law, upon the approach,' and he described three possible approaches – the judicial, the conceptual, and the functional.[29]

The judicial approach had been frankly hostile 'to the new institutions,' and here Willis expanded the analysis he had begun in *Parliamentary Powers*. He demonstrated the hostility by tracing its development in English decisions during the preceeding half century, and he condemned the approach, more by implication than expressly, because it was inconsistent with the preferences clearly expressed by the legislatures. He suggested three reasons. First, the agencies were created by statute, but the courts were hostile to statutes as a form of law. 'A statute is strictly construed. It is placed against the background of a common law whose assumptions are directly opposed to those of modern legislation.' Second, the courts were faithful to the common law and the 'uncompromisingly individualistic' values it expressed. The application of these values, especially as expressed in presumptions, 'goes far to nullify the effect of statutes which emphasize not the rights of the subject but the claims of the state upon him.' The third reason was that the courts were 'uncompromisingly hostile to the executive.'[30] These reasons may have permitted the inference that if only the judges would improve their processes and ways of reasoning, the results they reached would be better. He did not expressly suggest that the results were also determined by the general social or political values of the courts or by class power, although the general mood of his discussion suggested these influences. Allegations that the courts had been unsympathetic to the modern administrative state were familiar in the United States, but in England only a few scholars, again primarily Robson, Laski, and Jennings were making similar claims. In Canada, the issue had barely been raised.

Willis also condemned the conceptual approach. His discussion was provocative and insightful, even though it was vague at some crucial turns and ultimately incomplete. His understanding of conceptual reasoning can be illuminated by a brief reference to an otherwise unrelated article he wrote about conflict of laws, in which he described conceptual reasoning as 'the deduction of specific rules from a consistent legal theory of the nature of conflict of laws,' and contrasted it to a 'practical' approach that stressed 'justice and convenience.'[31] In 'Three Approaches' he began by asserting that concepts were necessary elements of legal reasoning, and he gave as examples of concepts, trust, bailment, and the distinction between judicial and administrative powers. The concepts were to be applied by courts to facts to resolve disputes, but sometimes two or more concepts seemed to apply. The choice among them was an expression of values and not a product of reasoning from the 'legal' premises, and the decision could be made only by resort to a theory – 'really not a question of law but of political science.'[32] The forms of legal thinking often obscured the nature of this choice, and concepts became ends in themselves and fixed in particular forms of words that obscured the original purposes and the theories behind them. His major example of the limitations of conceptual thinking was the efforts of the Donoughmore Committee to allocate functions of government by using the concepts judicial and administrative as though they had some firm and useful meaning.

In this discussion of conceptual reasoning, Willis had tackled deep and much-debated issues about legal reasoning. Much of the twentieth-century challenge to the traditional ideals was a denial of its vision of reasoning from general principles. From Holmes to the realists, legal thinkers asserted that the choices of principles were arbitrary, and that more than one result could be derived from any given principle. Willis shared these attitudes, although he did not elaborate them rigorously or express them in any original way. He did, however, understand how profoundly ideas could shape perceptions and conduct, and the dangers of responding to questions of values by reciting familiar and comfortable dogma.

Willis clearly preferred the functional approach, and distinguished it from the conceptual approach:

> The problem put is, how shall the powers of government be divided up? The problem is neither one of law nor of formal logic, but of expediency. The functional approach examines, first, the existing functions of existing governmental bodies in order to discover what kind of work each has in the past done best, and assigns the new work to the body which experience has shown best fitted to perform work of that type. If there is no such body, a new one is created ad hoc ... A proposal to empower a department to make regulations under a statute should not then, be met with the question, 'Is the legislature delegating legislative power?' but rather 'Is the department or the legislature itself better fitted to make a decision of this kind?'[33]

Lawyers cannot ignore function any more than they can ignore facts, and concern for the appropriate function of institutions without the word 'functional' existed long before the twentieth century; for example, in the doctrine of separation of powers, and the allocation of functions between judge and jury. In the United States, it appeared in thinking about administrative agencies in the late nineteenth century, and it emerged as a major and express approach in the 1930s. Willis was among the first scholars to apply it expressly and specifically to the design of the agencies. He used it to explain and justify the creation of particular kinds of agencies; for example, licensing agencies, and as the basis for proposals for supervising them. He had no doubt that some supervision was necessary, and that the courts were inappropriate, 'for they have no experience of administrative policy.' The appropriate institution was 'an independent body, composed of persons trained in the practice of the whole law pertaining to administration.'[34]

From 1936 to 1938 he published two articles, one case comment, and four book reviews, including enthusiastic and provocative reviews of Thurman Arnold's *The Symbols of Government and the Folklore of Capitalism*.[35] Willis shared Arnold's perceptions and way with words, although he tended to be caustic where Arnold was ironic. At Dalhousie, he taught only the traditional common law subjects until 1937, when he began a course in statutes and administrative law. During that summer, he wrote a short introduction to the course for his students, which appeared in 1938 as 'Statute Interpretation in a Nutshell.'[36] It was both a realistic guide to understanding the process of interpretation and a powerful attack on the traditional faith. Its iconoclastic attitude was expressed in the first few words, 'If you are trying to guess what meaning a court will attach to a section in a statute.' Guessing must have seemed inconsistent with the rule of law, if not impertinent. Willis asserted that the traditional sources and techniques did not and could not determine outcomes in difficult cases: 'No technique has much effect on final result.' The texts on statutory interpretation were unreliable, because they asserted 'one great sun of a principle – the "plain meaning" rule ... around which revolve in planetary order a series of minor rules of construction,' and the crucial element was not any one principle or technique, but the choice of approach. The texts took no account of the context of place and time, and they displayed what courts said, and not what courts did. 'What will they do, and not what they will say, is your concern.' Dictionaries and rules of grammar, such as the *ejusdem generis* rule, were equally unreliable, because they permitted wide ranges of choices. The plain meaning rule was rarely useful, because the growth of social legislation made 'wide and general terms' dominant, and it usually was no more than 'a device whereby to acheive some desired result.' The 'golden rule' was much the same, because the perception of an absurdity depended 'on the social and political views of the men who happen to be sitting on the case.'[37]

In difficult cases, the courts usually chose between the 'mischief rule' and presumptions. The mischief rule was 'sensible and ... thoroughly in accord with the constitutional principle of supremacy of Parliament,' but it was unworkable, because the rules that excluded evidence of parliamentary material made it impossible for judges to determine the policy and purpose. Again, it served merely 'to acheive a desired result.' Presumptions were a 'common law Bill of Rights,' although many of them, for example the presumptions against taking away property or common law rights, were opposed to the spirit of much of the social legislation, and none of them could determine the outcome of particular cases. Again, the crucial element was the approach and the attitude of the court.[38]

By 1938 much had been written about statutory interpretation, and assertions that words did not have plain meanings and that judges often had a choice that were far from novel. The 'Nutshell' was distinctive because of its effective unmasking of the traditional sources and techniques, and its emphasis on particular contexts and approaches. It gave lawyers seeking either to guess what a court might do or to persuade a court to reach a particular result a realistic understanding of the process of interpretation. It may have seemed dangerous – and impertinent – but it contained nothing that challenged the supremacy of Parliament or a rule of law, and it affirmed the obligation of courts to respect the purposes of the legislature and to make sense of a statute. However, despite its fame, it seems to me to be less perceptive and creative than 'Three Approaches,' and less carefully ordered.

Willis' next major article was 'Administrative Approaches and the British North America Act,' which appeared in the *Harvard Law Review* in 1939.[39] Its major purpose was to demonstrate that courts in England and Canada had imposed limitations on administrative powers that were similar to the constitutional requirements of separation of powers and due process in the United States. These limitations had been imposed despite legislative supremacy, through interpretation of statutes and the *British North America (BNA) Act*. The first part discussed the possibility that a faith in the separation of powers might support common law limitations on delegated legislative powers (delegated legislation). In the United States limitations had been imposed in the late nineteenth and early twentieth centuries and had been resurrected in the late 1930s. The Supreme Court of Canada and the Privy Council had approved these powers, but had left open the possibility of imposing limits. In 1937, trial courts in British Columbia and Alberta had characterized grants of wide rule-making powers as abdications of the legislative function, although an appeal to the Privy Council had upheld the particular powers. Willis thought that limits might still be imposed, although he did not explore their nature or extent. The second part of the article discussed section 96 of the *BNA Act*, which provided that the federal government 'shall appoint the Judges of the Superior District and County Courts in each Province.' The original purposes of this section are obscure, but it had been interpreted by the courts as forbidding the provinces from granting at least the powers that were exercised by

Superior Court judges at Confederation and perhaps from granting powers to perform any 'judicial' functions at all. Willis argued that this interpretation strained both the terms and any possible purposes of the section, and was a product of the courts' desire to protect their accustomed authority. 'We can only ... marvel at the way in which deeply held political beliefs succeed in establishing themselves in the most unlikely phrases of constitutions.'[40]

The last and most important part considered the work of the courts in review of administrative action. He expanded the insight, which he had introduced in the 'Nutshell,' that the courts had created a 'common-law bill of rights,'[41] and here he used the presumptions about access to the courts, and about procedure as examples. He argued that use of the presumption about access in interpreting privative clauses demonstrated a lack of respect for the declared preferences of the legislatures, and that the courts had again sought to protect their accustomed power:

> To set up the presumption in the teeth of [the] legislative history is to fly in the face of the legislature. They now use it ... as a means of controlling an expressed intent of which they happen to disapprove. The presumption is now, in substance, a rule of constitutional law masquerading as a rule of construction.[42]

The presumptions about procedure expressed important values, although Willis wondered whether in recent cases the courts had diminished the range of choice agencies were permitted to exercise and begun to require a trial-type hearing regardless of context. The observation that the results courts reach in England, the United States, and Canada – especially in administrative law – are often similar despite deep constitutional differences is now commonplace, but Willis was the first scholar to express it coherently, and his phrase – 'a common law bill of rights' – is wonderfully expressive.

In 1941 he edited a collection of essays, *Canadian Boards at Work*, for which he wrote a preface and short introductions to several parts. The purpose was to give 'a description of what Canadian boards in fact do.' In the preface, he described the growth of the administration more extensively than he had in *Parliamentary Powers*. Governments had undertaken a 'creative role' and legislature and courts were unable to provide 'creative realization of policy ... continuous realization of policy ... and specialized knowledge.' In Canada, the independent commission had become the dominant form of administration, perhaps because Canadians had a 'horror of politics' and this form 'helps to preserve the illusion that questions of policy can be kept out of politics.' He returned to his emphasis on commissions as 'governments in minia-ture,' and stressed the diversity 'in history, object and methods of operation.'[43] Again he stressed discretion, and saw that legislatures often left development of policy to the agencies:

> If anybody asks what, exactly, the legislature thought it meant by the in-definite expressions 'unjust discrimination' or 'public convenience and necessity,' there is no difficulty about the correct answer; it meant nothing. Their 'meaning' was deliberately left to the boards; the boards were ex-pected to put into these expressions the 'meaning' that experience de-manded; they were expected, in the economist's language, to invent their own economic theory, or in the language of a lawyer, to find their own law. And this they have done – with the result that we have in Canada an im-pressive body of administrative case law, which owes nothing to legisla-tures and practically nothing to courts but is not nearly as well known as it deserves to be.[44]

But the major theme of his contributions was the emphasis on what boards do; 'who, except a lawyer or a political theorist, cares what any board conceptually "is" as long as he knows what it in fact does?' No simpler statement of the functionalist creed could be made. He pursued this theme in two contexts – control of the agencies, and their pro-cedures. About controls by the courts and the legislatures he said, '[I]n practice these controls are almost always unreal ... but the absence of the traditional safeguards does not mean there are no safeguards at all; the professional pride which is not peculiar to judges and the glare of publicity which beats more fiercely on boards than it ever does on courts will be substitutes.' He returned to the argument he made in *Parliamentary Powers* – '[T]oo much attention is paid to what boards are permitted to do on paper and too little to what the individual board really does in real life ... which boards in fact behave irresponsibly and how and when, is the only question which there is any point in answer-ing.' The effect of studying what really happened would 'exorcise the bogey of the "new despotism" with which Lord Hewart and others have tried to frighten us.'[45]

His analysis of procedures perceived clearly the problem of the ap-propriateness of procedures and the limits of the trial-type hearing. Most lawyers 'assume that in the orthodox hearing before a court the technique of fair-minded investigation has reached a fixed and final form.'[46] He specified some of the pressing problems of procedure; for example, the utility of lawyers, the representation of the public interest, the need for openness, the utility of the common law rules of evidence, and the difficult balance between designing distinctive procedures for the particular contexts and having uniform and familiar procedures to enable lawyers to participate without being specialists.

> Problems like these – and these are the real problems of administrative procedure – cannot be met by the quoting of concepts culled from the philosophic blue; they can only be resolved by facts, finding out what actually goes on, and by experience, doing something and then seeing what happens.[47]

His perceptions of the issues to be thought about, especially the function of agencies in elaborating policy, the effectiveness of different kinds of controls, and the procedural needs and problems, was better than anything being written in England or Canada, although it was not as sophisticated and sustained as the best writing in the United States.[48]

Early in the early 1940s he wrote two more articles about law and government – 'Section 96 of the British North America Act' (1940) and 'Delegatus Non Potest Delegare' (1943).[49] Both were utterly different from the writing I have already described, because they were straightforward and straight-faced expositions of doctrine.[50] They demonstrated a powerful ability to see patterns and trends in cases, and to organize and generalize, but this ability alone would hardly make him worth writing about now.[51] They are an expression of a faith, which appears in other passages in his writing, that doctrine can make sense. They also demonstrate an ambivalence about lawyers. Despite the implications and power of his own writing, he often took the lawyers' enterprise seriously and wished them to take him seriously. He acknowledged this ambivalence in 1969 in a convocation address entitled 'What I Like and What I Don't Like about Lawyers.' He explained his title by saying, 'I have, all my working life, been torn between admiration and dislike of the whole lot – what in the jargon of today would be called a love-hate relationship.'[52]

In the decade from 1933 to 1943, Willis wrote a total of 22 items – two books, nine articles, two case comments, and one letter to the editor. Almost all were about law and government, and they expressed the thoughts and beliefs he held throughout his working life. The performance is remarkable, and it is all the more remarkable considering a heavy teaching load, administrative responsibilities, and worries that his school might vanish overnight and with it his job.[53] It was the best writing about law and government done in Canada in the 1930s, by lawyers, political scientists, or historians, and it was the best common law scholarship of any kind.[54] It deserves to be compared to the best writing done in England and the United States.

His later writing elaborated these beliefs and widened into other areas, especially criminal law, taxation, and legal education.[55] For the purposes of this study, four of the later articles can usefully be discussed and they can be divided into two pairs. The first is 'Administrative Law in Canada,' written for an international conference in 1961, and 'Canadian Administrative Law in Retrospect,' the Cecil Wright Memorial Lecture at the Faculty of Law at the University of Toronto in 1974.[56] The first was an attempt 'to *describe* in a dead-pan and non-polemical way for non-Canadians what seemed to me to be distinctively *Canadian* attitudes and methods.'[57] It served its purpose, but here it is interesting only for observations about the ways in which the experience in Canada combined the experiences in England and the United States, and for a provocative guess about Canadian legal history:

> Administrative law has never raised in Canada the storms of public controversy that it did in England and the United States. The reason may be that Canada has never been, is not, and never could be a laissez-faire state.[58]

The observation is correct, and the explanation parallels much of the thinking of the historians at the time, although the full explanation must include consideration of ideologies and the power of economic interests.

The 'Retrospect' summarized much of what he had thought throughout his life. He warned his audience that he was a 'government man,' a 'legislation man,' and a 'what actually happens man.' He contrasted 'what really happens' to the 'theology of administrative law,' and he made this plea to his audience: 'Do not, I beg of you, be global and theological: be specific and practical.' He also made a telling observation about narrowing visions of scholarship and teaching. He said that any administrative law course given in the 1970s 'will always be far more professional and far less political-science oriented today than it would have been in the thirties.'[59]

In the second pair of articles Willis fought dragons that he had fought long ago on the battlefields of the 1930s. The first was a case comment about *Canadian Wheat Board v. Hallet and Carey* and a letter to the editor in response to two attacks that it provoked,[60] and the second was 'The McRuer Report: Lawyers' Values and Civil Servants' Values,' which was a review of the first volume of the *McRuer Report*.[61] Both were full of exaggerations and oversimplifications aroused by the heat of battle, but they have passion and insight that are still striking and useful. The *Wheat Board* case arose out of the readjustment of the economy after World War Two. The *National Emergency Transitional Powers Act* gave the government power to 'make ... such ... regulations as it may ... deem necessary or advisable for the purpose of, (a) maintaining, controlling and regulating ... prices.' It decided to raise the floor price of barley, and, in order to avoid permitting commercial dealers to reap windfall profits, sought to expropriate the grain they held, pay them the old floor price, and resell it to them at the new price. Nolan, a dealer who lived in Chicago, challenged the regulation that implemented this policy, and the Supreme Court declared it *ultra vires*.

Willis was outraged by the result in favour of 'the Chicago Hampden,' and more outraged by the reasoning, and especially by its 'appalling air of unreality.' He alleged two reasons for this unreality. The first was 'the symbolical language of the law,' which was 'harmless enough if not allowed to conceal realities,' but unfortunately, the courts 'from time to time ... pass imperceptibly from the twilight of this symbolical language of the law into a Stygian fairyland peopled by bogies of dead tyrants.' Issues about the modern state were perceived as battles between Lord Coke and the Stuart despots. The second reason was presumptions, especially the presumption about property, which led lawyers 'to read measures implementing the twentieth century constitution through the spectacles of the nineteenth century constitution.' All of this learning about the 'lawyers' constitution' had led the Supreme Court to be 'unerringly wrong' in asserting the intention of the legislature, 'which it is their constitutional function to implement.' Willis did not explain how he determined the intention, but presumably his reasoning was that avoiding windfall profits was an incident of 'controlling prices.'[62] He was torn about the prospects of an appeal, because it might bring a sensible result at the cost of damage to the newly gained independence of Canadian courts. Whatever his preference might have been, the Privy Council vindicated his reasoning and reversed the Supreme Court.[63]

Two lawyers wrote separate letters to the editor, before the Privy Council decision might have given Willis some claim to respectibility, and shared the same horror at what he had said. To them, the choice at stake was between the rule of law and totalitarianism, and between private enterprise and socialism, and there was no doubt which choices they attributed to Willis and preferred themselves. Review of the agencies by the courts stood between civilization, and totalitarianism, Hitlerism, and Stalinism. 'Freedom in thought and speech must go hand in hand with a free economy ... in which there is some respect for private property ... It is not yet a crime to make a profit.'[64] Willis did not recant. In his reply, he restated his beliefs even more passionately, especially his beliefs about 'the immense gap between the legal theory of the State and the State as she actually operates – a source of perpetual astonishment to the bewildered layman,' which, he illustrated by saying, 'It is not yet a crime to make a profit, is only perfectly true in an economy which knows not price control.'[65]

The review of the *McRuer Report* demonstrated the same spirit. In 1964, the Honourable J.C. McRuer, then chief justice of the High Court of Ontario, was appointed a commissioner to enquire into 'personal freedoms, rights, and liberties.' In 1968 he submitted his first report, which was composed of three volumes.[66] The first was a statement of general principles, and it was an elegant and uncritical expression of faith in the traditional vision of the law about government and the basic common law principles of administrative law doctrine. The second volume was about the courts and the third was about specific governmental functions, such as expropriation and professional regulation.

In his review, Willis observed a difference between the 'abstract and legalistic' tone of the first, and the 'practical and sensible' tone of the second and third. He saw the first as 'characteristic of the "establishment" side of the thirties,' and wished for 'a posse of Davids,' to fight the Goliath. He fought against the preoccupation with 'ideology,' rather than the question 'who is now getting hurt by what and in what ways,' and against a bias in favour of lawyers' values – individual rights, the common law, and the courts. He summarized the entire approach of the volume in his discussion of judicial review by saying 'the Commission, however, once again approaches its problem globally, ideologically, and legalistically.' His comments were not unfair. The general approach of the commission was dominated by lawyers' thinking, and it failed to consider some of the basic issues of the modern administrative state; for example, procedures for policy-making and the ways of making the exercise of discretion efficient and humane.[67]

Willis' thinking about law and government can best be summarized by dividing it into three parts. The first is his observations and attitudes about government and its institutions, which were expressed in almost every piece he wrote, and especially in *Parliamentary Powers* and 'Three Approaches.' He perceived the nature and extent of the expansion of government, and its implications for the structure and functions of the legal institutions. He perceived a changing relation between the individual and the community, and how legislative policies were expanding the claims of the community against the individual, and circumscribing common law powers.[68] He seemed enthusiastic about these changes and about the errosion of the traditional ideals, although he never declared this enthusiasm openly. He had a great faith in experts, and he believed the courts should give liberal scope to the agencies on review. He expressed this attitude best in 1951: '[T]he judges ... [should] exercise this exceedingly delicate power with understanding and restraint; for it is the power to interfere with the normal functioning of a government system of which in these democratic days they are the least important arm.'[69] This first part of his thought was the least original part and least developed.

The second part was his functionalism and his concern for facts and 'what really happens,' in contrast to the abstractness of the traditional vision, its faith in comprehensive rules, and its preoccupation with doctrine, especially common law doctrine. In its most general form, this concern was a belief that facts were crucial to knowledge and understanding, and its more simple and specific form was the argument that the new despotism must be tested by looking at the exercise of powers and not their mere existence. Institutions should be assessed and designed according to their functions, and administrative law scholarship, in particular, should not be limited to abstract analysis of the doctrines of judicial review. The most useful subjects for study were confined and specific ones, and the most effective legal arrangements were ones designed for particular contexts. In 1968 Willis declared 'the principle of "uniqueness" is the principle for me.'[70]

The third part of his thought was a challenge to the traditional ideals for legal reasoning. In its most general form this challenge was a skepticism of conceptual thinking, and this skepticism was demonstrated most effectively in his analysis of the work of courts in statutory interpretation and review of administrative action, rather than in abstract

speculation about the nature of legal reasoning. He argued that interpretation and review were not apolitical and autonomous, and that the
traditional doctrines and techniques did not determine results and
often masked choices made by courts. He described some of the patterns and trends the choices made, especially the courts' determination
to protect their vision of the Constitution and their own power. His
explanations of these results usually emphasized institutional considerations; for example, the common law and its values, the general faith
in the traditional Constitution, and the rules about the legitimate sources
of meaning in statutory interpretation. He also asserted that the values
of the courts themselves determined results, but he did not generalize
about the nature of these values and he did not expressly discuss power
or class.

The most distinctive form of his challenge to the traditional ideals
were his comments about the constellation of ideals he called the lawyers' Constitution – the rule of law, the separation of powers, the
primacy of courts, the distinction between judicial and administrative
powers, and the rules about interpretation. This Constitution masked
unstated assumptions and values, and it was inaccurate, unworkable in
the modern government, and inconsistent with democratically declared
values. His most effective insight was the way in which lawyers divided their thoughts to accommodate both the Constitution and reality.
This insight appeared first in *Parliamentary Powers*, and he expressed it
best in 1943 in a comment about *Duncan v. Cammell, Laird & Co. Ltd*:

> I used to write articles attempting in my feeble way to inform the legal
> profession of the facts of modern government. That was an impertinent
> thing to do because they were even better informed on them than I was
> myself; but it was also … a useless thing to do because the lawyer seems to
> have two sides to his mind, one of them taking note of what really happens
> in government which he uses for everyday life, and the other unconsciously
> disregarding the facts of modern government which he uses when he comes
> to talk law.[71]

Although Willis never used the word 'ideology,' all of this analysis
was a striking demonstration of how ideas shape perceptions and understanding.

His writing did not express a comprehensive jurisprudence or a substantial program for reform, and it contained internal contradictions, and
excesses and limitations, some of which were the product of sheer exu-

berance. In retrospect, the faith in government and expertise did not consider adequately the difficulties of controlling the expert and the bureaucracy, the need to order the exercise of discretion, and the tangle between politics and expertise. The functional approach was not elaborated sufficiently to be much more than an exhortation, and the stress on facts did not consider the need to fashion some ordering conceptions that made facts significant or the great difficulties of designing and doing the kind of research he called for. The analysis of judicial reasoning did not offer a consistent account of the roles of doctrine. Some passages seemed to imply that doctrine had little or no effect and that results were products of the beliefs and values of the courts. Other passages seemed to imply that doctrine did have a substantial effect, although the nature and effect of the effect was not explained, and some articles and comments were entirely exposition and analysis of doctrine. But ultimately the greatest value of his thought is not the creation of a jurisprudence or a program. The value is the challenge to the traditional ideals. Much of these ideals remain and much of them are valuable, but they have been transformed. Our understandings of law are different, and the kind of challenge Willis made marks much of the difference.

Context can illuminate the nature and stature of his thought. One of the widely held propositions about Canadian legal history is that we did not have a realist movement, and doubtless we did not have the kind of transformation that the United States experienced. But we did have at least one realist – John Willis. He would protest at this label, because he would not like being labelled at all, and because he did not participate in any way in the realist movement as it defined itself. And it is, I suppose, a little late to revise the list of heroes and add an outsider. My assertion is, though, a useful beginning to understanding his context.

Who were the realists? They were a group of academics, most of them at a few eastern law schools, who built on earlier elements in American legal thought, especially insights of Holmes and the sociological jurisprudence of Roscoe Pound, and on general trends in the social sciences, especially scientific naturalism, which professed a mistrust of abstract logic and conceptual systems, and a faith in knowledge derived from observation and experiment. Its crucial assumptions were objectivism, particularism, and functionalism.[72] Against this background the realists made a transformation in American legal thought. They were not a unified school, and a short list of their characteristics may suggest more unity than is justified, but it is useful nevertheless. They believed that law must be openly and thoroughly instrumental, and they challenged conceptual reasoning and the vision of an apolitical and autonomous common law. They criticized the results the courts had reached and ultimately the values that produced these results. They mistrusted general and comprehensive approaches and solutions, and they stressed the importance of facts and particular contexts. And they did not in the end construct an enduring and comprehensive program. Does not this list also describe Willis?[73]

Despite these similarities, the influences that shaped his approaches and ideas are difficult to determine. His writing – the topics he chose, his style, and its organization and sources; his relative isolation in Dalhousie, and his later recollections – suggests that he did not steep himself continuously in the current legal literature and that his ideas were not derived from any specific source. His experience at Harvard, and especially the exposure to Frankfurter, shaped much of his thought, especially his interest in the law about government and his determination to study 'what really happens.' But he was not merely a faithful follower. The elements of his thought that distinguished him from Frankfurter and that he shared with the realists were obviously not a product of a common cultural and educational background with the realists – his background was much different. These elements may have been formed long before he became a legal scholar, in his youth and education in England. He may also have grasped the currents of social science thinking that were 'in the air' through his general reading. He read widely outside the law, and in a convocation address given in 1973 he advised the graduates to read. 'What you must do is feed your imagination; don't read respectable things like biography and history; read verse, read novels, ... read anything that makes you see into the life of things.'[74]

His writing had little influence in its own times. The courts and practising lawyers either ignored him or considered him a dangerous radical. One example is a poignant irony. At the time he wrote 'Three Approaches' and its attack on conceptual reasoning in administrative law, the courts in Ontario embraced a throughly conceptual approach to the distinction between judicial and administrative functions that shaped Canadian administrative law for decades.[75] The greatest understanding and influence of his writing came long after the 1930s, and my impression is that the expansion of visions of legal scholarship during the past decade has made teachers and students respond more enthusiastically to it than they did during the 1950s and 1960s.

My tribute to John Willis is almost done, and one of his own conclusions can be my conclusion. At the end of his letter to the editor about the *Wheat Board* case, he said,

My *Nolan* comment has obviously set up an emotional disturbance in the breasts of [the two critics]. I think I know why. I believe, and have believed for years that our constitution is changing and that no banging of constitutional bibles is going to stop it. As for me, I wish I was as 'enamoured' of the 'brave new world' as [they] think I am; but at any rate I refuse to be like [them], walking backward into the future lest a worse fate befall them.[76]

I pay tribute to the wit, the insight, and the courage.

NOTES

1 (1938) 16 *Can. Bar R.* 1.
2 Our understanding of these ideals is still incomplete, and whatever the state of our understanding may be, a short summary cannot avoid distortion and oversimplification. For a couple of generations our understanding has been shaped by the accounts of the progressives, especially Roscoe Pound. Recent scholarship is illuminating, although much remains to be done to explore the complexities of the thought and the differences among England, the United States, and Canada. For the United States, see R.W. Gordon, 'Book Review of White *Tort Law in America: An Intellectual History*' (1981) 94 *Harvard L.R.* 903; R.W. Gordon, 'Legal Thought and Legal Practice in the Age of American Enterprise,' in G. Geison, ed., *Professions and Professional Ideologies in America* (Chapel Hill: University of North Carlina Press, 1983); and D. Kennedy, 'Towards an Historical Understanding of Legal Consciousness: The Case of Classical Legal Thought in America, 1850–1940' (1980) 3 *Research in L. & Soc.* 3; for England, the best description is a book review, D. Sugarman, 'Book Review: The Legal Boundaries of Liberty: Dicey, Liberalism and Legal Science, a Review of Cosgrove *The Rule of Law: Albert Venn Dicey, Victorian Jurist*' (1983), 46 *Modern L.R.* 102. Even less has been done in Canada.
3 A.V. Dicey, *An Introduction to the Study of the Constitution* (London: Macmillan, 1885), especially c. 4.
4 A.V. Dicey, 'Droit administratif in Modern French Law' (1901) 17 *L.Q.R.* 302, and Dicey (1915) 31 *L.Q.R.* 148.
5 Lord Hewart, *The New Despotism* (London: Benn, 1929) 6.

6 Ibid. 14.

7 *Report of the Committee on Ministers' Powers* (Cmd. 4060, London 1932). The original chairman was the Earl of Donoughmore, who resigned and was replaced by Sir Leslie Scott. The terms of reference are on page 1.

8 The committee's comments on interpretation were probably provoked by one of its members, Harold Laski, who wrote a short personal note as an appendix to the report (at 135), in which he challenged the traditional approaches and stressed the element of choice, and recommended permitting use of a wider ranger of background materials in interpretation, especially explanatory memoranda. Discussions during the 1920s and 1930s attacked the restrictive rules on the use of background materials frequently, and far more often than the likelihood of opportunities to use them might have suggested. The issue might have seemed important because the use of these materials may have seemed to threaten the ideal of autonomy in a simple and dramatic way.

9 The principle was not rigid; for example, assigning judicial decisions to departments (although not to ministers themselves) could be justified by a large volume of cases, or a need for specialization or saving of cost. But the rule of law demanded that if judicial powers were assigned to departments, the courts should enforce a right to natural justice, and supervise decisions for errors of jurisdiction and law. The committee firmly rejected a proposal made by Robson for supervision by a specialized administrative court rather than the regular courts.

10 K. Llewellyn (1930) 30 *Columbia L.R.* 431; R. Pound (1931), 44 *Harvard L.R.* 697; and K. Llewellyn (1931) 44 *Harvard L.R.* 1222.

11 W.C. Chase, *The American Law School and the Rise of Administrative Government* (Madison: University of Wisconsin Press, 1982) gives a description of the events and participants.

12 J. Willis, *The Parliamentary Powers of English Government Departments* (Cambridge: Cambridge University Press, 1933).

13 More particularly, three kinds of powers were examined. The first was powers to make delegated legislation that included provisions making the rules as effective as if they were part of the statute or that made confirmation by the minister 'conclusive evidence' that the rules were properly made and authorized; the second was powers given to ministers to confirm 'schemes,' especially schemes for housing redevelopment, that included similar provisions to ensure validity; and the third was powers to modify statutes by order or delegated legislation.

14 *Parliamentary Powers*, supra note 12 at 4.

15 Some of the reviews were Corry (1934) 12 *Can. Bar R.* 60; Dobie (1933) 82

U. of Pennsylvania L.R. 198; E.C.S.W. (1934) *Cambridge L.J.* 428; Laski (1934) 47 *Harvard L.R.* 1453 ('This is the best book that has been published on delegated legislation in England. It has learning, it is well written, and it possesses what is still rare in books of law – a graceful power of wit'); MacDonald (1934) 20 *Cornell L.Q.* 536; Fairlie (1934) 27 *Am. Political Science R.* 994; Finkelman (1935) 1 *U.T.L.J.* ('Mr Willis's study remains the most outstanding contribution yet made to the subject of administrative legislation'); Fuchs (1934) 20 *St. Louis L.R.* 189; Robson (1934) 50 *L.Q.R.* 282 ('This is a book of the first importance, by virtue not only of the subject with which it deals but also because of the brilliant and profound treatment which it receives'), and Robson (again!) (1934) 34 *Columbia L.R.* 189 ('Mr Willis's book must undoubtedly rank as the most important treatise on delegated legislation which has so far been published in the English language'); Sayre (1934) 19 *Iowa L.R.* 652 ('the best treatment of delegated legislation in England that has so far appeared … well written, even brilliantly written'); Vaile (1934), 20 *Am. Bar Assoc. J.* 776;

16 *Parliamentary Powers*, supra note 12 at 13 and 51.
17 Ibid. 9. Willis understood that changes in legislation were often incremental and cumulative, like changes in the common law, and he stated this perception long before Horack's famous article in (1937) 23 *Iowa L.R.* 41. For example, '[T]he process of generalisation, the very life of the Common Law imperceptibly goes on in the field of legislation,' at 118.
18 Ibid. 33, 35, 113, and 157. See also 104, 132, 153, and 159–63.
19 Ibid. 58. Closely associated with this understanding was a belief, which he did not develop extensively, that effective legal arrangements must be designed for particular contexts, for example, at 157. This emphasis on facts and 'what really happens' was probably stimulated by Frankfurter: see Frankfurter (1927) 75 *U. of Pennsylvania L.R.* 614 at 620.
20 Ibid. 104 and 152. See also 57, 101, 104, 108, 152–6, and 166.
21 Ibid. 112. See also 81. His attitudes about statutory interpretation contrasted sharply with the traditional faith of the Donoughmore Committee.
22 Ibid. 51. See also 113 and 148.
23 Ibid. 42, 78, and 104.
24 Ibid. 113, 14, and 171–2.
25 Ibid. 5 and 51. See also 29 and 112.
26 'The Delegation of Legislative and Judicial Powers to Administrative Bodies' (1933) 18 *Iowa L.R.* 150; 'Book Review' [Moley and Wallace, *Administration of Justice*] (1933) 11 *Can. Bar R.* 705; 'Case Comment' [Right of a principal to sue on a promise under seal made to an agent in agent's name – trust of a chose in action – *Harmer v. Armstrong*, [1934] 1 Ch 65]

(1934) 12 *Can. Bar R.* 183, 7 *Aust. L.J.* 424, 1 *Solicitors' J.* 47; 'Book Review'
[Haines, *American Doctrine of Judicial* Supremacy] (1934) 12 *Can. Bar R.* 597;
and 'Parliament and the Local Authorities,' in H. Laski, I. Jennings, and W.
Robson, eds., *A Century of Municipal Progress: The Last Hundred Years*
(London: Allen & Unwin, 1936) 400.

27 'Three Approaches to Administrative Law' (1935) 1 *U.T.L.J.* 53. In 1942 he
sent a paper to his friend 'Caesar' Wright, the editor of the *Canadian Bar
Review*, and said, '[T]he only thing I beg of you is to not tone it down. In
1935 I wrote an article for Kennedy [the editor of the *U.T.L.J.*] and he toned
it down, and now … I find myself faced with a mass of milk and water
Willis which is much more disgusting than the real article' (Willis to
Wright, 29 December 1942, Wright Papers, University of Toronto Archives). I would be glad indeed to be able to read the original version.

28 Willis borrowed this effective phrase from a mid-nineteenth-century
article; for its origins, see H.W. Arthurs, *'Without the Law': Administrative
Justice and Legal Pluralism in Nineteenth-Century England* (Toronto: University of Toronto Press, 1985).

29 'Three Approaches,' supra note 27 at 59.

30 Ibid. at 60 and 61.

31 (1936) 14 *Can. Bar R.* 1, at 2 and 1.

32 'Three Approaches,' supra note 27 at 70.

33 Ibid. 75.

34 Ibid. 80.

35 (1936) 14 *Can. Bar R.* 457; (1936); 14 *Can. Bar R.* 1; 'Book Review' [Arnold,
The Symbols of Government] (1936) 14 *Can. Bar R.* 278; 'Case Comment'
[Jurisdiction of courts – action to recover damages for injury to foreign
land – *Albert v. Fraser*, [1937] 1 D.L.R. 39] (1937) 15 *Can. Bar R.* 112; 'Book
Review' [Jennings, *Cabinet Government*] (1937) 15 *Can. Bar R.* 579; 'Book
Review' [Arnold, *The Folklore of Capitalism*] (1938) 16 *Can. Bar R.* 417; and
'Book Review' [Curtis, *World Order*] (1938) 16 *Can. Bar R.* 154.

36 Supra note 1.

37 Ibid. 4, 2, 11, and 13.

38 Ibid. 14, 15, and 17.

39 (1939) 53 *Harvard L.R.* 251.

40 Ibid. 271.

41 Ibid. 274 and 281.

42 Ibid. 276. Again, he was the first Canadian scholar to present an insight
that eventually became part of the common stock; see J. Evans, H. Janisch,
D. Mullan, and R. Risk, *Administrative Law: Cases, Text, and Materials*, 2nd
ed. (Toronto: Emond Montgomery, 1984), c. 11.

43 Ibid. v–viii.

44 Ibid. 69–70.

45 Ibid. 2, 66, 70, and 71.

46 *Ibid. 117.*

47 *Ibid. 119.*

48 *See, for example, J.M.. Landis, The Administrative Process* (New Haven: Yale University Press, 1938), and a symposium (1937) 47 *Yale L.J.* 515.

49 Respectively at (1940) 18 *Can. Bar R.* 517, and (1943) 21 *Can. Bar R.* 267.

50 When he sent 'Section 96' to his friend 'Caesar' Wright, the editor of the *Canadian Bar Review*, he said, 'I have sternly repressed my incessant desire to be funny or caustic about constitutional law' (Willis to Wright, 19 June 1940, Wright Papers, University of Toronto Archives).

51 Evans et al., supra note 42 at 264, where a passage from 'Delegatus non protest delagare' is used to present the basic ideas about delegation. Another example of this ability is contained in the letter referred to in note 50, supra. He said that if he had a secure future at Dalhousie – he feared for its very existence – he would try to write a book on 'judicial control of administrative authorities, which would deal with such matters, inter alia as certiorari, persona designata, jurisdictional fact, bias, and a host of other matters which have to be dug out at the present from the most unlikely articles in Halsbury … This book could be based largely on a course I give on Judicial Control here.' In short he perceived 'administrative law' as a discrete and unified subject long before DeSmith wrote *Judicial Control of Administrative Action,* and made it apparent to the English. This perception probably began in his experience in the United States.

52 J. Willis, 'What I Like and What I Don't Like about Lawyers' (1976) 76 *Queen's Q.* 1, at 53.

53 See his own history of Dalhousie: *A History of Dalhousie Law School* (Toronto: University of Toronto Press, 1979), pt. II, s. 4.

54 This may he a debatable claim, but this is not the appropriate place to defend it thoroughly. Most of the writing in the journals was description and formal analysis of doctrine, and the efforts to do more were dominated by uplifting but vague invocations of Pound and Cardozo. There are some sparkling exceptions, especially in some of the writing by Wright, the young Laskin, and Kennedy (whose vision is underestimated), but none of them produced as much original and insightful scholarship during the 1930s as Willis. See Risk, 'Volume One of the Journal,' and 'W.P.M. Kennedy,' both in this volume.

55 *Editors' Note*: An appendix listing all of Willis' publications was included in the original version of this article but has not been reproduced here.

56 (1961) 39 *Can. Bar R.* 251; and (1974) 24 *U.T.L.J.* 225.

57 Ibid. 251. Emphasis in original.

58 Ibid. 253.

59 Ibid. 225–8.

60 'Case Comment' [Statute interpretation – real constitution versus lawyer's constitution – form versus substance – courts and public law – *Canadian Wheat Board v. Hallet and Carey and Nolan*, [1951] 1 D.L.R. 468] (1951) 29 *Can. Bar R.* 296; and 'Letter to the Editor' (1951) 29 *Can. Bar R.* 580.

61 'The McRuer Report: Lawyers' Values and Civil Servants' Values' (1968) 18 *U.T.L.J.* 351.

62 He did not deal with an issue raised by Rand J., whose judgment was the only one that did seem to him to take account of the twentieth-century realities, but who joined the majority, because the regulation did not obligate the government to offer the barley to the dealers, and was therefore not limited to the permitted purposes. Nor did the Privy Council deal with this issue.

63 Ibid. 229, 239, 302, and 303.

64 Ibid. 552, 578, and 580. These attacks were similar to attacks made on the realists at the end of the 1930s.

65 Ibid. 583.

66 Royal Commission, Inquiry into Civil Rights, *Report Number One* (Toronto: Queen's Printer, 1968).

67 'McRuer Report,' supra note 61 at 351, 356, and 359. Some evidence of the narrow visions of scholarship in the 1950s and 1960s, which he had politely suggested in the Wright lecture by talking about the scope of administrative law courses, is that he was the only academic to write in a substantial way about more than doctrine and technical detail in considering the report.

68 In his later writing, his respect for the claims of the community led to some strong arguments against civil liberties.

69 'Letter to the Editor,' supra note 60 at 585.

70 'McRuer Report,' supra note 61 at 359.

71 'Letter to the Editor' [Courts and the executive – *Duncan v. Cammell, Laird & Co. Ltd.* [1942] 1 All E.R. 587] (1943) 21 *Can. Bar R.* 51.

72 See E.A. Purcell, *The Crisis of Democratic Theory: Scientific Naturalism and the Problem of Value* (Lexington: University of Kentucky Press, 1973) for an account of the intellectual background of the realist movement.

73 *Editors' Note*: For further analyses of Canadian legal scholarship in the 1930s, and of its relation to realism, see R. Risk, 'Law Teachers' and 'Volume One of the Journal,' both in this volume.

74 (1973) *Law Society Gazette* 235, at 238.
75 This episode is described briefly in R.C.B. Risk, 'Lawyers, Courts and the Rise of the Regulatory State' (1984), 9 *Dalhousie L.J.* 31 at 46.
76 'Letter to the Editor,' supra note 60 at 585.

10

The Many Minds of W.P.M. Kennedy

Introduction

W.P.M. Kennedy is known to historians as the author of a book about Canadian constitutional history, although most of them probably know him only from reading Carl Berger's study of Canadian historians.[1] He is known to lawyers as a dean of the University of Toronto Law School, although most of them probably believe that he reigned in some obscure past, before 'Caesar' Wright succeeded him and 'real' legal education began in Ontario. These impressions are at best incomplete. Kennedy made a large contribution to his adopted homeland; he was an impressive scholar, and his vision of legal education is a chastening reminder to contemporary law schools that they were not the first to embrace the interdisciplinary study of law.

This paper is primarily about Kennedy's scholarship, which spanned five decades and a wide range of topics, from the Tudor prayer book to the modern administrative state. My title, 'The Many Minds,' suggests this impressive range, but perhaps it should end with a question mark. Whether there was one mind, or two, or many is a question that runs throughout my paper: what was the common ground, if any, between his writings about history and about law? And surely curiosity is stimulated by knowing that not only was he not a lawyer, but he had no formal legal education at all.

Early Years

He was born in Northern Ireland in 1879 and studied English and history at Trinity College, Dublin, graduating in 1900. All I know about the next 13 years of his life is that he wrote about Tudor history and supported himself at least part of the time by tutoring and teaching.[2] In 1913, he came to Canada and St Francis Xavier College, where he stayed for a year before going to the University of Toronto. Shortly after he came to Canada, he began to write about its constitutional history, at the same time continuing his Tudor scholarship. In the late 1920s, he shifted his interests to law and became head of the law school at the University of Toronto. During the next decade, he transformed the school and wrote extensively about Canadian life and politics, legal education, federalism, and the administrative state.[3]

If a study of his scholarship must be illuminated by a thorough understanding of his life, I fear my enterprise is doomed. Because Kennedy was reticent about his early years and destroyed his papers after he retired, I know little more about him than this short account, and I despair of ever knowing more.[4] I do have some impressions of him as a person, derived from his writing, the recollections of a few surviving colleagues and students, and his correspondence in the university records. He seems to have been romantic, passionate, authoritarian, compassionate, continually worried about his health, and inclined to see life's highs and lows in dramatic contrast. Obviously, though, these impressions are unreliable, even if they are relevant. Stories about him abound, but they are at least as unreliable as my impressions.[5] Thus I am limited to understanding his writing in the context of other writing about history and law, and the large sweeps of Canadian life, especially the rise of nationhood, the emergence of the regulatory and welfare state, and the Depression.

1910 to 1925: The Elizabethan Scholarship

Having began to study Kennedy as part of an interest in Canadian constitutional scholarship and legal education, I had mixed feelings upon discovering that he spent the first couple of decades of his scholarly career as a historian of Tudor England, specializing in Elizabethan ecclesiastical history. I was intrigued by the prospect that he was a more complex and more accomplished scholar than I had expected, chagrined at my own ignorance and relatively narrow interests, and dismayed by the prospect of reading about a topic that I barely remembered from undergraduate survey courses.

In 1908, at the age of 28, he published *Archbishop Parker*,[6] a biography of Queen Elizabeth I's first archbishop, and *The Interpretations of the Bishops*, a short study of a set of instructions about church affairs issued by the bishops in the early 1560s.[7] Two years later, he collaborated with his teacher and lifelong friend, William Frere (later Bishop Frere) in *Visitation Articles and Injunctions*, a collection of documents about the supervision of local churches by the bishops during the early years of Elizabeth I's reign.[8] In 1914, after he came to Canada, he published *Parish Life under Elizabeth*,[9] which dealt with the religious life in parish churches, including such subjects as the clergy, the church, the services, Puritans, and Catholics. Two years later came *Studies in Tudor History*,[10] a collection of essays, including studies of the reign of King Edward VII, the literature about the first and second prayer books, and the doctrine about the communion service. In 1924, almost 10 years later, came his largest work, *Elizabethan Episcopal Administration*,[11] extending the work he had done with Frere to the death of Elizabeth. It was composed of two volumes of documents preceded by a volume of introduction, which revisited and expanded the topics he had dealt with before, especially in *Parish Life*.

He saw the Tudors' policy towards religion as essentially secular: '[D]iplomacy and statecraft lie behind everything.'[12] Their dominant objective was to make England a unified nation, under the control of the state. Elizabeth perceived the issues about vestments, ritual, and doctrine from this perspective and this perspective alone. Her decisions were essentially compromises, made to appeal to the wide middle range of clerics and people, and to avoid strife between the Catholics and the Reformers. The rise of the secular state was central to this interpretation: '[W]e have been witnessing the writing of an extended chapter in the history of the Renaissance and Reformation state – *cujus regio, ejus religio* is the key.'[13] The sovereign that was emerging throughout Europe took the form of the nation state in England; Parliament became its representative, and the divine right of kings gathered the church into its power. These large themes and interpretations were derived from the mainstream of Tudor history in the early twentieth century, established primarily by Frederick Pollard of London University, whom Kennedy thanked in the preface to *Parish Life under Elizabeth*.[14]

Much of his writing was about the ways the Tudors' policies affected local churches. In the preface to *Elizabethan Episcopal Administration* he promised a study of 'the daily life of a people,' a 'sociological and political perspective,' and 'palpitating reality.'[15] In pursuing this objective, he demonstrated much respect for the minorities, the Roman Catholics and the Puritans, seeing them as the only people of real religious faith. He praised their devotion and courage, and lamented the destruction of the glorious Catholic parish churches and the loss of 'the beauty of Catholic worship and the traditions of Catholic piety.'[16] In contrast, most of the English people seemed to him to have lacked faith, and to have drifted into aimless pursuit of pleasure and material gain.

Canadian legal thought and legal education may seem to be far removed from these themes. What on earth can be the relation of pamphlet literature about the prayer book or a controversy about vestments to Canada and Canadian constitutional scholarship? Perhaps this Elizabethan scholarship was the first of the many minds of W.P.M. Kennedy, but I think not. As we shall see next, much of his writing about Canadian history continued some of its basic approaches, and, as I shall argue later, the interest in 'reality' was part of the path he took to modern legal thought.

The 1920s: Canadian Constitutional History

Shortly after he came to Canada, Kennedy began to write about Canadian constitutional history as well as continuing his writing about the Elizabethan church. In 1918, he published *Documents of the Canadian Constitution*,[17] a collection of documents intended for use by undergraduates, illustrating themes that were developed in a book that followed four years later, *The Constitution of Canada*.[18] It soon became a standard text, and its publication within two years of his major work in Elizabethan scholarship, *Elizabethan Episcopal Administration*, demonstrated his industry and his remarkable range of interests. The introduction of *The Constitution of Canada* declared the basic themes: liberty, continuity, and progress towards nationhood:

Canadian constitutional development begins in the ages of absolutism and grows down the centuries ... though it is a long journey back to the rock of paternalism which French pioneers struck in the pathless wilderness, yet even today in the full flood of liberty it is possible to discern in the mingled waters something of the far-off source ... Changes of direction could not prevent the stream from reaching inevitably the ocean of constitutional life.[19]

The book traced the stream of liberty from the 'stifling paternalism' of New France to Canada's autonomy within the British Empire. After short sections on the Proclamation of 1763 and the *Quebec Act*, Kennedy turned to the story of representative and responsible government in the Canadas. That story began with the *Constitutional Act* of 1791, which divided Upper and Lower Canada, and sought to reproduce in each 'the eighteenth-century British constitution.'[20] Four decades of tension and strife demonstrated that the new constitution was a failure. In Lower Canada, racial antipathy created an unbridgeable gulf between the elected French-Canadian assembly and the appointed British executive. In Upper Canada, 'a privileged social class, a privileged administrative group, and a privileged church had entrenched themselves behind the constitution,'[21] frustrating popular demands. In both colonies, the fundamental cause of failure was structural – the lack of responsible government: '[T]he Crown had no constitutional responsibility to the houses of assembly.'[22] Kennedy's analysis excluded entirely other considerations, such as class or regional conflict. In his eyes, the Upper Canadian reformers 'demanded reform for its own sake, for political ends.'[23]

Yet the solution was not apparent in 1838. Here Kennedy introduced a theme that was at the centre of much of his thinking for the next decade: the limitations of the traditional theory of sovereignty. Thinkers from Hobbes to John Austin had asserted that each state must have a sovereign, exercising omnipotent and unlimited power, and constitutional texts and jurisprudence texts repeated this theory, refining it in minor variations. Indoctrinated with this faith, neither Whigs nor Tories in England could imagine how a governor-general could be both responsible to Britain and a local assembly, or how Robert Baldwin could be loyal to Britain and at the same time devote himself to the cause of responsible government. 'The sovereignty of the crown seemed an insurmountable obstacle to colonial responsible government.'[24] The solution, and the threat to the traditional idea of sovereignty, was the distinction between colonial and imperial affairs, first proposed by Lord Durham in his Report, 'the greatest state paper in colonial history,'[25] and implemented by Lord Elgin in signing the Rebellion Losses Bill. 'The family compact was dissolved in political death, and John

Macdonald was already beginning to see in the future a combination of parties in which race and privilege were to surrender their places to constitutional nationalism.'[26]

The union of the Canadas in 1841 revealed another deep flaw in the Constitution. The combination of the two races in a unitary legislature paralyzed government. Federalism was the answer, and the Quebec Conference 'gave not only constitution to the colonies, but an example and an inspiration to states yet unborn within the Empire.'[27] After telling the story of Confederation, Kennedy continued with Canada's growth within Empire, first in independence in commercial matters, and then, from 1914 to 1922, to a comprehensive and proud autonomy.

The last few chapters turn to a survey of modern Canadian government, beginning with a detailed analysis of federalism, which needs to be considered at length in the light of its importance for the rest of Kennedy's scholarly life. His first major step was an exploration of the structure of Canada's federalism, based on the claim that it was a 'federation in essence,' not a confederation. That is, 'the national and local governments exercise coordinate authority and are severally sovereign within the sphere ... constitutionally granted to them.'[28] He pointed to some provisions of the *British North America Act* (*BNA Act*) that were at odds with this general nature, especially the provisions about the Senate, the federal government's power of disallowance, and its power to appoint the lieutenant-governors of the provinces. And he suggested that these powers were being curtailed and integrated into the dominant model.[29]

He continued by considering the source of this structure, beginning with an account of Confederation. The 'real nature' of the proposal debated in 1864 was 'nothing else than a thinly veiled legislative union.'[30] The need to make the proposal acceptable, though, made the *BNA Act* incomplete and left much to be settled by the courts, especially the Privy Council, which had made the 'federation in essence' during the 1880s and 1890s.[31] Kennedy saw its work as entirely benign, arguing that its approach, to interpret the Act as a British statute, had spared Canada from rending quarrels about the nature of its federalism. True, the status and the powers of the provinces had increased, but these interpretations had 'humanized' the Act and given it the 'elasticity of life' without violating its framework.[32]

Several claims in this analysis went astray. To say that Canada had been saved quarrels about the nature of her federalism ignored much of the politics of the late nineteenth century, when the provinces, led by

Ontario, aggressively sought power from the Dominion. Moreover, to say that the interpretations by the Privy Council had not violated the framework of the *BNA Act* masked a tension (if not a deep gulf) between his account of Confederation and the rise of the provinces.[33] Another difficulty was his understanding of interpretation. In asserting that the Privy Council had interpreted the *BNA Act* 'as a British statute,' Kennedy was referring to the approach it announced in *Bank of Toronto v. Lambe*; it would interpret the *BNA Act* 'by the same methods of construction and exposition which they apply to other statutes.'[34] This declaration expressed the dominant understanding of interpretation in the late nineteenth century: a statute was the expression of the will of the legislature, and its meaning was embedded in its terms. The task of the court was to determine this meaning by reading the terms, without considering evidence about the context and the making of a statute.[35] This understanding was, though, contrary to Kennedy's stress on the incomplete nature of the *BNA Act* and the contribution of the courts, for it denied that the courts made choices and exercised any creative function. And asserting that the courts had made a substantial contribution to Canadian federalism did not explain why they chose the model they did.

Following this analysis of federalism came a conclusion in which Kennedy looked proudly to the Empire: Canada was both loyal to Britain and substantially autonomous. The autonomy was, though, constrained by the appeals to the Privy Council, the need for British legislation to make constitutional amendments, and subordination in the conduct of foreign affairs. Here again he saw that the traditional theory of sovereignty obscured vision, limiting the apparent alternatives to complete independence or permanent inferiority. Realistic observation and modern theory rejected this dilemma: '[W]e must be content with the reality of relative autonomy, which alone provides, for men and for states, the condition of effective liberty and sane relationship.'[36] The Empire, and especially Canada's evolution, was not only a decisive challenge to traditional theory, but an example to a world seeking effective international order after the 'hideous clash of modern sovereignties.'[37] Thus Canada's history, which began 'in a paternal and conservative past, closes with the outlook of democratic and liberal hope.'[38]

His story of Canada's nationhood paralleled the story of the emergence of the English nation state under the Tudors. It was, as well, a story shared by most Canadian historians in the early twentieth century: the progress of Canada from a colony to independent nation, in which the struggle for responsible government was central. The major issue that divided historians was whether Canada's destiny was to remain a member of the Commonwealth, and it was a question about which Kennedy had no doubt. Among these historians, his scholarship was distinctive in its relatively rich analysis of the framework of federalism and its argument about the ways traditional sovereignty had shaped the story and limited the choices of the Empire and Commonwealth.

The 1920s: Commwealth and Federalism – and Sovereignty

During the early 1920s, Kennedy returned often to the ideas in the last few chapters of the text: federalism, Canada's autonomy within the Commonwealth, and the theory of sovereignty. In the aftermath of World War I, he saw the world endangered by nationalism, especially as it was enshrined in the sovereign state, and saw the Commonwealth as an alternative. It was 'the greatest living political witness to the interaction and interdependence of life, to the disappearance of the coercive state in favour of cooperating groups.'[39] Canada, too, offered a promising model for the future, exhibiting to the world responsible government, federalism, and Quebec – a nation within a state. Traditional ideas of sovereignty were at odds with these hopes, but 'all the historian or political thinker can hope to do is to look at things as they actually are,'[40] and if a formula is at odds with reality, 'so much the worse for the formula.'[41] 'Having cast down the Austinian idol, let us grind it to powder.'[42]

After the 1928 Commonwealth Conference, which declared the members to be autonomous and equal, Kennedy announced that 'the wheel of Empire has come full circle,'[43] and the claims of the Canadian revolutionaries had prevailed. The passing of the Statute of Westminster in 1931 was 'an inevitable development inherent in the grant of responsible Government in 1848.'[44] In 1938, on the centennial of Lord Durham's mission to Canada and in one of his last writings, Kennedy's faith reached its apotheosis. Responsible government and liberty were the central principle: at the signing of the Rebellion Losses Bill, 'the Dominion of Canada was in truth born; Dominions yet in the womb of time were endowed with their birthright; the British Commonwealth of Nations was made possible; and the Statute of Westminster – not forgetting its inevitable successors – flows in the clear logic of law answering life.'[45]

Most of these themes were expressed in a speech about the Irish Free State that he gave in Convocation Hall in 1924, where he mingled poetry, passion, and constitutional analysis. A quotation, albeit a long one (but one that eschews the poetry), is not only an illumination of the thought, but a glimpse into why he had a large and widespread reputation as a powerful, passionate speaker, and a stimulating teacher:

It is a magnificent thing that the Irish Free State, which brazenly and shamefully went a-whoring after the faithless leman of sovereign independence should forsake its barren amours and should seek to achieve creative independence in integral unity within a corporation. For this ... is the great paradoxical truth – and it is all the truer because it is a paradox: individual, group, national freedom and independence are only found and realized in the organic sense and experience of community. I believe then in the British Commonwealth because it realistically resolves that will-of-the-wisp of philosophy – unity in diversity – not the one from the many; but the one with and through because of the many. And my belief in the British Commonwealth rises to passionate heights because I see in it the magnificent witness that absolute sovereignty does not exist: that sovereignty not only is not one and indivisible but can be and actually is divided. I contemplate the British Commonwealth with keen delight, because it is the death knell of the Renaissance politiques, of Bodin, and of John Austin – for sovereignty is that pestilential legal fiction which has drenched this poor world in oceans of blood. Within the Commonwealth, then, the Irish Free State will realize her aspiration for independence, and within the Commonwealth she will acquire that relative but nonetheless real sovereignty which is sufficient for her needs and above all true to the facts. Is it not of high import that a land which worshipped so devoutly the Dagon of the nation-state in the temple of XIX century Philistia should become an integral party of our Commonwealth, whose destiny it may be under high heaven is to teach the world the constructive gospel of political realism?[46]

The dissatisfaction with the traditional theory of sovereignty that appeared so often in this early writing was a major current in the political thought of his times. The first challenge came from the great historian F.W. Maitland, in the introduction to his translation of O. Gierke's *Political Theories of the Middle Age.*[47] During the next few decades, the campaign was continued by a group of historians and political theorists commonly called the 'pluralists,' primarily J.N. Figgis, Harold Laski, and G.D.H. Cole. Proceeding from their central objective

– to protect individual liberty from the totalitarian tendencies of the modern state – they argued that each civil association had a personality, and that traditional theories of the state and sovereignty were unrealistic and oppressive.[48] Within the general context of this thought, Kennedy stressed the group life of the provinces and, more important, how realism and facts eroded the traditional theory.[49] This analysis gave Kennedy a sharp insight into Canadian history, a means of accommodating national autonomy and the Commonwealth, a perspective on federalism, and a vision of a sane world. More important, it was, as I have already suggested, part of his path towards challenging the dominant ways of thinking about law.

The 1930s: The New Career

By the end of the 1920s, Kennedy had written 10 books and more than a score of articles, notes, and reviews about Elizabethan history, Canadian constitutional history, and the Commonwealth. He was 50 years old, and if he had continued in the paths he had already taken, his life might now be worth note, but it would not be nearly as interesting as it was. At this point, though, he undertook a new career in legal scholarship and legal education.

Recall that he came to the University of Toronto in 1914, where he was first a member of St Michael's College, teaching English and history. In 1922, he shifted to the Faculty of Arts and Science,[50] teaching history and political science, including a course in 'Federal Constitutions.' In the late 1920s, he moved further towards law, a change recognized by his appointment as 'Professor of Law and Federal Institutions' in 1927. During the next decade, he poured immense energy into the law school, founded a major law journal, and wrote extensively about law – not only about federalism but about other topics such as administrative agencies and the family.

The 1930s: The Legal Thought

The most convenient beginning to this new and wide range of interests and writing is his general approach to law and legal thought. The central work is *Some Aspects of the Theories and Workings of Constitutional Law*,[51] a series of lectures he gave at Lafayette College in 1931, where he declared a manifesto that he would often revisit during the next few years.[52] He embraced a new world of legal thought, characterized by a 'socialization of law,' a 'social point of view,' or 'sociological jurisprudence,'[53] and at the same time rejoiced in the passing of the nineteenth-century world of laissez-faire, autonomous individuals and their rights, and the jurisprudence of Austin, Holland, and Salmond, to which 'no university law school pays any serious attention except for critical purposes.'[54]

He began *Some Aspects of Constitutional Law* by returning to the attack on the traditional ideas of the state, arguing again that it was simply one of the multitude of associations created by society, distinguished only by its particular purpose: the exercise of sovereign authority for the purposes of social order.[55] Founding himself on this understanding, he turned to the relation between the individual and the state, the function of the state, and individual rights. The individual could be understood only as a member of a community: '[H]e is not an *atom*, though an individual, not an *isolated fact*, though a person. His individuality, his personality – which in the final test make him say I – depend for their value to himself and to his necessary and inescapable environment, on the social life into which he is born and in which he lives.'[56] Because the state was made by the will of the citizens, there was no antithesis between individual and state. Instead, it was 'a great social engineer,'[57] created to promote liberty, and to enable the citizen 'to realize the good life' and be, 'in truth, *civis*.'[58] Thinking about rights as the centre of private law must give way to thinking about interests, without diminishing the centrality of the individual and the human personality. The 'individual interests should be secured only insofar as there is a social interest in securing them,' and the interests that deserved recognition must be 'viewed jointly and weighed against each other, to the end that the true social interests may be secured.'[59] The standard for designing and assessing laws was essentially functional: had they achieved their social ends?

Law-making in this new world would be difficult, far more difficult than it had been 'in a day of laissez-faire individualism.'[60] 'We must learn to create social machinery for making law if law is to serve social ends.'[61] Law makers would require a 'comprehensive survey of social values,'[62] and a 'carefully sifted examination of social facts,'[63] which must be drawn from social sciences. Lawyers must respond by learning new skills, and legal education must he transformed 'to save us from the black-letter lawyer … at a time when … we are still so ill-fitted to mold law to social ends.'[64] Law must be taught, not in isolation, but together with the other social sciences. Fearing that progress towards these ideals in Canada was being frustrated by precedent and conservative legal traditions, he hoped that the younger lawyers would become a 'vast social advance-guard of legal reform.'[65]

In 1937, five years after giving the Lafayette lectures, he wrote about a project he undertook with graduate students at the law school to apply these ideas in a study of family law, particularly adoption legislation.[66] The very topic itself demonstrates his wide range of interests and his acute perception of emerging topics and issues. He and the students prepared 'a scheme of social values'[67] for analysing the making of the legislation, its terms, and its effects – including, for example, the interest of the child in a good home, and the interest of the state in conserving resources. Their effort seems to have been entirely speculative, and apart from a reference to some testimony from social workers, there was no use of social science research. The experience was a chastening one, especially because of unforeseen perspectives and implications. Kennedy realized how difftcult and complex the work he had called for would be, and the dangers of a 'theoretical scheme' that did not fit facts.[68] 'We are singularly far from having developed a technique suitable for law-making in an age of newer values.'[69] His enthusiasm was, though, undiminished, and again he looked for reforms in legal education.

Understanding this thinking and its context can best begin by realizing that it was Kennedy's small contribution to a major watershed in legal thought: a rejection of nineteenth-century thought, an embrace of modernity, and a new understanding of the state. This watershed can, in turn, best be understood by turning our attention for a moment to the United States. There, from the beginning of the twentieth century onwards, scholars slew a dragon they called 'formalism' and proclaimed a new world under such banners as 'sociological jurisprudence' and 'realism.' For these scholars, 'formalism' was the legal thought of the late nineteenth century. At its centre, they saw a faith in the common law as central to the legal world, composed of changeless general principles, existing independently of values and politics, and classified by scholars and judges according to the needs of internal symmetry and elegance. Once properly arrayed, these principles could be applied to particular cases by judges in an objective, apolitical fashion. Choices about values were made by individuals and legislatures, not courts. This picture of the dragon was a caricature, but such is the fate of bodies of thought that are about to be slain.

The American scholars proclaimed a new vision with urgency and excitement. They argued that the common law was not and could not be autonomous and apolitical, because making and using its general principles required judges to make choices, both about the general doctrine and about the outcome of particular cases. All these choices should be made, not according to the dragon's standards of elegance and symmetry, but according to social need, and making them depended upon training in the modern social sciences. Moreover, statutes and administrative agencies must be given larger roles. In England, the only thinking that paralleled this transformation was in public law scholarship, in the borderland between law and political science.[70]

Kennedy's beliefs about the state as social engineer, the contrast between social interests and individual rights, the rejection of the legal thought of the nineteenth century, the call for functional standards, and the need for knowledge of the social context all seem greatly shaped by American legal thought in the 1920s, especially the writings of Roscoe Pound, whom he often explicitly acknowledged, although he often referred to Continental writers as well.[71] Yet threads in his earlier scholarship also became part of his legal thought. Recall that in his later work as a Tudor historian he promised a 'sociological and political perspective,' and 'palpitating reality.' Phrases of this kind were common in his writing during the mid 1920s, when the law school was far in his future and when he was writing about history and Empire.[72] Recall also that his challenge to the traditional theory of sovereignty was a rejection of the nineteenth century and an argument for realism, ideas that were central to modern legal thought. Thus Kennedy's Lafayette lectures were not a sharp break with his past, and if the question whether he had one mind or many is any more than an evocative title, the answer seems to be 'one, with many branches and changes.' Much more important, this analysis of one scholar's odyssey suggests that the emergence of modern legal thought had strong connections to trends in other disciplines.

Accompanying and overlapping this legal thought was his political faith: a rejection of nineteenth-century liberalism and an embrace of the new world of economic regulation and social welfare. In particular, his perception of the individual as fundamental and yet needing social structures to flourish, his belief that individual rights must give way to the needs of the community, and his respect for democratic change all suggest the 'new liberalism' of early-twentieth-century Britain, although he never extensively explored the political and economic structures of his vision. From this perspective, his legal thought can best be perceived as the enterprise of making a legal structure for the new world – one that had begun to emerge in Canada.

The Canadian Realists

Canadian legal scholars and students sometimes ask, Did Canada have a 'realist' movement similar to the upheaval in the United States? Those who ask this question usually believe the answer is 'no' without having read any of the writing from the 1930s. They assume, I suppose, that Canadians could never have done anything so bold. Yet the answer is surely 'yes.' During the 1930s, Percy Corbett, Alex Corry, Jacob Finkelman, Bora Laskin, Vincent MacDonald, Frank Scott, Herbert Smith, John Willis, and Cecil Augustus 'Caesar' Wright, as well as Kennedy, all proclaimed their own revolution. Among them, Kennedy was not only one of the first to make a major and comprehensive manifesto, but the most prolific and wide-ranging.[73]

Some of the Canadian scholars were greatly influenced by the thinking in the United States. Corry and Wright, for example, were shaped by their graduate work, Wright at Harvard under Pound, and Corry at Columbia. Yet others were not influenced by this source, or at least not influenced to the same extent as these two. Willis, although he was greatly impressed by Frankfurter during two years he spent at Harvard, was determined to oppose orthodoxy from his early days in England. For Scott, who seemed to have little interest in American scholarship during his formative years, his experiences as a graduate student in England seem central. MacDonald did not do graduate work and seemed to have read little of the realists. Laskin, like Wright, was influenced by studying at Harvard, but he was also shaped by Kennedy while he was an undergraduate at the law school. Finkelman, too, was greatly influenced by Kennedy, both as student and as colleague.[74]

The 1930s: Legal Education

The tangled history of law at the University of Toronto goes back to the mid-nineteenth century, but to understand Kennedy's role, we can begin in the mid-1920s, with an account of two of the degrees. One was the undergraduate honours BA program in political science, which permitted some specialization in law in its upper years; and the other was the LLB program, which began with a couple of years of preliminary work, for example, in the Arts faculty, and concluded with a thorough set of legal subjects. Both were taught by a small law department, composed of a few professors, supplemented by cross appointments.[75] Neither gave any professional qualification, because the sole route to becoming a lawyer was the school operated at Osgoode Hall by the Law Society of Upper Canada, the governing body of the profession. There, the program consisted of large doses of articling, together with lectures from practitioners and a few full-time teachers.[76]

In 1926, in the same year Kennedy was appointed professor, the scope for specialization in law in the BA was expanded, but still limited to the upper years. Late in 1927 he made a proposal for a separate honours BA in law, which was quickly approved.[77] During the 1930s, this BA was the principal degree, with the LLB in the background. Kennedy dominated the school, setting its general objectives, designing the curriculum, hiring the staff, admitting the students, and deciding their fates,[78] determined throughout to establish high standards for the staff, the students, and himself.[79] The faculty, including J. Forrester Davison, Finkelman, Hancock, and Laskin, were among the new generation and shared his faith.

His objectives were best stated in these two passages, one written in 1934 and the other in 1937:

[W]e have no professional ends to serve. We are concerned with legal *education* – to examine the law in relation to society, to probe into its social functionings, to create a body of citizens endowed with an insight into law as the basic social science, and capable of making those examinations into its workings as will redeem it from being a mere trade and technique and to make it the finest of all instruments in the service of mankind.[80]

The great general principle behind our work is the conviction that law is one of the greatest of university subjects ... the fundamental social science on which every aspect of our civilization must inevitably rest ... It must be taught amid the intellectual clash of university activities as well as in relation to the other social sciences.[81]

Passing by, for a moment, his belief that legal education must be part of a university, it is the word 'social' that demands attention. It appears over and over again in his other accounts of his school. The student in the professional law school, studying 'the traditional concepts of the lawyer ... knew nothing of the *social* meaning of it all, of its validity as *social* doctrine.' At Toronto, 'we relate law to life, not life to law.' Law must be designed, assessed, and taught, not in the abstract, but in the context of the complex relations and processes of modern society. Accompanying this emphasis was the rejection of the dragon called 'formalism.' In teaching constitutional law, 'I eliminate all the archaeology of Anson and Dicey.' In teaching jurisprudence, '[w]e spend no time over the historical or analytical jurisprudence. Austin, Salmon and such-like make way for the sociological jurisprudence as expounded by modern French, German, and American jurists.'[82]

His central vision was that law, especially the modern conception, would be taught in the university as a liberal education, with no immediate professional utility.[83] In published writing, Kennedy said little about the sources of this program. He paid vague tribute several times to inspiration from Lord Aitken and Lord Haldane,[84] and occasionally referred to American writing about legal education, but only to short, highly general passages, most of them written after the program was established.[85] In unpublished university records, though, he was much more forthcoming, and in large measure, the story is hardly startling: the source was British models, particularly the venerable programs at Oxford, Cambridge, and Dublin.[86] The combination of these models and his modern legal thought does, though, verge on irony, since these schools were bastions of nineteenth-century legal thought during the 1920s and 1930s.[87]

His curriculum was composed of law courses and arts courses, some of each kind in each of the four years. Among the law courses were legal history, jurisprudence, comparative law, international law, constitutional law, contracts, torts, property, criminal law, administrative law, industrial law, and municipal law. Some of these courses were remarkably modern, especially administrative law, of which he was especially proud, and labour law. Both were taught by Finkelman, but it was Kennedy who decided they should be in the curriculum and who would teach them.[88] The Arts courses were Roman history, philosophy, economics, and political science, but the social sciences that the modern legal thought called for, such as sociology, statistics, and psychology, were not included. To provide them at the University of Toronto in the 1920s and 1930s would have been a daunting undertaking at best, but the ultimate reason for this omission was probably a lack of a deep grasp of the implications of the legal thought he had embraced, and the hold of the British models. The liberal education and the legal thought were combined, but not integrated.

Kennedy encouraged research and writing, by both colleagues and students, seeing it as crucial not only to good scholarship, but to modern law reform. For the same reason, he expanded and promoted the graduate program.[89] In 1930, he began the Legal Studies Series, apparently intended to be a series of publications by the faculty and the Canadian Industrial Law Research Council, designed to provide 'objective, scientific, expert' advice about legislation for Canada's modern industrial state.[90] Neither seems to have amounted to much, but the experience in the United States in putting the modern legal thought to work was hardly more productive. Little is known about the teaching, and among the faculty, only Kennedy left a substantial record of his beliefs and practices. He prided himself on eschewing lectures, and teaching through discussion and cases. Asked by a student for an outline of Federal Law and Institutions, he said, 'I do not in the least work along lecture lines. The entire subject is worked by cases.'[91] Preparing notes of specified cases was a large part of each student's work in the course.[92]

Another innovation in the law school was the creation of the *University of Toronto Law Journal*, which Kennedy founded in 1935. Other law journals in Canada were dedicated to the needs of practising lawyers, tending to treat law as autonomous doctrine. Instead, Kennedy sought to 'encourage legal scholarship' and to 'foster comparative knowledge of the laws of the British Empire ... as expressions of organized community life, of ordered progress, and of social justice.'[93] As the *U.T.L.J.*'s first editor, he gathered articles from Willis, Wright, Corbett, Corry, and Finkelman for the initial volume, making it a remarkable display of the new approaches, one that was at least as sustained and ambitious as any North American journal.[94]

All this enthusiasm and innovation waned at the end of the 1930s; and during the next decade, the school lost its vitality and drifted. Major faculty members, especially Laskin and Hancock, left and were not replaced by scholars of the same stature. The vision of a liberal education faded as the objectives of the school became more and more oriented towards preparation for practice, a shift marked by the emergence of the LLB as the principal degree. Throughout, having approached and passed the age of retirement, Kennedy receded into the background, and was conspicuously absent from the discussions that swirled around the fate of the program at Osgoode Hall and the reorganization of legal education. In 1949, he was replaced as dean by 'Caesar' Wright.

The belief in a liberal education in law for undergraduates, independent of any professional qualifications, was at odds with the dominant

North American belief that a legal education could be both a liberal education that belonged in a university and at the same time a preparation for practice of the professional law schools. This was the belief that was quickly and firmly established at Toronto by Wright, erasing any memory of Kennedy. It remained dominant and virtually unquestioned for decades, accommodating all points in the political and jurisprudential spectrums. Yet during the past decade, the faith seems strained, and some scholars claim, like Kennedy, to have no professional ends.[95] He would have been pleased when the Curriculum Committee of his law school declared in 1998, at the outset of its effort to rethink the curriculum, that the central aspiration should be a 'rigorous liberal education in law.'[96]

The 1930s: The Administrative State

Kennedy wrote only one article and some short notes and reviews about the administrative state and administrative law, but his very interest in the field, let alone the content of what he wrote, illustrates the wide range of his interests. His thinking can best be understood against the background of the dominant understandings from the late nineteenth century onwards, which were articulated best by A.V. Dicey, the great English constitutional scholar. Individual liberty was the central value of the Constitution, and it was protected by the courts and the common law, which were the heart of the rule of law. The emerging administrative state was a threat to this liberty – and a threat to the preeminence of the common law and the courts. In the early years of the twentieth century, Dicey persuaded himself that liberty and the rule of law had been preserved by judicial review, but during the 1920s, as the state continued to expand, champions of the faith, such as Lord Hewart and C.K. Allen, proclaimed the passing of liberty, and the triumph of the 'New Despotism.'[97] Political beliefs and interests were aligned with constitutional faiths, for the rule of law protected property from regulation and redistribution, and protected the power and prestige of the lawyers and the courts. Critics such as William Robson, Ivor Jennings, Laski, and Willis challenged the rule of law during the late 1928s, but had virtually no impact on the dominant thought.[98]

In several book reviews written in the late 1920s and early 1930s, Kennedy seemed to share much of this orthodox perspective, proclaiming that the courts were crucial to the preservation of liberty and fearing that the rule of law was dead, Parliament had surrendered its

responsibility as a representative institution, and England was smoth-
ered under a bureaucratic administration. This early writing did, though,
include some distinctive thoughts, albeit expressed obliquely and in no
more than a few phrases. He understood that much of the administrative state was a response to the accumulation of private economic
power, and that both democratic preferences and the demands of justice had established it firmly in the constitutional order – if not in
lawyers' minds. He praised inquiry into the workings of the agencies –
the 'reality' of the administrative state.[99]

In a lengthy article published in 1934, he presented a fundamentally
different attitude, enthusiastically embracing the administrative state.[100]
His other writing suggests that he was pushed in this direction by the
evidence given to the Donoughmore Commission, the writing of the
critics, especially Jennings and Willis, and the impact of the Depression.[101] He began by describing the rise of the new state, and by pointing to the political and social faiths underlying the traditional approach:
'[W]e have the protests of Lord Hewart ... against this attempt to mete
out justice under auspices other than those which have been established
during the past few centuries.'[102] In this vision of justice

> [n]ew standards must be developed in all fields of human endeavour which
> will be in harmony with the new social philosophy of the age. Care of the
> sick, the poor, the aged and the infirm, elimination of slums, control of
> industry in the interests of humanity, protection of children, universal edu-
> cation, development of natural resources for the benefit of mankind all de-
> mand immediate attention. The views of social scientists as to the functions
> of the state have been revolutionized, but the legal technique and machin-
> ery necessary to cope with these new demands have been unable to keep
> pace with these theories.[103]

Faced by these developments, the role for academics was much different from what it had been for Kennedy's predecessors in the late nineteenth and early twentieth centuries. '[T]he teacher of the law or the
jurist is no longer merely a contemplative creature describing the law as
it exists. The very development of the administrative system has forced
him to be constructive, not only in interpreting the tendencies of social
existence, but also in assisting in molding and guiding them.'[104]

The new state demanded delegation of extensive discretionary powers to administrative authorities. For Dicey and his followers, discretion

was a fundamental threat to the rule of law, but for Kennedy, it was a useful tool for good government. In considering the contexts in which it should be permitted, he approved even contexts where the legislature had done no more than declare a general policy, leaving its implementation to the administration. His conclusion anticipated much modern thinking:

> The delegation of powers of this nature is never dangerous in itself, and is probably always justified by the circumstances. The danger, if any, lies in the manner in which these powers are administered .... the only safeguard against undue delegation ... lies in the intelligent realization of the new philosophy of government and the principles of social jurisprudence.'[105]

But how were these powers to be controlled? Making the traditional distinction between legislative and judicial powers, he argued that for legislative powers, the crucial challenge was to reconcile the tension between bureaucracy and democracy, and particularly to ensure control of the administration by the people through their representative institutions. Here, he was enthusiastic about the promise of review of regulations by the legislature and advisory committees, 'the most progressive advance so far.'[106] For judicial powers, the question was the efficacy of judicial review, although his understanding of the doctrine was straightforward, if not simplistic, demonstrating no general hostility to courts or lack of faith. He suggested a specialized branch of the court, but claimed, in a remarkable passage, which again anticipated modern thinking, that review could not be successful without standards, and he proposed that administrators should be induced both to develop these standards and to give reasons: 'It is only by such means that the administrator will be compelled to take thought and to offer reasoned decisions containing the principles upon which he acts.'[107]

In short, Kennedy had joined the critics of orthodoxy. Among Canadian lawyers, Willis was the only other one who wrote about the administrative state in such a substantial way. In one book and a couple of articles, Willis brilliantly attacked the courts and the common law, displaying immense faith in the state and its experts. Kennedy lacked Willis' critical power and imagination, but his ideas were a better anticipation of the developments in doctrine and thinking after World War II, when Canadian administrative law emerged as a substantial discipline.

The 1930s: Federalism

Recall that in the early 1920s the Privy Council's interpretations seemed to Kennedy to be benign – and the product of having interpreted the *BNA Act* by the general rules that governed the interpretation of any British statute. He did not return to federalism in any major way until 1929, when his mood was much different than it had been before.[108] His understanding of Confederation remained much the same, although now he emphasized the intention to make a strong federal government much more than he had earlier: '[t]he great central principle of Canadian federalism'[109] that the provinces would be subordinate to a strong Dominion government. This design was 'clearly grasped and carefully expounded'[110] by Macdonald, described by Lord Carnarvon in words that 'could scarcely be clearer,'[111] and accurately expressed in the *BNA Act*. Nonetheless, 'the most cherished aims of the founders have been nullified'[112] and the result was 'diametrically opposed'[113] to their intentions. The Dominion's power to legislate for the general good of Canada was reduced to an emergency power, and the provinces held the residue of power. There was 'a grave danger that the centrifugal forces, already numerous enough in Canadian national life, may be accentuated by this interpretation.'[114] The Privy Council was the villain. It had interpreted the *BNA Act* 'in the strictest terms as a statute,' and 'applied to it arbitrary rules of construction which ... have ... robbed it of its historical context and divorced its meaning from the intentions of those who in truth framed it.'[115]

The cause of this shift was a controversial series of decisions by the Privy Council during the 1920s,[116] which seemed to all scholars to have greatly diminished the powers of the federal government. The results of these cases may have been sensible, but the reasoning in the judgments, all written by Lord Haldane, seemed startling to contemporaries, and still seems to have little foundation after 70 years of scholarship. Whether this reasoning was a continuation of beginnings established by Lord Waston in the late nineteenth century or whether it was a substantially new departure has been debated since the 1930s, but the debate is of little significance for this story, because the texts and journals from 1900 demonstrate clearly that the protests began only in the late 1920s.

The first outcry was a remarkable case comment written in 1926 by Herbert Smith of the McGill Law School, a few pages that presaged mainstream constitutional scholarship from the 1930s to the 1950s.[117] Smith asserted that the Privy Council's misreading was caused by its failure to consider the discussions that preceded the making of the *BNA Act*, especially the debates in 1864. His purpose was not so much to give a warning to Canada as it was to challenge the general rule that prohibited considering context in interpreting statutes, using this blunder as an example of its typical effects. This rule was not often at stake in particular cases, simply because the making of most statutes, unlike a constitution, did not involve extensive, recorded discussions. It was, though, a lightning rod for challenge, perhaps because it was an expression of the centrality and power of the courts and the common law. Kennedy shared Smith's condemnation of the wreckage of the division of powers, but he did not grasp the full import of the argument about interpretation, and never considered it at any length.[118]

He did, though, see some benefit in what had happened, making an observation in 1930 that would be repeated by scholars decades later:

> I often wonder, however, with the inevitable divergencies in our national life due to race relations, geography and such like, whether the way of the Privy Council up to 1929 has not been the better way ... I am convinced that Macdonald's scheme ... would have broken down in an attempt to govern and direct from a centre a vast territory to which nature had not lent anything like a geographic unity.[119]

Here Kennedy spoke of 'delicate balancings,' again introducing an idea that became familiar much later, especially in the writing of William Lederman of Queen's University.[120] A few years later, though, he was apprehensive – 'I fear any further strengthening of provincial rights'[121] – and he wondered whether the balance had already been tipped too far. Fragmentation of authority threatened legislation about national resources, labour, old age pensions, interprovincial marketing, corporate regulation, and education, even though all were clearly of urgent national importance and all the more pressing as the ravages of the Depression continued.[122] One particular danger was the power of business interests. Regulation of conditions of labour such as hours of work and wages, for example, was threatened, because 'the interests at the local centres are often too strong to allow progress, and they are all too frequently able to strengthen their economic and financial purposes by an appeal to provincial rights.'[123] The Privy Council had not only misread the *BNA Act*, but it had frustrated the modern state. Kennedy did not, though, ever suggest that he had lost faith in federalism as a form of government, as did Laskin in the 1930s.

322 The Challenge of Modernity

In 1934, his gloom mounted as the Depression deepened:

The truth is that we have outgrown the *British North America Act*. The Dominion of Canada is attempting today to carry on the highly complex life of a modern industrial state under a constitution drawn up for a primitive community, scarcely emerging from pioneer agricultural conditions ... Worse still, under cover of all this has been preserved the legal, political and economic philosophy of laissez-faire utilitarianism.[124]

We have now a clear choice to make: shall we continue as a loose league of 'sovereign' provinces, into which the unfortunate judgments of the Privy Council had practically transformed us, surviving legally in order to break culturally and economically: or shall we boldly recognise that a nation of vast potential wealth and remarkable human achievements must not be sacrificed at a constitutional alter erected in a far-off pioneer past, and itself long since robbed of creative vitality by the barren processes of judicial obscurantism.[125]

In 1934 and 1935, the Conservative government enacted a cluster of statutes in response to the Depression, most of them collectively known as the New Deal. After the Privy Council declared most of them *ultra vires* in 1937, Kennedy's outrage reached its climax:

The federal 'general power' is gone with the winds. It can be relied on at the best when the nation is intoxicated with alcohol, at worst when the nation is intoxicated with war; but in times of sober poverty, sober financial chaos, sober unemployment, sober exploitation, it cannot be used, for these, though in fact national in the totality of their incidents, must not be allowed to leave their legal water-tight compartments; the social lines must not obliterate the legal lines of jurisdiction – at least this is the law and it killeth.[126]

Fundamental amendment was needed, and appeals to the Privy Council, according to Kennedy, must be abolished. 'We would have faced this issue long ago had we not too largely believed that constitutional and legal wisdom never really crossed the Atlantic.'[127]

Kennedy was not the only Canadian common law scholar to write about federalism. The other major writers were Smith, the author of the 1926 note, who returned to England in 1928, Frank Scott, also from McGill, and Vincent MacDonald, from Dalhousie. Kennedy, Scott, and

MacDonald all shared pride in Canada's independence and a set of beliefs about government: its functions had expanded to undertake economic regulation and social welfare programs, a strong central government was needed to implement these functions, the *BNA Act* had been designed to give Canada this government, and the Privy Council had grievously betrayed its design.

Scott is now doubtless the best known of the three, as a major Canadian poet, a founder of the Cooperative Commonwealth Federation, and a crusader for civil liberties. His major analysis of federalism during the 1930s appeared in 1931, where he began by announcing his conclusion: Canada's federalism was 'a legal morass in which ten governments are always floundering; a boon to lawyers and obstructionist politicians, but the bane of the poor public, whose pathetic plea is simply for cheap and efficient government.'[128] MacDonald's principal effort came in 1935, in the first volume of Kennedy's law journal, where he surveyed the doctrine at length and concluded that the *BNA Act*, as it had been interpreted, was no longer appropriate for Canada; amendment was needed, and even appeals to the Privy Council might be reconsidered.[129] In 1937, both joined in the outrage at the New Deal cases.[130] Among the three, Kennedy was the most prolific, by far, just as passionate and eloquent as Scott, but much less inclined to analyse the terms of the *BNA Act* and the doctrine. Their beliefs can usefully be called the 'model of the nation,' in contrast to the beliefs of the generation that preceded them, which had constructed a 'model of autonomy,' stressing not the division of powers, but the autonomy of the provinces. In turn, their model would be supplanted after World War II by a 'model of balance,' represented by such scholars as Lederman.

I have already suggested that all three were part of a small band of Canadian legal scholars whose thinking paralleled the American Realists. In the constitutional scholarship, the parallels are remarkable. The American scholars attacked *Lochner*,[131] in which their Supreme Court had struck down legislation setting minimum hours for bakers in the name of freedom of contract, for using misguided modes of legal reasoning and for frustrating progressive legislation. The Canadians attacked the Privy Council on just the same grounds: for its lamentable technique of interpretation and because it frustrated regulatory and social welfare legislation, which could be effected only by a strong federal government.

The 1930s: More Scholarship

Between 1931 and 1937, Kennedy embraced modern legal thought, transformed the law school, and wrote about the modern administrative state and federalism. But this impressive list did not exhaust his efforts. He was co-author of three books, although his contribution to each was probably modest,[132] and he wrote many articles, notes, and reviews about a wide range of subjects. Two examples of this range must suffice. First, for three years he wrote a column about Canada six or eight times a year in the *South African Law Times*,[133] about familiar topics such as Canadian life and politics, federalism and legal education, and about others such as international relations and torts cases. Second, he wrote reviews for each issue of his law journal. In the second issue, for example, he reviewed books about treasure trove, the Crown, South Africa, Ireland, Commonwealth constitutions, criminal procedure, defamation, India's constitutional history, international law, and the constitutions of the United States and Australia. As well as all this published writing, he prepared a report for the government about citizenship, including a proposed statute,[134] and did an extensive comparative study of constitutions for the Rowell Sirois Commission.[135]

Yet, readers may recall, he was not a lawyer,[136] and he had no sustained experience in practice or thinking about law before he became head of the law school, except in his writing and teaching about Canadian federalism. I can only speculate about the implications and consequences of this lack of training and experience. He walked like a duck and talked like a duck. More important, perhaps, he flew with ducks and taught ducks. But ducks come in all sorts of kinds, sizes, and shapes: what kind was he? Even after having read all his writing and much of it more than once, I remain unsure about his knowledge of doctrine and his capacity for legal analysis, such as interpretation of statutes and analysis of cases. He never undertook an extended analysis of doctrine and, in particular, he did not undertake an analysis of the Privy Council jurisprudence. He did not present any coherent account of constitutional interpretation, which was at the heart of the cases and seemed unaware of its complexities and implications. Yet short passages, especially in reviews, suggest knowledge of details of the doctrine of a handful of different subjects and some sense of the ways of thinking of the common law lawyers.[137] I am content to remain unsure and to think that the question is largely irrelevant to his accomplishments.

Conclusion

After the late 1930s, Kennedy wrote little,[138] and after he retired in 1949, he lived quietly until his death in 1963. His scholarship is now virtually unknown, and in his own law school, his distinctive accomplishment has been obscured by Wright's determination to make a different school, one dedicated to training lawyers for practice. Yet Kennedy deserves to be better remembered, for his love of Canada, his scholarship, and his vision for legal education.

NOTES

1 C. Berger, *The Writing of Canadian History: Aspects of English Canadian Historical Writing since 1900*, 2nd ed. (Toronto: University of Toronto Press, 1986) 40–3.

2 Between 1900 and 1902, he was a private tutor, and between 1910 and 1912, he taught school, but the intervening eight years are a blank to me. One small clue is that much later, in 1919, in a note to the president of the University of Toronto, Robert Falconer, he said that his first book, *Archbishop Parker* (London: Isaac Pitman, 1908) was written 'under the direction of Dr W.H. Hutton, St John's College, Oxford' (Kennedy to Falconer, box 59a, accession A67-0007, Office of the President (Falconer) [hereinafter Falconer Papers], University of Toronto Archives). There is, though, no record of him as a student at St John's during this period.

3 The major sources of information about his life are A. Brady, 'William Paul McLure Kennedy' [1964], Proceedings of the Royal Society of Canada 109; newspaper clippings in the University of Toronto Archives; letters about his appointment in the St Francis Xavier University Archives; a transcribed interview with his son Gilbert, in the University of British Columbia Library; and personal conversations with another son, Frere. These sources give several towns as his birthplace, and both 1880 and 1881, as well as 1879, as the year.

4 Here is most of the little more I know. His father was a Presbyterian minister, sent from Scotland to Northern Ireland, and he was raised in the faith of his family. In his early years, sometime between his graduation from Trinity College and coming to St Francis Xavier, he converted to Roman Catholicism, and in the early 1920s, he forsook that faith for the Church of England. In 1915, shortly after coming to Toronto, he

married and had two children, but soon afterwards, in 1919, his wife died in the influenza epidemic. In 1921, he married again and had two more children.

5 Among stories about Kennedy is a reputation for his magnifying his involvement in important political affairs and his friendships with major figures in the political and scholarly worlds. This sort of reputation is hard to prove or disprove, and the task is especially difficult because there are no personal papers. Having considered the claims he made in his writing and gathered as much as I can about the reality, my impression is that, yes, he was inclined to exaggerate, but his reputation is itself also an exaggeration. Whatever the truth may be, though, the question is largely irrelevant to my topic.

6 Supra note 2.

7 *The Interpretations of the Bishops* (London: Longmans, Green, 1908).

8 *Visitation Articles and Injunctions* (London: Longmans, Green, 1910). Throughout his life Kennedy listed this book as one of his publications, naming himself and Frere as co-authors. The book itself named Frere alone as the author, and in its preface, Frere thanked Kennedy for help with the first of the three volumes. I use the word 'collaborated' to comprise all the possibilities.

9 *Parish Life under Elizabeth* (London: Manresa Press, 1914).

10 *Studies in Tudor History* (London: Constable, 1916).

11 *Elizabethan Episcopal Administration* (London: A.R. Mowbray, 1924). The dedication was to Frere, as a tribute to a friendship 'which … has known neither deviation nor shadow caused by turning.' This opaque phrase was presumably a reference to Kennedy's departure from Roman Catholicism a few years before.

12 *Parish Life under Elizabeth*, supra note 9 at 28.

13 *Elizabethan Episcopal Administration*, vol. 1, supra note 11 at 76.

14 Supra note 9. For Pollard, see R. O'Day, *The Debate on the English Reformation* (London: Methuen, 1986) at 202–6; and J. Kenyon, *The History Men* (London: Weidenfeld and Nicholson, 1983). I have been unable to discover the particular connection between Pollard and Kennedy, although presumably it was made during the eight years between 1902 and 1910, about which I know so little.

15 Supra note 11, preface.

16 *Parish Life under Elizabeth*, supra note 9 at 44.

17 *Documents of the Canadian Constitution* (Toronto: Oxford University Press, 1918).

18 *The Constitution of Canada* (London: Oxford University Press, 1922). Harold

Laski gave praise, saying in a review that Kennedy had written 'what is likely long to remain the standard introduction to the study of the Canadian constitution': 'Book Review' (1929) 35 *New Republic* 159 at 159. In his correspondence with Justice Oliver Wendell Holmes Jr he said in 1923 that it was 'quite excellent,' and two years later he demonstrated his penchant for forgetting, saying that among his recent reading, it had given him 'great pleasure': M. DeW. Howe, ed., *Holmes-Laski Letters* (Cambridge, MA: Harvard University Press, 1953) at 476 and 808. In 1938, Kennedy published a second edition of *The Constitution of Canada* (London: Oxford University Press, 1938), which had four additional chapters, taken almost entirely from articles he had published during the 1930s.

19 *Constitution of Canada*, 1st ed. at 1. This introduction and the book it promised put Kennedy firmly in the Whig tradition, which, for my purposes, is effectively described by J.W. Burrow: '[O]ne thing that is definitive in the sense of a Whig interpretation … is confidence: confidence in the possession of the past … The past may be revered; it is not regretted, for there is nothing to regret. Whig history that earns the name is, by definition, a success story: the story of the triumph of constitutional liberty and representative institutions. But if it is celebration, it is not brash or heedless; it is, rather, an invitation to national jubilation, at which the shades of venerated ancestors are honoured guests, or, as Burke puts it, "canonized forefathers"': J.W Burrow, *A Liberal Descent: Victorian Historians and the English Past* (Cambridge: Cambridge University Press, 1981) at 3. More particularly, the Whig themes in the text paralleled the version of the tradition that Pollard established for early twentieth-century Tudor history, which emphasized the nation, the Constitution, and Parliament. For accounts of Pollard, see supra note 14.

20 *Constitution of Canada*, supra note 18 at 85. The British hoped that the French Canadians 'would finally sink race, religion, and traditions, and rush to accept the British constitution out of sheer jealousy, lest Upper Canada should enjoy a monopoly in such a life-giving, wonder-working scheme': Ibid.

21 Ibid. 161.

22 Ibid. 164.

23 Ibid. 161.

24 Ibid. 165.

25 Ibid 168.

26 Ibid. 259; see also 177–80 and 250 for discussions of sovereignty and responsible government. A few years later, Kennedy published a substantial biography of Lord Elgin: *Lord Elgin* (London: Oxford University Press,

1926). For him, Baldwin and Elgin were Burrow's 'canonized forefathers' (see Burrow, supra note 19).

27 *The Constitution of Canada*, supra note 18 at 301.

28 Ibid. 408.

29 Ibid. 407 and 408. Much of this analysis of structure was taken from an article he wrote a year before, 'The Nature of Canadian Federalism' (1911) 2 *Can. Hist. R.* 106. His target was Lord Haldane's ruminations in *A.G. Australia v. Colonial Sugar* [1914] A.C. 237 (P.C.), where he suggested that Canada was not a truly federal state, making the distinction between federation and confederation. In 1924, Kennedy tackled disallowance at length: 'Disallowance of Provincial Acts in the Dominion of Canada' (1924) *J. Comparative Legislation* 84.

30 *The Constitution of Canada*, supra note 18 at 404.

31 The centre of this story were cases such as *Hodge v. The Queen* (1883) 9 A.C. 117 (P.C.), and *Maritime Bank of Canada v. New Brunswick*, [1892] A.C. 437 P.C.). For an account of the details, see R.C.B. Risk, 'The Supreme Court under the Influence' (1990) 40 *U.T.L.J.* 687.

32 *The Constitution of Canada*, supra note 18 at 431. This account of structure was followed by a short chapter on the distribution of legislative power, where he presented sections 91 and 92 as granting general powers: a power to legislate about local matters to the provinces and a power to legislate about national or general matters to the Dominion. This analysis was followed by an account of some approaches and principles for deciding cases, such as the aspect rule. None of this was original, and much of it came from the texts written by A.H.F. Lefroy, who taught constitutional law at the University of Toronto from 1900 until his death in 1919. In 1918, Kennedy wrote the 'Historical Introduction' to Lefroy's last text, *A Short Treatise on Canadian Constitutional Law* (Toronto: Carswell, 1918), in which Kennedy presented an early version of some of the ideas in the text, especially the centrality of responsible government, and paid tribute to him in the preface of *Canadian Constitutional Law*. For an account of Lefroy, see R.C.B. Risk, 'A.H.F. Lefroy,' in this volume.

33 A good example of this tension is his description of the 1880s and 1890s as the 'golden age of provincial rights, where the Privy Council was gradually bringing to light the essentially federal nature of the Canadian constitutlon': *The Constitution of Canada*, supra note 18 at 422. The 'essential nature' that the Privy Council made was fundamentally at odds with Kennedy's 'real nature' of Confederation.

34 (1887), 12 A.C. 575 (P.C.) at 579.

35 For a typical statement of this faith see P.B. Maxwell, *The Interpretation of*

Statutes (London: William Maxwell, 1875) 1. If the terms were not clear, common law principles were the background for illumination, but this possibility was barely relevant to constitutional interpretation.

36 *Constitution of Canada*, supra note 18 at 56.
37 Ibid. 458.
38 Ibid. 56.
39 W.P.M. Kennedy, 'The Conception of the British Commonwealth' [1921] *Edinburgh R.* 227 at 227. This was a review article, which included praise for McIlwain's *American Revolution*. McIlwain argued that the American Revolution was a conflict between two fundamentally irreconcilable theories of sovereignty – one the orthodox faith in the single sovereign, and the other a faith that sovereignty could be divided. Kennedy observed that the rupture caused by this conflict had been avoided in Canada by the grant of responsible government, referring back to his analysis in the constitutional history text. Here, though, he introduced another new idea: that the passing of mercantilism and the coming of laissez-faire international economic policy in Britain contributed to the constitutional change.
40 W.P.M. Kennedy, 'Canada's National Status' [1922] *North American R.* at 305–6.
41 Ibid. 310. John Skirving Ewart immediately challenged this conception of the Empire and sovereignty, relying on the traditional doctrine: J.S. Ewart, 'Canada's National Status: A Reply' [1922] *North American R.* 772. Kennedy replied in 'Canada's National Status: A Last Word' [1923] *North American R.* 202.
42 'The Conception of the British Commonwealth,' supra note 39 at 238.
43 W.P.M. Kennedy, 'Theories of Law and Constitutional Law of the British Empire,' in [1929] Minutes of Proceedings of the Fourteenth Annual Meeting of the Canadian Bar Association,' 152 at 164.
44 W.P.M. Kennedy, 'The Statute of Westminster' [1933] *Juridical R.* 330 at 330; see also W.P.M. Kennedy, 'The Imperial Conferences, 1926–1930: The Statute of Westminster' (1932) 48 *L.Q.R.* 191.
45 W.P.M. Kennedy, 'The Centenary of Lord Durham's Mission to British North America, 1838–1938' (1938) 50 *Juridical R.* 136 at 140. At the end of the 1920s, Kennedy wrote a chapter about Canada in volume 6 of the *Cambridge History of the British Empire* and a handful of more general essays about Canada, including 'The Political Development of Canada' [1927] *Edinburgh R.* 209; and 'Sixty Years of Canadian Progress' (1927) 132 *Contemporary R.* 291, both of which demonstrated his affection for his adopted homeland, a wide range of knowledge, a strong conventional morality, and a faith in British institutions and peoples contrasted to

immigrant 'foreigners,' who would be a threat to Canadian ways unless they were properly educated.

46 Kennedy Papers, Fisher Rare Book Library, University of Toronto. (These papers are a small collection, containing only the final manuscripts of a couple of books, this speech, and a copy of his syllabus for a constitutional course.) He published a more scholarly and less colourful study shortly before this speech: 'Significance of the Irish Free State' [1923] *North American R.* 316.

47 O. Gierke, *Political Theories of the Middle Age* (Cambridge: Cambridge University Press, 1900).

48 For accounts of these papers, see D.N. Nicholls, *The Pluralist State* (Oxford: St Martin's Press, 1975), and P.Q. Hirst, *The Pluralist Theory of the State* (London: Routledge, 1989). Among them, Kennedy seems especially to have been influenced by Laski; see H. Laski, *Studies in the Problem of Sovereignty* (New Haven: Yale University Press, 1917), and *The Foundations of Sovereignty* (London: George Allen and Unwin, 1921).

49 In the preface to *Elizabethan Episcopal Administration*, vol. 1, supra note 11, Kennedy offered one distinctive idea, which has disappeared into the sands of time: the first challenge to the traditional idea of sovereignty was the Oxford movement. 'In their essence the Tracts for the Times were anti-Austinian ... the Tractarians greeted the breaking dawn of the realist conception, which finds in the state neither omnicompetence nor all-embracing and absolute sovereignty. In the final winnowing of history, this may perhaps prove itself to be the most vital contribution made by the Oxford movement.'

50 Presumably this shift was related to his departure from the Roman Catholic faith.

51 *Some Aspects of the Theories and Workings of Constitutional Law* (New York: MacMillan, 1932). He gave four lectures, the first about legal thought, and the remaining three about the Canadian Constitution, culture, and government.

52 See especially a couple of articles about federalism and family law: W.P.M. Kennedy, 'The Workings of the British North America Acts, 1867–1931' (1936) 48 *Juridical R.* 57; and 'Some Aspects of Canadian Family Law' (1937) 49 *Juridical R.* 1. He also talked about these ideas in his writing on legal education, which I will consider later.

53 These three phrases appear in *Some Aspects of Constitutional Law*, supra note 51 at 23, 20, and 22. 'Sociological jurisprudence' is the best known, having been made famous by Roscoe Pound; Kennedy used it frequently, but by no means exclusively. 'Socialization of law' was first used by Laski, whose

writings Kennedy knew well. See, for example, H. Laski's 'Introduction' to L. Duguit, *Law in the Modern State* (New York: B.W. Huebsch, 1919).

54 'Workings of the BNA Acts,' supra note 52 at 57.

55 He added an analysis about obligation derived from French writers, especially Hariou: The citizens' will to accept this essential purpose of the state founded their obligations to obey its day-to day policies. As well, because the state was made by the will of the citizens, 'it is not some mystical sovereignty that coerces ... [I]t is no longer necessary to ask where ultimately sovereignty lies': *Some Aspects of Constitutional Law,* supra note 51 at 9.

56 'Workings of the BNA Acts,' supra note 52 at 58.

57 *Some Aspects of Constitutional Law,* supra note 51 at 15.

58 'Workings of the BNA Acts,' supra note 52 at 58 and 59.

59 'Some Aspects of Family Law,' supra note 52 at 18.

60 Ibid. 18.

61 *Some Aspects of Constitutional Law,* supra note 51 at 27.

62 Ibid. 24.

63 Ibid. 28.

64 'Some Aspects of Family Law,' supra note 52 at 18.

65 *Some Aspects of Constitutional Law,* supra note 51 at 23.

66 'Some Aspects of Family Law,' supra note 52.

67 Ibid. 17.

68 Ibid. 14.

69 Ibid. 18. See also 'Testators' Dependents Relief Legislation' (1935) 20 *Iowa L.J.* 317.

70 The American thought has been extensively explored. Among recent books, see, for example, N. Duxbury, *Patterns of American Jurisprudence* (Oxford: Clarendon Press, 1995); M.J. Horwitz, *The Transformation of American Law 1870–1960: The Crisis of Legal Orthodoxy* (New York: Oxford, 1992); L. Kalman, *Legal Realism at Yale* (Chapel Hill: University of North Carolina Press, 1986); and J.H. Schlegel, *American Legal Realism and Empirical Social Science* (Chapel Hill: University of North Carolina Press, 1995). The English thought has not been considered nearly as extensively, but a good, recent survey is M. Loughlin, *Public Law and Political Theory* (Oxford: Clarendon Press, 1992).

71 See, for example, the references in the first chapter of *Some Aspects of Constutional Law,* supra note 51. When he said that law-making would require a 'comprehensive survey of social values' (see the text accompanying note 62), he referred to French writers, and not to Pound, as North American readers might have expected.

72 In a review of McIlwain's *American Revolution*, Kennedy made a call 'to facts, to realism, to pragmatism at a time when vague phrases are beginning to do duty for serious political thinking': (1924) 5 *Can. Hist. R.* 168 at 170. In the speech about the Irish Free State given in the same year (supra note 46), he pleaded over and over for realism in understanding its constitution.

73 Wright also published a manifesto in 1932: C.A. Wright, 'An Extra-Legal Approach to Law' (1932) 10 *Can. Bar R.* 1. Kennedy's Lafayette lecture, written at about the same time, was more comprehensive and more deeply grounded. Note, though, that the new thinking was present in the law schools a few years earlier than any of this writing; see, for example, a letter from Donald MacRae, dean at Dalhousie Law School, to John Falconbridge, dean at Osgoode, 2 July 1924. The context of this letter was a request by the president of the University of Toronto, Robert Falconer, to Falconbridge for suggestions for a new appointment in law. Falconbridge in turn asked MacRae and forwarded the reply to Falconer on 15 July 1924. MacRae recommended one young scholar who had done graduate work at Harvard, because 'he has had experience with sociological jurisprudence,' concluding with praise for Harvard and criticism of Oxford. (box 98, Falconer Papers, supra note 2).

74 For Wright, see C.I. Kyer and J. Bickenbach, *The Fiercest Debate: Cecil A. Wright, the Benchers, and Legal Education in Ontario, 1923–1957* (Toronto: Osgoode Society for Canadian Legal History and University of Toronto Press, 1987). For Corry, see J.A. Corry, *My Life and Work: A Happy Partnership* (Montreal and Kingston: McGill-Queen's University Press, 1981). For Willis, see R.C.B. Risk, 'John Willis: A Tribune,' in this volume. For Scott, see S. Djwa, *The Politics of the Imagination: A Life of F.R. Scott* (Toronto: McClelland and Stewart, 1987); S. Djwa and R. St J. Macdonald, eds., *On F.R. Scott: Essays on His Contributions to Law, Literature, and Politics* (Montreal and Kingston: McGill-Queen's University Press, 1989); and M. Horn, 'Frank Scott, the League for Social Reconstruction, and the Constitution,' in J. Ajzenstat, ed., *Canadian Constitutionalism: 1791–1991* (Ottawa: Canadian Study of Parliament Group, 1992) 231. For MacDonald, see J. Willis, *A History of Dalhousie Law School* (Toronto: University of Toronto Press, 1979) 100, 104–5, and 121–4. For Laskin, see Laskin's recollections in an oral interview (3, accession B76-001, University of Toronto Archives); D. Reaume, 'The Judicial Philosophy of Bora Laskin' (1985) 35 *U.T.L.J.* 348; and R.C.B. Risk, 'Law Teachers' and 'On the Road to Oz,' both in this volume.

75 This account, which is based on the calendars, is greatly over-simplified,

and throughout I have used the name 'the law school' for convenience, even though there were several different names and institutional structures. There is no comprehensive study of law at the University of Toronto.

76 See B.D. Bucknall, T.C.H. Baldwin, and J.D. Laskin, 'Pedants, Practitioners and Prophets: Legal Education at Osgoode Hall to 1957' (1968) *Osgoode Hall L.J.* 137; and Kyer and Bickenbach, supra note 74 at c. 2 and 4.

77 See the correspondence of Kennedy to John Brebner (the Registrar) 27 December 1928, box 1, accession A82-0041, Law School Papers [hereinafter Law School Papers], University of Toronto Archives; and of Kennedy to Falconer, 21 December 1928, box 115, the Falconer Papers, supra note 2.

78 Kennedy's comprehensive control can be seen throughout the law school papers. He retreated to the north every summer, continuing to govern the school by correspondence; see, for example, his correspondence in the law school papers with Finkelman during the summers, especially in the second half of the 1930s. For his own account of his control over admissions, see 'A Project of Legal Education, II: The Student and his School Preparation' [1937] 1 *Scots L.T.* 17, although his extended summers in the north suggest that he was not always as thorough as he implied there. For particular examples of his control over admissions and petitions, see a set of letters about graduate students written in 1932 to the secretary of the School of Graduate Studies: 'I do not intend to allow any of our candidates to present themselves for the final examination for D. Phil this year' ... 'It will be impossible for me to accept him' ... 'I cannot accept him for graduate work in law' ... 'So I suspended the rule for this year': 20 March 1932, 9 November 1932, and 25 January 1932, box 2, Law School Papers, supra note 77. For examples of his control over hiring see his correspondence about J. Forrester Davison (ibid., 1927 and 1928, box 1); F.A. Vallat (ibid., 1932 to 1934, box 2); Moffat Hancock (ibid., Kennedy to Hancock, 14 December 1936; Finkelman to Kennedy, 7 July 1937; and Kennedy to Finkelman, 9 July 1937, box 3); E.R. Hopkins (ibid., box 3, 1935 and 1936); and Bora Laskin (ibid., Auld to Kennedy, 29 July 1936, and Kennedy to Finkelman, 9 August 1936, box 3). He was remarkably gracious when his attempts at hiring were frustrated or when faculty members left, even in a few cases when coldness or even anger might have been understandable. Much later, Laskin recalled the faculty in daily procession across the campus to lunch, with Kennedy always in the lead (oral interview, supra note 74, 8 May 1975, at 55).

79 Replying to a student at Princeton who hoped for a teaching job, Kennedy said, 'There will be no openings in the Department for many years to

come, as I intend to keep the standards so high that the total number of
students will never be high': supra note 77, to M. Ayearst, 13 December
1927, box 1, Law School Papers.

80 W.P.M. Kennedy, 'Law as a Social Science' (1994) 3 *South African L.J.* 100 at
100.

81 W.P.M. Kennedy, 'A Project of Legal Education' [1937] *Scots L.T.* 1 at 1. See
also W.P.M. Kennedy, 'Legal Subjects in the Universities of Canada' (1933)
10 *J. Soc'y Public Teachers of Law* 29; W.P.M. Kennedy, 'A Project of Legal
Education, II,' supra note 78; W.P.M. Kennedy, 'A Project of Legal Education, III: Undergraduates and Graduates' [1937] *Scots L.T.* 21; and W.P.M.
Kennedy, 'Some Experiments in the Teaching of Law' (1941) 7 *Cambridge
L.J.* 399.

82 'Law as a Social Science,' supra note 80, at 101.

83 Kennedy did, though, often stress the utility of this education for law-
making and public service in contrast to practice.

84 Kennedy referred several times to a speech given by Lord Atkin in 1933
('Law as an Educational Subject' [1934] *J. Soc'y Public Teachers of Law* 23),
but it was given long after his program was designed. He also referred to
discussions with 'my lifelong friend' Lord Haldane ('Law as a Social
Science,' supra note 80 at 100) and to his help 'in the actual drafting of the
courses': 'Legal Subjects in the Universities of Canada,' supra note 81 at 26.

85 In the United States, programs at Columbia, Yale, and Johns Hopkins had
some similar elements, but none had at its heart an undergraduate liberal
education in law. For a survey of American legal education, including
these decades, see R. Stevens, *Law School: Legal Education in America from
the 1850s to the 1980s* (Chapel Hill: University of North Carolina Press,
1983). See also Schlegel, and Kalman, both supra note 70.

86 The first evidence is a statement made to the president and the Board of
Governors in February 1928 signed by all the faculty but almost certainly
written by Kennedy. It speaks of their hope to develop 'an honours course
in law similar (mutatis mutandis) to that in the Faculty of Arts at Oxford,
Cambridge, Dublin (and, in a lesser degree, recently at London)' (supra
note 2, box 121 Falconer Papers). During the next few years, Kennedy
referred often to these models in his law school correspondence (see, for
example, Kennedy to R. Brossard, 9 February 1929, and Kennedy to A.
Kellar, 9 February 1929, box 1, Law School Papers, supra note 77). Much
later, in an undated memorandum written in the mid 1940s for President
Sydney Smith, he spoke again of these models. More particularly, he
spoke of meeting Lords Haldane and Atkin in 1925, and making plans
with them for education in law as 'a social science' and the combination of

legal subjects and the liberal arts: box 025(02), A68-0007, Papers of the President (Smith), University of Toronto Archives. I have no other authority for this meeting, but both Lords Haldane and Atkin declared their support of teaching law in the university. See, for example, Atkin, supra note 84, and Haldane's Commission on the University of London (Royal Commission on University Education in London, 145–9).

87 For a survey of legal education in England in the 1920s and 1930s, see B. Abel-Smith and R. Stevens, *Lawyers and the Courts: A Sociological Study of the English Legal System, 1750–1965* (London: Heinemann, 1967) at 165–85.

88 Kennedy's role was confirmed in a conversation with Professor Finkelman.

89 W.P.M. Kennedy, 'Graduate Studies in Law' [1935] *Scots L.T.* 113.

90 'Extra-Academic Activities in Legal Education' [1938] *Scots L.T.* 77 at 78. Three monographs appeared in 'Legal Studies Series': W.P.M. Kennedy and D. Wells, *The Law of the Taxing Power in Canada* (Toronto: University of Toronto Press, 1931); W.P.M. Kennedy and J. Finkelman, *The Right to Trade* (Toronto: University of Toronto Press, 1933); and, much later, F.E. Labrie and J. Westlake, *Deductions under the Income War Tax Act* (Toronto: University of Toronto Press, 1948). The difficulties of the new scholarship are suggested by the fact that all three are essentially doctrinal analysis, with a few vague exhortations about law adapting to changing political needs and contexts. Finkelman and Laskin did research and writing for the Research Council, but none of it was published.

91 Kennedy to R. Fordham, 27 December 1927, box 1, Law School Papers, supra note 77; see also Kennedy to B. Park, 21 March 1928, box 1, ibid.: 'I have no lecture notes of any sort or description. If I had, I should not pass them on to a student as that would be almost a guarantee that he would fail.' His own notes or syllabus for his Comparative Constitutional Law course was thoroughly grounded in the cases (Kennedy Papers, supra note 46).

92 In 1938, Kennedy failed a student for his egregious lack of work in this requirement, 'one of the more important subjects,' and required him to annotate a supplemental list of cases, 'in full and directly from the reports.' After the student produced 220 pages of annotations, Kennedy relented and recommended that he pass (J.A. Renwick, box 3, Law School Papers, supra note 77).

93 'Foreword' (1935) 1 *U.T.L.J.* 2.

94 For an account of this volume, see R.C.B. Risk, 'Volume One of the Journal,' in this volume.

95 See supra note 80.

96 Report of the Curriculum Committee, 8 April 1996, 5, Faculty of Law, University of Toronto. Wright would have despaired, even though a few pages later, the Committee added, 'We aim not simply to provide a liberal legal education, but a professional legal education.'

97 Dicey's great text, *An Introduction to the Law of the Constitution* (London: MacMillan, 1885), was central, but his views cannot be completely understood without considering a short note written in 1915: 'The Development of Administrative Law in England' (1915) 31 *L.Q.R.*, 148.

98 For a survey of this English background, see M. Loughlin, supra note 70.

99 W.P.M. Kennedy, 'Book Review of *Administrative Powers over Persons and Property* by E. Freund' (1928) 6 *Can. Bar. R.*; W.P.M. Kennedy, 'Book Review of *An Introduction to British Constitutional Law* by A .B. Keith, and *Constitutional Law* by E.C.S. Wade and G.G. Phillips' (1931) 45 *Harvard L.R.* 605; W.P.M. Kennedy, 'Three Views of Constitutional Law' (a review of *An Introduction to British Constitutional Law* by A.B. Keith, *Bureaucracy Triumphant* by C.K. Allen, and *Constitutional Law* by E.C.S. Wade and G.G. Phillips) (1931) 9 *Can. Bar R.* 553; W.P.M. Kennedy, 'Book Review of *Bureaucracy and Administrative Law* by J. Beck' (1932) 10 *Can. Bar R.* 611; W.P.M. Kennedy, 'The Growth of Administrative Law' [1932] *South African L.T.* 173; W.P.M. Kennedy, 'The St Lawrence Treaty, Administrative Tribunals, Comparative Law' [1932] *South African L.T.* 219; and 'Some Aspects of Constitutional Law,' supra note 51 at 20.

100 W.P.M. Kennedy, 'Tendencies in Canadian Administrative Law' (1934) 46 *Juridical R.* 203.

101 W.P.M. Kennedy, 'Some Recent Legal Literature' [1934] *South African L.T.* 196.

102 'Tendencies in Canadian Administrative Law,' supra note 100, at 204.

103 Ibid. 221.

104 Ibid. 214. Kennedy took great pride in the courses and research at the law school; see ibid. 208 and 223.

105 Ibid. 222–3.

106 Ibid. 219.

107 Ibid. at 228.

108 W.P.M. Kennedy, 'Law and Custom in the Canadian Constitution' [1929] *Round Table*. This article was reprinted in Kennedy's *Essays in Constitutional Law* (London: Oxford University Press, 1934), which was a reprinting of a handful of articles; and much of it was used in *Some Aspects of Constitutional Law*, supra note 51, and in the second edition of *The Constitution of Canada*, supra note 18.

109 *Essays*, supra note 108 at 89.

110 Ibid.

111 Ibid. 90.

112 Ibid. 84.

113 Ibid. 93.

114 Ibid.

115 Ibid 85.

116 *Reference Re The Board of Commerce Act, 1919, and the Combines and Fair Prices Act, 1919* [1922] 1 A.C. 191 (P.C.); *Fort Frances Pulp and Paper Co. v. Manitoba Free Press* [1923] A.C. 695 (P.C.); and *Toronto Electric Commissioners v. Snider* [1925] A.C. 396 (P.C.).

117 H.A. Smith, 'The Residue of Power in Canada' (1926) *Can. Bar R.* 432.

118 Kennedy's understanding of the significance of these cases for the division of powers, especially for national economic regulation, was demonstrated in two reviews written about the same time Smith's comment appeared, but this very understanding is in contrast to his lack of discussion of the modes of interpretation. See 'Book Review' of *Problems of Industrial Arbitration in Canada*' [1926] *American Econ. R.* 135, and 'Book Review' of *The Mechanism of the Modern State* by J.D.A. Marriott' (1927) *Can. Hist. R.* 160.

119 'Book review of *The Canadian Constitution as Interpreted by the Judicial Committee* by E.R. Cameron' [1930] 8 *Can. Bar R.* 703 at 708. See also 'The Interpretation of the Constitution' [1932] *South African L.T.* 57; and 'Radio: Aviation: Insurance' [1932] *South African L.T.* 240. Like a few other scholars, Kennedy saw some hope for change in a handful of judgments in the early 1930s, although he added a skepticism that was eventually justified.

120 He suggested the idea of balance even earlier, in a brief passage in the introduction to his constitutional history text, where he spoke of Canada as having 'a genius for balance of centrifugal and centripetal forces': *The Constitution of Canada*, supra note 18 at 5.

121 *Some Aspects of Constitutional Law*, supra note 51 at 102.

122 'Then came the crash ... Then the whole problem of industrial control came to the front in a manner never before experienced – fair competition, hours of labour, rates of wages, minimum wages for men, marketing organizations, the capitalization of companies, mass production – all provincial subject-matters, but now erected, before the forces of a compelling world agony, into questions of vital national importance': W.P.M. Kennedy, 'The Constitution in the Melting Pot' [1934] 3 *South African L.J.* 157 at 158.

123 *Some Aspects of Constitutional Law*, supra note 51 at 102.

124 W.P.M. Kennedy, 'Crisis in the Canadian Constitution' (1934) 24 *Round Table* 803 at 815.

125 Ibid. 819. See also W.P.M. Kennedy, 'The Workings of the *British North America Acts, 1867–1981*' (1936) 48 *Juridical R.* 57, for his mounting despair. Here (at 68–73) Kennedy called for abolition of appeals to the Privy Council and set out a proposal for making amendments to the *BNA Act*, which required approval of the federal government and two-thirds of the provinces (except for some matters entirely within the domain of the federal government and some other matters of 'fundamental' importance, for which approval of all the provinces was needed). He had presented this proposal to the Special Committee on the *BNA Act* of the House of Commons in the previous year, 1935.

126 'The British North America Act: Past and Future' (1937) *Can. Bar R.* 393 at 398–9. This comment was part of a symposium of which Kennedy was the editor. See also 'The Constitution of Canada' [1937] *Politica* 357. In a letter to Henry Davis, a member of the Supreme Court, Kennedy said, 'I think Lord Atkin has gone slightly coo-coo': Kennedy to Davis, 1937, box 3, Law School Papers, supra note 77.

127 'The British North America Act: Past and Future,' ibid., 398. He continued, 'The time has come to abandon tinkering with or twisting the *British North America Act* – a curiosity belonging to an elder age. At long last we can criticize it, as the stern demands of economic pressure have bitten into the bastard loyalty which gave to it the doubtful devotion of primitive ancestor worship. We must seek machinery to do in Canada certain things: i) to repeal the *BNA Act* in toto; ii) to rewrite completely the constitution; to provide reasonable and same and workable constituent machinery; ... iv) to abolish all appeals to the Judicial Committee' (ibid. 399). A decade before, he had been much more sanguine about the appeals: see, for example *The Constitution of Canada*, supra note 18 at 398, and W.P.M. Kennedy, 'Nationhood in the British Commonwealth' (1926) 131 *Contemporary R.* 555 at 560– 1. In the early 1930s, Kennedy claimed that the *Statute of Westminster* permitted the Dominion government to bar appeals from federal courts, a claim that was vindicated in *British Coal Corporation v. The King* [1934] A.C.. 500 (P.C.). See 'Book Review' of *National Sovereignty and Judicial Autonomy in the British Commonwealth* by H. Hughes' (1931) 9 *Can. Bar R.* 675 at 676; 'Book Review of *The Statute of Westminster, 1931* by R.P Mahaffy' (1932) 7 *Can. Bar R.* 672 at 672; 'The Statute of Westminster,' supra note 44 at 338–40; 'The Imperial Conferences, 1926–1930: The Statute of Westminster,' supra note 44 at 223–7; and W.P.M. Kennedy, 'British Coal Corporation v. The King: Three Com-

ments' (1935) 13 *Can. Bar R.* 614. During 1938, Kennedy corresponded with C.H. Cahan, a prominent Conservative member of Parliament, who was planning to introduce a bill to abolish appeals. The two exchanged about a dozen letters, in which Kennedy gave advice about arguments and strategy. Cahan Papers, vol. 1, MG 27 III B 1, NA.

128 F.R. Scott, 'The Development of Canadian Federalism' [1931] *Procs. Can. Political Science Assoc.* 231 at 231.

129 V.C. Macdonald, 'Judicial Interpretation of the Canadian Constitution' (1936) 1 *U.T.L.J.* 260.

130 F.R. Scott, 'The Consequences of the Privy Council Decisions' (1937) 15 *Can. Bar R.* 485; and V.C Macdonald, 'The Canadian Constitution Seventy Years Later' (1937) 15 *Can. Bar R.* 401. Both these articles were part of the symposium edited by Kennedy, supra note 125.

131 *Lochner v. New York* 198 U.S. 45 (1905).

132 Kennedy and Finkelman, *The Right to Trade*, supra note 81; Kennedy and Wells, *The Law of the Taxing Power*, supra note 90; and W.P.M. Kennedy and H. Schlosberg, *The Law and Custom of the South African Constitution* (London: Oxford University Press, 1935). The first two were based on theses written by graduate students, and in both, the structure and most of the text were the same as the thesis. (The theses are in the University of Toronto Archives.) All I can determine about the third comes from Schlosberg's recollections in his autobiography. According to him, Kennedy contacted him 'out of the blue,' suggesting such a book, encouraging him to write it, and offering to help to persuade the publisher to accept it. After working on a manuscript for five years, he sent it to Kennedy, who revised it, and sent it to the Oxford University Press. (The autobiography was written after Schlosberg had changed his name: Henry John May, *Red Wine of Youth* [Cape Town: Cassell, 1946] at 21–3.) In a letter to J.C. Smuts, written in August 1934, Kennedy spoke of 'putting the last touches' on the book (Kennedy to Smuts, 18 August 1934, vol. 237, A1, J.C. Smuts Collection, National Archives of South Africa).

133 I have no idea how and why this endeavour in journalism began, although the connection may have been made through Schlosberg.

134 *Report to the Honourable Secretary of State for Canada on Some Problems in the Law of Nationality* (Ottawa: King's Printer, 1930).

135 Having been retained, at $24 per day, to do a study of comparative federalism, Kennedy produced reports on the United States, Australia, Switzerland, and Argentina. All were descriptions of structure and doctrine, with very little reflection and commentary. Simply reading them, though, suggests that they must have taken a lot of time, and some

evidence of his work habits is reflected in his correspondence about his bills; he said that he worked 30 days in December, including Christmas Day.

136 The Arts program he took at Dublin did not include any law courses, even constitutional law or history, required or optional. I cannot be entirely certain that he did not encounter law in some way during the decade or so after he graduated, about which I know so little. Nonetheless, his work as a Tudor historian alone seems to make the possibility a remote one.

137 See, for example, 'Book Review of *An Historical Introduction to Land Law* by W.S. Holdsworth' (1929) 7 *Can. Bar R.* 59; 'Book Review of *Constitutional Laws of the British Empire* by L. LeM. Minty' (1929) 7 *Can. Bar R.* 146; 'Book Review of *Source Book of Constitutional History* by D.O. Dykes' (1931) 17 *Am. Bar Assoc. J.* 338; 'Book Review of *A Treatise on the Doctrine of Ultra Vires* by H.A. Street' (1931) 17 *Am. Bar Assoc. J.* 681; 'Book Review of *Cases on International Law* by C.G. Fenwick' (1937) 2 *U.T.L.J.* 217; and 'Book Review of *Gatley on Libel and Slander in a Civil Action with Precedents of Pleadings and Dominion and American Cases*, ed. R. O'Sullivan' (1940) 3 *U.T.L.J.* 463.

138 In two articles about the Constitution, he returned to all that he had said since the mid-1930s, adding only an analysis of terms of sections 91 and 92 of the *BNA Act* derived from the O'Connor Report (W. F. O'Connor, *Report to the Senate of Canada on the British North America Act*, 1939). See W.P.M. Kennedy, 'The Terms of the "British North America Act"' in R. Flenley, ed., *Essays in Canadian History in Honour of G.M. Wrong* (Toronto: Macmillan, 1939); and W.P.M. Kennedy, 'The Interpretation of the British North America Act' (1943) 8 *Cambridge L.J.* 146. For an account of the O'Connor Report and the way it influenced scholars during the 1940s and 1950s, see R.C.B. Risk, 'The Scholars and the Constitution,' in this volume. A third article about the Constitution was a comprehensive and straightforward description: W.P.M. Kennedy, 'The Judicial Process and the Canadian Legislative Process' (1940) 25 *Washington U.L.Q.* 215. His last writing was W.P.M. Kennedy, 'The Office of the Governor General in Canada' (1953) 36 *Can. Bar R.* 994, in which he returned to responsible government and Canadian autonomy, saying gracefully, '[M]y armour is on the walls.'

11

Canadian Law Teachers in the 1930s: 'When the World Was Turned Upside Down'

Introduction

This paper is a study of the scholarship done by the teachers in Canadian common law schools in the late 1920s and the 1930s. A few of them are now remembered, albeit dimly, but most are now forgotten, and today, law teachers have no sense of them as a distinctive generation. Yet they produced a wide range of impressive scholarship, and introduced changes that continue to shape legal thinking. When I told one of them, John Willis, that I was interested in this period, he captured both the accomplishment and a distinctive mood in a single phrase by exclaiming that it was 'when the world was turned upside down.'[1] I seek to understand what he meant, and more particularly, to explore the changes they made in ways of thinking about law, legal institutions, and their own roles.[2] At least 40 individuals taught in the common law schools during this period, although many of them stayed for only a year or two before leaving to go into practice.[3] Some were at the forefront of changes, some followed a few gasps behind, and some continued in the established ways of thinking. A list of the ones who did distinctive scholarship, as judged both by their contemporaries and in hindsight, may be useful, even if only to recite some names that may be familiar: Vincent MacDonald, Horace Read, Forrester Davison, Sidney Smith, and John Willis, all at Dalhousie University; Herbert Smith, Percy Corbett, and Frank Scott at McGill University; John Falconbridge and 'Caesar' Wright at Osgoode Hall; W.P.M. Kennedy, Jacob Finkelman, and Larry MacKenzie at the University of Toronto; Alex Corry and Russell Hopkins at the University of Saskatchewan, and Bora Laskin. (Laskin did not have a teaching job until 1940, and therefore does not quite fit into the round dates I have set for myself. I have included him nonetheless because he eventually became such an important academic and judicial figure.)[4]

They worked in conditions that are a far cry from the present. The teaching and marking loads were far greater than present ones. Whatever their relations with their colleagues at their own schools, they had little communication with the teachers at other schools. There were no organizations for meetings, or exchanges of ideas and information; distances were great; and their meagre budgets offered little support for travel. They did correspond with each other, but not in any widespread, regular way; instead, most of the correspondence was between friends, or about administrative matters. Their major sources of ideas and information were not Canadian, but journals and books from England and the United States.

The Major Themes Introduced

The distinctive moods and ideas appeared first in a few isolated phrases in the late 1920s and 1930s,[5] and were announced early in 1931 with remarkable breadth and clarity in two manifestos, one by 'Caesar' Wright and the other by W.P.M. Kennedy. Although Wright's given names were Cecil and Augustus, they gave way to the 'Caesar' throughout his life. In 1931, he was at the beginning of a career that stretched from the late 1920s to the late 1960s. Born in 1900 in London, Ontario, he went to Osgoode Hall Law School after getting a degree in Arts at the University of Western Ontario. He then went to Harvard Law School for graduate work, and returned to Osgoode to teach in 1926. His manifesto was a talk given in January 1931, to the Law Club at the University of Toronto.[6] Among the audience was a Bora Laskin, then in his first year. At the very end of my paper, I shall suggest that this coincidence was a remarkable portent.

Wright began his talk by declaring a new mood:

The day of faith and credence seems going, ... and in its place, we have a general spirit of skepticism followed often by a move towards the empirical and pragmatic ... Practically all legal writings of the present time are permeated with a spirit of skepticism as to all our former ideas of law.[7]

Law was woefully inappropriate for the 'modern industrial era.' In elaborating its failings, he emphasized the ways of common law reasoning. It had been autonomous from its social context, and its goals had been dominated by a quest for internal coherence and elegance. It had been 'a subject to be studied and developed in and for itself.' Analysis of this kind of – 'analyzing and comparison of the rules of law themselves' was still a large part of lawyers' work, but it was not alone enough. As well, law must be studied as 'a means to an end … The end of law must always be found outside the law itself.' He was especially concerned about the needs of business, arguing that the proper approach was 'from the standpoint of what business requires from law, rather than from that of what the law demands from business.'[8]

Entangled with this call to make law serve the needs of contemporary society was an approach he had suggested in the phrase 'the empirical and pragmatic.' The essential notion was that the law should be tested by its results. Speaking of the old beliefs that no longer commanded allegiance merely because they were old, he said, '[T]here is … a demand that they work and above all produce results … Today our concern is not so much with what law is, but why it is and what it is for.' Closely related to this demand was an emphasis on facts, contrasted to the doctrine. '[N]ot what the courts say they are doing but what they actually do is the important inquiry today.'[9]

In the past, the claims of individuals against each other and against the state were labelled rights, which were typically perceived to be hard-edged and absolute. Yet the contemporary society that law must serve was complex, changing, and interdependent, a world for which these rights were entirely inappropriate. A more efficient way of recognizing and reconciling the various claims was to assign interests, which could be evaluated, adjusted, and balanced.

Last of all, Wright saw the need to reform legal education, although he did not make any proposals, except to say that students must be enabled to understand the needs of business, and 'adapt the formulas of a pre-commercialized age to the new situations.'[10]

Kennedy's manifesto was given a few months later, in a set of public lectures at Lafayette University.[11] [*Editors' Note*: The section on Kennedy's life and approach to legal education has been deleted; an extensive discussion of both can be found in 'The Many Minds of W.P.M. Kennedy,' in this volume.]

In contrast to Wright, he was at the last stage of his career – a long and remarkable one. Born in 1879 in Northern Ireland and educated at Trinity in Dublin, he began his scholarly career as a historian of Elizabethan England, publishing a small handful of books about ecclesiastical affairs. He came to Canada in 1913, perhaps because he was unable to get a job in an English university, and after spending a couple of years at St Francis Xavier College, in Nova Scotia, he moved to the University of Toronto. He became interested in Canadian constitutional history, and wrote a survey in 1922, which became a standard text. In the late 1920s, his interests shifted again, first to contemporary constitutional affairs, and then to a wide range of legal subjects. At that time, law was a small branch of the Faculty of Arts, limited to the upper years. Frustrated in his hopes of becoming head of either political science or history, Kennedy managed to have law made a separate department, and himself made its head – and as its head, invited Wright to give the talk that was Wright's manifesto.[12]

Speaking to the American audience, Kennedy lamented that '[o]ur progress is slow, our legal traditions extremely conservative,' and our law contains 'many ancient and obfuscated features which are still far out of tune with the complex civilization of a modern state.' He feared 'the dead hand of legal precedent' but saw hope, especially because 'our younger lawyers are in close touch with your legal literature which has become a vast social advance-guard of legal reform.' He was pleased that 'in some degree, our law is taking on a social point of view.' This word 'social' was pervasive throughout the lectures, used in such phrases as 'sociological jurisprudence,' 'social standards,' 'a social point of view,' and 'the socialization of law.' The essential idea it expressed was that the law must be 'in functional agreement with social demands'; that is, it must be made to serve the needs of this society, not its own internal elegance or some past society.[13]

The complexity of modern life required different ways of understanding social conduct; for example, a shift away from an understanding of crime as a particular event to 'a social evil which may be anticipated and prevented.'[14] This complexity and a new conception of the individual required that individual rights and duties should no longer be the central elements of the legal framework. Like Wright, he argued that they should be replaced by social interests, a concept that suggested overlap, accommodation, and balancing.[15]

Law-making of this kind required a thorough knowledge of social facts and values, so that law would not be based on 'undigested principles or the untried theories of social cranks.' He returned several times to this need for facts, saying, for example, '[We] must learn to create social machinery for making law, if law is to serve social ends ... [T]he processes of lawmaking must themselves be socialised.' And it was clear that he included courts in this requirement. Turning to the education of lawyers, he argued that law 'must not be taught *in vacuo*, apart from the other social sciences.' Their training must include 'history, economics, sociology, political science and philosophy.'[16]

All these new ways of thinking about law were to be in the service of a new politics: the individual, even though the basic element of civil society, must not be conceived as the autonomous individual of the nineteenth century, 'the older individualism.'[17]

The two manifestos shared a bundle of assumptions, ideas, and beliefs, which can be gathered into five themes. The first is that they shared the sense of excitement and urgency that John Willis remembered so clearly decades later. Even though this mood is implicit in all the other themes, it is important enough to be made separate. The second, and closely related, theme was an assumption, sometimes explicit, and implicit when it was not declared, that the world was fluid and changing. Third, they rejected the past – both its ways of thinking about law and its politics. Fourth, in the place of the past, they sought new ways of thinking about law that would be – in their words – 'functional' and 'realistic,' and that would serve the changing needs of their own, modern, society. And fifth, they would be participants in making this new world, not merely observers. These themes were widely shared during the next decade, displayed in scores of articles, case comments, and book reviews.

Kennedy and Wright also differed. Their few words about legal education alone represented a deep gulf. Kennedy sought to make a humane and liberal education, and Wright sought to prepare students to practise law. I shall not, though, explore this difference here. More important for my purposes, Kennedy considered a wider range of sources; he had less interest in common law doctrine; he considered more of the contemporary political and economic context; and he expressed his political faiths more openly – the short reference to 'the older individualism' was revealing. Just as the themes they shared were widely shared among the other scholars, these differences between the two manifestos represented significant differences. Together, the shared themes and the differences were what made this generation distinctive, and they are what I seek to explore.

A Map of What Follows

For the most part, I will proceed by discussing a parade of scholars and their writing about a single subject, taking some of them alone and others in groups. This parade will be ordered by separating common law and public law subjects. I do not wish this distinction to serve any rigorous theoretical purposes. Instead, I wish simply to mark off writing about common law doctrine from writing about topics that entailed the extensive use of legislation, even though this legislation required interpretation. As we shall see, this distinction marks a major difference in the scholarship, which, as we shall see, was a difference that separated Wright and Kennedy.

This much is straightforward, but two long passages, which follow immediately, create the need for a map, or at least an assurance that I have a plan. Both provide essential background. The first is an account of legal thought in late-nineteenth-century England, which is needed because it was dominant throughout the legal profession in Canada until the 1920s, and we have already seen how much effort the scholars devoted to rejecting it. The second passage is a description of challenges in the United States to this nineteenth-century thought, which is needed because one of my central arguments is that these challenges influenced the scholars greatly.

England in the Late Nineteenth Century: The World Left Behind

English legal thought was the predominant model for Canadian lawyers in the late nineteenth century. It has been given several names, which tend to be associated with different perspectives. For example, 'formalism' is usually used by modern scholars continuing the campaign of rejection, especially in the ritual slaying that still takes place in first-year classrooms. Instead, I shall use the simple term 'the nineteenth-century tradition.'

The common law was its essence and foundation, pervading the day-to-day work of lawyers, their courts, their Constitution, their ceremonial speeches, and their ways of understanding their work and their world. I shall limit the description here to the common law in the sense of doctrine made primarily by judges, and postpone considering the public law elements. The basic elements of this common law were its principles, arranged among subjects such as contracts and property, and ideally consistent with each other.[18] Beliefs about the sources of these principles were complex and contested, but it is sufficient for me to suggest that in England, most lawyers assumed that they were induced from the decided cases, and ultimately expressed the experience of the community, elaborated by the judges. The principles changed over time, although the process of the change and the values at stake were rarely explored.

Courts determined disputes, by finding the facts and then selecting and applying the appropriate principle. Even though they changed, the principles were stable enough to enable making these decisions. The outcomes might be contested, but they could and must be reached by reasoning from the principles, independent of context, values, or social need.[19] A lawyer's prediction, or a judge's decision might be influenced by some considerations outside this structure of authority, but such an outcome would be a mistake – a failure to reason properly.

The primary job of scholars was to synthesize and teach these principles. In England, after the accumulation of great changes in central topics such as torts and contracts, and the abolition of the forms of action, the common law desperately needed reconstitution. A small group at Oxford, including Anson, Dicey, Markby, and Pollock, wrote great texts synthesizing the principles from this mass of cases for students and for lawyers to use in their daily work.

In Canada, these ways of thinking were adopted as a matter of course, and continued to be virtually the only way of thinking from the late nineteenth century to the late 1920s. The leading scholar was A.H.F. Lefroy, who taught at the University of Toronto, and explored questions that were pressing at the turn of the century: did judges make law, how did they make it, and what were their sources?[20]

This common law and its ways of thinking were an expression of political values as well as the technical apparatus for the work of a profession. In short, they were the legal structure of mid-nineteenth-century liberalism, and from this perspective, the texts the scholars wrote were making or legitimating an ideology. The core tenets were that individuals were to have autonomy to make choices about their lives, free from interference by other individuals or the state, and that their liability to others was to be determined by the expressions of their wills or by conduct that failed to meet objective standards. The state, through the courts, simply enforced their choices by applying the principles, objectively and without discretion.

American Legal Thought in the Early Twentieth Century: The Coming World

Challenges to this thinking began in the United States in the late nineteenth century and flourished early in the twentieth century. Oliver Wendell Holmes was the beginning, albeit an enigmatic one. In a few short aphorisms – 'the life of the law has not been logic, it has been experience,' and 'general propositions do not decide concrete cases' – he seemed to prophesy much of what was to happen. Early in the twentieth century, scholars now labelled the Progressives emerged, in a context shaped by pragmatism, by the burgeoning social sciences, and by political turmoil and calls for a new social order. The major figures were Roscoe Pound, at Harvard Law School and later its dean, and Benjamin Cardozo, a judge of the New York Court of Appeals.

The titles of two of Pound's articles capture much of their spirit: 'Mechanical Jurisprudence'[21] and 'Sociological Jurisprudence.'[22] Calling for 'pragmatism as a philosophy of law'[23] he protested at the abstraction from social life, the pursuit of an elegant internal structure, and the faith that results could be deduced 'mechanically' from general rules. The common law

> must be judged by the results it achieves, not by the niceties of its internal structure; it must be valued by the extent to which it meets its end, not by the beauty of its logical processes or the strictness with which its rules proceed from the dogmas it takes for its foundation.[24]

Instead, common law reasoning should be instrumental and seek social welfare. For Pound, the objective was 'putting the human factor in the central place and relegating logic to its true position as an instrument,'[25] and for Cardozo, 'The final cause of law is the welfare of society.'[26] Lawyers should become, in Pound's phrase, 'social engineers,' a function that included paying more attention to facts and to enlisting the social sciences. Nonetheless, the Progressives believed that legal reasoning could be and should be objective. For them, the common law was a coherent structure, and systematization of its doctrine was a coherent and useful enterprise. Its principles were not rigid rules, but guidelines that governed all but a few difficult cases, which would be decided in the light of social welfare and be the impetus for change. The similarity to Wright's manifesto is both obvious and important to my story, and I shall return to it later.

In the late 1920s and 1930s, another group appeared – the Realists. Even though they created much excitement and controversy, they cannot be separated sharply from the Progressives. Their common ground makes isolating the differences between them difficult, and these difficulties are compounded by the diversity among the Realists themselves. Nonetheless, the sharpest difference was that the Realists tended to be skeptical about the coherence of the common law, arguing, for example, that its principles were intelligible only in the context of particular facts, and could not provide determinate outcomes. Instead, in deciding disputes, much depended upon the context and the judge. The Realists did not, though, deny a large element of predictability. Instead, they sought stability and objectivity in the social sphere, and turned to the social sciences, especially the behavioural sciences, for guidance for both courts and scholars.

The Common Law: The Scholarship Introduced

Most of the writing by my scholars was about the common law, and such subjects as contracts, property, estates, and torts. Most of it was comments about recent cases, and the rest was short articles, often prompted by a case or series of cases, or book reviews. This emphasis on the common law is hardly startling. These scholars perceived their function to be not only to educate lawyers, but to support their daily work as practitioners and judges. Because the welfare and regulatory state was still in its beginnings, the bulk of this work was directed at the ordering of private affairs, and the common law and the interpretations of a few statutes that consolidated or modified it.

Most of this writing was exposition and analysis of the doctrine. Sydney Smith is a remarkable example. After serving in the war, getting a degree from Dalhousie and doing graduate work at Harvard, he returned to teach at Dalhousie in 1921, where he introduced the case method. After a few years of growing popularity as a teacher, he went to Osgoode Hall, and returned to Dalhousie as dean in 1929. He left law teaching in 1934 to be president of Manitoba University, and later president of the University of Toronto. In 1957, he moved to the political world, becoming minister of external affairs under John Diefenbaker, and died shortly afterwards.

Between 1928 and 1934, Smith wrote over 80 case comments, as well as a large handful of book reviews and a couple of short articles. The range of topics and his knowledge of doctrine were remarkable, and far beyond the reach of legal scholars today. The comments, which were no more than a few pages long, typically described the case and its context in the doctrine, and demonstrated either that it expressed an important principle in an interesting way, or was at odds with the settled doctrine. Values and social and economic implications were never considered, except for a few expressions of a faith in individual responsibility and effort.

Yet understanding Smith is not so simple as reading all these comments might suggest. In the late 1920s, he wrote to a colleague, Horace Read, that he hoped to be remembered for 'molding and shaping of Canadian destiny through the instrumentality of law, rather than an erudite analysis of the rule in Shelley's case'; he spoke of 'law as a social science' and hoped that Dalhousie would become a 'centre of creative legal thought.'[27] Later, in discussing teaching materials, he said that he wanted to make the students 'respond to the new social idea ... To treat legal principles as a mere tool for a livelihood ... would leave the science of law, in this new country, out of step with the mark [?] of the other social sciences, and in it lurks a social danger.'[28]

How can these ambitions be reconciled with his scholarship? To say that he just did not understand what he was saying, or that he was not able to do what he dreamed of doing, assumes that he lacked intelligence, which was simply not true. Another possibility is that he did not have time to do the more adventurous scholarship. True, his teaching, his administrative duties, and his work as an assistant editor of the *Canadian Bar Review*, all made a remarkable load, but it doesn't explain the lack of regrets or even a few small tries. The beginning of a more promising explanation is the realization that these comments were designed primarily to assist the practising profession. I shall seek to develop this possibility later, in discussing Caesar Wright.

A handful of other scholars did the same kind of writing as Smith, especially Gordon Cowan and George Crouse of Dalhousie, Frederick Read of Manitoba, and John Weir of Alberta. Among them, Read and Weir demonstrated distinctive power and thoroughness, but none of them undertook any analysis of the nature of the common law or its reasoning, described context, or looked for justification to social need or values.

The large amount of this kind of writing – modest exposition and analysis of doctrine within the limits of the nineteenth-century tradition – is hardly surprising. Even in a period of challenge and change, most of the scholars did what scholars like them had done for decades. Even though they were aware of the changes, and sympathetic to them, and even though some professed to have embraced them, their day-to-day work continued in the familiar ways.

The Common Law: Falconbridge and the Conflicts of Laws

In the common law writing, two scholars towered over the others: John Falconbridge and Caesar Wright. In short, Falconbridge represented the world that was being left behind, and Wright represented the world that was emerging.

Falconbridge was born in 1875, and practised from 1899 to 1915, when he began to teach at Osgoode Hall, where he stayed throughout his long career. His output was immense. Before 1940, he wrote texts on mortgages, negotiable instruments, and banking, and over 60 articles and case comments. The largest and most interesting part of this writing was about conflicts. He was regarded in England as one of its dominant scholars, being often cited and discussed.

Conflicts was a battlefield during the 1920s and 1930s. The dominant approach was a traditional one, expressed most famously by Joseph Beale, of Harvard, the Reporter for the *Restatement of Conflicts*, which appeared in 1934, having been preceded by drafts, which appeared in the 1920s. At its centre was the notion of vested rights, created by the courts of one jurisdiction, which another court would enforce. The doctrine was a self-contained, internally consistent set of rules, derived from a few basic principles, such as the territorial sovereignty of nations. The English doctrine was much the same, although much less conceptual and hierarchical.

Challenges to Beale began in the 1920s, especially from the Realists. In 1924, Walter Wheeler Cook argued '[o]n the basis of actual observation of what courts have done and are doing,'[29] that the forum did not enforce a right created by another jurisdiction, but instead enforced 'a right created by its own law,'[30] and its decision must be defended entirely 'on the basis of social convenience and practical expediency.'[31] In the same year, Ernest Lorenzen challenged the enterprise of deducing the doctrine from a few basic principles,[32] and four years later, in 1928, Hessel Yntema argued that principles could have meaning only in particular contexts and could not control decisions.[33]

Almost all of Falconbridge's writing during the late 1920s and early 1930s was straightforward exposition and synthesis of the doctrine; for example, a survey of the entire subject for his text on Bills and Notes, or studies of particular corners, such as contracts or administration of estates.[34] Here, he was occasionally critical of particular decisions, but only for their failure to conform to authority.

Two changes appeared after the mid-1930s. First, he sought to suggest new ways of ordering the doctrine, and to make proposals for change more openly than he had before. In pursuing these objectives, he invoked a wide range of European literature, as well as the more familiar English and American sources. An example is two articles about renvoi, a renowned and problematic doctrine.[35] In the first, in 1930, he sought to demonstrate that renvoi was not a part of the English law, by undertaking a thorough analysis of the cases.[36] Nine years later, in 1939, he treated it in a more expansive way, discussing individual cases less and seeking, instead, to clarify the doctrine and openly suggesting a compromise among the competing views.[37]

Second, and more important for my purposes, he made an effort to take account of the challenges to the traditional approach. In 1935, in a review of Beale's text, he referred to the debate about the basic principle of 'vested rights,' and said, 'It would seem better ... to say nothing about the power of a law or state to create a right, and rather to say that the proper law in a given situation should be chosen with the object of reaching a socially satisfactory result. Inevitably, each country must decide for itself what rules of conflict of laws are likely to reach such a result.'[38]

But this was a review. In his own work, he did not integrate this approach with the general structure of his reasoning or his proposals for changes in doctrine. For example, in 1937, he discussed characterization – the process of determining 'the juridical nature' of a problem.[39] He analysed the nature of the question and the different contexts in which it arose, and then discussed a series of cases and problems, making only a few small references to the challenges.[40] His analysis demonstrated he had no doubt that characterization was an objective process. Determining the 'judicial nature' of an issue might be difficult and debatable, but it did not entail any consideration of social context or values. In contrast, four years before, Cook had mocked the assumption that lines between categories had an objective existence, permitting them to be discovered by some 'mechanical or logical process.' Classifications were inescapably surrounded by a 'twilight zone or penumbra,' and meaningful distinctions could only be made by considering the purposes for which each one was made.[41]

Two years later, in his 1939 article on renvoi, Falconbridge went a bit further towards embracing the challenges. Considering the doctrine of renvoi generally, he disapproved of accepting it or rejecting it on 'supposedly logical ... grounds.' Turning to characterization he said, '[I]t is sometimes a good thing to look before you leap,' and made the radical suggestion that a court could peek at the content of a foreign law that might be chosen to govern the problem before it, to help it reach 'a reasonable economic or social result.' He did not, though, pursue the implications of this suggestion, instead saying that they needed 'further consideration.'[42]

In short, Falconbridge continued to be committed to the nineteenth-century tradition. He read the challenges, and respected them, but did not make substantial changes in his basic approaches. Happenstance, though, may have been significant. The challengers were some of the more enthusiasic Realists. He might have been tempted more if they had chosen some other field, and some moderate Progressives had written about conflicts.

At the end of the decade, another major conflicts scholar emerged, Moffat Hancock. After graduating from the law school at the University of Toronto in 1933 and Osgoode Hall, he did graduate work at Michigan, and returned to Toronto in 1937. From there, he went to Dalhousie and then to Stanford, where he became one of the major contributors to the postwar rearrangements of conflicts scholarship. He wrote little about conflicts while he was at Toronto – a review, a case comment, and an article – but enough to suggest the future of his ideas, and the difference between him and Falconbridge. In 1937, while he was still a student, he declared allegiance to the challengers, approving both Yntema and Lorenzen.[43] Three years later, he tackled choice of law in torts cases, especially the meaning of a notoriously vague passage in an old English case.[44] Seeking a 'functional approach' and eschewing 'purely logical deductions' and 'mechanical reasoning,' he offered a reading of this passage that was grounded in basic purposes of the conflicts doctrine; for example, the interest of states in enforcing their laws for conduct occurring within their boundaries.

Within months, Falconbridge challenged this reading in a case comment,[45] relying on a close reading of the passage, its 'natural construction,'[46] and the tendency of the cases. Again, within months, another case offered Hancock an opportunity to revisit the topic.[47] Suggesting that the English doctrine originated at a time when courts were wary about applying the law of other states, he defended the American doctrine, which was similar to his proposed formulation of the English doctrine, because it was flexible, offering the court an opportunity to distinguish between mere differences and results that were 'harsh or unjust.'[48]

The Common Law: Caesar Wright and Torts

Wright needs careful study, simply because he was a major figure, arguably the dominant figure, in scholarship and education from the mid-1930s to his death in 1967. Between 1928, when he began to teach, and 1940, he published about 120 pieces, the vast majority of them after 1935. Seven were articles about the common law, legal education, and the profession, and the remainder were divided almost equally between book reviews and case comments. The book reviews covered a vast range of topics, including jurisprudence, biographies, and texts. The case comments were virtually all about cases involving the common law, and they too covered a vast range of topics, including torts, wills, contracts, and evidence. Amidst this wealth, the case comments were the major and the most revealing part of his writing, and among them, the comments about torts were representative.[49]

Many of these comments were powerful scholarship, and are all the more impressive in light of the realization that many of them must have been written in an evening or two. His most common undertaking was to criticize a court's reasoning for being confused, inconsistent, or at odds with the established doctrine, and then to demonstrate how the reasoning should have been done. An example is his comment on an Ontario case, *Hutson v. United Motor Service*.[50] The claim was for damage done to a building leased by the plaintiff to the defendants, who had sought to clean the floor using gasoline, which exploded in some unexplained way. The Court of Appeal allowed an appeal from a trial judgment dismissing the action. Wright approved the result, but criticized the judgments for failing to distinguish between two different grounds of liability: negligence and strict liability. Each had its own distinct elements, which the judgments had jumbled together. Having demonstrated this confusion and presenting the proper structure of the doctrine, Wright went on to explain how the doctrine of *res ipsa loquitur*, which one judgment had mentioned in an aimless way, applied to the doctrine of negligence.

As well, Wright often criticized confusion, inconsistency, or gaps in the doctrine itself, rather than the court's reasoning, usually proposing a reformulation. An example is a comment written in 1939 about *Paine v. Cone Valley Electricity Supply*, a trial decision in England.[51] It dealt with a question left by the watershed decision in *Donoghue v. Stevenson*, which had held that a manufacturer could be liable in negligence to a consumer. In *Paine*, a worker was injured by a defective piece of electrical equipment supplied to his employer by its manufacturer. The liability of the employer was clear, but whether the manufacturer was liable depended upon the answer to the question that had been left unanswered in *Donoghue*: what was the significance of the possibility that the employer could have inspected the equipment before installing it? Wright's proposal was that the duty of the manufacturer continued, regardless of an opportunity for inspection by a stranger, and that a separate inquiry could be made to determine whether the stranger also owed a duty to the plaintiff.[52]

The crucial element of his proposal was a decision of the Supreme Court about the liability of an occupier of land, in which the court held that the occupier was liable to a plaintiff, even though the plaintiff knew about the danger that caused the injury (and reduced the damages by the degree of his negligence). Wright argued that this result could only make sense if the occupier's duty continued regardless of the plaintiff's carelessness. Therefore, in considering products liability, a failure to inspect by the injured plaintiff should not bar recovery, and consistency required that a failure to inspect by a stranger should be treated the same way.

This reasoning, and by implication the justification for his proposal, was derived from the basic principles of the established doctrine. Wright never challenged these principles, nor did he seek justification for his proposals in some general theory of liability, or consider the social context; for example, industrialisation, the rise of the large corporation, or the Depression. He often said that the modern world was bustling, complex, and changing, but he did not explain how these features shaped the doctrine or his thinking.

Nonetheless, the accumulation of comments suggests a large measure of his beliefs. The beginning was the basic principles of the doctrine: liability should be based primarily upon negligence, supplemented by intentional torts and strict liability.[53] Within this structure, he preferred results that imposed liability on enterprises for the losses caused by their activities. An example is his discussions of vicarious liability, one of his favourite topics, beginning with his comment on *Kerr v. T.G. Bright*, a decision of the Ontario Court of Appeal.[54] The plaintiff's husband was killed by a motorcycle carelessly driven by a person whom the defendants had hired to deliver wine. Her claim that the defendants were vicariously liable succeeded in the Ontario Court of Appeal. The result pleased Wright, but the reasoning did not.

Using both English and American sources he synthesized the general principles about liability for an agent in both contract and tort. For tort, the liability was based on control – did the defendant have a right to control the conduct of the agent? Having finished this synthesis, he argued that the inconsistent results of the cases demonstrated that the notion of control was not 'capable of satisfactory or uniform application under prevailing business conditions.' Instead, it was a conclusion that followed from some other considerations. Having reached this stage, he went on to assert that 'vicarious liability is an economic and social, rather than a legal problem,' and that if an agent had become integrated into the defendant's business, liability was 'only fair.'[55]

He pursued this analysis of control at length in a series of comments about cases involving the liability of hospitals for the liability of nurses.[56] In 1936, commenting on a set of cases from England, New Zealand, and Canada, be spoke of 'the futility of arguing pure control.' The results depend upon 'some other factor which does not appear in the text-book rules,' and upon the answer to 'a broader question, does a hospital board undertake to supply properly qualified nurses.' He did not declare his preference expressly, but it was clear enough: he believed this undertaking should be implied.[57]

He did not explain or justify this preference, but not because he lacked the power to undertake the task. Instead, he was simply not much interested in theory. He did not explain or justify his preference to impose liability on enterprises for the losses created by their activities, by considering, for example, internalizing the costs of business, deterrence, passing costs on to consumers, or widespread spreading of losses, and he did not explain its relation to the basic principle of negligence. Thinking about these questions was beginning to appear in American periodicals,[58] but in Canada, only George Curtis, at Dalhousie University, explored them, in an article proposing loss-spreading as the basis for vicarious liability.[59] Outcomes of this kind shared the same basic justifications as workers' compensation schemes, which had already been established. As well, they paralleled the more explicit beliefs and programs of the welfare and regulatory state that were being debated in the public law scholarship; for example, unemployment insurance schemes.

Having sought to understand Wright's ideas about torts, I turn to his beliefs about the common law. Here, he sought a delicate balance between three elements: the structure of principles, a need to make choices in deciding particular cases, and continual change to respond to changing social needs.

He spoke often of principles as the basic structure and content of the common law, sometimes adding such adjectives as 'fundamental' or 'working.' They were generalizations from decided cases, and he had no doubt that they could be formulated and understood independent of any particular context, and used to decide cases. One of the major responsibilities of the profession, especially the academics, was to formulate them carefully, and to design and use precise and consistent terminology. The restatements undertaken by the American Law Institute were the outstanding fulfillment of this responsibility, one to which Wright referred often, and about which he wrote his longest piece of the decade.[60]

The principles were essential for deciding cases, but alone they were not enough. Wright disdained the belief that they could always simply be applied to facts to produce decisions, scorning it as a 'slot machine' or 'static or mechanical' conception of deciding. This disdain, usually expressed as a rejection of 'logic,' was widely shared throughout this generation. Therefore courts must make choices, and these choices must involve 'some conception of the value of the result.'[61] Whether Wright believed that these choices must be made in every case, or whether there were some that could be decided by a straightforward application of principles was not entirely clear. A few short passages in general discussions were conflicting, but his discussions of cases in the comments clearly demonstrated an assumption that many cases, probably the vast majority, could be, and should be, decided without discretion, and for the others, the principles were essential guidelines for ordering thinking.

Wright had no doubt that principles changed. '[T]he static or mechanical concept of law has never at any stage in our legal history been true nor can it be true. That our law has changed and will change, is undoubted.'[62] The change came from the challenge of difficult cases, ones that did not fit comfortably within the terms of an existing principle. The decisions in these cases depended upon 'logic, a view as to what is expedient, [and] some notion of the social or economic implications of the problem before the court.'[63] In using 'logic' in this context, he was not referring to the belief that general principles could decide all cases. Instead, he probably meant a combination of technical craft and the limits of the changes that seemed to be permitted by the existing structure. In 1931, he said, '[T]he courts may not make law out of thin air ... they are limited by the existing legal material before them. But they can shape and reshape that material by choosing different starting points.'[64] He said no more about the limits of change, but my understanding is that he meant the courts must respect the basic structure and principles of the doctrine. Nor did he consider the force of precedents at any length, but his case comments demonstrate that he considered them to be useful guidelines and often a sufficient justification, but just as often not compelling. Within these limits, the standards or contents of the changes must come from 'something external'[65] – from some social need or value outside the doctrine. He said little, though, about these sources, except for several comments about the need for law to meet the needs of business.[66] In general, he seemed to accept the prevailing values of the contemporary society, and to assume that these values were unproblematic.

The manifesto also declared an 'empirical and pragmatic' approach. These words pointed to the developments in philosophy at the turn of the century,[67] but for Wright – and all the other scholars of this generation except Kennedy – these changes were in a very dim background. Instead, these words were a call for the law and its institutions to be continuously tested by current social need, and a suggestion of a fluid and changing world. Associated with this 'empirical and pragmatic' approach, was a need to be 'realistic' in reading judgments and doctrine. By saying this, Wright did not mean an inquiry into the social effects of the decisions. Instead, he usually meant that the doctrine masked the considerations that pushed a court to a result. The considerations he uncovered were not, though, ones like class, power, value, or the underlying reasons for allocating losses. Instead, they were ideas that were consistent with the general structure of the doctrine.

These understandings of the common law were the rejection of the past that Wright had announced in his manifesto. This rejection was complex, because he shared more with his ancestors than he acknowledged. Like most of the scholars of his generation, he created a caricature for the purpose of a ritual slaying.[68] Lefroy, too, believed that the common law changed, that it sometimes was incomplete, and that judges made choices, and he was no less vague than Wright about the sources for making changes.[69] Nonetheless, there were two large differences between them. First, the nineteenth-century scholars had much more faith than Wright in the power of precedent and the feasibility of deducing results from principles, independently of context. This was the 'logic' that he and most of his generation scorned. Second, Wright believed that larger changes were needed, and needed urgently.[70] Yet these differences alone do not explain the forcefulness of the rejection. It was amplified by a rejection of the politics that the nineteenth-century doctrine embodied. As we have seen, Wright did not openly declare his own politics. Nonetheless, he shared the prevailing liberal beliefs of most Canadian intellectuals.

His beliefs about the common law were not original or distinctive. Instead, they were the mainstream of the Progressive thought that was dominant in the United States during the 1920s, when he did his graduate work at Harvard. Pound, especially, seems to have had a large influence on Wright. One moment that might serve as a symbol came on 22 February 1926, when Pound lectured about 'the deficiencies of nineteenth century legal thought,' and Wright took extensive notes.[71]

He turned continually to the United States for guidance. It was there, and not in England, that the models were to be found for common law reasoning, for legal education, and for the role of scholars. He pointed to the American cases and scholarly literature, especially the Restatements, as sources of ideas for change, and to its schools, scholars, and texts as inspirations for the Canadians.[72] When he became editor of the *Canadian Bar Review*, he avowedly sought American contributions.[73] In contrast, he saw the English legal thought as unimaginative and parochial. Its prevailing Austinian positivism was 'as deadening to the spirit as it is unproductive of result, excluding as it did, assessing law by any social or moral standards.[74] It was, though, the developments in the early part of the century that Wright turned to – Pound and the Progressives. He demonstrated little interest in the Realists, as did the other Canadian teachers. They cited the writing of the Realists only rarely, and in a few short passages, they disapproved their more radical ideas.[75]

Wright's beliefs about common law reasoning were in tension with his thinking about torts. He scorned autonomous analysis of doctrine, and called for realism, responsiveness to social change, and 'an extralegal approach to law.' Yet, as we have seen, his case comments did not discuss values or context. Instead, he adopted the prevailing values, assuming they were widely shared and unproblematic, and the familiar contexts of middle-class urban life. Not even the Depression intruded.

To look for an explanation of this tension by reading his work more closely is to look for thinking he never did, and to dwell on its existence is to miss the heart of his efforts. Wright was well read, but he did not care much for theory. The dominant purpose that ran through all his work was to educate lawyers: the courts who had to decide cases, lawyers who had to argue before them, and students who had to be trained for both jobs. They were the audience for whom he wrote. The limits of useful criticism and proposals, and the limits of leadership were the limits of the changes courts could make, and to criticize them was just not part of this task. In this light, much of his general declarations were a call for work by someone else, perhaps at some other time.

This emphasis on the profession is difficult to explain. One possible reason was a simple delight in using his immense powers of analysis. Another is his passionate beliefs about a legal education: it should be a professional education, yet freed from the dead hand of the Benchers at Osgoode Hall. His writing demonstrated the useful work that could be done by scholars, and at the same time accepted the prevailing economic order – which lawyers usually prefer.

Last of all in this discussion of Wright, I remember that many pages ago, I suggested that Falconbridge and Wright represented the world that was disappearing and the world that was emerging. The differences between them were much the same as the differences between Wright and the scholars in the nineteenth century. Both of them believed that principles were the centre of the common law, and that these principles changed in response to changes in their social contexts. A sense of excitement and urgency, though, shone through Wright's work. He had much less respect for precedent, and argued, in a way that Falconbridge never did, that judges often must choose between results that the doctrine permitted. He stressed change more, and was more inclined to criticize and to advocate change. For Falconbridge, the role of scholar was deferential, and his main function was to synthesize; for Wright, it was to educate the profession to better ways of thinking and its responsibilities. And last, Falconbridge looked primarily to England and secondarily to Europe for ideas and models, and Wright looked primarily to the United States.

An Introduction to the Public Law Subjects and the Constitution

So far, I have considered a couple of the common law scholars, Falconbridge and Wright. I turn now to the scholars who wrote about the

Constitution, interpretation, and administrative agencies, gathering these subjects under the heading 'public law.' This turn marks major differences in the scholarship, which were the differences suggested by the differences between Wright's and Kennedy's manifestos.

First, a brief introduction to the lawyers' understandings of the Constitution in the late nineteenth century is needed. The classic exposition was Dicey's *Law of the Constitution*, written in 1885 as a text for students.[76] In the introduction, he set himself the task of describing and classifying the 'first principles.' He saw three, although only the first two are significant here.[77] The first was the sovereignty of Parliament. Parliament had power to make any law it wished, and no other institution had power to override its laws. For our purposes, this principle is straightforward, even though explaining it led Dicey into long technical analysis; for example, about law-making by courts and about federalism. The second principle was the rule of law, which had three parts. First, no individual could be coerced by the state 'except for a distinct breach of law established in the ordinary legal manner before the ordinary Courts of the land.' Contrasted to this ideal were 'wide, arbitrary, or discretionary powers of constraint.' The second part was formal equality: government and its officials were subject to the law in the same way as all individuals. The individual was free to do whatever she wished, unless restrained by a law enforced by the courts. Both these principles had been at the heart of the ideal of constitutional government for generations, generating images of the tyranny of the Stuart kings and their overthrow. Third, the Constitution was the accumulation of 'judicial decisions determining the rights of private persons.' It was the courts that made the Constitution. In this way, liberty was embedded in the fabric of the law, and better protected than it was by the elegant statements of paper constitutions – especially the flimsy European constitutions. Throughout, the liberty of the individual was the central value, and it was best protected by the courts. This union of the common law, the courts, and lawyers was central to the Constitution that Dicey articulated for the lawyers of his generation.

Federalism

The Canadian Constitution combined Dicey's British constitution and federalism. This proposition, both simple and adventuresome, was declared in 1867 in the *British North America [BNA] Act*: the provinces 'desired to be federally united into one dominion ... with a Constitution similar in principle to that of the United Kingdom.' The importance of federalism in Canadian political life made the Constitution a central topic for these scholars and the one that they wrote about most passionately.

An account of the nineteenth-century understandings can best be presented by returning to Lefroy, who wrote about constitutional law as well as the common law, especially a massive text about the division of powers that appeared in 1897.[78] Like Dicey, he sought to synthesize principles, setting out 68 of them, each followed by an extensive discussion of the cases from which it was derived. The cases were analysed in ways that tended to make them consistent with each other, and the principles were constructed in ways that made a coherent pattern. Both were divorced from their social and political context, including Confederation itself, which was barely mentioned, and the struggle between the Dominion and the provinces that raged while Lefroy was writing.

The interpretation of the *BNA Act* was far from as consistent and coherent as Lefroy believed, both at the time he wrote and after his death. Most scholars agree that by the middle of the 1930s, the power of the Dominion government was much weaker than the makers of Confederation had intended, and less than any reasonable reading of the *BNA Act* would permit. When and how this reduction happened is still debated, but a reasonably safe suggestion is that much of it was done by Lord Haldane in three cases decided during the 1920s. The last of these three was *Toronto Electric Commissioners v. Snider*, decided in 1925.[79] In the following year, H.A. Smith, who taught at McGill, wrote a case comment, which set the frame for analysis for the next decade, at least.[80]

Smith arrived in Canada in 1921, from England, where he had been born and educated. For eight years, he was a powerful force, teaching and writing about a wide range of subjects, and making ambitious proposals for reforming legal education.[81] In his comment about *Snider*, he argued that the Privy Council had misunderstood the structure of sections 91 and 92, making the Dominion's power to legislate for 'peace, order and good government' one that was to be used only in emergencies, rather than an omnibus power to legislate for the benefit of the country. The result was that Canada had a constitution 'the precise opposite of that which our fathers hoped and endeavoured to attain.'[82] Smith argued further that the reason the Privy Council went astray was its misguided approach to interpretation, which I shall consider in the next section. In short, it failed to consider the context of the making of the *BNA Act*, and the clearly expressed vision of the founders they would have found there.

After Smith left, three Canadian scholars emerged: W.P.M. Kennedy, who has already been introduced, Frank Scott, of McGill, and Vincent MacDonald, of Dalhousie. Scott, the youngest, is still an awesome figure. After studying humanities at Oxford in the early 1920s and taking a law degree at McGill, he began to teach in 1928. Even then, he was not only a legal scholar, but also a poet, a socialist activist, an advocate for civil liberties, and sympathetic to French-Canadian culture. During the next four decades, he pursued all these paths with passion, becoming a major poet and a founder of the CCF, defending civil liberties against the Duplessis regime, and offering Canada a vision of a bicultural country.[83] Compared to such remarkable figures as Kennedy and Scott, MacDonald was relatively straightforward. After getting a law degree from Dalhousie, he practised in Toronto and Halifax before returning to Dalhousie to teach in 1930, where he became dean in 1934.[84] Among the three, Kennedy was the most prolific, by far, writing seven substantial pieces between 1929 and 1937, as well as a handful of short notes. MacDonald and Scott each wrote half as much.

All three continued the attack on the Privy Council, largely in the framework Smith established. The makers of Confederation intended to make a strong national government, responsible for all matters of general or national scope, and expressed this vision clearly in the *BNA Act*. The Privy Council ignored the terms and their context, and the result was that the Dominion had far less power than had been intended, and the provinces had far more. Canada's federalism was fundamentally different from the federalism its makers had intended.

During the first few years of the attack, from Smith's comment in 1926 to around 1930, the protests were about the technique of interpretation – the failure to consider the context. In the early 1930s, a different kind of protest emerged: the mistaken interpretation had rendered the Dominion unable to perform crucial functions. This protest had two branches, both based on a firm belief that the original design of the *BNA Act* – to create a strong Dominion government – was the appropriate allocation of powers for the modern nation Canada had become. The first branch of the protest was about the power to implement treaties. Canada must be able to make treaties and to implement them, and the powers to perform these functions should be assigned to the Dominion. The Dominion government doubtless had power to make treaties, but its power to implement them was at best problematic. Second, Canada should establish a welfare and regulatory state, and only the Dominion could undertake this function, but its power was at best partial and incomplete. These scholars were the first to declare this vision of Canada in a sustained way: a modern nation, having power to determine its own international obligations, and a strong Dominion government, with responsibility and power to guide the making of a modern state.

Most of the writing was about the second branch. At the outset, it was a protest about the confusion caused by uncertainty about the teams of the division of powers. For example, in 1932, Scott asked, 'What has become of our federalism? It is a legal morass in which ten governments are always floundering; a boon to lawyers and obstructionist politicians, but the bane of the poor public whose pathetic plea is simply for cheap and efficient government.'[85] At the same time, though, he was concerned about the shrinking of the Dominion's powers, and gave as examples its inability to regulate the grain market, water power in the St Lawrence River, airplanes, and unemployment insurance, all subjects of national importance. In the same year, Kennedy feared that the powers and the independence of the provinces could be exploited by 'vast economic interests,' observing that 'the interests at the local centres are often too strong to allow progress, and they are all too frequently able to strengthen their economic and financial purposes by an appeal to provincial rights.'[86]

As the ravages of the Depression mounted, the protests became passionate. In 1934, Kennedy declared a crisis:

> The truth is that we have outgrown the *British North America Act*. The Dominion of Canada is attempting to-day to carry on the highly complex life of a modern industrial state under a constitution drawn up for a primitive community, scarcely emerging from pioneer agricultural conditions ... Worse still, under cover of all this has been preserved the legal, political and economic philosophy *of laissez-faire* utilitarianism ... Upheld with an almost suicidal tenacity, provincial 'rights' have become national wrongs ... We have now a clear choice to make: shall we continue as a loose league of 'sovereign' provinces, into which the unfortunate judgments of the Privy Council had practically transformed us, surviving legally in order to break culturally and economically? Or shall we boldly recognise that a nation of vast potential wealth and remarkable human achievements must not be sacrificed at a constitutional altar erected in a far-off pioneer past, and itself long since robbed of creative vitality by the barren processes of judicial obscuranticism?[87]

A year later, MacDonald said simply that the Constitution is 'ill-adapted to our new status within the empire, to our present social and economic organization and needs, and to prevailing political theories which indicate the propriety or necessity of a greater degree of national control over, and governmental intervention in, matters of social welfare and business activity.'[88]

When the Privy Council declared most of the New Deal legislation *ultra vires* in 1937, the three joined in a remarkable symposium in the *Canadian Bar Review*. They all agreed that the *BNA Act* as it had been interpreted was a denial of the intentions of the makers, and was now woefully inappropriate for a modern nation. There was no hope for change from the courts, and therefore it must be amended and appeals to the Privy Council must be terminated. Scott, after retelling the story of the frustration of the original design, said, 'None but foreign judges ignorant of the Canadian environment and none too well versed in Canadian constitutional law could have caused this constitutional revolution.'[89] A few pages later, speaking of the restrictions on cooperation between the Dominion and the provinces, he said,

> This legalistic straining at technicalities will do little to enhance the prestige of the courts ... Canada has suffered a national set-back of grievous proportions. A federal government that cannot concern itself with questions of wages and hours and unemployment in industry, whose attempts at the regulation of trade and commerce are consistently thwarted, which has no power to join its sister nations in the establishment of world living standards, and which cannot even feel on sure ground when by some political miracle it is supported in a legislative scheme by all the provinces, is a government wholly unable to direct and to control our economic development ... It would seem ... that the doctrines of *laissez-faire* are in practice receiving ample protection from the courts.[90]

The rejection of the nineteenth-century beliefs and the embrace of the regulatory and welfare state were obvious throughout, together with an urgent need to respond to the Depression. Seen from this perspective, these protests are a remarkable parallel to the protests of scholars in the United States to *Lochner v. New York*.[91] Perverse interpretations, shaped by political faiths from the nineteenth century, had frustrated making the modern state. At the same time, the distance from scholars in the late nineteenth century like Lefroy was made clear by the role of scholars as critics, their open belief that the law must express the needs and values of the present, and their aspiration to create the new state.[92]

Interpretation

The furor about federalism was a part – a dramatic one – of a much wider question: how should courts interpret statutes and constitutions? Again, the beginning is an account of the thinking in the late nineteenth century. The basic principle was that the courts must determine and implement the intent of the legislature. The primary step in making this determination was to decide whether the words being interpreted had a clear meaning, and if they did, it must be followed, even if it was contrary to the known preferences of the legislature, or to the court's sense of justice or the public good. These lawyers did not, though, contrary to what is sometimes now assumed, believe that words always had clear meanings, considered either alone or in their textual context. If the words did not have clear meaning (or if the meaning led to a startling result) most texts agreed that the court must reconstruct the intent of the legislature.

Nonetheless, this call for an inquiry into intention was obscured, even sometimes negated, by sharp restrictions on the sources the courts could consider. Among the sources that were permitted, the primary ones were the common law and other statutes. What had happened in the legislature when the statute was discussed was put firmly beyond bounds. In this scheme, the dominant source of meanings became the common law, especially its presumptions, such as the preferences for property and individual liberty.[93]

Two Canadian examples illustrate this approach. The first is Lefroy's federalism text. For him, interpretation of the *BNA Act* entailed discerning the meaning embedded in its terms. Many of these terms were terse and general, leaving much to be determined by courts, but even for this purpose, he rejected considering 'the demands of public policy and the public welfare.'[94] The second example is a debate about the decision of the Privy Council in the *Royal Bank* case, which need not be described at length. Two quotations will suffice. Replying to a claim that no one could doubt the 'perfect justice or wisdom' of the Privy Council's decision, Lefroy said,

All I can assume to discuss is law, not perfect justice or wisdom. Law may be, and ought to be, just and wise. But whether it is or not, is a matter with which a lawyer, as such, has nothing to do. That is what the old philosopher Hobbes meant when he laid down the dictum so shocking to weak minds, that 'no law can be unjust.'[95]

Another participant, Henry Labatt, agreed. Faced with the claim that the Privy Council was ignorant of Canadian conditions, he argued that its ignorance was really a blessing:

A controversy determined by jurists of ample practical experience, who consider the law and the facts with the intellectual detachment of college professors forming an opinion in regard to the soundness of abstract doctrines, may well be said to have been determined under ideal conditions.[96]

The first appearance of a new world was the case comment about *Snider* by Herbert Smith, which was introduced in the last section. He agreed that the object of interpretation was to discover the intent of the legislature as expressed in the words of the statute, but he argued that meanings depended upon purposes and contexts. Therefore, evidence about the making of a statute, such as parliamentary debates and public speeches, should be considered. Yet the English courts had deprived themselves of this information by an 'arbitrary and unreasonable rule.'[97] This argument was ultimately much more than an attack on a small corner of doctrine. It was, as well, a challenge to the power of the courts to govern interpretation by imposing the common law presumptions and to preserve values that were being threatened by the rise of the welfare and regulatory state.

To understand the Canadian scholarship that followed Smith, it is necessary first to understand developments in the United States that began in the late 1920s and early 1930s. An exchange in 1930 between Max Radin and James Landis is a landmark.[98] Radin denied that the search for the intent of the legislature could be a meaningful undertaking. For issues that had not been foreseen, the legislature could have had no intent at all. Moreover, a legislature could not have an intent in any meaningful sense, for the legislators who supported a typical statute shared a multitude of different understandings of its meanings, and most of them had little or no knowledge of its details. The chances that they would all have the same intent about a particular issue were smaller than 'infinitesimally small.'[99] The text did, though, set limits beyond which the judge must not go, and within which a choice must be made. Radin's claim became famous:

Somewhere, somehow, a judge is impelled to make his selection – not quite
freely as we have seen, but within generous limits as a rule – by those
psychical elements which make him the kind of person that he is. That this
is pure subjectivism and therefore an unfortunate situation is beside the
point.[100]

In his reply, Landis argued first that an intent about the particular
issue at stake was much more likely to be apparent than Radin had
suggested, especially from looking at the evidence of legislative history.
More important, if no intent in this sense were discoverable, he proposed that the court be guided by the purpose of the statute, that is, by
the general policy of the legislature. '[L]egislative purposes and aims
are the important guideposts for statutory interpretation.'[101]

In Canada, three major articles appeared during the next handful of
years, written by Alex Corry, John Willis, and Vincent MacDonald.
Corry and Willis were in the mainstream of change. Both explicitly
rejected the nineteenth century and proposed a new approach. Because
Willis did the more effective job of the rejection, and Corry contributed
more to the new approach, they can be best presented by taking Willis
first.

Willis was born in England, was educated at Winchester and Oxford.
In 1929, he went to Harvard for two years, where he studied under
Felix Frankfurter. Upon returning to England, his hopes for a teaching
job were frustrated by the Depression, so he went to Dalhousie to take a
job for a year and stayed in Canada for the rest of his life. To me, he was
the most imaginative scholar of this generation. Even as late as the
1970s and 1980s, he continued to be admired by administrative law
scholars.

'Statute Interpretation in a Nutshell'[102] appeared in 1937, written in
the preceding summer as a guide for students about to take his new
course in legislation. Still a delight to read, it is one of the landmarks in
the campaign to demolish the traditional approach. The central message was announced at the outset, and clear throughout. The traditional
sources of meaning were all hopeless guides for 'guessing' (a suggestive word that he used throughout) what a court would do, and for
guiding a judge. The words could not determine results, especially in
the world of the modern regulatory and welfare state, in which 'wide
and general language' abounded. Nor could precedent. Instead, the
doctrine offered a set of approaches among which judges could choose
freely, and which served, in the end, to justify some 'desired result' –

some result desired by the judges. In the same way, the courts chose whether to invoke a presumption and among them, which one to choose. 'What will they do and not what will they say, is your concern.'[103]

Yet, although demolition was the main aim of 'Nutshell,' Willis did not say that interpretation was inescapably no more than an expression of personal and political attitudes. In one short passage, in talking about the common law doctrine, he came to the mischief rule – the courts should be guided by the 'mischief' at which the statute was aimed. This approach was 'so sensible and so thoroughly in accord with the constitutional principle of the "supremacy of Parliament"' that it was 'amazing' to find it used so rarely.[104]

Corry is now widely known as a political scientist, and few remember that he began his academic career as a law teacher. Born in southwestern Ontario, he farmed during World War I and then went west to study law at the College of Law of the University of Saskatchewan. After graduating and articling for a year, he went to Oxford for another law degree. In 1927, he returned to Saskatchewan to teach at the College of Law, remaining there until the 1934–5 academic year, when he spent a year's leave at Columbia Law School. After returning to Saskatchewan for a year, he went to Queen's University, forsaking law as his primary interest for political science.[105] 'Administrative Law and the Interpretation of Statutes'[106] appeared in 1936, a few months after he returned from Columbia.

Corry's rejection of the past was based on Radin. Both words and intent were hopeless guides to meaning, for words typically had no clear meanings, and intent was a myth.[107] The words did, though, set limits, within which the judge must choose. Like Landis, Corry argued that the judge must respect and implement the purpose of the legislature, grounding this obligation on society's basic commitment to democracy.[108]

> Though the intention of the legislature is a fiction, the purpose or object of the legislation is very real. No enactment is ever passed for the sake of its details; it is passed in an attempt to realize a social purpose.[109]

This purpose was 'very real,' an ascertainable fact, and therefore the judge was not a 'despot,' even though the judge's opinions about 'the proper functioning of the state and its relation to the individual' must shape the choices about some ambiguities about details. Only rarely was the judge left to 'trust himself.' This 'real' purpose was a particular form of the social record in which Pound and Wright sought guidance.[110]

Looking at his footnotes and the surrounding literature, especially the exchange between Radin and Landis, Corry's proposals made a significant step in the mainstream of change. He embraced Landis' idea of purpose, but presented it more fully. More important, not only did he ground the obligation in democracy, he saw it as an obligation to cooperate with the legislatures. As well as rejecting the past, Corry, like Willis, instructed his readers to watch what courts did, rather than what they said. This admonition was a rejection of a faith in doctrine, paralleling Wright's call to be 'realistic' and the rejection of 'logic.'

For both Willis and Corry there was much more at stake than a preference for the word 'purpose' rather than the word 'intention.' Like Wright, although much more openly, and like the protests at the decisions about federalism, their thinking about interpretation was part of a campaign for a change in politics. The older approach to interpretation, especially the presumptions about property and individual liberty, defied statutes that were intended to regulate property and redistribute wealth. A new doctrine was required by a new society. The fighting edge of the talk about purpose, whatever its analytical difference from intent may have been, was an attack on the common law and its values as a source of meaning, and a demand that judges respect these social and political changes and interpret statutes generously. In the introduction to 'Administrative Law and the Interpretation of Statutes' Corry spoke of the modem world in which 'the activities of the state are increasing rapidly day by day,'[111] and suggested that often 'efficient administration is being embarrassed by judicial interpretation.'[112] And at the end of the discussion of interpretation, he gave judges a blunt warning about the consequences of recalcitrance:

> [T]here is no other way in which judges can supply the necessary co-operation for maintaining an orderly process of social change. The modern state everywhere is engaged in adjusting itself to the machine age. We are attempting to do under forms of law in an orderly way what is accompanied elsewhere by violent upheavals, quite regardless of law, of rights, or of individuals. That is the meaning of the statutes which give us social legislation and state control over various forms of economic life. At present the judges interpret and apply these statues and thus can further or obstruct their objects. Unless they are familiar with the aim and purpose of the leg-

islation so as to aid in the adjustment, the orderly process will fail or pass to other hands.[113]

Like Corry, but at much greater length and more colourfully, Willis demonstrated that the courts had frustrated modern legislation, especially by invoking presumptions. The presumptions that counselled against interpretations that changed the common law or interfered with established rights and property were tolerably accurate expressions of legislative attitudes in the nineteenth century, for legislatures then were not inclined to take such radical steps.

> But times have changed ... If in 1937, a court resorts to these old presumptions, it is doing something very different from attempting to ascertain the probable intention of the legislature, it is flying in the face of the legislature. Only one conclusion can be drawn from the present judicial addiction to the ancient presumptions and that is that the presumptions have no longer anything to do with the intent of the legislature, they are a means of controlling that intent. Together they form a sort of common law 'Bill of Rights.' English and Canadian judges have no power to declare Acts unconstitutional merely because they depart from the good old ways of thought; they can, however, use the presumptions to mould innovation into some accord with the old notions. The presumptions are in short 'an ideal constitution' for England and Canada.[114]

If these two articles were in the mainstream, the third, written by MacDonald, was certainly not. Yet it is one that has a remarkable appeal to modern scholars. It dealt with the power to implement treaties, and particularly with section 132 of the *BNA Act*, which gave the Dominion power to implement obligations of Canada 'as part of the British Empire arising under treaties between the Empire and ... foreign countries.' These terms seemed to be limited to treaties entered into by Britain for its colony, and inapplicable to treaties made by Canada as an independent nation. Moreover, if intent was the test, surely the British Parliament in 1867 could barely have conceived of a colony having such a power, let alone have decided to confer it. Did it have any effect after Canada had become an independent nation?

In 1933, after the Privy Council gave several confusing interpretations of section 132, MacDonald wrote 'Canada's Power to Perform Treaty Obligations.'[115] The essence of his argument was that the basic purpose of section 132 was to give the federal government power to implement all of Canada's international obligations. Even though its particular terms were designed for the obligations of Canada as a colony, it should be interpreted 'progressively and liberally'[116] to give the same general power, decades later, after Canada had become an independent nation. The courts must

> effectually translate into modern terms the language of 1867 so that it will speak with equal vitality today with regard to circumstances essentially similar to those envisaged for its application in 1867. A constitution is never to be outgrown but to speak permanently and to be given a progressive construction which will keep it an apt instrument of government even in its application to circumstances not foreseen by its framers.[117]

MacDonald's argument depended upon a crucial distinction between, on the one hand, the particular contexts and outcomes that the makers had in mind and the particular terms they had used – which he usually labelled 'intent,' and, on the other hand, the general policy of the legislature, which he labelled 'purpose,' 'essential purpose,' 'spirit,' 'dominant intention,' and 'general policy.' What made him distinctive was not simply giving priority to purpose, rather than intent, for we have seen that other scholars, especially Landis and Corry, made this argument at the same time, and made it more clearly. Instead, what was distinctive was his argument that interpretation should be shaped by the contemporary context, and that it might be at odds with the particular perceptions of the original intent and even the terms that expressed that intent. Much of the classic literature had proclaimed the need for law to respond to changing needs and contexts, but no scholar had been so bold as MacDonald.[118]

Administrative Law

In England, the expansion of the welfare and regulatory state brought much debate and much protest from the legal establishment. The protest was aimed, of course, at the new politics of regulation and redistribution. As well, though, it was aimed at the institutions and doctrine that implemented the changes, especially the expanded functions of the executive. The foundations of these constitutional protests were articulated in Dicey's text, especially in his version of the rule of law. The new state threatened liberty by displacing the courts and the common law, and giving arbitrary powers to the executive, which became the modern embodiment of the Stuart kings.

The protests continued throughout the 1920s, and in response, the government appointed the Committee on Ministers' Powers in 1929, just before Lord Chief Justice Hewart published his famous tirade, *The New Despotism*.[119] In Canada, the legal establishment made the same protests and lauded Lord Hewart when he came on a lecture tour. In contrast, the Canadian legal scholars embraced the new state and the politics it expressed, and the Depression made their embrace passionate. Among these, Willis, Corry, Kennedy, Jacob Finkelman, and E.A. Hopkins were outstanding.[120] They probably did not think much about their intended audience, but the journals in which they wrote and the terms and analysis they used pointed to the legal profession. Their message, though, was different from Wright's, because they sought to make a larger change in attitudes and commitments than he did.

Willis was the jewel. His first major publication, *The Parliamentary Powers of English Government Departments*,[121] appeared in 1933 as a response to *The New Despotism*. Two years later, he wrote 'Three Approaches to Administrative Law,'[122] in which the central theme was the design of the new institutions. Two years later, in 1938, came 'Statute Interpretation in a Nutshell,' followed quickly by two more articles. The first, 'Administrative Law and the British North America Act,'[123] elaborated an argument that he introduced in the 'Nutshell.' American lawyers would feel more at home in Canada than the absence of Bill of Rights might suggest, for the Canadian courts had employed interpretation and presumptions to fashion parallel protections of property and contracts. The second, 'Section 96 of the British North America Act,'[124] developed one thread of this argument at length. Under the cloak of interpreting this 'innocuous section,' the courts had created a substantial limitation on the powers of provincial legislatures to create agencies exercising judicial powers, thereby smuggling the doctrine of separation of powers into the Canadian Constitution. As well, in 1941, just beyond my round ending date of 1940, he edited a collection of essays, entitled *Canadian Boards at Work*.[125]

Corry wrote two articles. The first, 'Administrative Law in Canada,'[126] which appeared in 1933, described the new politics and the need for new institutions it had created. Throughout, his analysis was sensible and useful, although it lacked the imagination of Willis or of his own article about interpretation. The second appeared in 1936 – the same year as the interpretation article, and presaged his shift to political science. It dealt with the public corporation, and especially its promise to solve the central problem of the twentieth century: 'to make economic government ... responsible to the public weal.'[127] As well, he did a study for the Rowell-Sirois Commission, which is well known to Canadian scholars, even though it was never published. Entitled 'The Growth of Government Activities since Confederation,'[128] it was just what its title promised: a detailed description of the expansion of government, which was a large accomplishment and still useful, even though by 1939 none of it was distinctive.

Kennedy wrote only one major article, 'Aspects of Administrative Law in Canada,'[129] which appeared in 1934. It demonstrated his remarkably wide range of interests, and an enthusiasm for change and a perceptiveness that were remarkable in someone who was then 65 years old and had already done major scholarship in an entirely different field and was at the same time administering the law school and writing about constitutional law. It included a self-congratulatory account of the work being done at his school, including the introduction of a course in Administrative Law in 1931, the first in Canada, which Kennedy assigned to a young faculty member, Jacob Finkelman.

Finkelman graduated from Kennedy's school in 1926, worked for a year to save his tuition, and spent three years at Osgoode Hall. He was appointed a lecturer in 1930, becoming the first Jew appointed to a permanent position at the university. In 1936, he published his major contribution to administrative law, 'Separation of Powers: A Study in Administrative Law.'[130] Three years later, in 1939, he wrote 'Government by Civil Servants,'[131] where he dealt more generally with the new state. Last in this group came Russell Hopkins, who was born on the prairies, graduated from the Law School at Saskatchewan, and went to Oxford as a Rhodes scholar. After teaching at Kennedy's school for a year, he returned to Saskatchewan for financial and family reasons, replacing Corry. His 'Administrative Justice in Canada'[132] was a comprehensive survey of the thinking that had accumulated since the late 1920s.

All these scholars shared a belief that this new state was a product of fundamental change in social values and demands. Phrases such as 'new social standards,' 'new standards,' and 'new social philosophy' appeared throughout their writing, and Corry announced, 'Socialistic legislation ... is the mainspring of administrative discretion.'[133] They also believed that this change was a response to political demands by segments of society that had been disadvantaged by the workings of nineteenth-century economic liberalism. Their understanding of laissez-faire, a term they commonly used, may have been simplistic, but they firmly believed that it was harsh and unfair. Finkelman's account was more forceful than the others, but they would not have disagreed:

> Then came the rude awakening. The romance was ended. Laissez-faire had failed to bring happiness to the masses of mankind. In fact, the untold misery and suffering and the social waste which followed in the wake of the new industrial system caused a revulsion of feeling which is gradually undermining even the positive achievements of the past century ... [T]he operation of that doctrine doomed millions of people to want and privation.[134]

They were not philosophers and only Kennedy speculated about the theory of this new state. Building on theories of the new state, including the English pluralists and, likely, another faculty member at the University of Toronto, Robert MacIver,[135] and scattered European writers, he argued that the state should be conceived not as an abstract sovereign, but as an association constructed by society to achieve shared purposes. In the Lafayette lectures, his manifesto, he argued,

> [W]e must ... conceive of the state as a definite group-life ... established by society as a means to achieve certain purposes ... It is not a mere policeman standing on guard to see that we get our share of liberty and of rights, and that our neighbour gets his ... In other words, the state is a great social engineer and its laws ... are socially created rules of social engineering.[136]

Beginning with this understanding, he turned to the relation between the individual and the state, arguing that the individual could only be understood and could only flourish as a member of a community, and that because the state was made by the will of the citizens, there was 'no antithesis between individual and state.' Instead, the function of the state was to enable the citizen 'to realize the good life,' and be, 'in truth, civis.'[137] His thinking about the state also included a challenge to the Austinian sovereignty of the state that was at the heart of nineteenth-century English legal theory. As early as the middle 1920s (thinking not about the administrative state, but about federalism and the struggles to make the League of Nations), he declared sovereignty to have been vanquished by both theory and facts. 'No one seriously follows John Austin, and sovereignty is as dead as Queen Anne.'[138]

Even though the others eschewed such flights of theory, they were not content merely to observe and record the changes. Instead, they were participants. In short, paralleling the writing about federalism and interpretation, they sought to help construct and legitimate the legal structure of this new state and the legal structure of the new liberalism.[139] Kennedy proclaimed this new role, and called on scholars to be creative in pursuing it:

> [T]he teacher of law or jurist is no longer merely a contemplative creature describing the law as it exists. The very development of the administrative system has forced him to be constructive, not only in interpreting the tendencies of social existence, but also in assisting in moulding and guiding them.[140]

The basic ideas about this structure emerged in England during the 1920s, and were accepted by the Donoughmore Committee in 1932.[141] The existing institutions of government, particularly the legislatures and the courts, were adequate to perform the limited functions of the nineteenth-century state, but they did not have the time, the knowledge and expertise, or the appropriate structures and procedures to perform the new functions. Appropriate institutions must be created, if they did not already exist, and given the necessary powers.

The Canadian scholars echoed these arguments, most of them in a moderate way. Willis, though, was fervent about the need to respect expertise. In *Parliamentary Powers* he asked, '[W]hy should our system of government be conceived of as a pyramid with the courts at the apex ... and the actions of the Civil Service, the best informed and most forward looking body of persons in England today, regulated from the point of view of an outside jurisdiction?'[142] Forty pages later, he said that the purpose of most delegation was 'to give full play to the determinations of the expert.'[143] None of the others went so far, and Finkelman had reservations, wondering, in particular, whether the Canadian civil service had developed the necessary professionalism.[144] None of them wondered about a tension between democracy and the experts, although their frequent use of the distinction between policy – the responsibility of the legislature – and implementation and detail – the responsibility of the experts – suggests their answer.

The Canadian scholars realized that even though the new state had been accepted, questions of design remained and would change as needs and values changed. They saw a fluid future, in which change would be constant, and flexibility and experiments would be needed, often using phrases such as 'experimental laboratories' and 'new experiments.'[145] They tended to look to experience and 'reality' as guides to action, and some, especially Willis, Finkelman, and Kennedy expressly called for research into 'what really happens,' a call corresponding to the calls for realism and what courts did. Moreover, most of them were sensitive to the Depression, which amplified their sense of urgency, and to the distinctive circumstances of Canada.

Willis was the one who thought most about these questions of design. In 'Three Approaches' he said the central question was 'how to fit into our constitutional structure these new institutions whose growth seems inevitable.'[146] This question was essentially a choice of an approach to designing institutions. After concluding that the approach of the courts and the 'conceptual approach' were utterly inadequate, he suggested a 'functional approach':

> The problem put is, how shall the powers of government be divided up? The problem is neither one of law nor of formal logic, but of expediency. The functional approach examines, first, the existing functions of existing governmental bodies in order to discover what kind of work each has in the past done best, and assigns the new work to the body which experience has shown best fitted to perform work of that type. If there is no such body, a near one is created ad hoc.[147]

Here, 'functionalism' had much the same meaning as 'empirical and pragmatic' had for Wright. The agencies must be designed and assessed to serve current, concrete social need, and not some abstract ideal. Later, in *Canadian Boards at Work*, Willis specified some particular issues of design, and suggested a connection between his functionalism and the earlier developments in philosophy by saying that an agency must be understood by knowing what it did.[148]

This thinking about designing the new institutions and powers was entangled with the response to the claims of critics that Parliament, the courts, and individual liberty were all threatened. One thread of these claims, based on the principle of separation of powers, was that judicial powers should not be given to the executive or agencies, or at least that any delegation should be restricted and mistrusted, to protect individual liberty and abuse of power. The new powers threatened to offend the principle. In England, the outcome was expressed in vague phrases such as 'quasi-judicial.' In Canada, Finkelman made the most elaborate response. Separation of powers was not a part of the Constitution or the common law, and it was not and should not be a rigid rule.[149] Precision was both impossible and undesirable. Instead, the allocation of functions should 'serve practical ends ... grow[ing] out of necessity and common sense.' In particular, the courts needed discretion, to 'balance between working efficiency and the life of the individual citizen.'[150] Willis made another closely related response: the rigid form of the principle was an unworkable and incoherent product of lawyers' tendency to 'conceptual thinking.' 'Difficulties arise ... as soon as maxims enunciating generalities acquire particular and fixed meanings ... [T]here is no essential distinction between the three supposedly distinct types of powers.'[151] The only test was, what sorts of questions were courts best equipped to administer – the functional test.

The major claim of the critics, though, was simply that the agencies recklessly intruded upon liberty, through mistake or excessive zeal. Here, the scholars made two kinds of responses. The first, made by Willis alone, was a stark demonstration of the importance of facts and experience, contrasted to abstract faiths and doctrines. The claim was wrong, because there had been no abuses. Speaking of powers to modify statutes, he said,

> It is easy to understand a lawyer's horror at this section, for there is nowhere any provision for control by the courts ... No one can deny that there is some risk involved in so wholesale a delegation, but so far there has been no suggestion of hardship to individuals or of usurpation of the parliamentary power. The generality of the words used is not in itself important; the proper question is what has in fact been done under those words ... I was almost disappointed to find that the orders were uniformly uninteresting.[152]

The second response, which was the more common one, took different forms, but its essence was that the intrusions upon liberty were typically limitations of property interests entailed in programs of regulation and redistribution that had been chosen democratically. The critics were simply defying democratic choice, and the courts had shared this defiance by hostility to the new state. Willis was the most expansive and insightful. Throughout, his claims were not sweeping abstract generalizations, but instead, grounded upon the results of the cases. For example, in both 'Nutshell' and 'Administrative Law' he analysed cases about presumptions, and in 'Three Approaches' he considered cases on discretions and procedural requirements, where much of the doctrine was about the highly technical limits of the prerogative writs, and where the results were 'a direct product of judicial hostility.'[153]

He saw the values of class and property as the major source of the hostility. In *The Parliamentary Powers* he pointed to '[t]he scandals from a social point of view ... whereby great improvement schemes were held up for months by slum owners upon technical points,'[154] and in his account of presumptions in 'Administrative Law' he said,

> The years of depression since 1929 have induced legislatures to pass laws which are right out of line with traditional ways of thought and therefore distasteful both to those guardians of the past, the lawyers, and to their wealthy clients who have, of course, been adversely affected by these laws. Once more the old ghost of Lord Coke stalks abroad.[155]

But class and property were not the entire source of hostility. By training and experience, the minds of lawyers were shaped to have a predilection for the common law and its principles, and for courts, contrasted to the statutes that made the new state, the agencies that administered it, and their discretions

> to a lawyer a statute does not speak the living language of the day. Lawyers' ears are attuned to the accents of a forgotten past, new commands are faintly apprehended through the fog of the Common Law.[156]
> A statute is strictly construed. It is placed against the background of a common law whose assumptions are directly opposed to those of modern legislation ... The common law has much to say about private rights, little of public duties. It is uncompromisingly individualistic. Rights of property and freedom from personal restraint are sacred ... The judges have never forgotten the part which their predecessors took in the struggle between king and commons: as men they are uncompromisingly hostile to the executive.[157]

In these responses to the critics, both Finkelman and Willis argued that the doctrine had not given coherent, determinate results. Neither suggested that doctrine was inescapably indeterminate or that judicial decisions were inescapably the product of politics or chance, and their own common law writing demonstrated a faith in the enterprise. Instead, their protests were aimed at the use of rigid abstract concepts, divorced from context, experience, and function. These arguments suggest the American Realists, although the suggestion depends greatly upon a choice of identity for the Realists. Neither of them offered any references to make the connection, and a much firmer connection was to the rejection of 'logic.' Their aim was not so much to analyse judicial reasoning as it was to demonstrate the effect of class and professional prejudice.

In a sharp contrast to postwar scholarship, supervision of the agencies was rarely a major topic or a major battleground. Instead, the discussions tended to be sanguine, except for some support for rejecting review by courts on functional grounds and creating an administrative court instead.[158] Kennedy was the most imaginative. He considered the potential role of legislatures in supervising rule-making by the executive, stressing the need to protect democratic principles and encouraging advisory committees. He also suggested a specialized branch of the courts for review; and, most remarkable, he made a suggestion that would become part of modern thinking decades later: the most promising way to facilitate review was to encourage the agencies 'to develop their standards consciously, and by requiring the publication of reasons for their decisions.'[159]

The Public Law Scholarship Reviewed

Much of this writing about public law was simply excellent, especially compared to writing in England, which was scant indeed. Saying this, though, does little more than please my national pride. More important, it was different from the contemporary Canadian common law scholarship in three important ways.[160]

First, it openly espoused political beliefs, especially campaigning for the new liberalism, and it openly considered context. Like Wright, all of these scholars, except Scott, shared the prevailing liberal faiths of most Canadian intellectuals. Because Scott's writing about public law was primarily about federalism, and because the making of a socialist state required the same strong central government as the new liberalism did, he did not differ from them. Perhaps the reason for this openness may be that the new state, which the scholars wanted so much, would be made by the legislature, and the courts were at best supplementary institutions, and at worst, undemocratic obstacles. The lessons that law cannot be separated from its context and that the legislature should make the major social changes were needed only in a world in which the courts were at the centre of the scholars' legal visions, and not in a country where legislatures were supreme and that had used the state so much to make its economy. The need for detachment and objectivity in doing common law analysis was not as pressing for this work.

Second, it was greatly influenced by the English experience, especially the rise of the regulatory and welfare slate, the debates at the end of the 1920s, and the pervasive perception of the tension between individual liberty and government tasks. Lord Hewart and his cohort needed to be refuted. Except for Corry's article about interpretation, the experience and writing in the United States was mentioned only very rarely, and the contrast of its appeal to Wright neatly reflected the delicate and shifting balance of the two empires in Canadian life generally. Third, it contained little analysis of doctrine – and almost all of the analysis it did contain was directed towards responding to critics, not describing doctrine to help lawyers. Again, the reason may be simply that this analysis was not among the most pressing issues.

Labour Law: Herein of Bora Laskin and the State of the Art

As the devastation of the Depression mounted during the 1930s, the struggle between workers and employers intensified. Violence often erupted, and the state often intervened to support the employers. Late in the decade, the conflicts began to appear more and more frequently in the courts, and two scholars began to write extensively about the results. One was Jacob Finkelman, whom we have already seen in the discussion of administrative law, and the other was Bora Laskin. Born in Fort William, he came to the University of Toronto and Kennedy's school in 1930, where he heard Wright's manifesto. After graduation, he went to Osgoode Hall for three years, at the same time working for an MA at Toronto. In 1936–7, he went to Harvard for an LLM, and then returned to Toronto, where he worked for a commercial legal publisher and involved himself in labour research and education, until Kennedy appointed him in 1940, at the very end of my story.[161]

Both Finkelman and Laskin believed in the legitimacy and utility of collective bargaining and peaceful picketing. Finkelman declared, perhaps a bit hopefully, '[T]he social utility of trade unions in the modern industrial community has become almost axiomatic.'[162] They also shared the belief that the courts had too often imposed the values of their class and the nineteenth-century faith in individual liberty.

Finkelman's major contribution was a long article about picketing,[163] in which his major objective was to 'analyze the decisions ... for the purpose of discovering the principles, if any, upon which the courts proceed.'[164] This might well have been the purpose of a scholar in the late nineteenth century, but as well as providing a guide for the profession, Finkelman sought to demonstrate confusion and inconsistency in the doctrine, and a pervasive hostility to labour, and as well to demonstrate that both were greater in Canada than in England. Speaking of the lingering effects of the nineteenth century, he spoke about the way half-forgotten ideas from the past can shape attitudes:

> [T]he notion that there exists a right to trade has coloured the whole interpretation of the legal principles relating to trade unions and has often beguiled the courts into resting judgments on vague generalisations relating to freedom of trade and individual liberty, rather than on relevant legal principles. In fact, anyone reading the voluminous judgments relating to trade-union activities cannot but feel that the approach of the courts has been instinctive (the act complained of is abhorrent to their economic, social, and political predilections: such conduct must be circumvented) rather than properly judicial and impartial.[165]

Laskin's major contributions were two articles, both comments on recent Canadian cases, both written while he was at Harvard, both demonstrating his support for labour, and both shaped by American scholarship and his teachers. The first,[166] which dealt with the trial judgments in a couple of cases from Manitoba, began by advocating the use of American cases as guides for deciding labour issues, and criticizing the courts for blindly following English cases that had been repudiated by statute. Instead, the courts should be willing to use the statutes themselves as starting points for common law development that accommodated the changing social values, an idea that seems lilkely to have been stimulated by reading Pound or Landis.

In the cases that prompted the article, the court barred picketing in the absence of lawful strike. Laskin disagreed, arguing that the picketing was justified by 'the remoter interests of labour generally. '[M]ore than the sanctity of profits is involved in these controversies.'[167] As well, assuming the workers could picket, the court prohibited statements about working conditions that used such terms as 'unfair.' Laskin was scornful. '[T]he bare statement of unfairness as an opinion honestly held should not be objected to in a country which still boasts of freedom of speech.'[168] Moreover, he argued, both in this article and in a comment written after the Manitoba Court of Appeal affirmed the trial judgment, that the court's assessment of fairness tended to express its economic faiths, which were equally likely to be the faiths of the past – the faith in individualism and freedom to contract.[169] Therefore, statements should not be prohibited unless they were defamatory, deceptive, or intimidating.

The second article, about the labour injunctions to restrain picketing,[170] began with a long account of the injunction and its abuses in the United States. Here it was an Ontario case that prompted Laskin to write. Workers had picketed, and after an injunction was granted, some union members who were not employees but who knew the injunction had been granted, began to picket. The Ontario Court of Appeal held they were guilty of contempt, and Laskin was again scornful, arguing that the effect of the holding was that an injunction granted to enforce a private right had been turned into a public criminal prohibition against the whole community. Unless the courts exercised their equitable jurisdiction 'with a spirit of social understanding,'[171] their role was likely to be circumscribed by legislation.

Laskin returned to labour only once more during the decade,[172] but he wrote about 30 articles, comments, and reviews about a wide range of other topics. Among them, the major one was 'The Protection of Interests by Statute and the Problem of "Contracting Out,"' written while he was in his second year at Osgoode Hall, in 1936, but not published until 1938.[173] As its title suggests, it dealt with the question when courts should permit an individual from making a contract to give up a benefit or protection given to him or her by statute. Again, the introduction revealed much of his general thinking. Two themes in particular were important. The first was his version of the underpinnings of the new state. The nineteenth-century theories, which had made the individual will paramount, failed to understand that individuals could 'be rendered so helpless through economic privation as to be incapable of having a free will.' Change was needed, 'by throwing the weight of the state behind those interests which the individualistic legal theories of an evanescent period have proved pitifully inadequate to protect.' The second was his beliefs about the role of courts and legislatures. In the past, the courts had sometimes changed law to respond to social change, but their potential was spent. '[T]he responsibility for the protection of new interests and the legal recognition of new social forces must hereafter be primarily the concern of the legislature and not of the courts.'[174] These thoughts were heady stuff for a young student, and suggest that he had been introduced to the new ideas at Kennedy's school.

At the end of this long introduction, he set out the basic principle: whether contracting out of a protection given by statute could be surrendered depended upon the policy of the statute. The bulk of the article followed: a thorough description of what the courts had done. In the conclusion, he returned to this basic principle, and the question of how to determine the policy of a statute. Here, Laskin presented an elegant survey of the developments of the 1930s, especially Corry's article: the rejection of literal meaning and the will of the legislature, the shift to purpose, the need to understand the context of making the statue, and the need for cooperation between courts and legislatures.[175]

In a few comments about common law topics, especially torts, he repeated his admonition to think in terms of interests, not rights, and suggested that the reasoning must always be 'tentative.'[176] In writing about interpretation, he repeated the need to respect 'motivating considerations' and the changes in the public philosophy.[177] When the Supreme Court invoked the freedom of commerce to sanction a tavern owner's refusal to serve a coloured person, he argued it had imposed the right to trade, an economic faith from the past, which had been displaced by comprehensive legislative regulation. Instead, the court should have interpreted this legislation as prohibiting discrimination.[178]

He wrote about administrative law only once, in a short note apparently prompted by a Supreme Court decision by his former teacher, Felix Frankfurter.[179] Here he asserted that regulation was necessary, and the task was to balance 'the maximum of administrative regulation required ... with the minimum of arbitrary interference in the life of the citizen.'[180] The major purpose of the note seemed to be to introduce American sources, especially Frankfurter, to Canadian lawyers.

None of Laskin's major ideas about legal reasoning and institutions was distinctive. Instead, Canadian scholars had introduced all of them in the first half of the decade. One symbol of this accomplishment was the first volume of the *University of Toronto Law Journal*, which Kennedy established, and which appeared in the academic year of 1935 and 1936, just as Laskin was beginning to write. It was a dazzling collection of the new thinking: Corbett on the new international law, which we will see in a moment, Wright on the *Restatement of Torts and Agency*, Willis on administrative law, MacDonald on federalism, Corry on interpretation, Finkelman on separation of powers, and a host of reviews that shared the same stances. Yet Laskin was nonetheless remarkable. He incorporated virtually all the innovations in a wide range of subjects, and can best be understood as representing the state of the art of legal thinking at the end of the 1930s.

International Law

Only two scholars had a sustained interest in international law: Larry MacKenzie, at Toronto, and Percy Corbett, at McGill. Both were interesting and important figures, albeit for very different reasons. MacKenzie was born in Nova Scotia, served in the war, and then went to Dalhousie. After obtaining degrees in Arts and Law, he worked at the International Labour Office for a couple of years, before coming to Toronto in 1926. The list of his scholarship was long, but most of it was short, descriptive notes and book reviews. The few substantial pieces demonstrated enthusiasm and good judgment, but little analysis or imagination. His abilities lay in managing and leading people, not scholarship. He left Toronto in 1940 to be president of the University of New Brunswick, and later became president of the University of British Columbia.[181]

Corbett, who was born in Prince Edward Island, obtained two degrees in Arts at McGill, before going to Oxford as a Rhodes scholar, where he obtained a BCL. He stayed as a junior fellow and wrote his first article about International Law, an inquiry into the legal nature of the League of Nations.[182] The task was urgent. According to the prevailing doctrine, made in the late nineteenth century, sovereignty was the central concept and the nation states were the sole form of international authority. Even more than in the domestic world, taming the past was crucial to a modern international order. Corbett sought to enable the construction of international institutions that were not nation states, by separating sovereignty from personality.

In 1935, after he had returned to Montreal and joined the faculty at McGill, he revisited the task of finding an escape from sovereignty in 'Fundamentals of a New Law of Nations.'[183] It was, he declared, unacceptable simply because it was unrealistic. Observation revealed a community of states, bound together by interdependence and extensive common interests, and accepting order in their relations. 'No state can, for any considerable period, successfully withstand the common will of a strong majority in this society.'[184] The doctrine of sovereignty persisted only because 'the legal mind is notoriously conservative; it persists in clinging to theories and twisting the new facts of life to fit them, rather than admit new theories to account for the facts.'[185] He derived much of his analysis from European thinkers, especially from Hans Kelsen and his Vienna school.[186]

Perspective

The sense of excitement and urgency, the making of new roles, the rejection of the nineteenth-century legacy, and the embrace of new ways of thinking about law and a new state were all large changes. Of course, much of the common law ways of thinking remained, but enough was done to justify Willis' exclamation: he and his colleagues had turned their world upside down.

After the War, the United States became the dominant, often the exclusive, exemplar for legal scholars, and England was usually dismissed as mired in the past or simply ignored. At the same time, the distinctive elements of the Canadian public law scholarship disappeared. Analysing cases, albeit done with a sense of urgency, became a much larger component of scholarship, even in constitutional law and administrative law, and the open expression of political beliefs disappeared. In the background of this change were the emergence of the legal process school in the United States, and the determination of the Canadian scholars to establish and legitimate their professional schools.

This story, especially the triumph of the American thought, can be encapsulated, albeit oversimplified, by seeing it as the triumph of Wright over Kennedy, and especially by looking again at Laskin. He acknowledged much later how much Kennedy had influenced him while he was an undergraduate. Nonetheless, a few years afterwards, Wright became Laskin's mentor. Laskin looked to American models just as much as Wright did, and wrote a flock of case comments that looked just like Wright's.[187] After the War, the two became the most powerful figures in scholarship and education, and what was distinctive in Kennedy's manifesto and public law scholarship disappeared.

Yet this look at the future is not part of my story. It has been, instead, the story of a generation that needs to be remembered, especially in a time when Canadian law schools seem to be looking for a new identity.

NOTES

1 All I can remember about this conversation is that it took place by phone after Willis retired, and was living in Sandy Cove, Nova Scotia. I thank Jim Phillips for reading early drafts of this article and making suggestions, and Philip Girard, not only for suggestions but for letting me read drafts of his forthcoming biography of Laskin.

2 I do not mean to suggest that law schools in Canada did not flourish and do interesting work before the 1930s. McGill, especially, was a sparkling school throughout the 1920s.

3 The number 40 does not include many part-time teachers, who were typically practitioners.

4 There was only one major Canadian scholar who did not fit into my topic at all: D.M. Gordon, a practising lawyer in Victoria, British Columbia, who wrote primarily about Administrative Law. For him, see K. Roach, 'The Administrative Law Scholarship of D. M. Gordon' (1984) 34 *McGill L.J.* 1.

5 See W.P.M. Kennedy, 'Theories of Law and the Constitutional Law of the British Empire,' in *Minutes of Proceedings of the Fourteenth Annual Meeting of the Canadian Bar Association* (Toronto: Carswell, 1930) at 152, reprinted virtually completely in W.P. M. Kennedy, *Some Aspects of the Theories and Workings of Constitutional Law* (New York: Macmillan, 1931) (Austin and sovereignty are no longer taken seriously); John D. Falconbridge, 'The Revolt of the Silk Merchants' (1929) 7 *Can. Bar R.* 23 (law should be studied as a social science); P.E. Corbett, 'Book Review of *Essays in Jurisprudence and the Common Law* by Arthur L. Goodhart' (1931) 9 *Can. Bar R.* 451 (Austin presents only simple and rigid dogma, and is a paralyzing influence); J. Finkelman, 'Book Review of *Foreign Relations of the Federal State* by H.W. Stoke' (1931) 9 *Can. Bar Rev.* 603 (scholars are inclined these days to eschew theoretical discussions, and to deal with concrete problems); H.E. Read, 'The Divorce Jurisdiction Act, 1930' (1931) 9 *Can. Bar R.* 73 (the need for law to express social need and conditions, and references to Pound and Cardozo).

6 C.A. Wright, 'An Extra-Legal Approach to Law' (1932) 10 *Can. Bar R.* 1.

7 Ibid. 1.

8 Ibid. 15, 2, and 13.

9 Ibid. 1, 5; emphasis in original.

10 Ibid. 15.

11 Kennedy, *Some Aspects*, supra note 5.

12 For an account of Kennedy's life and scholarship, see R.C.B. Risk, 'The Many Minds of W.P.M. Kennedy,' in this volume.

13 '[W]e maintain personality as something inviolate and incommunicable and ultimate and, at the same time, we maintain that "self" must imply other "selves." In a word, the individual and the social have a necessary reciprocal implication': *Some Aspects*, supra note 5, at 23–4. The earlier quotations in this paragraph are taken ibid., 22–3, 20, and 25.

14 Ibid. 21.

15 In speaking of the shift from rights to interests, he said, '[B]efore law takes any interests within its protection there must be a previous comprehensive survey of social values': ibid. 24.

16 Ibid. 21, 27, and 25.

17 Ibid. 21, and see above, note 13.

18 In the United States, scholars tended to pursue an ideal form, in which subsidiary principles were arranged beneath these primary ones, and the entire structure was internally consistent and coherent, without gaps or overlaps. In contrast, the scholars in England did not pursue this ideal with nearly the same rigour.

19 The obligation to follow single precedents, which was established late in the century, complicated this structure, but not in ways that need be pursued here.

20 For an account of Lefroy's life and scholarship, see R.C.B. Risk, 'A.H.F. Lefroy,' in this volume.

21 'Mechanical Jurisprudence' (1908) 8 *Columbia L.R.* 605.

22 'The Scope and Purpose of Sociological Jurisprudence' (1911) 24 *Harvard L.R.* 591, and (1912) 25 *Harvard L.R.* 140 and 489.

23 Pound, 'Mechanical Jurisprudence,' supra note 21, at 609.

24 Ibid. 605.

25 Ibid. 609–10.

26 B.H. Cardozo, *The Nature of the Judicial Process* (New Haven: Yale University Press, 1921) 65.

27 Sydney Smith to Horace Read, 3 February 1934, box E-16, MS 1-13, Dalhousie University Archives.

28 Sydney Smith to Norman Rogers, 13 January 1933, box E-19, MS 1-13, Dalhousie University Archives.

29 'The Logical and Legal Bases of the Conflict of Laws' (1924) 33 *Yale L.J.* 457 at 464.

30 Ibid. 469.

31 Ibid. 467.

32 'Territoriality, Public Policy, and the Conflict of Laws' (1924) 33 *Yale L.J.* 736.

33 'The Hornbook Method and the Conflict of Laws' (1928) 37 *Yale L.J.*
468.
34 See, for example, 'Conflict of Laws Relating to Bills and Notes' (1925) 6
Can. Bar R. 356 and 430; 'Contract and Conveyance in the Conflict of Laws'
(1933) 51 *U. of Pennsylvania L.R.* 661 and 517; and 'Administration and
Succession in the Conflict of Laws' (1934) 12 *Can. Bar R.* 66 and 125.
35 Fortunately, for my purposes, it need not be fully described; it is enough
to say that in its simplest form, it raised the spectre of two jurisdictions
playing Ping-Pong – the doctrine of the first one specifying the second
as the jurisdiction whose doctrine would govern the problem, and the
doctrine of the second saying that such a problem should be solved by the
doctrine of the first one or a third one. The question was, what should the
first one do? Accept the renvoi, which was required by the doctrine named
'renvoi' or solve the problem by applying the domestic law of the second?
36 'Renvoi and Succession to Movables' (1930) 46 *L.Q.R.* 465, and (1931) 47
L.Q.R. 271. Clearly, he disapproved of the doctrine, but apart from
pointing out a few strange results it could cause, there was no demonstration of disadvantage or advantage, and more generally, no reference to
social need and values.
37 'Renvoi, Characterization, and Acquired Rights' (1939) 17 *Can. Bar R.* 369.
38 'Book Review of *A Treatise on the Conflict of Laws* by J.H. Beale' (1935) 13
Can. Bar R. 531 at 533.
39 'Characterization in the Conflict of Laws' (1937) 53 *L.Q.R.* 235 and 537. See
also 'Conflict of Laws: Examples of Characterization' (1937) 15 *Can. Bar R.*
215.
40 At the outset, he referred to challenges and their quest for the means of
reaching 'desirable social or economic result(s)' instead of 'the mechanical
application of rules,' and then said that his purpose was the more modest
one of discussing specific problems and making suggestions about the
doctrine: Falconbridge, 'Characterization in the Conflict of Laws,' 244. As
well, he made a short reference to reaching a 'socially desirable result' in
making new rules for situations that did not fall within the existing ones:
ibid. 246.
41 . '"Substance" and "Procedure" in the Conflict of Laws' (1933) 42 *Yale L.J.*
333 at 334, 335. Cook did not, though, deny that most problems were
comfortably within the core of a classification, and that logic was nonetheless useful.
42 Falconbridge, 'Renvoi,' supra note 37, at 370, 373, 374, and 397. This
suggestion was likely prompted by reading an article by David F. Cavers

of Harvard Law School: 'A Critique of the Choice of Law Problem' (1933) 47 *Harvard. L.R.* 173.

43 'Book Review of *Principles of Conflict of Laws* by G.W. Stumberg' (1937) 2 *U.T.L.J.* 449.

44 'Torts in the Conflict of Laws: The First Rule in *Phillips v. Eyre*' (1940) 3 *U.T.L.J.* 400.

45 'Case Comment on *Phillips v. Eyre*' (1940) 18 *Can. Bar R.* 308.

46 Ibid. 311.

47 'Case Comment on *Dalton v. McLean*' (1940) 18 *Can. Bar R.* 642.

48 Ibid. 645. Again, he rejected the 'mechanical application of verbal formula': ibid. 646.

49 For a survey of the entire span of Wright's tort scholarship, see R.B. Brown, 'Cecil A. Wright and the Foundations of Canadian Tort Law Scholarship' (2001) 64 *Sask. L.R.* 164.

50 'Case Comment on *Hutson v. United Motor Service*' (1936) 14 *Can. Bar R.* 514.

51 'Case Comment on *Paine v. Colne Valley Electricity Supply*' (1939) 27 *Can. Bar R.* 214

52 As well, he proposed that a failure to inspect by the plaintiff be considered as contributory negligence, and not a bar to recovery, not, at least, in most provinces in Canada, where legislation had established that contributory negligence was not a bar to liability and, instead, the damages would be limited by the proportion of the plaintiff's fault.

53 His understanding of the foundations was derived from American literature, especially from Bohlen, his teacher, and from Fowler Harper. A text by Harper appeared in 1933, and Wright's review was not only his first writing about torts, but embodied much of what he would say during the next five years. See C.A. Wright, 'Book Review of *A Treatise on the Law of Torts* by F.V. Harper' (1935) 1 *U.T.L.J.* 193.

54 'Case Comment on *Kerr v. T.G. Bright*' (1937) 15 *Can. Bar R.* 285.

55 Ibid. 291, 292. In the Court of Appeal, Rowell, C.J.O., had gone further, by saying that more and more business was done by corporations, who could act only through agents, who would usually be unable to pay a damage award. The employer could insure against liability, and the cost would ultimately be borne by the general public. Wright said simply that he agreed, and no more.

56 'Case Comment on Hospital Liability' (1936) 14 *Can. Bar R.* 699.

57 Ibid. 704, 701.

58 G.L. Priest, 'The Invention of Enterprise Liability: A Critical History of the Intellectual Foundations of Modern Tort Law' (1985) 14 *J. Legal Stud.* 461.

59 'Vicarious Liability for Tortious Acts' (1936) 14 *Can. Bar R.* 725.

60 'The American Law Institute's *Restatement of Contracts and Agency*' (1935) 1 *U.T.L.J.* 17.

61 'Law and the Law Schools' (1938) 16 *Can. Bar R.* 579 at 583, 585.

62 Ibid. 583–4.

63 Ibid. 584.

64 Wright, 'Extra-Legal Approach,' supra note 6, at 15.

65 Wright, 'Law Schools,' supra note 61, at 585.

66 One example is his 1931 manifesto (Wright, 'Extra-Legal Approach,' supra note 6). In one unusual passage, he spoke of the values of comparative law as a source of ideas. See Wright, 'Law Schools,' supra note 61, at 600.

67 See, for example, J.T. Kloppenberg, *Uncertain Victory: Social Democracy and Progressivism in European and American Thought, 1870–1920* (New York: Oxford University Press, 1986).

68 For a good account of the similarities and differences, see A.J. Sebok, *Legal Positivism in American Jurisprudence* (Cambridge: Cambridge University Press, 1998) 83–112.

69 See Risk, 'A.H.F. Lefroy,' in this volume.

70 There were two other differences, less important for my purposes: first, the rejection of the past was accompanied by the removal of any interest in the study of history, either as a guide or for its own value, and, second, Lefroy was much more inclined to make binary distinctions, rather than distinctions of degree.

71 Jurisprudence Notes at 157–67, box 001 (Lecture Notes), Accession B82-0028, Papers of Cecil A. Wright, University of Toronto Archives,.

72 See, for example, Wright, 'Law Schools,' supra note 1, at 588, 596; Wright, 'Restatement,' supra note 60; and the following, all by C.A. Wright: 'Book Review of *Legal Essays: In Tribute to Oren Kipp McMurray*, ed. Max Radin and A.M. Kidd' (1935) 13 *Can. Bar R.* 425; 'Book Review of *Principles of Contract* by the Right Honourable Sir Frederick Pollock' (1936) 14 *Can. Bar R.* 753; 'Book Review of *Selected Cases on Commercial Contracts* by A. Cecil Caporn' (1938) 16 *Can. Bar R.* 73; 'Book Review of *Readings in Jurisprudence* by Jerome Hall' (1939) 17 *Can. Bar R.* 365.

73 See, for example, Cecil A. Wright to Roscoe Pound, 8 October 1935, in box 3, Wright Papers, supra note 71; and Cecil A. Wright to Warren Seavey, 31 October 1936, in ibid., box 10.

74 Wright, 'Review of *Readings*,' supra note 72, at 366. In the late 1930s, Wright did, though, see hope in some small signs of change; see, for example, 'Book Review of *Legal Essays and Addresses by the Right Honourable Lord Wright of Durley*' (1940) 18 *Can. Bar R.* 71.

75 C.A. Wright, 'Book Review of *A Digest of English Civil Law* by Edward Jenks et al.' (1938) 16 *Can. Bar R.* 505; J. Willis, 'Book Review of *The Administration of Justice* by Raymond Moley and Schuyler C. Wallace' (1933) 11 *Can. Bar R.* 705; B. Laskin, 'Book Review of *The Law in Quest of Itself* by Lou L. Fuller' (1940) 18 *Can. Bar R.* 660; and Speech of Frederick C. Cronkite to the Law Society of Saskatchewan (1937), Saskatoon, Speeches and Articles, MG 33, S1, University of Saskatchewan Archives,. The only sustained account of the Realists was J. Finkelman, 'Williston on Contracts' (1940) 3 *U.T.L.J.* 387.

76 A.V. Dicey, *The Law of the Constitution* (London: Macmillan, 1885).

77 The third was a minor account of conventions.

78 A.H.F. Lefroy, *The Law of Legislative Power in Canada* (Toronto: Toronto Law Book and Publishing, 1897–8).

79 [1925] A.C. 396 (P.C.).

80 'The Residue of Power in Canada' (1926) 4 *Can. Bar R.* 432.

81 For accounts of his career see R.A. Macdonald, 'The National Law Programme at McGill: Origins, Establishment, Prospects' (1990) 13 *Dal. L.J.* 211 at 256–61; and R. St J. Macdonald, 'An Historical Introduction to the Teaching of International Law in Canada' (1974) 12 *Can. Yearbook of Int'l Law* 67 at 72–4.

82 Smith, 'Residue of Power,' supra note 80, at 434.

83 See S. Djwa, *The Politics of the Imagination: A Life of F.R. Scott* (Toronto: McClelland and Stewart, 1987); and S. Djwa and R. St J. Macdonald, eds., *On F.R. Scott: Essays on His Contribution to Law, Literature, and Politics* (Montreal and Kingston: McGill-Queen's University Press, 1983) 54.

84 See J. Willis, *A History of Dalhousie Law School* (Toronto: University of Toronto Press, 1979).

85 'The Development of Canadian Federalism' (1931) 3 *Procs. Can. Political Science Assoc.* 231 at 231.

86 *Some Aspects*, supra note 5, at 101.

87 'Crisis in the Canadian Constitution' (1934) 24 *Round Table* 803 at 815–16, 819.

88 'Judicial Interpretation of the Canadian Constitution' (1935) 1 *U.T.L.J.* 260 at 282.

89 'The Consequences of the Privy Council Decisions' (1937) 15 *Can. Bar R.* 485 at 489.

90 Ibid. 491–2. Kennedy agreed: 'We must no longer live in the vain world of delusion that the Judicial Committee will do for the Act what the Supreme Court of the United States has been able to do ... We would have faced this issue long ago had we not too largely believed that constitutional and legal

wisdom never really crossed the Atlantic': 'The British North America Act: Past and Future' (1937) 15 *Can. Bar R.* 393 at 398. MacDonald said simply that the decisions 'go a long way towards depriving Canada of adequate legislative power to meet effectively pressing national necessities': 'The Canadian Constitution Seventy Years After' (1937) 15 *Can. Bar R.* 401 at 421.

91 198 U.S. 45 (1905).

92 The scholarship about federalism was almost the only topic within the usual range of the term 'constitulional.' There was, in particular, little writing about individual rights, and virtually all of it was by Scott. In 1930, in 'The Privy Council and Minority Rights' (1930) 37 *Queen's Q.* 668, he challenged the argument that the appeals to the Privy Council protected minority rights, demonstrating that what it had done was to protect provincial rights, not minority rights. During the next few years, he published a handful of powerful indictments of efforts to restrict the political activities of labour leaders and communists.

93 These ideas are considered at greater length in R.C.B. Risk, 'Here Be Cold and Tygers: A Map of Statutory Interpretation in Canada in the 1920s and 1930s' (2000) 63 *Sask. L.R.* 195.

94 *Legislative Power*, supra note 78 at 475.

95 '*Royal Bank of Canada v. The King*, Letter to the Editor' (1914) 50 *Can. L.J.* 622 at 624.

96 'Power of Provincial Legislatures to Enact Statutes Affecting the Rights of Non-Residents: A Reply to Some of My Critics' (1915) 51 *Can. L.J.* 265 at 287.

97 'Residue of Power,' supra note 80, at 433.

98 M. Radin, 'Statutory Interpretation' (1930), 43 *Harvard L.R.* 563; and J.M. Landis, 'A Note on "Statutory Interpretation"' (1930) *Harvard L.R.* 886.

99 Radin, supra note 98, at 870.

100 Ibid. 881.

101 Landis, supra note 98, at 892.

102 'Statute Interpretation in a Nutshell' (1938) 16 *Can. Bar R.* 1.

103 Ibid. 11 and 2.

104 Ibid. 14. Like Smith, he said that the refusal to consider the legislative materials made this approach 'unworkable.'

105 See J.A. Corry, *My Life and Work: A Happy Partnership: Memoirs of J.A. Corry* (Montreal and Kingston: McGill-Queen's University Press 1981).

106 (1936) 1 *U.T.L.J.* 286. The discussion of interpretation was a few pages sandwiched between an introduction about the ways courts had dealt with the modern administrative state, and a long account of the history of interpretation in private law contexts in the eighteenth and nineteenth centuries.

107 This claim about words, which appeared throughout the writing of this
generation, misunderstood its target, for most writers in the late nineteenth century did not claim that words always had clear meanings. The
crucial difference, and one which was not clearly expressed, was that
Corry and his generation assumed, contrary to the earlier scholars, that
the uncertainty of words was pervasive, and that a text alone would
rarely give clear meanings about realistic problems.

108 He did not explain the difference between intent and purpose, but it was
the distinction Landis had made, between a specific meaning about the
particular problem and the general policy of the legislature. This distinction was far from radical. It had been a part of the late-nineteenth-century
approach, but at its margin, as a circumscribed inquiry when no clear
meaning was apparent.

109 Corry, 'Administrative Law,' supra note 106, at 292.

110 Ibid. 292, 291, and 293.

111 Ibid. 288.

112 Ibid.

113 Ibid. 243.

114 Willis, 'Nutshell,' supra note 102, at 17.

115 (1933) 11 *Can. Bar R.* 581.

116 Ibid. 599.

117 Ibid. 582. A few years later, in 1935, he made the same argument in a
comment about *British Coal v. The King*, [1935] A.C. 500 (P.C.), in which the
Privy Council decided that Canada could bar appeals to the Privy Council
in criminal cases, using remarkably convoluted reasoning based on the
premise that this power had been included from the outset. The result
pleased MacDonald, because it confirmed Canada's status as an independent nation, but the reasoning did not, because in 1867 the British Parliament would hardly have intended to give such a power to a colony.
Instead, be argued, the Privy Council should openly have acknowledged
Canada's independence and interpreted the *BNA Act* as giving the power,
even though the interpretation would have been different in 1867. Courts
should read constitutions 'as speaking the language of today against the
background of present legal and political facts': 'British Coal Corporation
and Others v. The King: Three Comments' (1935) 13 *Can. Bar R.* 615 at 632.
The 'general policy' of a constitution should prevail, even if it required
'occasional disregard of the intention of the draftsmen': Ibid. 633.

118 The Privy Council paid no attention. In *Canada (A.G.) v. Ontario (A.G.)
(Labour Conventions)* [1937] A.C. 326 (P.C.) it decided that section 132 was
limited to treaties made by Britain for Canada.

119 *The New Despotism* (London: Benn, 1929).

120 Three others need mention. J. Forester Davison graduated from Dalhousie and did graduate work at Harvard Law School. After returning to Canada for a few years, he moved to the United States, where he collaborated with Frankfurter on a casebook. Among the handful of articles and comments he wrote about Canadian topics, only one had lasting significance: 'The Constitutionality and Utility of Advisory Opinions' (1938) 2 *U.T.L.J.* 254. Nigel Tennant, who also graduated from Dalhousie and did graduate work at Harvard, wrote one article, 'Administrative Finality' (1928) 6 *Can Bar R.* 497, which pointed to the importance of this new field. It sought to synthesize the doctrine of review, and at the end, suggested that an appeal to the courts was not likely to give a better decision than the administration had made, and that better appointments were a more effective means of obtaining good decisions. John Humphrey, of McGill, who later became an important figure in the international field, wrote an article about review and administrative courts: see infra note 158. See also R.B. Brown, 'The Canadian Legal Realists and Administrative Law scholarship, 1930–1941' (2000) *Dal. J. Legal Studies* 36.

121 *The Parliamentary Powers of English Government Departments* (Cambridge: Harvard University Press, 1933).

122 'Three Approaches to Administrative Law' (1935) 1 *U.T.L.J.* 53.

123 (1939) 53 *Harvard L.R.* 251.

124 (1940) 18 *Can. Bar R.* 517.

125 *Canadian Boards at Work.* (Toronto: Macmillan, 1941). Although he wrote little in this collection, the very undertaking demonstrated one large strand of his approach: the importance of 'what really happens.' Between 1933 and 1941, as well as these six pieces, Willis wrote a clutch of reviews, including two sparkling reviews of books by Thurman Arnold, and two articles about entirely different topics, the nature of joint bank accounts, and a comparison of English and American approaches to conflicts of laws. The range of topics is impressive, and so is the range of approaches. Most of these pieces combined careful analysis of doctrine, with political critique, and middle-level theory.

126 'Administrative Law in Canada' (1933) 5 *Procs. Can. Political Science Assoc.* 190.

127 'The Fusion of Government and Business' (1936) 2 *Can. J. Economics and Pol. Science* 301.

128 'The Growth of Government Activities,' study prepared for the Royal Commission on Dominion–Provincial Relations, 1939, unpublished.

129 'Aspects of Administrative Law in Canada' (1934) 46 *Juridical R.* 203.
130 'Separation of Powers: A Study in Administrative Law' (1936) 11 *U.T.L.J.* 313.
131 'Government by Civil Servants' (1939) 17 *Can. Bar R.* 166.
132 'Administrative Justice in Canada' (1939) 17 *Can. Bar R.* 619.
133 'Administrative Law,' supra note 126, at 194. In 'Aspects of Administrative Law in Canada' Kennedy spoke of a new social philosophy that was committed to '[c]are of the sick, the poor, the aged, and the infirm, elimination of slums, control of industry in the interests of humanity, protection of children, universal education, development of natural resources for the benefit of mankind, all demand immediate attention': supra note 129, at 221.
134 'Civil Servants,' supra note 131, at 171–2 [emphasis in original].
135 MacIver's major work was *The Modern State* (Oxford: Clarendon Press, 1926). Kennedy never referred to it, but it was published when he was beginning to think about these topics, and his ideas paralleled much of its thinking.
136 *Some Aspects*, supra note 5, at 8–9, 14–15.
137 'The Workings of the British North America Acts, 1867–1931' (1936) 48 *Juridical R.* 57 at 58–59.
138 *Some Aspects*, supra note 5, at 57.
139 They might usefully be added to historians' understanding of the 'government generation'. See D. Owram, *The Government Generation: Canadian Intellectuals and the State, 1900–1945* (Toronto: University of Toronto Press, 1986).
140 'Aspects of Administrative Law,' supra note 129, at 214.
141 *Report of the Committee on Ministers' Powers*, Cmd. 460, in *Sessional Papers*, vol. 11, 1931–2, 341.
142 Supra note 121, at 113.
143 Ibid. 157.
144 Book reviews of *The Administrative Process* by J.M. Landis, *State and Federal Grants-in-Aid* by H.J. Bitterman, and *Women Servants of the State, 1870–1938: A History of Women in the Civil Service* by H. Martindale, all in (1940) 3 *U.T.L.J.* 519 at 520.
145 See, for example, Hopkins, 'Administrative Justice in Canada,' supra note 132, at 621; and Corry, 'Administrative Law in Canada,' supra note 126, at 191.
146 Supra note 122, at 54.
147 Ibid 75.
148 Supra note 125, at 2.

149 'Separation of Powers,' supra note 130. It was not a part of the Constitution because Parliament, the executive, and the judiciary had each
exercised all three functions: legislative, executive, and judicial. Nor was
it part of the common law, because the courts had not developed any
clear and consistent meanings of the functions. In both these paths, the
reasoning was grounded upon experience and 'reality.'

150 Ibid. 341, 342.

151 Three Approaches,' supra note 122, at 71.

152 *Parliamentary Powers*, supra note 121, at 151–2.

153 'Three Approaches,' supra note 122, at 52.

154 Supra note 121, at 42.

155 Supra note 123, at 273.

156 Willis, *Parliamentary Powers*, supra note 121, at 51. The same thought
appears at 171.

157 Willis, 'Three Approaches,' supra note 122, at 60–1.

158 Willis firmly advocated review by an administrative court, in 'Three
Approaches,' ibid. at 79–81; John Humphrey, of McGill, agreed, in
'Judicial Control Over Administrative Action with Special Reference to
the Province of Quebec' (1939) *Can J. Economics and Pol. Science* 417, but
on the basis of awkward doctrinal reasoning. Two others suggested that
such a step might be necessary: Corry, in 'The Growth of Government
Activities,' supra note 128, at 15–18, and Kennedy, 'Aspects of
Adminislrative Law,' supra note 129, at 224–8.

159 'Aspects of Administrative Law,' supra note 129, at 228.

160 Note that it is the subject matter that seems to make the difference and
not the identity of the scholars. Most of the scholars who did the major
public law scholarship also did major pieces of common law scholarship
without a trace of these distinctive differences. See, for example, J.A.
Corry, 'The Custom of a Month's Notice' (1932) 10 *Can. Bar R.* 331; V.C.
MacDonald, 'Statutory Conversion of Land into Goods' (1931) 9 *Can. Bar
R.* 691; and J. Willis, 'The Nature of a Joint Account' (1936) 14 *Can. Bar R.*
457.

161 I have taken this account of Laskin's life from the drafts of Philip Girard's
biography. *Editors' note*: This book has now been published; see P.V.
Girard, *Bora Laskin: Bringing Law to Life* (Toronto: Osgoode Society for
Canadian Legal History and University of Toronto Press, 2005).

162 'The Law of Picketing in Canada' (1940) 2 *U.T.L.J.* 67 and 344 at 69.

163 Ibid.

164 Ibid.

165 Ibid. 76.
166 'Picketing: A Comparison of Certain Canadian and American Doctrines' (1937) 15 *Can. Bar R.* 14.
167 Ibid. 13.
168 Ibid. 16.
169 In a case comment in the same year, Laskin spoke bluntly about choices of this kind: 'A court which makes a choice here is exercising a purely legislative function. It is not desirable, nor is it possible to shut the judiciary off from legislative considerations. But the notions that a court may adopt here, if it decides to act, must be in line with the current mores of the community': 'Case Comment on *Allied Amusements Ltd. v. Reaney & Kershaw Theatres Ltd.*' (1937) 15 *Can. Bar R.* 813 at 817.
170 'The Labour Injunction in Canada: A Caveat' (1937) 15 *Can. Bar R.* 270.
171 Ibid. 283.
172 'Case Comment on *Moscrop v. London Passenger Transport Board*' (1949) 18 *Can. Bar R.* 810, which used the case as a springboard for general comments about the need for strong unions and legislative support for industrial democracy.
173 (1936) 16 *Can. Bar R.* 669.
174 Ibid. 673, 670, 671.
175 The introduction and this conclusion were remarkably detached from the account of the cases. Perhaps they were added later.
176 'Case Comment on *Camden Nominees Ltd. v. Slack*' (1940)18 *Can. Bar R.* 393 at 394.
177 'Case Comment on *Beresford v. Royal Insurance Co. Ltd.*' (1938) 16 *Can. Bar R.* 393 at 405. See also B. Laskin, 'Case Comment on *Industrial Standards Act*' (1937) 15 *Can. Bar R.* 660, and 'Case Comment on *Tolton Manufacturing Co. Ltd. v. Advisory Committee*' (1940) 18 *Can. Bar R.* 657.
178 'Case Comment on *Christie v. York Corp.*' (1940) 18 *Can Bar R.* 314. See also B. Laskin, 'Case Comment on *Burton v. Power*' (1940) 18 *Can. Bar R.* 646, a case about speech in public places, where Laskin demonstrated that the freedom of speech really depends upon the permission and discretion of the police, and argued for firmer standards.
179 'Case Comment on Administrative Tribunals' (1940) 18 *Can. Bar R.* 227. This comment was not signed, but considering both the style and the subject matter, it was almost certainly written by Laskin.
180 Ibid. 227.
181 For an account of MacKenzie's career, see P.B. Waite, *Lord of Point Grey: Larry MacKenzie of U.B.C.* (Vancouver: University of British Columbia Press, 1987).

182 'What Is the League of Nations?' (1934) 5 *Brit. Yearbook of Int'l L.* 119. For an illuminating account of this article and early-twentieth-century international law thought generally, see D. Kennedy, 'International Law and the Nineteenth Century: History of an Illusion' (1997) 17 *Q.L.R.* 99.

183 (1935) 1 *U.T.L.J.* 3.

184 Ibid. 8.

185 Ibid.

186 His other contributions to international law were a couple of descriptive books about Canada's role in international affairs and a bundle of reviews. At the outset of his scholarly career, he wrote a handful of articles and a short book about Roman Law, and during the 1930s, he continued his interest in European sources by introducing Canadian lawyers to the thinking of Francois Geny.

187 See, for example, 'Case Comment on *In the Goods of Knight*' (1939) 17 *Can. Bar R.* 677; 'Case Comment on *Johnson v. Summers*' (1939) 17 *Can. Bar R.* 148; 'Case Comment on *Spencer Clarke & Co. Ltd. v. Goodwill Motors Ltd.*' (1939) 17 *Can. Bar R.* 604; 'Case Comment on *Commercial Credit Corp v. Niagara Finance Corp. Ltd.*' (1940) 18 *Can. Bar R.* 120; 'Case Comment on *Lockhart v. Stimson and C.P.R.*' (1940) 18 *Can. Bar R.* 205; 'Case Comment on *Staples v. Isaacs*' (1940) 18 *Can. Bar R.* 573; 'Case Comment on *United Australia Ltd. v. Barclays Bank Ltd.*' (1940) 18 *Can. Bar R.* 62; 'Case Comment on *Weld Blundell v. Synott*' (1940) 18 *Can. Bar R.* 504.

PART THREE

Postwar Developments

On the Road to Oz: Common Law Scholarship about Federalism after World War II

Introduction

I can state the purpose of this essay in a few words: it seeks to reconstruct the Canadian common law scholarship about federalism from the late 1940s to the early 1970s. Such a brief account, though, is far from being an adequate prospectus for any reader who wonders whether to devote an hour or so to my enterprise. Some elaboration is needed.

Federalism has been one of the large themes of Canadian public life since Confederation. It has been studied from all sorts of perspectives, for all sorts of purposes, and by all sorts of scholars. I am interested in the scholarship of lawyers, particularly the common law academic lawyers. They were not the only lawyers who wrote thoughtfully about federalism, but they were nonetheless a distinctive group, and well worth studying. I wish to explore two themes in their scholarship. The first is their beliefs about federalism. What kind of federalism did Canada have, and what kind should it have? What was the allocation of powers between the federal government and the provinces, and what should it be? Here, we shall see a shift from an emphasis on a strong federal government at the outset to a belief in a 'carefully balanced federalism' and cooperation. The second is their beliefs about ways of thinking about law, especially the ways in which courts made, and should make, their decisions. What were their beliefs, for example, about the interpretation of a constitution, the role of precedent, and whether current needs and values should be considered? Here, we shall see much less change, for all my scholars denied that doctrine alone could provide adequate guidance and maintained that the courts should seek the welfare of contemporary society, differing only slightly in the emphasis they gave to this theme and in their beliefs about how the courts should perform this task.

In addition, I wish to consider three minor themes, which are entangled with each other and with the major ones. The first is the perceptions of the Privy Council, which was a villain at the outset, then benign or even a hero, and last merely a piece of the distant past. The second is the scholars' attitude towards their own, Canadian, history, which, as we shall see, they tended to ignore; and the third, which may or may not be related to their lack of interest in their history, is their dependence on models of scholarship in the United States.

The first two postwar decades were dominated by three scholars – Frank Scott, Bora Laskin, and William Lederman – whom I shall discuss at length. And, fearing that my prospectus lacks vitality so far, I hasten to remind anyone who knows Frank Scott that no story that includes him can be entirely dull. In the mid-1960s, a group of younger scholars emerged, although none of them become dominant in the same way that the first three did. I shall discuss them only briefly, concluding with an equally brief account of the large differences in legal scholarship that began a decade later and that make a deep gulf between this period and the present – a gulf that will eventually explain my title.

The Contexts of Scholarship: The Doctrine and Modern Federalism

The doctrine that prevailed after the war was made by the Privy Council between the late nineteenth century and the 1930s. Its implications and the influences that shaped it have been debated at great length, but a reasonable conclusion is that, by the end of nineteenth century, the basic structures of the governments had been established and the division of powers remained as the major, even the sole, battleground. The early decisions, which are the most difficult to interpret, seem to expand the powers of the provinces, although knowing what happened afterwards may encourage this interpretation. During the 1920s, Lord Haldane gave a notorious trio of judgments that clearly and greatly diminished the powers of the federal government.[1]

Throughout the 1930s, this doctrine was attacked by scholars, especially W.P.M. Kennedy, at the University of Toronto; Frank Scott, at McGill; and Vincent MacDonald, at Dalhousie. All three were proud of Canada's new stature as a twentieth-century nation and enthusiastic about the emerging regulatory and welfare state. All three believed that the objective of Confederation, clearly expressed in the *British North America (BNA) Act*, was to give Canada a strong national government, and that the Privy Council had betrayed this wise design. What was important about their writing was not the validity of this belief – for, on any reasonable reading of the *BNA Act* and Haldane's decisions, it was substantially correct, or, at least, surely not unreasonable – but the way they made the betrayal central in their writing. As the ravages of the Depression mounted, their belief became passion, for they were convinced that only a strong Dominion could mount the response that was so urgently needed. And in 1935, when the Privy Council declared most of the New Deal statutes *ultra vires*, they were outraged, for Canada seemed to have been condemned to constitutional paralysis. I shall call their vision of federalism the 'model of nation' and assert, without stopping to offer an explanation, that it supplanted the 'model of autonomy,' based on mutually exclusive spheres of power, which had been made by scholars in the late nineteenth century.[2]

After World War II, the regulatory and welfare state expanded greatly. Old age pensions, for example, were expanded in 1951, unemployment insurance was established in 1956, and nationwide health care in 1957. Guided by Keynesian economics, the state undertook responsibility for economic stability through fiscal and monetary policy. The federal government took the initiative for these measures, with the support of all the provinces except Quebec, which alone remained aloof. Sensitivity to its claims to autonomy, coupled with the restrictions on the legislative power of the federal government, created a preference for fiscal arrangements, especially shared cost programs, rather than legislation. As the federal government and the provinces, except Quebec, undertook continuing cooperation to implement these measures, the boundaries of jurisdiction ceased to mark the limits of the functions of the governments. Early in the 1960s, the Quiet Revolution in Quebec led to claims for increased autonomy and power, and to a growing sense of urgency and crisis in English-speaking Canada.

The 1950s and 1960s: Frank Scott, Bora Laskin, and William Lederman

After the War, Frank Scott continued a many-sided career he had begun in the 1930s, continuing to write until the mid-1960s. Laskin's most productive years as a scholar were from the early 1940s to the mid-1960s, and Lederman's were roughly a decade later, from the mid-1950s to the 1970s. For all three of them, federalism was the dominant subject in their constitutional scholarship. I shall consider them separately, first, and then seek to explain their ways of thinking against the background of twentieth-century legal thought.

Scott still looms larger than life. Born in 1899 in Quebec City and educated at McGill University and at Oxford, he was a member of the Faculty of Law at McGill, a major Canadian poet, a founder of the CCF, and a crusader for civil liberties.[3] Among his immense pile of writing of many different kinds – poems, political manifestos, submissions to government, legal writing, and letters to editors – were more than a dozen scholarly articles written between the mid-1940s and 1965 that dealt with federalism in a substantial way.

Here Scott continued to embrace the model of nation that he had helped to make in the 1930s, retelling the story of betrayal and arguing that its outcome was the frustration of good government. The size and scope of modern economic and social problems were beyond the grasp of the provinces, both because they lacked the financial resources – a lack the Depression had already amply demonstrated – and, more importantly, because the problems sprawled beyond provincial boundaries. 'Provincial autonomy becomes national inactivity.'[4] Only a strong federal government could ensure redistribution to mitigate regional inequality, and only such a government could undertake the large, complex programs of the modern regulatory and welfare state. In economic affairs, private business interests, having concentrated their power greatly, went effectively unregulated by the uninterested or incapable provinces, flourishing in 'the anarchy that results from big issues being left to small jurisdictions.'[5]

Aggressive American corporations had easily invaded Canada, ruthlessly exploiting her natural resources. 'Only under an unplanned capitalism would one find Canadian children receiving a scanty education in overcrowded schools, while Texan shareholders reap huge profits from Canadian oil and natural gas.'[6] He saw that private economic power was government conducted for private gain. 'We do not escape government, but we do have a choice between public and private government'⁷ – a choice that led to him to his faith in a strong central government. Throughout, Scott passionately advocated a socialist state, arguing that socialism was not at odds with the basic principles of Canadian federalism.

Scott saw clearly how structures and practices of federalism were being changed and how 'Keynes became a kind of post-natal Father of Confederation.'⁸ Speaking of the modern welfare state, and especially of the need to diminish regional inequalities, he said that 'it requires a more co-operative kind of federalism than we have had in the past and more instruments of co-operation there can be no doubt. Federal–provincial conferences seem here to stay.'⁹

He also saw the implications for constitutional law and lawyers:

> The emergence of fiscal and monetary policy as economic regulators has become so important a factor today as almost to make us forget the question of legislative jurisdiction. It seems to have by-passed Sections 91 and 92 of the B.N.A. Act. The lawyers are moving out and the economists are moving in.¹⁰

As well, Scott saw the implications for democratic responsibility of conferences among mandarins and politicians. Observing the 1961 conferences on patriation, he anticipated the debates about the Meech Lake agreement by saying that

> [w]hat is happening at the Attorneys-General Conference is mostly confidential and cannot be discussed here. This is itself a fact of some importance. It is our country and our future that is being planned and we – the citizens – should have our chance to be heard at the appropriate time before our governments have taken up fixed positions.¹¹

Quebec's distinctive role in Canadian federalism was another large theme, one that had not been present in Scott's writing in the 1930s. He believed deeply in a vision of Canada as a partnership between two cultures, and, as a member of the Commission on Bilingualism and Biculturalism, he advocated equality between the two languages. He believed just as deeply, though, that autonomy had not been necessary for the preservation of Quebec's culture in the past and would not be necessary in the future. Private economic power and the scale of modern technology made it a foolish hope to entrust a culture to a small, autonomous government. The partnership Scott envisioned could flourish within the framework originally established by the *BNA Act*.

Throughout these articles, Scott wrote much about context and values: about current politics, the changing practices of federalism, the emergence of autonomy in Quebec, technological trends, the concentration of economic power, the expansion of American investment, and his own passionate beliefs about Canadian federalism and socialism. To read these articles is to read a colourful, opinionated, and intelligent history of the times. At the same time, they contained little analysis of the doctrine. For example, Scott did not undertake a thorough analysis of the course of the betrayal, not even of Lord Haldane's trilogy, which began while Scott was a law student and concluded when he was a young lawyer in Montreal. He did not often discuss recent cases, and in his accounts of the contemporary issues of doctrine that concerned him, such as taxation powers or the regulation of investment, he did not parse cases or discuss principles such as the aspect rule, necessarily incidental effects, or paramountcy, preferring to limit himself to generalizations and conclusions. For example, he concluded that the trade and commerce power gave the federal government almost no power to regulate direct investment, since 'the Privy Council long ago laid down the ridiculous rule that federal authority to regulate trade and commerce did not include regulation of any particular trades _ in which Canadians would otherwise be free to engage in the provinces';[12] both the conclusion and the reason were sensible, but in drawing it he analysed neither this complex doctrine and its awkward inconsistencies nor the trends in contemporary cases. Nor did he discuss the nature of judicial reasoning or the functions of courts in any sustained way.

Bora Laskin was born in Fort William, Ontario, in 1912 and enrolled in the University of Toronto in the early 1930s. After obtaining a BA in 1933, he turned to the law school, then headed by W.P.M. Kennedy, receiving an MA in 1935 and an LLB in 1936. Next, with Kennedy's encouragement, he went to Harvard, where he studied for an LLM under Felix Frankfurter. After returning to Toronto, he languished until Kennedy hired him in 1940. Five years later he was enticed to Osgoode Hall by 'Caesar' Wright, and in 1949 he returned to the University of Toronto, following Wright, who had resigned from Osgoode Hall to become dean at Toronto. Here, Laskin was a dominant figure in common law scholarship until he was appointed to the Ontario Court of Appeal in 1965. Soon afterwards he was elevated to the Supreme Court, becoming chief justice in 1970.

His earliest writing was a series of about 15 comments between 1940 and 1947. In 1947, he wrote 'Peace, Order, and Good Government Re-examined,'[13] his first major effort and still probably his best-known article. Four years later, in 1951, came a collection of teaching materials, *Canadian Constitutional Law*,[14] and an article, 'The Supreme Court of Canada: A Final Court of and for Canadians.'[15] The five years from 1955 to 1959, his most productive period, included a couple of important case comments and four substantial articles, about characterization, section 96, agricultural marketing programs, and the *Bill of Rights*.[16] His last article before being appointed to the Court of Appeal, written in 1963, was about paramountcy.[17] After his appointment, Laskin continued to write scholarly articles that gave some useful insights into his beliefs about judicial reasoning but added little to his thoughts about federalism.

Almost all Laskin's writing before his appointment was dominated by analysis of doctrine, either cases or issues defined in terms of doctrine, and by a concern with ways of reasoning. Typically, he set out the doctrine surrounding each topic, exposing the inconsistencies of the results and the inadequacies of the reasoning. What did a case decide? Was it consistent with the earlier cases? What were its implications for unsettled problems? His concern with ways of reasoning included common law reasoning, for example, the nature of precedent, but it was directed much more at the general principles for deciding federalism cases and at such topics as characterization, the 'necessarily incidental' principle, and the relation between paramountcy and validity. Characterization was the central issue for Laskin, and he revisited it often. The audience he had in mind seems to be primarily, perhaps entirely, lawyers – the judges who would decide cases, the counsel who would argue them, and the students who would become the lawyers and the judges.

In contrast to the emphasis on doctrine and technique, there was little description of context and values. Until he became a judge, Laskin said virtually nothing about the changing practices of federalism or the turmoil in Quebec. Nor did he consider any of the scholarship done in civilian law schools. He did not declare his own preferences for Canada's federalism in any express, sustained way, nor did he demonstrate any significant interest in Canadian history – not even Confederation, or the searing experience of the Depression. Yet there can be no doubt at all that he did not intend his writing to be a disembodied exercise in technical analysis. That he cared deeply not only about legal analysis but about Canada is demonstrated by both an obvious sense of urgency in this writing, demonstrated most clearly in 'Peace, Order, and Good Government Re-examined,'[18] and the testimony of colleagues and students. I shall return to this tension between the mode of scholarship and the passion, but first I turn to considering his beliefs about federalism and ways of thinking.

Laskin had a deep and abiding belief that Canada should have a strong national government. The story of betrayal ran throughout his writing, appearing briefly in the case comments in 1940s and most fully and famously in 'Peace, Order, and Good Government Re-examined.' He argued that the Privy Council, abetted by an obedient Supreme Court, had greatly and unjustifiably diminished the powers of the federal government, creating a 'destructive, negative' autonomy for the provinces.[19] Haldane was the major villain, Duff his willing collaborator.

Laskin did not analyse the boundaries of the federal power at any substantial length, however, or give examples, except for the regulation of agricultural products and nuclear energy.[20] Instead, he spoke generally of a need for power to deal with problems of a national scope. In contrast, he did not consider the power of the provinces in any general and sustained way. In itself, this is not remarkable – for him, their powers were not pressing or problematic. He did not, though, thoroughly consider the implications of assigning large powers to both levels of government. He did not consider, for example, the implications for the structure of the powers, for the doctrine of paramountcy, and for cooperative federalism. In the 1963 article about paramountcy he expressed a preference for the narrowest of the apparent tests for conflict – 'conflict in _ actual operation' – not for some reason based on substantive principles of federalism but because it was the most 'manageable and demonstrable.'[21]

Looking backwards, we can see that Laskin's beliefs about federalism were essentially the same as those of Frank Scott and the scholars of the 1930s: the model of nation, based on the belief that Canada needed a strong central government, and the cruel betrayal by the Privy Council. Perhaps his beliefs were shaped by his early experience. He had gone to Toronto, the heart of central Canada, as little more than a youth, and to a law school where Kennedy was at the peak of his powers. Moreover, the model of nation seemed appropriate immediately after the war, when the federal government was taking the initiative in making the modern state. But there were two important differences between Laskin and the earlier scholars. First, he stressed the doctrine far more than they did, analysing the cases at great length and presenting the ways of reasoning needed to decide them properly. Second, they perceived the betrayal primarily as the abandonment of the original design of Confederation, a design that they hoped the courts would restore; Laskin, in contrast, did not look to the past for guidance.

Turning from federalism to ways of thinking about law, Laskin's writing continually attacked the courts for their techniques of reasoning. Typically, his attack was made in phrases that were virtually a code. For example, in 'Peace, Order, and Good Government Re-examined,' he condemned 'cold abstract logic,' 'rigid abstractions,' 'inflexible concepts,' and an unwillingness to consider 'the context of our society and its contemporary problems.'[22] In later writing, he lamented that a 'legal logic' prevailed even though 'its social underpinning has disappeared';[23] he condemned 'wooden reasoning' and 'conceptualism' that did not serve the contemporary constitutional or social order;[24] and he rejected 'the hypnosis of empty words'[25] and 'mechanical jurisprudence.'[26]

The meaning of these phrases was revealed most clearly in his discussions of characterization. He considered it first, like much of his thinking, in 'Peace, Order, and Good Government Re-examined,' where he argued that the Privy Council had failed to use the aspect rule sensibly. For example, in the economic regulation cases, it had seen only local purposes and effects, failing to recognize the national interest and sweep of the regulatory schemes. These thoughts were expanded in the 1955 article on characterization, which was a response to an article by David Mundell, a Toronto lawyer who later became a senior counsel in the Ontario government.[27] Mundell asserted that characterization was entirely objective – a determination of fact, involving no weighing or choice by the judge – and that the Privy Council had been consistent in its labours. Laskin's response scorned this 'naiveté' and the 'delusion that constitutional adjudication is "pure" law, divorced from social, or economic, or political (in the highest sense) beliefs.' 'A verbal mechanism will not assist in deciding cases.'[28]

What he was rejecting in all these phrases was the faith that answers to constitutional questions were embedded in words and doctrine – the text of the *BNA Act* and the precedents – to be discovered or extracted by judges without making choices or exercising discretion. For him, choice was inescapable. Two representative passages are 'a selective process is involved and this necessarily means a choice among competing factors'[29] and 'constitutional adjudication involves considerations of policy and hence of social and political and economic beliefs.'[30]

Not only was the failure to acknowledge choice inadequate, it was often misleading, for wooden recitals of doctrine too often masked outcomes determined by the social and economic preferences of the judges.[31] His target in all these attacks was not simply the Privy Council but also the Canadian judges, especially the Supreme Court, now supreme in authority as well as in name but apparently inclined to follow the inadequate and misleading ways of reasoning of the past.

Laskin's dominant objective throughout these attacks was to educate his generation about the errors of the courts and about how to reason more openly and effectively. The scholars of the 1930s had also condemned the Privy Council, but they were not read much, if at all, after the war, and in any case they did little analysis of the cases and said little about ways of reasoning. Remembered in this way, 'Peace, Order, and Good Government Re-examined,' Laskin's casebook, and his teaching can be seen as an inspiration for a generation of students.

If choice was inescapable, though, what was the significance of the text and precedent? Laskin said little of a general nature about either. About text, he said almost nothing, although presumably he would have believed that it set some limits within which the choice was to be made. He was only a little more forthcoming about precedent. In 1951, borrowing a phrase from Cardozo, he hoped that the liberated Supreme Court would understand that 'consistency in decisions is merely a convenience and not a necessity.'[32]

But what were the standards or criteria for making the choices? Laskin's answer, which he repeated often, was that they must be responses to contemporary needs and conditions. For him, the betrayal by the Privy Council was its failure to consider the 'profound social and economic changes'[33] that had taken place since Confederation, and he hoped that courts would come to consider legislation 'in the context of our society and its contemporary problems.'[34] Usually, in discussing particular issues and cases, he seemed to assume that the proper choices were embedded in the facts. An example is his analysis of two cases in the late 1950s that seemed to him to give hope for a revival of the federal power to regulate trade and commerce. One was *R. v. Klassen*,[35] in which the Manitoba Court of Appeal upheld the federal regulation of a small, local grain transaction as part of regulation of the national grain market under section 91(2) of the *BNA Act*, and the other was *Pronto Uranium Mines v. Ontario Labour Relations Board*,[36] in which the Ontario

High Court assumed that the regulation of nuclear fission was within 'Peace, Order, and Good Government' and upheld federal regulation of labour relations in uranium mining. Laskin argued that in each of these cases the proper characterization was derived from a perception of functional relationships. For example, in *Pronto Uranium*, the outcome was 'an assessment of the facts,' especially the relation between the mining of the uranium and nuclear fission: '[T]he functional interrelationship of any group of operations may be such as to make all of them reasonably susceptible to uniform treatment.'[37]

Beyond this sort of demonstration, Laskin did little to elaborate the nature of the choices to be made or to explain how they might be made. The pursuit of contemporary needs and conditions precluded looking to history – to Confederation, the *BNA Act*, or the accumulated experience of a century – and in 1965 he declared, '[H]istorical records have, of course, but a limited value in constitutional interpretation (especially as we move farther from them in time), and this is so even where they speak clearly.'[38] Nor did he consider the significance of values and the possible need to choose among conflicting values. Perhaps the need for a strong central government was the basic value, although he did not explain whether it was derived from the *BNA Act* or from contemporary social need. He seemed to assume that a social consensus existed, not only about the basic principles but also about the relative values of different undertakings and activities, which the courts could read in an objective and dispassionate way. In the 1950s, this was a tempting assumption and probably a prevailing one, once Quebec's claims were marginalized. In the midst of Canada's peace and prosperity, social and economic divisions seemed relatively minor.

Laskin's inspiration of a generation of students and his towering stature in Canadian scholarship and teaching are unquestioned. I am puzzled, though, by tensions in his work: between the call for an escape from 'legal logic' and the emphasis on doctrinal analysis; between the call for recognition of contemporary values and the lack of illumination from the contemporary context; and between his love of Canada and his lack of interest its past. All of these tensions are captured for me in 'Peace, Order, and Good Government Re-examined' and in the way his passion about the betrayal of Canada was expressed in doctrinal analysis that seems distant from the Depression and the needs of the welfare state.

Bill Lederman was born in 1916, four years later than Laskin, in Saskatoon, Saskatchewan, a thousand miles west of Fort William. After

obtaining degrees in Arts and Law from the University of Saskatchewan
in the late 1930s, he enlisted in the army. Following the war, he began
his teaching at Saskatchewan and then did graduate work at Oxford on
a Rhodes scholarship he had been awarded just before he enlisted. He
went to Dalhousie in 1949, and then to Queen's in 1958, serving as dean
until 1968 and remaining there until his death in 1992.

Lederman's first article about federalism was an extended study of
classification, written in 1953.[39] A set of four articles in the 1960s completed his major ideas: in 1962, he wrote about paramountcy;[40] in the
next year, he considered treaties, making a proposal about 'Peace,
Order, and Good Government';[41] and a year later, he introduced the
idea that Canada's federalism was 'balanced.'[42] The last of this series of
articles appeared in 1967, and in it he considered the structure of
cooperative federalism.[43] Lederman expanded the ideas in these articles until the late 1970s. Most importantly, he elaborated ideas about
federalism as a balance; judicial reasoning, especially interpretation
and precedent; cooperative federalism; and the nature and doctrine of
the 'Peace, Order, and Good Government' power. As well, he began to
consider the appearance of Quebec's claims to greater powers and
autonomy. Like Laskin, however, he did not explore any of the scholarship done in civilian law schools.

By the end of the 1970s, Lederman had written almost 30 articles –
more or less the same number as Laskin. Almost all of this writing was
about relatively general topics, such as characterization, paramountcy,
and cooperative federalism, and about trends in the division of powers.
Little of it was intensive analysis of doctrine and patterns of cases.
Lederman tended, instead, to suggest sweeping trends, discussing a
handful of major cases without unravelling them in great detail. Even
his proposals for reformulating doctrine included little detailed analysis, instead presenting the proposal and its justifications in general
terms. The few articles that were avowedly accounts of doctrine took
much the same form: extended expositions of doctrine, with the cases
used primarily as reference points or relegated to the footnotes.

Lederman often invoked social and political contexts; for example, he
alluded often to the practices of cooperative federalism, the Depression,
and the ferment in Quebec. His audience included lawyers but not, I
think, lawyers alone. His writing was accessible to a wider range of
academics than Laskin's, and perhaps also to politicians, in a way that
suggests the public service traditions of both Queen's and Saskatchewan.

As in my discussion of Laskin, I shall consider Lederman's beliefs about Canadian federalism and then his beliefs about ways of thinking. His vision of federalism, which I shall call the model of balance, was composed of two central elements, balance and cooperation, which he first articulated in 1965, in the same article.[44] I shall consider balance first. In the original article, Lederman asserted that Canada had 'a balanced federal constitution – one that maintains and develops reasonable equilibrium between centralization and provincial autonomy'[45] Clearly, he intended both to describe and to approve the contemporary world. This idea reappeared several times in his writing during the next 10 years, especially in 1975, when he spoke of 'a carefully balanced federalism that accommodated old and new diversities as well as ensuring essential unities.'[46] Moreover, he argued that the balance had not been made by the *BNA Act*, which was 'simply ambiguous or incomplete.'[47] Instead, it had been made by the courts, 'painstakingly, by judicial interpretation and precedent over many years.'[48] He saw that the courts had changed the equilibrium from time to time during the twentieth century, to take account of new needs, although he did little to trace the changes through the cases or to describe the contexts and the needs.

Lederman invoked balance in an imaginative way in proposals he made for the 'Peace, Order, and Good Government' power. The first such proposal, which he made in 1963, was about treaties.[49] He rejected both giving the federal government exclusive power and giving it no power at all: one would threaten the autonomy of the provinces, while the other would frustrate Canada's participation in the modern international community. Instead, he proposed that 'Peace, Order, and Good Government' be a power to implement treaties that had 'genuine and important national aspects.'[50]

More than a decade later, Lederman made a more general proposal. In its background was a concern he had expressed several times before about the handful of relatively broad powers in the *BNA Act*, especially the 'Peace, Order, and Good Government' power, that he saw as threats to autonomy and balance. Considering 'Peace, Order, and Good Government,' the central question was what standards or test should determine whether a subject came within its scope. His answer was, 'First, the new subject must require country-wide regulation at the national level. Secondly, new subject must also have an identity and unity that is quite limited and particular in its extent.'[51] This was the test adopted shortly afterwards by Betz J. in the *Reference Re Anti-Inflation Act*[52] and established as authority in *R. v. Crown Zellerback*.[53] Continuing his concern about broad powers, he argued that power should not be given over sweeping and all-pervasive subjects such as labour, pollution, and economic growth. Instead, subjects must be divided into meaningful levels of specifics and particulars, and comprehensive legislative programs should be made through cooperation. Moreover, the need for stability meant that changes must be made gradually and that getting past this threshold should be difficult. Other scholars made suggestions for this doctrine, but Lederman's contribution was the most thorough.[54]

Lederman introduced the second element of his beliefs about federalism, cooperation, briefly in 1965;[55] elaborated his thoughts at length in 1967;[56] and revisited them several times afterwards.[57] Again, he both described the contemporary world and approved of it. Cooperation between the central and local governments was a necessary and valuable element of any modern federalism because of the interdependence that was embedded in the modern social, political, and economic worlds. The governments could not remain in separate spheres. No matter how carefully their powers were drafted, many important subjects – he often took the environment as an example – had overlapping local and national perspectives that could not be untangled and must be 'harmonized' and 'coordinated.'[58]

The major means for achieving this coordination were delegation and conditional grants, both of which he discussed at length. Another reason for cooperation was to achieve regional equality through income transfers from the federal government, typically through conditional grants.

Lederman saw cooperation and its techniques as essentially benign. Conditional grants did pose some threat to a balanced federalism, by threatening to make differences among provinces, but not to autonomy, since 'each party has real bargaining power.'[59] Moreover, whatever dangers did exist were greatly outweighed by advantages, especially that of providing welfare and health services more widely than would have been otherwise. More generally, Lederman denied that cooperation through agreements between governments threatened democracy, on the grounds that cabinet government ensured responsibility. Scott saw the future outcry more clearly. Despite his sanguine assessment of cooperation, Lederman did insist that the legal structure of the division of powers was basic and must be maintained, to give the governments their balanced powers, and changed only slowly and carefully, to ensure stability.

Lederman's model of balance was a more accurate account of developing doctrine and contemporary practice than the model of nation. From its perspective, he saw the Privy Council and the Supreme Court in a much different light than did Scott, Laskin, and the scholars of the 1930s. They had made this balance, and made it reasonably well. The villains, except Haldane (and even he was not harshly criticized) became benign, and even heroes, for Lord Watson's judgment in the *Local Prohibition* case, especially its balance between provincial autonomy and national concern, was the 'primary words of wisdom.'[60] Both Lederman's vision of federalism and his perception of the Privy Council were major shifts in constitutional scholarship.

Moreover, both marked a deep difference between Lederman and Laskin, a difference that may have been shaped by time and geography. The four years that separated their birthdays were a short period, but a crucial one, for it brought Lederman to early adulthood during and after the war, and in a Canada much different from that of the 1930s. The thousand miles between their birthplaces put him in the middle of the prairies and in Saskatoon, a long cultural and political distance from Toronto, Kennedy's law school, and the model of nation.

In terms of ways of thinking about law, the basic elements of Lederman's beliefs were much the same as Laskin's. Doctrine – precedent and the terms of statutes – did not determine outcomes, at least not often. The courts must often choose, and they must make their choices wisely and with restraint, taking into account the needs of contemporary society. Lederman presented these beliefs primarily in his discussions of two interrelated topics, characterization and interpretation. His major effort to describe characterization was his first article about federalism, written two years before Laskin's debate with Mundell.[61] It was the foundation of much of his own thinking and a landmark in Canadian legal thought.

Drawing on basic principles of definition and classification, Lederman wrote that 'there are as many possible classifications of a rule of law as that rule has distinct characteristics or attributes that may be isolated as criteria of classification.' This led him to the conclusion that it was usually possible to characterize a statute in ways that put it within the powers of either the provinces or the federal government. The choice among the possible classifications could not be made by relying on logic, 'for logic merely displays the many possible classifications.' The court must instead ask, 'Is it better for the people that this thing be done at a national level, or at a provincial level,' or by both? Put in a different and more colourful way, '[W]ho is the better physician to prescribe in this way for this malady?' To make this choice, the courts must consider 'the relative value of uniformity and regional diversity, the relative merits of local *versus* central administration, and the justice of minority claims.' The considerations should be 'weighed carefully,' and 'widely prevailing beliefs' should be influential. For some problems, though, he perceived that these considerations would not give a clear answer and that the judge must make the choice alone.[62]

These beliefs about characterization combined with the idea of the balance of powers to make another change in perceptions of federalism – about the nature and relation of the powers of the governments – a change that was implicit in all that Laskin said, although it was more clearly articulated by Lederman. The sharp-edged, mutually exclusive spheres of the late nineteenth century and the model of autonomy were gone, replaced by spheres that I can best describe as fuzzy and overlapping. The federal and provincial powers overlapped, both because the terms of sections 91 and 92 overlapped and, more importantly, because characterization was essentially a choice. The function of courts had changed in a corresponding way. Instead of policing the boundaries of the spheres, they weighed and balanced competing claims to power, in a way that I shall seek to explain in a moment. It is this combination of the balanced powers and the courts as makers of the balance that makes the name 'the model of balance' appropriate.

Lederman's beliefs about interpretation paralleled these beliefs about characterization.[63] Two modes were available, and the choice between them was 'the central issue' of constitutional law. The first approach was the 'literal or grammatical,' which emphasized words. It was the method that had been dominant in the Privy Council and the Supreme Court, but it was hopeless; words alone could not determine outcomes. Lederman's favourite example of the failure of words alone was the way in which the *BNA Act* had been read in diametrically different ways by W.F. O'Connor, in his Report to the Senate, and by a Canadian historian, G.P. Browne, in *The Judicial Committee and the British North America Act*.[64] Words could limit choices and focus thinking, however. The second approach, preferable by far, was the 'sociological' approach, which linked the words to 'the ongoing life of the country.' The most promising prospect for improvement in interpretation lay in 'judicial appreciation of social, political, economic and cultural facts that gave the various aspects of challenged statutes their relative importance.'[65]

In his 1953 article on classification, Lederman suggested that precedents – the outcomes of earlier choices – would often not determine the choices. 'The degree of certainty and predictability their operation can provide is often much overestimated or misconceived,' he wrote, and often judges would confront the choices 'just as starkly as the original constitution-makers themselves.'[66] He did not expressly return to this question, but, during the next two decades, he came to have a far greater faith in the stability and continuity of precedent, a faith illustrated by his claim that the balance of federalism had been made by the courts, by his stress on the need for stability of doctrine, and by his proposals for changes in the doctrine.[67]

All these beliefs about judicial reasoning were, again, much the same as Laskin's, although expressed much more fully, and, like Laskin, he said little to analyse the nature of the choices or to explain how the courts might make them, except by suggesting that they have ample evidence, in the fashion of a Brandeis brief. He seemed to assume that two sets of claims would appear and be weighted, but he did not suggest what the interests or considerations might be or explore the process of weighing them. He referred to history more than Laskin did, but he never explored Canadian history to understand the process of change, for lessons about its federalism, or for guidance about the nature of the society that the courts must understand. Instead, his history tended to be a vague teleological force in the background or a selective Whiggish story.

Lederman accomplished much. His writing in the mid-1960s began a shift in perceptions of the Privy Council; his vision of federalism as balance was both an accurate perception of the contemporary political practice and a rich insight into the judicial process, anticipating much of the thinking of the Supreme Court; and, last, he contributed much to the current doctrine, especially the doctrine about national concern.

Judicial Reasoning: The Sources

I now turn to speculating about the sources of the beliefs of all three scholars – Scott, Laskin, and Lederman – about legal reasoning. In short, my impression is that they derived their beliefs primarily from the thinking that emerged in the United States early in the twentieth century. I shall consider Laskin and Lederman first, simply because Scott was so distinctive.

My argument requires a hasty survey of legal thought in the twentieth century. Major changes began in the United States around the turn of the century. The beginnings were some of the striking insights and aphorisms of Oliver Wendell Holmes. After him, early in the twentieth century, came the Progressives, notably Roscoe Pound and Benjamin Cardozo. The very titles of some of Pound's articles suggest their program: 'Mechanical Jurisprudence,'[68] 'Sociological Jurisprudence.'[69] They rejected late-nineteenth-century thought, which they labelled 'mechanical jurisprudence,' because of its faith (or the faith they attributed to it) that doctrine alone could and should determine outcomes. Instead, they argued, judges could not escape making choices.

This attack on the power of doctrine to determine outcomes let a cat out of the bag, and much of twentieth-century legal thought can be seen as an effort to domesticate it, and especially to prevent it from being a political alley cat. The answer of Pound and his generation was that these choices should be deliberately made to promote the social welfare. The law was not an end itself, or an elegant set of abstract principles, but a means to the social good. Doctrine and precedent were not authoritative commands but guidelines directed to this same purpose. When Pound called for a 'sociological jurisprudence,' he used the word 'sociological,' not in any modern sense, but to mean 'social'; in the same sense, he argued that lawyers should be social engineers. Reform was desperately needed. It should be made primarily by legislatures, and their work should be respected and implemented by the courts.

All these ideas, and many of the particular words and phrases, were at the centre of the thought in the 1950s. Laskin referred to very few authors, but he paid tribute to Cardozo, whose ideas in *The Nature of the Legal Process* seemed to him in 1972 to be 'as fresh today as they were in 1921.'[70] Lederman invoked Cardozo, Pound, Cohen, and Dickinson, and his analysis of the inescapable need to make choices may have been influenced by Felix Cohen.[71] For Laskin, the influence of these thinkers may well have come directly from his early mentors: Kennedy, Frankfurter, and Wright. Lederman is more of a puzzle. Oxford was a bastion of traditional thought when he did his graduate work there after the war, hardly likely to stimulate the sorts of ideas he expressed in the article about classification he wrote a few years later. Perhaps he was given a push by teachers at Saskatchewan, and perhaps he gathered the ideas from the extensive reading in legal theory he began while he was at Oxford.[72]

A younger generation, usually called the Realists, emerged in the late 1920s and 1930s, led by such scholars as Karl Llewellyn, Jerome Frank, and Thurman Arnold. Historians of American legal thought debate the measure of continuity between them and the Progressives, as well as the contribution of each to the longer story. My sense is that the Realists continued both the Progressive attack on late-nineteenth-century thought and the belief that judges must seek the social welfare. They tended, though, to have more regard for legislatures, to see more indeterminacy in doctrine, and to look more to the emerging social sciences for guidance. From the perspective of more than half a century, much of the thought that was distinctively realist seems to have been an exciting detour, and the Progressives seem to have made a larger lasting contribution. Certainly the Realists had virtually no influence on Laskin or Lederman. Both expressly disavowed the indeterminacy of Realist thinking, and both had a strong faith in doctrine, albeit as guidelines and standards, not as inflexible rules. Moreover, neither expressed any significant interest in the social sciences.

But what about the influence from contemporary legal thought in the United States? During the 1950s, Canadian law schools began to make Harvard, Yale, Columbia, and Chicago their models. The dominant mode of thinking in these schools, so dominant that it seemed to be the natural, normal way in which every good scholar thought, is labelled the 'legal process.' It was composed of two major themes, the first of which was legal institutions: the distinctive expertise of lawyers was to understand the appropriate functions and procedures for legislatures, courts, and administrative agencies. The second was reasoned elaboration. Courts did not make unconstrained choices about values; instead, they reasoned to elaborate widely shared principles and purposes. These themes were shaped by a need to escape the threat of the indeterminacy suggested by the some Realists and were founded on a faith in a widely shared set of fundamental values.

My impression is that this thought did not have a large impact on Laskin, Lederman, and their generation, at least not in their thinking about federalism. They emphatically shared with the legal process the faith that the functions of courts were reasoned and objective, but this faith was not distinctive to the postwar period. They did not invoke the major themes of the legal process or refer to its major thinkers. Perhaps they had matured before the legal process became dominant; perhaps it did not seem to have much to contribute to the problems of federalism; and perhaps it was simply not attractive to them, based as it was on distinctive American issues, especially the need to tame Realism. But they did share a mood with the legal process scholars, which I can best describe as an emphasis on professionalism, a word that expresses, at least for me, the emphasis on doctrine and technique and a distance from context and values. Two possible sources for this mood were, first, a faith in shared values and a peaceful society, which may have tempted a sense that the job of lawyers – and law teachers – was to implement these values; and, second, the pervasive need to establish the postwar law schools as professional schools, which may have tempted law teachers to demonstrate their usefulness to the professional enterprise and to shy away from debates about values, especially because their own were likely to be to the left of the practising profession and their clients.

I return to the suggestion that the thinkers in the early twentieth century were the shaping influence for Laskin and Lederman, and that little influence came from the Realists and the legal process. This may be a surprising idea, but I derive some comfort from recent American writing that emphasizes the continuing influence of the Progressives.[73]

But what about their own Canadian past? In the 1930s a handful of scholars, including Kennedy, Scott, and MacDonald, enthusiastically embraced the new world introduced by the Progressives. They were aware of contemporary scholarship in the United States, and of some parallel scholarship undertaken by a hardy few in England, and some of them seem to have been directly influenced by the Progressives, especially Pound. Others, though, seem to have been shaped by a more varied set of influences.[74]

In looking back from the 1960s to the 1930s, we must not base any comparisons primarily on Kennedy and Scott alone, for they were distinctive individuals. Nonetheless, looking not only at them but at MacDonald and such other scholars as Caesar Wright, Percy Corbett, John Willis, Alex Corry, and Jacob Finkelman, it seems to me that Laskin and Lederman were different, especially because of their mood of professionalism. In contrast, the earlier scholars spoke more about context and about the values that supported their sense of betrayal. Perhaps I can suggest a different mood by saying that they were more openly passionate and excited, and it is the phrase 'more openly' that is crucial.

Frank Scott Revisited

Scott shared much with Laskin and Lederman, but differed, too, in complex ways that I find difficult to describe and even more difficult to explain. His vision of federalism was substantially the same as Laskin's, the model of nation, although he was more forthcoming about why a strong federal government was needed. About the judicial process he said very little. My understanding, and 'guess' might be a more appropriate word, is that his basic beliefs were substantially the same as the others'. Doctrine did not determine outcomes, and law was a social construct which should be made to serve social purposes. But he was less consistent and more opportunistic in his use of doctrine than either Lederman or Laskin, and more inclined to adopt whatever approach seemed appropriate for the task or cause at hand.

The most obvious differences were Scott's open declaration of his values and his extensive use of context. True, there was a difference of this kind between Laskin and Lederman, but it was not nearly as large as the difference between Scott and the other two. This difference made Scott's audience wider that even Lederman's, suggesting that his objectives may have included educating – no, persuading – Canadian citizens. More than the different audience, though, and more than a different style, this difference may suggest that he saw a closer relation between law, and its context, and politics, although I should not suggest that Scott had made some careful analysis about the relation. Perhaps, whatever other reasons there are for Scott's distinctiveness, he was rooted in the 1930s.

The Generation of the 1960s

A new group of scholars emerged in the mid-1960s. Most of them were Canadians, relatively young, and at the outset of their careers: Dale Gibson at the University of Manitoba, Noel Lyon at the University of British Columbia (UBC) and at Queen's, Ken Lysyk at UBC, Colin McNairn at Toronto, Barry Strayer at Saskatchewan, and Paul Weiler at Osgoode Hall. Two other members of the group were somewhat different. The first, Albert Abel, was an American and considerably older that the others, having taught in the United States for about 20 years before coming to Toronto as a result of a friendship with Laskin. The second of the two, Edward McWhinney, was an Australian who did graduate work at Yale before coming to Toronto and began to write a few years before the others. Whatever else they all had in common, virtually all had done graduate work in the United States, at Harvard or Yale.[75]

Most of their writing was primarily analysis of doctrine, and much of it was straightforward exposition, with little critical analysis or sustained evaluation.[76] Writing of this kind had been virtually absent since the early twentieth century, and it must have seemed greatly needed in a world that had changed so much during more than half a century. As well, these scholars, like Laskin and Lederman, may have felt the need to establish their schools as professional schools and felt that exposition might support this objective by demonstrating that scholars could participate in the mainstream of lawyers' work. Some of this writing made proposals, especially about 'Peace, Order, and Good Government'[77] and about treaties,[78] and some of it included criticism of the results or the reasoning of the cases,[79] although the amount of this criticism and its vehemence were far less than in the writing of the 1930s or in Laskin's 'Peace, Order, and Good Government Re-examined.' Very little of it dealt with the work of the Privy Council, and that which did treated it with little passion, as history or as an example of reasoning to be avoided.[80] Throughout, these discussions of doctrine tended to be detached from context, with little consideration of the changing practices of federalism. For example, there was little writing about the spending power, taxation, and delegation, or about the ways in which the courts and their doctrine were no longer determining the allocation of the functions of government.

A large handful of articles about Quebec appeared in the second half of the 1960s, most of them describing the issues and the conflicting claims in a general way and proposing some degree of accommodation.[81] At the same time a cluster of articles appeared about amendment, especially about the Fulton-Favreau proposal.[82] These scholars did little to propose a new constitutional framework for Canada, however. Albert Abel made the most elaborate structure, which disappeared from sight almost entirely unnoticed.[83] Apart from these discussions of Quebec and efforts by Abel and Lysyk, there were few express discussions of the structure and the allocation of powers.

There was not much discussion of ways of thinking about law. Most of this group seemed to share the beliefs of Laskin and Lederman and to feel little need for discussion or analysis. Two of them did tackle the task of rethinking: Noel Lyon and Paul Weiler. Both wrote in 1967, and both began with a ritual slaying of their nineteenth-century ancestors, especially their faith in 'logic' and their recitals of doctrine that masked choices about values. This task hardly needed doing in the world of legal theory, for it was the same task that had been begun in the early twentieth century, but, like Laskin and Lederman, Lyon and Weiler believed that the enemy was still alive and well in the contemporary courts, and especially in the Supreme Court. They later turned to alternative models of reasoning, which seem to have been shaped by their graduate work and which were the first significant efforts in the Canadian literature to go beyond simple exhortations about responding to social context and values. Lyon's proposal was 'policy science,' derived from his graduate work at Yale under Laswell and McDougall.[84] Weiler, in turn, seems to have been influenced by his graduate work at Harvard, and especially by the legal process.[85]

With only a few, marginal, exceptions,[86] this group continued the forgetting of their Canadian history that had begun in the mid-1950s, as well as the tendency to rely on American models. For example, Lyon and Weiler cited little Canadian literature – and almost none that reached beyond legal materials. Weiler declared that in making the changes to escape from the past, 'we will be decades behind the same developments in our neighbour to the south,' as though following in its neighbour's footsteps were desirable and unproblematic.[87]

Conclusion: Dorothy's Trip to Oz

My purpose extends only to the early 1970s, and therefore I shall not dwell on the scholars who followed after the mid-1960s group, for example, Katherine Swinton and Peter Hogg. Instead, I wish to conclude by considering the large changes that began in the mid-1970s, which have made a deep gulf between contemporary scholars and the scholars I have sought to reconstruct. The major landmarks were the appearance of new approaches, such as Critical Legal Studies and Law and Economics, and turmoil in law schools, typically about curriculum and standards for appointments. As well, my sense is that at the same time, scholars' understandings of themselves changed. The earlier scholars thought of themselves as lawyers, teaching students to become lawyers; contemporary scholars, in contrast, tend to think of themselves, instead or as well, as members of a university, studying and teaching law as a social, historical, and theoretical enterprise.

The best way to describe how these changes manifested themselves in constitutional scholarship is to imagine that one of my earlier scholars, say one who was working in the 1960s, was swept up in a tornado and deposited in midst of the conference of constitutional scholars held at the University of Toronto in October 2000, arranged by Patrick Macklem and David Schneiderman. My displaced scholar would have found the conference a strange world, as Dorothy found Oz, in which the participants spoke a language that was both familiar and full of unexpected twists and turns.

Looking at the topics for discussion at the conference and the current projects of the participants, Dorothy would soon have realized that federalism had been displaced as the dominant focus of scholarship by rights, both individual and collective, especially the rights granted by the *Charter of Rights and Freedoms*. She would also have sensed that attitudes towards doctrine had changed. It would quickly have been apparent to her that none of the topics for the panels contained doctrinal terms and that only a few of the participants made analysis of doctrine central in any of their current projects. Her first impression might have been that for the most part, the inhabitants of Oz were simply ignoring doctrine, but eventually she would have understand that this impression was far too simple; they were, after all, studying and talking about law and legal institutions, but she would have had trouble figuring out just what their interests were.

After listening to the discussions for a while, here are some of the themes she might have observed. First, these scholars were interested in the basic nature of constitutions and rights; for example, they talked about the Constitution as dialogue or as process, and about preserving what has been distinctive and valuable about Canada. Of course, she too was interested in constitutions and rights, but they tended to seek fundamental ideas more than she did, to be more openly and explicitly concerned about social context, and to be shaped by the 'interpretive turn' that she had flown over in the tornado. They were also concerned with techniques of legal reasoning, especially interpretation, the justifications for review, and the forms of argument in constitutional cases. Again, these were familiar ideas to her, but these scholars were more theoretical than she, less interested in seeking immediate utility for specific decisions, and much more interested in political implications. Here she was especially disoriented, being equally concerned with technique but in an apolitical way. She would also have perceived that many of the discussions and the projects of the participants included comparisons to other countries, far more than she had ever imagined undertaking in her own work. And in observing these comparisons, she would have realized that, for most of the participants, the United States was no longer the sole model or ideal. As well, they were explicitly concerned about current issues, from globalization and citizenship to particular incidents. In her own work, she might have made current issues such as the environment into topics, but her object would usually have been to synthesize the doctrine that related to the topic. In contrast, they were more concerned with the impact of the topic on the doctrine and the appropriate responses the legal system might make. In this way, their work was much more normative than hers had ever been, measuring doctrine and making proposals in the light of explicit moral standards. She had her own social and moral beliefs, but she was not as comfortable integrating them into her thinking about law.

Throughout, she would have been struck by the presence of civilian scholars from Quebec. In contrast to the question she often heard at home, 'What does Quebec want?' she would have seen that the participants sought to understand their different interpretations of Canada and its history, their different ways of reasoning. And last of all, she would have noticed that interest in Canadian history, so long forgotten, had reappeared.

As she listened to them talk, these scholars would have seemed to have a wider range of interests and knowledge than she had. She would have sensed that they had read a lot of philosophy, history, economics, and feminist literature (and she might even have wondered whether Foucault was a straw scarecrow). At first, she might have thought that the result was interdisciplinary scholarship, which was then fashionable at home, but, on reflection, she might have interpreted it as an expansion of discipline instead. If she wandered around halls, their offices might have stressed this difference. Her own office was filled with law reports, legal periodicals, and texts, but their offices contained a lot of books that seemed at first to have little to do with law. Seeing these books and remembering that scholars in the other disciplines had spent their lives studying them, she might have wondered whether these the inhabitants of Oz had fully grasped the nature and limits of their enthusiasms.

If she ventured to talk to them about the conference and her own work, they might have thought she was simply 'uninteresting,' and she, in turn, might have thought that they had lost their way, forgetting the essential tasks of teaching students to become lawyers and exhorting judges to reason better. My sense is that each impression would contain some truth and some misunderstanding. They might not have respected or even understood her passion to teach lawyers and judges or her ability to do traditional doctrinal analysis. On the other hand, she might have underestimated or not even understood the wider range of knowledge and perspectives they brought to bear on doctrine and legal institutions. Unless, perhaps, she was Frank Scott.

NOTES

1 The cases are collected in P. Macklem et al., *Canadian Constitutional Law*, 2nd ed. (Toronto: Emond-Montgomery, 1997).

2 The 1930s are described in R.C.B. Risk, 'Many Minds of W.P.M. Kennedy,' and the late nineteenth century is described in R.C.B. Risk, 'A.H.F. Lefroy' and 'Constitutional Scholarship,' all in this volume.

3 See S. Dijwa, *The Politics of the Imagination: A Life of F.R. Scott* (Toronto: McClelland & Stewart, 1987).

4 F.R. Scott, 'Centralization and Decentralization in Canadian Federalism' (1951) 29 *Can. Bar R.* 1095, reprinted in F.R. Scott, *Essays on the Constitution* (Toronto: University of Toronto Press, 1977) 251 at *Essays* 274.

5 F.R. Scott, 'Federal Jurisdiction over Labour Relations: A New Look' (1960) 6 *McGill L.J.* 153 at 162, reprinted in Scott, *Essays*, supra note 4 at 346.

6 F.R. Scott, 'Social Planning and Canadian Federalism,' in M. Oliver, ed., *Social Purpose for Canada* (Toronto: University of Toronto Press, 1961) 394 at 406.

7 F.R. Scott, 'Canadian Federalism: The Legal Perspective' (1967) 5 *Alberta L.R.* 263, reprinted in Scott, *Essays*, supra note 4 at 364.

8 'Our Changing Constitution' (1961) 55 *Trans. Royal Society* 83, reprinted in Scott, *Essays*, supra note 4 at 397. A similar statement (or overstatement) is 'Maynard Keynes put more substance back into federal powers than Lord Haldane had ever taken out': Scott, 'Social Planning,' supra note 6 at 397.

9 'Our Changing Constitution,' supra note 8 at *Essays* 400.

10 Ibid. 397.

11 Ibid. 401.

12 'Social Planning,' supra note 6 at 400–1.

13 B. Laskin, 'Peace, Order, and Good Government Re-examined' (1947) 25 *Can. Bar R.* 1054.

14 *Canadian Constitutional Law* (Toronto: Carswell, 1951). My copy of the casebook is the only scrap of paper that survives from my three years as an undergraduate at the Faculty of Law. In the fashion of generations of schoolchildren, I decorated the title page, making Laskin say, 'I hate Haldane, Duff and Mundell.' My understanding of him more than 40 years ago may have been just as accurate as it is now, and it was certainly much shorter and simpler.

15 B. Laskin, 'The Supreme Court of Canada: A Final Court of and for Canadians' (1951) 29 *Can. Bar R.* 1038.

16 'Case Comment on *Pronto Uranium Mines v. Ontario Labour Relations Board*' (1957) 35 *Can. Bar R.* 101; 'Comment (*Regina v. Klassen*)' (1959) 37 *Can. Bar*

R. 630; 'An Inquiry into the Diefenbaker Bill of Rights' (1959) 37 *Can. Bar R.*
77 (only part of this article is about the federalism issues, but it is a long
part); 'Municipal Tax Assessment and Section 96 of the British North
America Act: The *Olympia Bowling Alleys* Case' (1955) 38 *Can. Bar R.* 993;
'Provincial Marketing Levies: Indirect Taxation and Federal Power' (1959)
13 *U.T.L.J.* 1; and 'Tests for the Validity of Legislation: What's the Matter?'
(1955) 11 *U.T.L.J.* 114; In 1963, he wrote a short article on amendment,
'Amendment of the Constitution' (1963) 15 *U.T.L.J.* 190.

17 'Occupying the Field: Paramountcy in Penal Legislation' (1963) 41 *Can. Bar R.* 234.

18 18. Supra note 13. The article is strewn with such criticisms as 'cold,
abstract logic' (1059), 'a sense of unreality' (1059), 'There can surely be
nothing more remarkable in judicial annals' (1067), the 'sham quality'
of the reasoning (1075), 'He has fashioned the Procrustean bed; let the
constitution lie on it' (1077), an opinion 'almost shocking in its casualness'
(1079), and reasoning that is 'a monument to judicial rigidity and to a
complacence which admits of no reasonable explanation' (1080).

19 Ibid. 1085.

20 See 'Comment (*Pronto Uranium Mines*)' and 'Comment (*Regina v. Klassen*),'
supra note 16.

21 'Occupying the Field,' supra note 17 at 244. He suggested that the
considerations for choosing a test to determine when two statutes were in
conflict were 'accommodating federalism, or efficient administration of
regulatory schemes, or, perhaps as a last resort, the purpose of the
paramount legislature': ibid. 236.

22 'Peace, Order and Good Government Re-examined,' supra note 13 at 1059,
1060, 1077, 1082.

23 'Supreme Court of Canada,' supra note 15 at 1071, 1070.

24 'Provincial Marketing Levies,' supra note 16 at 3, 21.

25 'Comment (*Pronto Uranium Mines*),' supra note 16 at 105.

26 'Canadian Federalism: A Scott's Eye View in Prose and Poetry' (1968) 14
McGill L.J. 494 at 498.

27 B. Laskin, 'Tests for the Validity of Legislation under the British North
America Act' (1954) 32 *Can. Bar R.* 813.

28 'Tests for the Validity of Legislation,' supra note 16, at 115, 117, 114.

29 Ibid. 122.

30 Ibid. 123.

31 Laskin made this assertion most clearly in 'Peace, Order, and Good
Government Re-examined,' saying that the results were not caused by a
mistaken technique of statutory interpretation, as scholars in the 1930s had

often argued, but by a 'conscious and deliberate choice of a policy which required manipulations which can only with difficulty be represented as ordinary judicial techniques': supra note 13 at 1086. He did not, however, explain what this policy was.

32 'Supreme Court of Canada,' supra note 15 at 1075. Much later, in 1963, he said that 'precedent is no longer a conclusive test of the merit of a constitutional pronouncement of the Supreme Court': 'Occupying the Field,' supra note 17 at 236.

33 'Supreme Court of Canada,' supra note 15 at 1075.

34 'Peace, Order and Good Government Re-examined,' supra note 13 at 1082.

35 (1959) 20 D.L.R. (2d) 406 (Man. C.A.). See also Laskin, 'Comment (*Regina v. Klassen*),' supra note 16.

36 [1956] O.R. 862, 5 D.L.R. (2d) 342 (H.C.). See also Laskin, 'Comment (*Pronto Uranium Mines*),' supra note 16.

37 Laskin, 'Comment (*Pronto Uranium Mines*),' supra note 16 at 103.

38 'Municipal Tax Assessment,' supra note 16 at 999.

39 Bill Lederman, 'Classification of Laws and the British North America Act,' in J.A. Corry, F.C. Cronkite, and E.F. Whitmore, eds., *Legal Essays in Honour of Arthur Moxon* (Toronto: University of Toronto Press, 1953), reprinted in Lederman, ed., *Continuing Canadian Constitutional Dilemmas* (Toronto: Butterworths, 1981) 229.

40 'The Concurrent Operation of Federal and Provincial Laws in Canada' (1962) 9 *McGill L.J.* 185, reprinted in Lederman, *Continuing Canadian Constitutional Dilemmas*, supra note 39 at 250.

41 'Legislative Power to Implement Treaty Obligations in Canada,' in J.A. Aitchison, ed., *The Political Process in Canada* (Toronto: University of Toronto Press, 1963), reprinted in Lederman, *Continuing Canadian Constitutional Dilemmas*, supra note 39 at 350.

42 'The Balanced Interpretation of the Federal Distribution of Legislative Powers in Canada,' in P.A. Crepeau and C.B. Macpherson, eds., *The Future of Canadian Federalism* (Toronto: University of Toronto Press, 1965) 91.

43 'Some Forms and Limitations of Co-operative Federalism' (1967) 45 *Can. Bar R.* 409, reprinted in Lederman, *Continuing Canadian Constitutional Dilemmas*, supra note 39 at 314. In the same year, he also published 'The Process of Constitutional Amendment for Canada' (1967) 12 *McGill L.J.* 371.

44 'Balanced Interpretation,' supra note 42.

45 Ibid. 267.

46 'Unity and Diversity in Canadian Federalism: Ideals and Methods of Moderation' (1975) 53 *Can. Bar R.* 597, reprinted in Lederman, *Continuing Canadian Constitutional Dilemmas*, supra note 3, 285 and 281.

47 'Thoughts on Reform of the Supreme Court of Canada' (1970) 8 *Alberta L.R.* 1; reprinted in Lederman, *Continuing Canadian Constitutional Dilemmas,* supra note 39, 195 at 197.

48 'Unity and Diversity,' supra note 46 at *Continuing Canadian Constitutional Dilemmas* 291.

49 'Legislative Power,' supra note 41.

50 Ibid. at *Continuing Canadian Constitutional Dilemmas* 291. This suggestion reappeared decades later amid controversies about globalization and North American free trade; see, for example, R. Howse, 'The Labour Conventions Doctrine in an Era of Global Interdependence' (1990) 16 *Can. Bus. L.J.* 160.

51 'Unity and Diversity,' supra note 46 at *Continuing Canadian Constitutional Dilemmas* 292.

52 [1976] 2 S.C.R. 373.

53 [1988] 1 S.C.R. 401.

54 See G. LeDain, 'Sir Lyman Duff and the Constitution' (1974) 12 *Osgoode Hall L.J.* 261, and D. Gibson, 'Measuring National Dimensions' (1976) 7 *Manitoba L.J.* 17.

55 'Balanced Interpretation,' supra note 42.

56 'Forms and Limitations,' supra note 43.

57 See, for example, 'Cooperative Federalism: Constitutional Revision and Parliamentary Government in Canada' (1971) 78 *Queen's Q.* 7, reprinted in Lederman, *Continuing Canadian Constitutional Dilemmas,* supra note 39 at 374.

58 Ibid. at *Continuing Canadian Constitutional Dilemmas* 377.

59 'Forms and Limitations,' supra note 43 at *Continuing Canadian Constitutional Dilemmas* 333.

60 Ibid. 294.

61 Lederman, 'Classification of Laws,' supra note 39.

62 All quotations in this paragraph are taken from ibid., at *Continuing Canadian Constitutional Dilemmas* 238, 242. The image of the physician was suggested to Lederman by a comment by Lord McMillan in 1943 in the *Alberta Debt Adjustment* case, which presumably he watched while on leave from military service; see 'Thoughts on Reform,' supra note 47, at *Continuing Canadian Constitutional Dilemmas* 197–8. Lederman set out his beliefs about legal reasoning, especially about choice, a few years later, in 'The Common Law System in Canada,' in E. McWhinney, ed., *Canadian Jurisprudence: The Civil Law and Common Law in Canada* (Toronto: Carswell, 1958) 34.

63 His ideas were expressed most clearly in 'Thoughts on Reform,' supra note 47.

64 See W.F. O'Connor, *Report to the Senate Relating to the Enactment of the British North America Act* (Ottawa: King's Printer, 1939), and G.P. Browne, *The Judicial Committee and the British North America Act* (Toronto: University of Toronto Press, 1967).
65 The quotations in this paragraph are taken from 'Thoughts on Reform,' supra note 47 at *Continuing Canadian Constitutional Dilemmas* 197, 196, 198.
66 'Classification of Laws,' supra note 39 at *Continuing Canadian Constitutional Dilemmas*, 243.
67 Here, both Laskin's and Lederman's articles on classification having been surveyed, a short detour is needed to explore an article written five years before Lederman's by Eugene LaBrie. Born and raised on the prairies, like Lederman, LaBrie obtained both an LLB and an LLM at the Faculty of Law of the University of Toronto in the early 1940s and joined its staff in 1945. In 1949, he published 'Canadian Constitutional Interpretation and Legislative Review' (1949) 8 *U.T.L.J.* 298. Its major message was that the central issue in review was characterization; the judges had 'virtually unfettered discretion' (at 310); outcomes were determined by their social outlook and political philosophy; and beliefs, text, rules, and precedent offered little or no guidance. The argument parallels much of the more extreme realist literature, and it was the first sustained appearance in Canadian constitutional scholarship of a powerful challenge to doctrine. LaBrie soon left constitutional law to begin a long career in the tax field, both in practice and as a scholar. The article was rarely cited, even during the few years following its publication, and it soon disappeared.
68 (1908) 8 *Columbia L.R.* 101.
69 'The Scope and Purpose of Sociological Jurisprudence' (1911) 24 *Harvard L.R.* 591 and (1912) 25 *Harvard L.R.* 160.
70 B. Laskin, 'The Institutional Character of the Judge' (1970) 7 *Israel L.R.* 329 at 330.
71 See F. Cohen, 'The Ethical Basis of Legal Criticism' (1931) 41 *Yale L.J.* 201. Lederman's claim that sometimes the judge would have to make the choice alone may have been suggested by a similar claim in M. Radin, 'Statutory Interpretation' (1930) 43 *Harvard L.R.* 863.
72 He described his early interest in theory in correspondence about his appointment at Dalhousie: Appointments, Law School Records, Dalhousie University Archives.
73 See N. Duxbury, *Patterns of American Jurisprudence* (Oxford: Clarendon Press, 1995), c. 4; and T. Grey, 'Modern American Legal Thought (A Review of N. Duxbury, *Patterns of American Jurisprudence*)' (1997) 106 *Yale L.J.* 493, for this observation and for the survey of the American legal

thought described in the preceding few paragraphs of the text. The observation may help explain the gulf between Denise Réaume, who treats Laskin as a Progressive (although without the name and the context), and Paul Horwitz, who argues that Laskin belongs in the legal process camp. See D. Réaume, 'The Judicial Philosophy of Bora Laskin' (1985) 35 *U.T.L.J.* 438, and P. Horwitz, 'Bora Laskin and the Legal Process School' (1995) 59 *Sask. L.R.* 77.

74 For the Canadians, see R.C.B. Risk, 'Volume One of the Journal,' in this volume, which may greatly overestimate the influence of American legal thought, and especially of the Realists.

75 Lysyk was the only exception, having done his graduate work at Oxford.

76 See, for example, D. Gibson, 'The Constitutional Context of Canadian Water Planning' (1969) 7 *Alberta L.R.* 71; K. Lysyk, 'The Unique Constitutional Position of the Canadian Indian' (1967) 45 *Can. Bar R.* 513; C. McNairn, 'Transportation, Communication and the Constitution' (1969) 47 *Can. Bar R.* 355.

77 D. Gibson, 'Measuring National Dimensions,' supra note 54, and K. Lysyk, 'Constitutional Reform and the Introductory Clause of Section 91: Residual and Emergency Law-Making Authority' (1979) 57 *Can. Bar R.* 531.

78 See, for example, E. McWhinney, 'The Constitutional Competence within Federal Systems as to International Agreements' (1966) 1 *Can. Legal Stud.* 165.

79 A. Abel, 'The Anti-Inflation Judgment: Right Answer to the Wrong Question' (1976) 26 *U.T.L.J.* 409; D. Gibson, 'And One Step Backward: The Supreme Court and Constitutional Law in the Sixties' (1975) 53 *Can. Bar R.* 621; P. Weiler, 'The Supreme Court and the Law of Canadian Federalism.' (1973) 23 *U.T.L.J.* 307;

80 See, for example, M. MacGuigan, 'The Privy Council and the Supreme Court: A Jurisprudential Analysis' (1966) 4 *Alberta L.R.* 419.

81 F.E. Cronkite, 'Thoughts on the Constitution of the Second Century' (1967) 32 *Sask. Bar R.* 236; M. Cohen, 'The Canadian Federal Dilemma' (1968) 14 *McGill L.J.* 357; G. LeDain, 'Reflections on the Canadian Constitution after the First Century' (1967) 45 *Can. Bar R.* 402; E. McWhinney, 'Federalism, Constitutionalism, and Legal Change: Legal Implications of the Revolution in Quebec' (1964) *Future* 157; E. McWhinney, 'The New Pluralistic Federalism in Canada' (1967) 2 *Themis* 169; E. McWhinney, 'Social Revolution and Constitutional Revolution in Canada: Some Reflections on the Philosophy of Legal Change' (1967) 12 *McGill L.J.* 479.

82 See, for example, E.A. Alexander, 'A Constitutional Straitjacket for Canada' (1965) 43 *Can. Bar R.* 262, and a symposium in (1967) 12 McGill L.J.

83 Abel argued that strong government was needed to match private power and to protect against absorption into the United States. For federalism, he emphasized Canada's pluralism and proposed decentralization, arguing that this was the original design. He gave the power to manage the economy to the federal government, limiting its spending power to its legislative sphere, and the residue to the provinces. The proposal was incomplete when Abel died, and those parts that were finished were published posthumously: J. Laskin, 'Albert Abel's Constitutional Charter for Canada' (1978) 28 U.T.L.J. 261. See also A. Abel, 'A Chart for a Charter' (1976) 25 *U. of New Brunswick L.R.* 20, and 'The Neglected Logic of 91 and 92' (1969) 19 *U.T.L.J.* 487.

84 'A Fresh Approach to Constitutional Law' (1967) 45 *Can. Bar R.* 554.

85 'Two Models of Judicial Decision-Making' (1968) 46 *Can. Bar R.* 406.

86 There were two major pieces that were avowedly historical. The first was A. Smith, *The Commerce Power in Canada and the United States* (Toronto: Butterworths, 1963), which described and analysed the course of the doctrine in both countries thoroughly, but with little regard for its context. The second was B. Strayer, 'Saskatchewan and the Amendment of the Canadian Constitution' (1967) 12 *McGill L.J.* 443, which treated context more fully.

87 'Two Models of Judicial Decision-Making,' supra note 85 at 406.

1981   David H. Flaherty, ed., *Essays in the History of Canadian Law: Volume I*

1982   Marion MacRae and Anthony Adamson, *Cornerstones of Order: Courthouses and Town Halls of Ontario, 1784–1914*

1983   David H. Flaherty, ed., *Essays in the History of Canadian Law: Volume II*

1984   Patrick Brode, *Sir John Beverley Robinson: Bone and Sinew of the Compact*
David Williams, *Duff: A Life in the Law*

1985   James Snell and Frederick Vaughan, *The Supreme Court of Canada: History of the Institution*

1986   Paul Romney, *Mr Attorney: The Attorney General for Ontario in Court, Cabinet, and Legislature, 1791–1899*
Martin Friedland, *The Case of Valentine Shortis: A True Story of Crime and Politics in Canada*

1987   C. Ian Kyer and Jerome Bickenbach, *The Fiercest Debate: Cecil A. Wright, the Benchers, and Legal Education in Ontario, 1923–1957*

1988   Robert Sharpe, *The Last Day, the Last Hour: The Currie Libel Trial*
John D. Arnup, *Middleton: The Beloved Judge*

1989   Desmond Brown, *The Genesis of the Canadian Criminal Code of 1892*
Patrick Brode, *The Odyssey of John Anderson*

1990   Philip Girard and Jim Phillips, eds., *Essays in the History of Canadian Law: Volume III – Nova Scotia*
Carol Wilton, ed., *Essays in the History of Canadian Law: Volume IV – Beyond the Law: Lawyers and Business in Canada, 1830–1930*

1991   Constance Backhouse, *Petticoats and Prejudice: Women and Law in Nineteenth- Century Canada*

1992   Brendan O'Brien, *Speedy Justice: The Tragic Last Voyage of His Majesty's Vessel Speedy*
Robert Fraser, ed., *Provincial Justice: Upper Canadian Legal Portraits from the Dictionary of Canadian Biography*

1993   Greg Marquis, *Policing Canada's Century: A History of the Canadian Association of Chiefs of Police*
F. Murray Greenwood, *Legacies of Fear: Law and Politics in Quebec in the Era of the French Revolution*

1994   Patrick Boyer, *A Passion for Justice: The Legacy of James Chalmers McRuer*
Charles Pullen, *The Life and Times of Arthur Maloney: The Last of the Tribunes*
Jim Phillips, Tina Loo, and Susan Lewthwaite, eds., *Essays in the History of Canadian Law: Volume V – Crime and Criminal Justice*
Brian Young, *The Politics of Codification: The Lower Canadian Civil Code of 1866*

1995   David Williams, *Just Lawyers: Seven Portraits*

Hamar Foster and John McLaren, eds., *Essays in the History of Canadian Law: Volume VI – British Columbia and the Yukon*

W.H. Morrow, ed., *Northern Justice: The Memoirs of Mr Justice William G. Morrow*

Beverley Boissery, *A Deep Sense of Wrong: The Treason, Trials and Transportation to New South Wales of Lower Canadian Rebels after the 1838 Rebellion*

1996 Carol Wilton, ed., *Essays in the History of Canadian Law: Volume VII – Inside the Law: Canadian Law Firms in Historical Perspective*

William Kaplan, *Bad Judgment: The Case of Mr Justice Leo A. Landreville*

F. Murray Greenwood and Barry Wright, eds., *Canadian State Trials: Volume I – Law, Politics, and Security Measures, 1608–1837*

1997 James W. St.G. Walker, *'Race,' Rights, and the Law in the Supreme Court of Canada: Historical Case Studies*

Lori Chambers, *Married Women and Property Law in Victorian Ontario*

Patrick Brode, *Casual Slaughters and Accidental Judgments: Canadian War Crimes and Prosecutions, 1944–1948*

Ian Bushnell, *A History of the Federal Court of Canada, 1875–1992*

1998 Sidney Harring, *White Man's Law: Native People in Nineteenth-Century Canadian Jurisprudence*

Peter Oliver, *'Terror to Evil-Doers': Prisons and Punishments in Nineteenth-Century Ontario*

1999 Constance Backhouse, *Colour-Coded: A Legal History of Racism in Canada, 1900–1950*

G. Blaine Baker and Jim Phillips, eds., *Essays in the History of Canadian Law: Volume VIII – In Honour of R.C.B. Risk*

Richard W. Pound, *Chief Justice W.R. Jackett: By the Law of the Land*

David Vanek, *Fulfilment: Memoirs of a Criminal Court Judge*

2000 Barry Cahill, *The Thousandth Man: A Biography of James McGregor Stewart*

A.B. McKillop, *The Spinster and the Prophet: Florence Deeks, H.G. Wells, and the Mystery of the Purloined Past*

Beverley Boissery and F. Murray Greenwood, *Uncertain Justice: Canadian Women and Capital Punishment*

Bruce Ziff, *Unforeseen Legacies: Reuben Wells Leonard and the Leonard Foundation Trust*

2001 Ellen Anderson, *Judging Bertha Wilson: Law as Large as Life*

Judy Fudge and Eric Tucker, *Labour before the Law: The Regulation of Workers' Collective Action in Canada, 1900–1948*

Laurel Sefton MacDowell, *Renegade Lawyer: The Life of J.L. Cohen*

2002 John T. Saywell, *The Lawmakers: Judicial Power and the Shaping of Canadian Federalism*

Patrick Brode, *Courted and Abandoned: Seduction in Canadian Law*

David Murray, *Colonial Justice: Justice, Morality, and Crime in the Niagara District, 1791–1849*

March 26/07